Creating Business Value with Information Technology: Challenges and Solutions

Namchul Shin
Pace University, USA

IRM Press
Publisher of innovative scholarly and professional
information technology titles in the cyberage

Hershey • London • Melbourne • Singapore • Beijing

Acquisitions Editor:	Mehdi Khosrow-Pour
Managing Editor:	Jan Travers
Development Editor:	Michele Rossi
Copy Editor:	Lori Eby
Typesetter:	Amanda Appicello
Cover Design:	Integrated Book Technology
Printed at:	Integrated Book Technology

Published in the United States of America by
    IRM Press (an imprint of Idea Group Inc.)
    701 E. Chocolate Avenue
    Hershey PA 17033
    Tel: 717-533-8845
    Fax: 717-533-8661
    E-mail: cust@idea-group.com
    Web site: http://www.idea-group.com

and in the United Kingdom by
    IRM Press (an imprint of Idea Group Inc.)
    3 Henrietta Street
    Covent Garden
    London WC2E 8LU
    Tel: 44 20 7240 0856
    Fax: 44 20 7379 3313
    Web site: http://www.eurospan.co.uk

Library of Congress Cataloging-in-Publication Data

Creating business value with information technology : challenges and solutions / [edited by] Namchul Shin.
    p. cm.
  Originally published: Hershey, PA : Idea Group Pub., 2002.
  Includes bibliographical references and index.
  ISBN 1-931777-91-8 (paper)
  1. Information technology--Management--Case studies. 2. Industrial management--Technological innovations--Case studies. 3. Strategic planning--Case studies. I. Shin, Namchul, 1962-

HD30.2.C73 2003
658.4'038--dc21

               2003040688

eISBN 1-59140-088-0

Previously published in a hard cover version by Idea Group Publishing.

British Cataloguing in Publication Data
A Cataloguing in Publication record for this book is available from the British Library.

New Releases from IRM Press

- **Multimedia and Interactive Digital TV: Managing the Opportunities Created by Digital Convergence**/Margherita Pagani
  ISBN: 1-931777-38-1; eISBN: 1-931777-54-3 / US$59.95 / © 2003
- **Virtual Education: Cases in Learning & Teaching Technologies**/ Fawzi Albalooshi (Ed.)
  ISBN: 1-931777-39-X; eISBN: 1-931777-55-1 / US$59.95 / © 2003
- **Managing IT in Government, Business & Communities**/Gerry Gingrich (Ed.)
  ISBN: 1-931777-40-3; eISBN: 1-931777-56-X / US$59.95 / © 2003
- **Information Management: Support Systems & Multimedia Technology**/ George Ditsa (Ed.)
  ISBN: 1-931777-41-1; eISBN: 1-931777-57-8 / US$59.95 / © 2003
- **Managing Globally with Information Technology**/Sherif Kamel (Ed.)
  ISBN: 42-X; eISBN: 1-931777-58-6 / US$59.95 / © 2003
- **Current Security Management & Ethical Issues of Information Technology**/Rasool Azari (Ed.)
  ISBN: 1-931777-43-8; eISBN: 1-931777-59-4 / US$59.95 / © 2003
- **UML and the Unified Process**/Liliana Favre (Ed.)
  ISBN: 1-931777-44-6; eISBN: 1-931777-60-8 / US$59.95 / © 2003
- **Business Strategies for Information Technology Management**/Kalle Kangas (Ed.)
  ISBN: 1-931777-45-4; eISBN: 1-931777-61-6 / US$59.95 / © 2003
- **Managing E-Commerce and Mobile Computing Technologies**/Julie Mariga (Ed.)
  ISBN: 1-931777-46-2; eISBN: 1-931777-62-4 / US$59.95 / © 2003
- **Effective Databases for Text & Document Management**/Shirley A. Becker (Ed.)
  ISBN: 1-931777-47-0; eISBN: 1-931777-63-2 / US$59.95 / © 2003
- **Technologies & Methodologies for Evaluating Information Technology in Business**/ Charles K. Davis (Ed.)
  ISBN: 1-931777-48-9; eISBN: 1-931777-64-0 / US$59.95 / © 2003
- **ERP & Data Warehousing in Organizations: Issues and Challenges**/Gerald Grant (Ed.)
  ISBN: 1-931777-49-7; eISBN: 1-931777-65-9 / US$59.95 / © 2003
- **Practicing Software Engineering in the 21st Century**/Joan Peckham (Ed.)
  ISBN: 1-931777-50-0; eISBN: 1-931777-66-7 / US$59.95 / © 2003
- **Knowledge Management: Current Issues and Challenges**/Elayne Coakes (Ed.)
  ISBN: 1-931777-51-9; eISBN: 1-931777-67-5 / US$59.95 / © 2003
- **Computing Information Technology: The Human Side**/Steven Gordon (Ed.)
  ISBN: 1-931777-52-7; eISBN: 1-931777-68-3 / US$59.95 / © 2003
- **Current Issues in IT Education**/Tanya McGill (Ed.)
  ISBN: 1-931777-53-5; eISBN: 1-931777-69-1 / US$59.95 / © 2003

Excellent additions to your institution's library!
Recommend these titles to your Librarian!

To receive a copy of the IRM Press catalog, please contact
(toll free) 1/800-345-4332, fax 1/717-533-8661,
or visit the IRM Press Online Bookstore at: [http://www.irm-press.com]!

Note: All IRM Press books are also available as ebooks on netlibrary.com as well as other ebook sources. Contact Ms. Carrie Skovrinskie at [cskovrinskie@idea-group.com] to receive a complete list of sources where you can obtain ebook information or IRM Press titles.

Creating Business Value with Information Technology: Challenges and Solutions

Table of Contents

Preface

Many questions raised by managers and researchers over the last two decades on the business value of information technology (IT) have not yet been settled. Firms invest in IT in order to improve, their business performance. However, some firms fail to improve while others succeed. The overall benefits realized from IT vary enormously from firm to firm. Computerization does not automatically create business value, although it is one essential component. Just as important are organizational changes such as new strategies, new business processes, and new organizational assets. The critical question facing information systems (IS) managers is not only "Does IT pay off?" but also "How can we best use IT and related technologies?" However, little is known about successful strategies for creating business value with IT, what characteristics of firms create more value from IT, and what types of IT contribute to increase in business value.

This book tackles these questions from a number of unique perspectives. The first chapter, by Tallon and Kraemer, investigates the relationship between strategic alignment and IT payoffs at the process level. By focusing on how IT supports key processes, it provides a comprehensive assessment of the link between strategic alignment and IT business value. The authors operationalize the degree of strategic alignment and IT business value based on executives' perceptions, which they use to examine empirically the relationship between the two. They find a positive and significant relationship between strategic alignment and IT payoffs. They also uncover evidence of an alignment paradox, which shows that while strategic alignment can lead to increased payoffs from IT, this relationship is only valid up to a certain point.

Shams and Wheeler's chapter provides interesting insights into the informational aspects of strategic alignment. The authors define strategic alignment in terms of three semiological dimensions: pragmatics, semantics, and syntactics. They use these three perspectives to demonstrate the importance of these informational dimensions in the analysis of strategic alignment. The authors also introduce organizational dynamics as a fourth dimension to address time-related changes.

The chapter by Setzekorn, Rai, and Melcher examines empirically the mediating effects of supply chain coordination strategy and manufacturing IT infrastructure on the relationship between business complexity and firm inventory productivity. To cope with the diversity and volatility associated with a firm's product markets, firms deploy extensive manufacturing IT infrastructure, which can improve inventory turnover by reducing the need for inventory buffers. However, without a supply chain coordination strategy, they experience significantly lower inventory turnover. The authors provide evidence for the importance of supply chain coordination strategy, which is complementary to IT investment, for better (i.e., higher) inventory turnover.

Navarrete and Pick's chapter empirically studies the impact of IT investments on organizational performance in the Mexican banking industry by employing multiple performance measures: profitability, efficiency, productivity, and performance indexes. It provides an interesting look at the relationship between IT and business value at the firm level in a context different from the United States. The authors find that there is a lack of correlation between IT spending and indexes of profitability and efficiency, but that there are positive and significant correlations between IT spending and indexes of productivity and performance. They also provide insights into economic and industry factors affecting IT business value in the Mexican banking industry, such as the historical aspects of the industry and the effects of changes in ownership.

The chapter by Shin examines empirically the relationship between IT and coordination costs, and the relationship between IT and firm productivity by considering the value derived from IT's reduction of coordination costs and its improvement of coordination. The author finds that IT is strongly associated with lower coordination costs and that IT contributes to firm productivity by reducing coordination costs and improving coordination of economic activities.

Based on the case of the Mexican banking industry, Navarrete and Pick's next chapter analyzes empirically the relationship between IT expenditure and the monetary value (the real and perceived market values) of banks. They find that IT spending has a positive impact on the value of the firm when it reflects the change of ownership or the control of the organization, and that firms spending more on IT do not tend to reach higher selling prices. They discuss the model and the results in terms of the productivity paradox.

Gupta and Sharma investigate how e-commerce enhances business value. The authors introduce an e-commerce framework and show how this framework affects critical value activities such as production, logistics, customer service, sales, and marketing—and the way these factors create business value. They discuss business value at the industry and the firm levels separately. They also discuss the emergence of new intelligent enterprises and learning organizations that are made possible by the wide adaptation of an e-commerce framework.

Stahl's chapter provides interesting insights into the business value of IT from an ethical perspective. Discussing the relationship between business and moral value, the author introduces a theory of values based on the assumption that higher-order values come into play in the case of value conflicts. According to the author, this theory can help management make better decisions by incorporating these higher-order values into the decision-making process. This can lead to solutions that are morally and financially superior.

The chapter by Chinburg, Sharda, and Weiser proposes a methodology that facilitates the mapping of network security to business needs using classification schemes, the Open System Interconnection, and Porter's value chain, along with a decision-support tool called analytical hierarchy process. According to the authors, by relating the two classification schemes using the decision-support tool, this methodology can provide an effective way of determining network security needs that will create business value.

Shin and Kinsella's chapter investigates the business value of Internet-based virtual private networks (IVPN) in managing communications among distributed business entities. Based on two case studies, the authors propose a decision model of the IVPN, which can be used for the assessment of its strategic value and risks, as well as for the design of virtual telecommunication networks in organizations.

Ghahramani's chapter discusses an optimization model for telecommunication systems that can evaluate business value and utility for every activity in the systems design and development process, thereby enabling systems designers and developers to determine the business value of telecommunication systems. According to the author, this model is capable of facilitating higher business profitability and productivity by enhancing systems' strategic goals such as customer service and product position and quality.

The chapter by Craig studies the link between EC strategy and firm performance, focusing on small- and medium-sized manufacturing enterprises. The study shows that small- and medium-sized enterprises (SMEs) gain disproportionately from EC. The author finds that, for SMEs, a higher proportion of stronger performers are found in the group that makes EC a strategic priority. He also finds that, for all firms that view EC as strategically important, SMEs have more to gain than larger firms. A higher proportion of these are strong performers, compared to larger firms.

Based on earlier studies on successful use of IT in small business, Poon's chapter analyzes how management can effectively help small firms to benefit through Internet commerce. By examining the management factors that contribute to Internet commerce benefits among small businesses, the author finds three factors that make a distinct contribution to success: (1) pushing for Internet technology adoption, (2) setting up new business initiatives through Internet commerce, and (3) convincing others to use Internet commerce.

Singh's chapter discusses the opportunities and challenges of e-commerce experienced by small businesses in Australia. It is an exploratory study based on interviews conducted with 20 small e-business owners. Based on his findings, the author provides suggestions to enhance the value of e-commerce in small organizations.

Research on IT business value is valuable not only for academics but also for practitioners, because knowledge obtained through this kind of research can provide managers with a more precise rationale for making IT investments. When IT initiatives fail, it is usually because they are not supported by business case and value propositions. Thus, research on this area should continue for the purpose of obtaining and sharing solutions toward the unsettled and challenging questions surrounding the relationship between IT and business value.

Acknowledgment

I would like to acknowledge the help of all involved in the collation and review process of the book, without whose support the project could not have been satisfactorily completed. A further special note of thanks goes also to all the staff at Idea Group Publishing, whose contributions throughout the whole process from inception of the initial idea to final publication have been invaluable.

Deep appreciation and gratitude is due to Susan Merritt, Dean of School of Computer Science and Information Systems, Pace University, for ongoing sponsorship in terms of generous allocation of summer research grants and other editorial support services for coordination of this year-long project.

I wish to thank all of the authors for their insights and excellent contributions to this book. Most of the authors of chapters included in this also served as referees for articles written by other authors. Thanks go to all those who provided constructive and comprehensive reviews, especially Paul Tallon of Boston College, whose reviews set the benchmark.

Special thanks also go to the publishing team at Idea Group Publishing. In particular to Michele Rossi and Jan Travers, who continuously prodded via e-mail to keep the project on schedule and to Mehdi Khosrow-Pour, whose enthusiasm motivated me to initially accept his invitation for taking on this project. This book would not have been possible without the ongoing professional support from them. Finally, I want to thank my wife, Joy, for her love and support throughout this project.

Namchul Shin, PhD
New York, NY, USA

Chapter I

Investigating the Relationship between Strategic Alignment and IT Business Value: The Discovery of a Paradox

Paul P. Tallon
Boston College, USA

Kenneth L. Kraemer
University of California, Irvine, USA

Although business executives remain skeptical about the extent of payoffs from investment in information technology (IT), strategic alignment or the alignment of information systems strategy with business strategy continues to be ranked as one of the most important issues facing corporations. In this paper, we report on the results of a process-level study to investigate the relationship between strategic alignment and IT payoffs. An analysis of survey data from 63 firms finds a positive and significant relationship between strategic alignment and IT payoffs, a relationship that holds for all firms, irrespective of their strategic intent or goals for IT. However, in exploring minor differences in strategic alignment between firms with different goals for IT, we uncovered evidence of an alignment paradox. *This paradox shows that while strategic alignment can lead to increased payoffs from IT, this relationship is only valid up to a certain point beyond which, paradoxically, further increases in strategic alignment appear to lead to lower IT payoffs. Finally, we offer some suggestions for why this paradox might exist, specifically around issues of environmental uncertainty, industry clock-speed, and the need for organizational flexibility.*

INTRODUCTION

Although executives continue to voice concern for payoffs from investment in information technology (IT), strategic alignment or the alignment of information systems (IS) strategy with business strategy, has emerged as one of the most important issues facing executives in Europe and America (CSC, 2000; Price Waterhouse, 1996). Although IT business value and strategic alignment are often treated separately, researchers argue that a firm's inability to realize sufficient value from IT is due in part to an absence of strategic alignment (Henderson & Venkatraman, 1993; Prairie, 1996). If, as these researchers suggest, IT payoffs are indeed a function of strategic alignment, then an absence or deficiency in payoffs from IT may point to a misalignment between the business and IT strategies. Equally, if a corporation tries to reposition or change its strategic alignment, consideration may need to be given to any subsequent shift in the value the corporation realizes from IT investment, with downstream implications for firm performance. This question—long debated by academics and IS practitioners—leads to the first and most important question in this paper, namely, what is the nature of the relationship between strategic alignment and IT payoffs, and in particular, does strategic alignment have a positive impact on IT business value?

Although low levels of strategic alignment may undermine payoffs from IT, some researchers sound a word of caution for corporations who try to improve IT payoffs through strategic alignment. For example, Jarvenpaa and Ives (1994) argue that for corporations competing on a global scale, tight fit between the IS and business strategy might reduce strategic flexibility and force a firm down a path from which it cannot escape.[1] If this argument is valid, then there is a point beyond which increased alignment may weaken a corporation's ability to respond to environmental threats and opportunities, with the possibility that a reduction in flexibility may also erode IT payoffs. This would then imply that beyond a hypothetical inflection point, greater strategic alignment could, paradoxically, lead to lower IT payoffs. This leads to our second and final research question in which we ask if there is an *alignment paradox*, such that beyond a certain point, increased strategic alignment could, by limiting a corporation's ability to react favorably to environmental challenges, result in lower payoffs from IT? If our findings support the existence of an *alignment paradox*, then in subsequent research, we may question if IS executives are willing to accept less than perfect alignment in order to maintain some sense of strategic flexibility, even if this decision should entail a less than optimal level of IT payoffs.

In this paper, we explore both of these questions in the context of a process-oriented model of IT business value and strategic alignment—both variables are examined at the process-level rather than at the firm level. In the next section, we motivate this choice through a review of recent literature on strategic alignment and IT payoffs. After this, we present a theoretical model and hypotheses to more fully investigate the relationship between strategic alignment and IT business value. We then describe how the model was tested using data from a series of matched surveys. This is followed by a review of our results and a discussion of an *alignment paradox* uncovered by our analysis. Finally, we conclude and identify areas for further research.

LITERATURE REVIEW

The field of business policy, from which strategy research has emerged, has its origins in the concept of matching or aligning organizational resources with environmental threats and opportunities (Andrews, 1980). Accordingly, a business strategy reflects decisions that align corporate resources and capabilities with environmental threats and opportunities (Andrews, 1980; Bourgeois, 1985). This interpretation has implications for how we define and interpret strategic alignment. For example, by viewing strategic alignment as a snapshot of the link between business and IS strategies, we can focus on the content of strategic alignment, or specifically on what aspects of IT are aligned with what aspects of the business strategy. Previous research on strategic alignment has often applied this approach. For example, Reich and Benbasat (1996) apply the term "linkage" to "the degree to which the IT mission, objectives, and plans support and are supported by the business mission, objectives and plans" (p. 56). Similarly, Broadbent and Weill (1993) define strategic alignment as "the extent to which business strategies were enabled, supported, and stimulated by information strategies" (p. 164).

One way to identify the content of strategic alignment is to identify if the business plan links or refers to the IT plan, and vice versa (Broadbent & Weill, 1993; Kearns, 1997; Reich & Benbasat, 1996). However, in reviewing whether strategic alignment has been achieved, we accept that cross-referencing between the written IS and business plans (which would illustrate the content of strategic alignment) is at best a surrogate or proxy for "true" alignment, because planned strategy can be different from realized strategy (Mintzberg, 1978). This would imply that efforts to relate strategic alignment to IT payoffs should extend beyond an examination of the content of written plans to include measures of actual or realized IS and business strategy and from this, to compute an actual measure of realized strategic alignment to compare against a measure of realized IT business value.

Where studies of strategic alignment exclude measures of firm performance, there is often an implicit assumption that greater levels of strategy alignment are preferable to lower levels of strategic alignment. Among those studies that have considered the performance impacts of strategic alignment, there is often a wide variation in the type of performance metrics used. For example, Venkatraman (1989a) and Chan, Huff, Barclay, and Copeland (1997) use metrics such as net margin, market share, revenue growth, return on investment, cash flow and profitability. Yet, with the exception of Chan et al. (1997), the empirical literature has remained silent on the degree to which strategic alignment has impacted IT business value (where IT business value mediates the link between strategic alignment and firm performance). In that study, four items measured the impact of IT on efficiency, managerial effectiveness, market linkages and product/service enhancement. However, in combining these IT business value items with three items on end-user information satisfaction to form a variable labeled "IS effectiveness," their research could only offer an indirect assessment of the link between strategic alignment and IT business value. However, as the main focus of this research is on the link between strategic alignment and IT business value, this research – insofar as we are aware – represents the first time that this relationship has been empirically tested.

Research on IT Business Value

One of the most comprehensive bodies of research on the performance impacts of IT employs econometric techniques. As such, econometrics can provide useful insights into a range of IT impacts using theories of production economics, information processing or industrial organization (Bakos & Kemerer, 1992). Although the performance impacts of IT span multiple dimensions (Tallon, Kraemer, Gurbaxani, & Mooney, 1997), econometric studies tend to view IT impacts in one dimension such as value added or productivity. Therefore, a criticism of econometric methods involves their limitations in capturing impacts such as quality improvements, increased managerial effectiveness and enhanced customer relations. While econometric techniques may offer a high degree of objectivity, they provide somewhat limited insights into the process by which IT payoffs are created and, therefore, ultimately measured. In order to provide such insights, researchers advocate a behavioral or perception-based approach to IT business value using multiple process-level measures at various points throughout the corporation. While there are several ways to model business processes, one of the best known ways is the "value chain"—a framework that divides a firm's activities into distinct business processes (Porter, 1985). By considering the impact of IT on each process and on inter-process linkages, executives can obtain a more detailed understanding of how IT investments impact firm performance. Furthermore, while econometric techniques employ financial or objective measures of IT payoffs, we may consider using executives' perceptions to identify and assess payoffs from IT at the process-level.

Executives' Perceptions of IT Business Value: Fact or Fiction

The use of perceptual measures as a proxy or surrogate for objective measures of IT payoffs has been criticized by some researchers who believe executives may give an inaccurate assessment of IT payoffs due to personal biases and the complex nature of the IT evaluation process. Research has alleviated some of these concerns by showing, for example, that executive perceptions correlate with objective measures of firm performance. In one study by Venkatraman and Ramanujam (1987), senior executives were asked to rate their company's performance against that of major competitors using criteria such as sales growth, income growth and return on investment. In finding a strong correlation between perceptual and objective measures, the authors suggested that "perceptual data from senior managers . . . can be employed as acceptable operationalizations of [business economic performance]" (p. 118). In other research, executives' perceptions of IT business value were found to correlate with economic measures of IT performance such as revenues per IT dollar, net income per IT dollar and firm-wide productivity (Tallon, Kraemer, & Gurbaxani, 1998).

Further supporting the use of executives' perceptions in evaluating payoffs from IT, DeLone and McLean (1992) argue that business executives are ideally positioned to act as key informants in a qualitative assessment of IT impacts in their firms. There is a twofold basis for this argument. First, as direct consumers of IT, business executives can rely on personal experience when forming an overall perception of how IT has impacted different aspects of firm performance at the process level (Davis & Olson, 1985; Rockart & Flannery, 1983). Second, as business executives become more involved in IT investment decisions, they are increasingly exposed to the views of peers and subordinates as to the performance of previous IT investments (Watson, 1990). Taken together, these arguments confirm that business executives are an important source of information on IT impacts, thereby supporting the use of executives' perceptions in evaluating payoffs from IT investment.

THEORETICAL MODEL AND HYPOTHESES

While previous research on strategic alignment considers business and IS strategy at the firm level, a key contribution of our research is to focus instead on the process level in order to gain deeper insights into the relationship between strategic alignment and IT payoffs. As outlined above, the value chain divides a business into a sequence of processes, allowing us to locate primary business activities and IT support for these activities. By focusing on how IT supports key processes, we hope to provide a more comprehensive assessment of the link between strategic alignment and IT business value.

A second contribution of this research is our definition of strategic alignment and related approach to measuring it. While strategic alignment is typically defined as a measure of the extent to which IT supports the business strategy, this paper employs a two-dimensional definition based on the notion of *IT shortfall* (IT fails to support the business strategy) and *IT underutilization* (business strategy fails to utilize existing IT resources to the fullest extent possible). In Figure 1, we provide a graphical representation of these dimensions of IT shortfall and underutilization by depicting the bidirectional relationship between the business and IT strategy. The interaction between both strategies will feature prominently in measuring strategic

Figure 1: Dimensions of Strategic Alignment

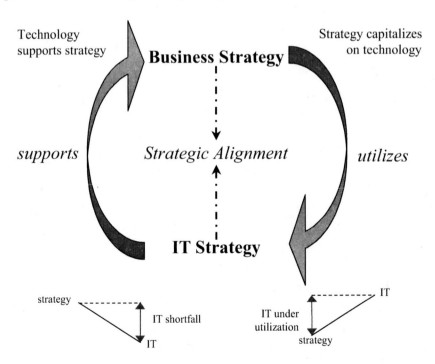

alignment. For example, perfect strategic alignment will exist when the IT strategy fully supports the business strategy and when the business strategy, in turn, has fully capitalized on the capabilities offered by the IT resources. This suggests that misalignment can occur through a lack of IT support for the business strategy (possibly caused by a lack of IT spending) or, alternatively, by failure to capitalize on IT resources (possibly caused by excessive spending on IT or by failure on the part of executives to understand the business opportunities presented by IT).

Strategic Alignment and IT Business Value

The espoused positive relationship between strategic alignment and payoffs from IT has been a core belief of IS researchers for the past decade, though there has been little empirical evidence to confirm or refute this belief. With reference to Figure 1, efforts to improve strategic alignment involve eliminating or at least reducing the gap between business and IT strategy, where a gap refers to either IT shortfall or IT underutilization. For example, in the case of IT shortfall, where the implementation of the business strategy is hampered by inadequate levels of IT support, increased IT spending or a reallocation of existing IT resources toward the most critical processes can help a firm achieve its business goals. In the case of IT underutilization, the introduction of new business activities around existing IT capabilities can help a corporation make more effective use of its IT resources.

If IT provides strong support for the business strategy consistent with high levels of strategic alignment, there is likely to be a small gap between the business and IS strategy (meaning low levels of IT shortfall). Business executives should subsequently find that this high level of IT support allows IT to have a significant impact on key performance criteria within each business process. If, on the other hand, there is a low level of support for the business strategy, consistent with misalignment between the IS and business strategy, business executives will likely find that IT has a lower impact on firm performance. This argument leads to the following hypothesis:

Hypothesis 1: Higher levels of strategic alignment lead to higher levels of IT business value.

Strategic Intent for IT

While theory might suggest that alignment between the business and IS strategy contributes to greater payoffs from IT, it is unclear if this relationship will hold for all corporations. For example, if IT is seen as a strategic resource and critical to the future success of the business, then by implication, strategic alignment may be seen as a competitive necessity and every effort may be made to achieve and maintain strategic alignment. However, if IT is only seen in a support or nonstrategic role, there may be less emphasis on strategic alignment. For example, McFarlan, McKenney, and Pyburn (1983) argue that "where information services are—and should be—in the support role,... less effort needs to be made to ensure alignment of IS and corporate strategy" (p. 156). Meanwhile, if IT is seen as a vehicle for organizational change, executives may feel that a more intense form of strategic alignment or a tighter fit between the business and IS strategy is warranted. This argument suggests that strategic intent or corporate goals for IT may be related to strategic alignment, and that therefore, we should consider some mechanism for measuring strategic intent for IT.

Based on Porter's argument that firm performance is related to two strategic foci: operational effectiveness and strategic positioning (Porter, 1996), we created a two-dimensional framework using these foci to represent strategic intent for IT. There are critical differences between each dimension. For example, operational effectiveness entails performing similar activities better than rivals, while strategic positioning entails performing different activities or performing similar activities but in different ways. Firms that focus on operational effectiveness "get more out of their inputs than others because they eliminate wasted effort, employ more advanced technology, motivate employees better, or have greater insight into managing particular activities... operational effectiveness includes, but is not limited to,

Figure 2: Classification of Firms by Strategic Intent for IT

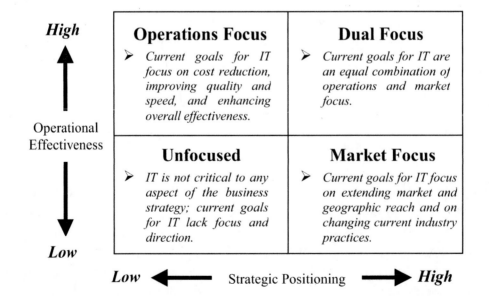

efficiency" (Porter, 1996, p. 62). Greater efficiency comes from using IT to control or reduce operating costs and to improve factor productivity, while effectiveness comes from using IT to increase flexibility and responsiveness to changing market needs. Alternatively, the primary emphasis in operational effectiveness is on using IT for internal purposes though this does not exclude the use of IT for market-oriented ends. In contrast, strategic positioning involves using IT to achieve greater market reach or to identify entirely new market opportunities. As shown in Figure 2, we can use this relationship between goals for IT and business foci to create an a priori classification of firms based on whether companies use IT for operational effectiveness, strategic positioning or both.

Using a "low" to "high" scale for both dimensions, we constructed a 2 x 2 framework. Firms in the lower left quadrant have little or no focus on operational effectiveness or strategic positioning and are labeled *unfocused* as a way to highlight their apparent indifference toward IT. For firms in this quadrant, strategic alignment is unlikely to be a major concern. In contrast, firms in the upper left quadrant have clearly defined goals for IT around operational effectiveness, but with less emphasis on using IT for strategic positioning. We label these firms as *operations focus* to reflect their use of IT to control operating costs and boost the effectiveness of business operations by improving quality, speed, flexibility and time to market. Firms in the lower right quadrant have a reverse emphasis on IT—they focus more on using IT for strategic positioning than for operational effectiveness. Such *market focus* firms use IT to achieve strategic positioning or to create a value proposition for their customers. While market focus firms concentrate their IT spending on more external or market-based initiatives, they may still be proficient at using IT in operations, though this is purely a way to support their market-based objectives. Finally, a significant number of firms recognize that IT can support operational effectiveness and strategic positioning simultaneously. Corporations with this *dual focus* approach use IT for operational effectiveness and strategic positioning. Consequently, IT is likely to be key to the success of these companies, and executives are likely to emphasize the need for a tight fit between the business and IS strategy.

In considering each of these foci (unfocused, operations focus, market focus and dual focus), as we move from being unfocused through dual focused, there is likely to be an increasing emphasis on strategic alignment and using IT to support the business. This leads to the following hypothesis:

Hypothesis 2*: Corporations with more strategic goals for IT will have higher levels of strategic alignment, while those with less strategic goals (where IT is in a purely support role) will have lower levels of strategic alignment.*

DATA COLLECTION AND ANALYSIS

Previous research by the authors involved the development of a 30-item survey instrument to measure payoffs from IT at the process level, where the value chain was used as a process model of the firm. The 30 items were divided across six business processes (i.e., process planning, supplier relations, production and operations, product and service enhancement, sales and marketing and customer relations), with five items per process. All items were based on an extensive review of the literature. As a way to focus responses on realized rather than expected impacts, the following lead-in question was applied: "To what extent does IT boost firm performance in the following areas? Please restrict your appraisal to value already realized rather than value expected in the future." All items were rated on a seven-point Likert scale, where "1" denotes "not at all" (low payoffs), and "7" denotes "to a great extent" (high payoffs). The set of business value items was subsequently validated in a global survey of 304 corporations that also included four items to measure strategic intent or corporate goals for IT [see Tallon, Kraemer and Gurbaxani (2000) for a more detailed description of the survey validation].

Having validated the business value items, the next stage of the research was to develop items for business and IS strategy. To facilitate a more direct assessment of the link between strategic alignment and IT business value, the text of the 30 IT business value items was duplicated in two independently developed surveys designed to measure business and IS strategy, respectively. As the original IT business value items reflected realized IT payoffs, it was felt that measures of business and IS strategy should focus on strategy as implemented rather than strategy as formulated. Consequently, in the business strategy instrument, the lead-in question for the same set of 30 items was: "To what extent have the following items been implemented as part of your business strategy?" Meanwhile, in the IS strategy instrument, IS strategy was operationalized as IT use, where the lead-in question preceding the 30 items was: "To what extent is your company using IT for each of the following?"

After some initial testing among a small set of companies and the incorporation of comments received from a panel of CIOs, the surveys were mailed to a sample frame of single segment, single line-of-business corporations[2] identified through the S&P Compustat database. Different respondents were identified for each of the surveys as follows: IT business value (CEO, COO, CFO or a functional VP), business strategy (strategic planner or corporate development officer) and IS strategy (CIO, CTO or senior IT manager). At part of a parallel study, surveys were also sent to executives in publicly traded businesses in Ireland (the same criteria for number of segments and respondents was applied).

Using a matched survey approach meant that we could only consider data collection for any company to be "complete" if we received at least one IT business

Table 1: Survey Response Rates

	U.S.	Ireland	Total*
Sample Frame			
Corporations (single segment)	477	64	542
Respondents			
Business Executives	118	31	151
IT Executives	90	20	111
Strategic Planners	<u>80</u>	<u>24</u>	<u>105</u>
Individual respondents	288	75	367
Survey Matching (within firm)			
Complete set of surveys received	46	16	63
Missing one survey (match 2 only)	33	5	38
Missing two surveys (match 1 only)	<u>56</u>	<u>12</u>	<u>68</u>
Corporations responding	135	33	169
Response Rate (% of sample frame)			
Corporations responding	28.3%	51.6%	31.2%
Complete surveys (fully matched)	9.6%	25.0%	11.6%

Totals are inclusive of responses from a Dutch firm that returned 4 surveys.

value survey, one IS strategy survey and one business strategy survey. Whereas we mailed IT business value surveys to at least one business executive, we only mailed one copy of the business and IS strategy surveys to the individuals identified above. A detailed summary of all responses received is shown in Table 1. Complete data (or fully matched surveys) was received for 63 corporations, giving an overall response rate of 11.6%. An analysis of nonresponding companies found no evidence of response bias on measures of revenues, profitability, employee count or total assets.[3] Furthermore, no significant country differences were found in comparing the 46 U.S. and 17 E.U. (i.e., Irish and Dutch) companies for which complete data had been received

Modeling Strategic Alignment

Venkatraman (1989b) devised a framework showing six perspectives of fit from the strategy literature—perspectives that can be used to reflect alignment between the business and IT strategy. Of these, moderation is the most appropriate, because this captures the interaction between the business and IS strategies as indicated in Figure 1. Although there are different ways to model moderation, earlier research by Chan et al. (1997) revealed that an interaction or product term was more appropriate and parsimonious than more complex polynomial forms. To model this interaction between the business and IS strategy, each of the 30 items from the IS strategy survey was paired with (and multiplied by) the corresponding item in the business strategy survey to produce 30 strategic alignment terms (recall: the text of the items in each survey was identical so that one-to-one matching was possible). Because analysis on the business and IS strategy items in their respective surveys found that the items factored into six process groups, the 30 strategic alignment items were grouped into the same process headings, and averages were taken to yield six process-level measures of strategic alignment.

As part of the measurement process, it was also recognized that firms could react differently to strategic alignment. For example, a corporation that saw IT as being critical to the business process might be disappointed with a particular measure of strategic alignment, while another corporation that used IT for support purposes alone might appear indifferent with the same measure of strategic alignment. To allow for this, we introduced weights to represent the importance of IT to each business process. Data on the importance of IT in each process was collected from respondents in each survey and was averaged to give an overall measure of IT importance in that process. So, at the conclusion of this step, for each of the 63 firms in our dataset, we had, for each of the six processes in the value chain, a measure of business strategy, IS strategy, strategic alignment and IT business value.

Finally, we examined data on strategic intent for IT as a way to classify firms into one of the four cells shown in Figure 2 (specific details of the classification technique are given in Tallon et al., 2000). Table 2 summarized the results of this classification.

It is interesting to note from Table 2 that no companies were assigned to the market focus cell. In previous research (Tallon et al. 2000), it was noted that market focus firms accounted for some 8% of the total population of corporations, and that these companies tended to be smaller in revenue terms and were almost exclusively based in the business and professional services sector. This included, for example,

Table 2: Classification of Firms by Strategic Intent for IT

Strategic Intent for IT	Number	%
Unfocused	13	20.6
Operations Focus	26	41.3
Market Focus	-	-
Dual Focus	24	38.1

firms involved in outsourcing, consulting and health care management services. Besides the fact that there were only 63 firms with complete data in the present study and that 8% of this number would represent only 5 firms, our decision to focus on large multibillion dollar companies in areas such as manufacturing, transport and utilities, wholesale and retail and financial services meant that there was a low probability that smaller, market focus firms would be identified in our later survey.

REVIEW OF FINDINGS AND DISCUSSION

An analysis of the business and IS strategy data for each of the six processes reveals some interesting facts. As indicated in Figure 3, strategic alignment is highest in production and operations and customer relations, indicating that there is a significant degree of IT support for business activities in these processes. Meanwhile, strategic alignment is lowest in sales and marketing, suggesting low levels of IT support for these activities and perhaps signaling a problem for firms that consider sales and marketing activities to be important to the success of their business.

In the arguments leading to the first hypothesis, we suggested that strategic alignment could have a positive impact on IT business value such that in processes where strategic alignment is higher, we might expect to find evidence of higher IT

Figure 3: Relating Strategic Alignment to Business and IS Strategy

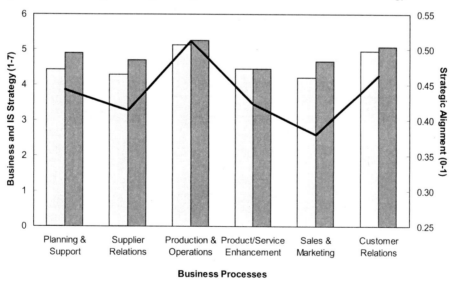

Figure 4: Strategic Alignment and IT Business Value (H1)

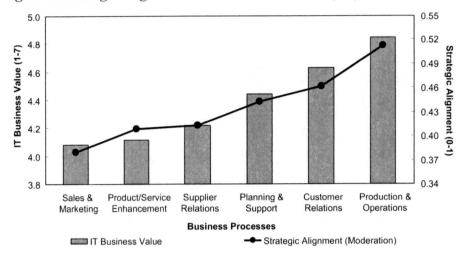

business value. Even when we consider that companies may have different strategic intent or goals for IT, there is still a basis for arguing that this relationship between strategic alignment and IT business value will be sustained across all corporations.

As shown in Figure 4, when we compare each process-level measure of strategic alignment in Figure 3 with the corresponding process-level measure of IT business value, a positive relationship emerges (the processes on the bottom axis in Figure 4 have been sorted to make this association more apparent). This relationship indicates that IT business value is related to strategic alignment such that increased IT business value may result from greater alignment between the business and IT strategies. Consistent with our earlier comments on Figure 3, production and operations and customer relations have the highest level of IT business value and strategic alignment, while sales and marketing has the lowest level of IT business value and strategic alignment. In summary, therefore, there is support for Hypothesis 1, from which we can conclude that an inability to realize payoffs from IT is due, at least in part, to an absence of, or deficiency in strategic alignment.

Investigating the Existence of an Alignment Paradox

The second hypothesis asked if firms with more focused or strategic goals for IT would report increased levels of strategic alignment. As shown in Table 3, when we examined strategic alignment for each of the three foci—unfocused, operations focus and dual focus—a pattern of results emerged that suggested that as firms pursue more strategic goals for IT, they also reported increased levels of strategic alignment. Specifically, unfocused firms had lower levels of strategic alignment throughout the value chain indicating consistently low levels of IT support for the business strategy. Meanwhile, operations focus firms had higher strategic

Table 3: Strategic Alignment by Strategic Intent for IT (Hypothesis 2)

Value Chain Processes	Strategic Alignment (Range: 0-1)			
	Unfocused	Operations Focus	Dual Focus	F (sig.)[1]
Process Planning and Support	0.393	0.437	0.477	1.019
Supplier Relations	0.325	0.341	0.486	1.917
Production and Operations	0.455	0.503	0.499	0.259
Product and Service Enhancement	0.391	0.401	0.462	0.367
Sales & Marketing Support	0.352	0.373	0.402	0.364
Customer Relations	0.376	0.454	0.518	1.399

[1] F statistics are not significant.

alignment throughout the value chain, though particularly in production and operations, consistent with using IT for efficiency and effectiveness. Finally, dual focus firms had the highest level of strategic alignment across the value chain, with the highest values being found in production and operations and customer relations, processes that are consistent with using IT for internal (efficiency and effectiveness) and external (marketing and customer) purposes.

Although Table 3 provides support for Hypothesis 2 in that firms with more focused goals for IT realize higher levels of strategic alignment, a one-way analysis of variance failed to find significant differences in process-level measures of strategic alignment, though significant differences had been found for IT business value. Because there is a positive link between strategic alignment and IT business value, it seems unusual that there were no significant differences in terms of strategic alignment. One possible reason for this would be if strategic alignment exhibited diminishing marginal returns so that the gain in IT payoffs from each successive increase in strategic alignment would be smaller. Another reason could be that for dual focus firms especially, increased strategic alignment, while helping to increase IT payoffs, could somehow have an adverse impact on the ability of the corporations to be flexible in how they respond to external events. For corporations that fail to identify this possibility and instead pursue ever-higher levels of strategic alignment, there might be an adverse outcome in which greater strategic alignment in fact leads to a decline in payoffs from IT.

To investigate this further, we created a scatter graph containing, for each firm, a firm-level measure of strategic alignment and IT business value (these measures are averages of the six process-level measures). As seen in Figure 5, when we fitted a second-degree polynomial curve to the data for each focus type, the shape of each curve suggested that higher levels of strategic alignment eroded IT payoffs. While we may have expected the critical level for dual focus firms to be higher than for

Figure 5: An Alignment Paradox (Scatter Plot)

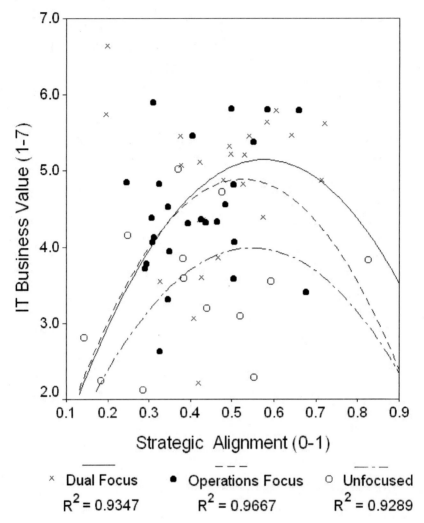

× Dual Focus	● Operations Focus	○ Unfocused
$R^2 = 0.9347$	$R^2 = 0.9667$	$R^2 = 0.9289$

operations focus or unfocused firms, that did not occur, as the critical level of strategic alignment for all three foci was almost the same, falling in the range 0.48 to 0.56. It was also interesting to find in Figure 5 that for each focus type, there are only a small number of firms to the right of the critical point, meaning that for the vast majority of corporations, strategic alignment is still positively related to IT business value. Nevertheless, for each focus type, the inverted shape of each curve supports the existence of an alignment paradox. Consequently, efforts to improve IT payoffs through strategic alignment are only likely to succeed up to a point. As we move beyond that point, further increases in strategic alignment may have an adverse impact on IT payoffs—a paradoxical outcome that holds for all firms, irrespective of their strategic intent for IT.

Factors Related to the Alignment Paradox

Identifying what factors determine the location of this point is important to understanding the limits of the relationship between strategic alignment and IT payoffs and to being able to find ways to avoid any adverse impacts of strategic alignment. One factor that may play a role in the location of this point is the extent of environmental uncertainty and corporations' desire to maintain flexibility in order to respond to external events. For example, in a turbulent environment where corporations are faced with multiple challenges, flexibility in the business or IS strategy may be the difference between success and failure. If corporations are tightly aligned, they may not be able to initiate the necessary changes in the business strategy. IT legacy systems that had supported a previous business strategy and around which the corporation has grown may become a limiting factor as corporations strive to alter the business strategy. In a more stable environment, corporations may be more willing to pursue strategic alignment, because the need to retain flexibility is not as important as in a turbulent setting.

To investigate the possible impact of environment on strategic alignment, we included a series of questions on clock-speed in the business strategy survey. Clock-speed refers to industry variables such as length of product life cycle, percentage of revenues received from new product launches, pace of product price changes and rate of customer turnover (Mendelson & Ziegler, 1999). Corporations in high clock-speed industries such as semiconductors, PC hardware production or biotechnology face highly dynamic environments characterized by frequent product changes and falling product prices. Respondents to the strategic planner's survey were asked to identify these operational indicators for a flagship product or service. Because firms in the same industry are likely to report the same clock-speed, we split our data into industry groups using two-digit SIC codes, and then further split the companies in each sector into smaller subgroups according to strategic intent for IT. This allowed us to focus on the largest sectors in our data: manufacturing, transport/utilities, wholesale/retail and financial services.

As shown in Table 4, when we examined clock-speed by sector and by focus type, we found that in each sector, dual focus firms had higher clock-speed than unfocused and operations focus firms. This means that dual focus firms have shorter product life cycles (and faster product launches) and receive a higher percentage of sales from products launched over the last two years. For example, in financial services, dual focus firms earn over 60% of their revenues from recent product launches compared with 26% for operations focus firms. Dual focus firms also have a product life cycle of only 32 months as against 78 months for operations focus firms. If we try to relate these measures of clock-speed to measures of strategic alignment from Table 3, we find that firms with greater clock-speed also report higher strategic alignment, but the addition of the data in Figure 5 might then suggest

Table 4: Industry Clock-speed—Key Operational Indicators

	Manufacturing	Transport and Utilities	Wholesale and Retail Trade	Financial Services
Length of Life Cycle of Product / Service (months)				
Unfocused	49.6	-	15.0	-
Operations Focus	62.5	102.0	36.3	78.0
Dual Focus	59.3	32.0	21.0	32.0
Percentage of Sales from Products/Services Launched in the Last Two Years (%)				
Unfocused	31.8	-	22.5	-
Operations Focus	28.7	10.5	26.0	25.5
Dual Focus	50.8	18.0	57.5	61.7

that this relationship between clock-speed and strategic alignment is incomplete. Specifically, while dual focus firms may have higher strategic alignment, there is a possibility that due to having higher clock-speed, they are somehow forced to rethink any move that involves an increase in strategic alignment if at the same time, this could lead to a reduction in the payoffs they realize from their IT investment.

From a managerial viewpoint, it is important to recognize that environmental uncertainty and clock-speed are opposite sides of the same coin. In a sector with shrinking product life cycles, falling prices and frequent product launches, there is likely to be a great deal of uncertainty. Faced with this, efforts to pursue tighter strategic alignment by adopting certain types of IT may not be optimal in the long-term if this entails, for example, locking a corporation into a particular limiting IT infrastructure or set of technology choices. If changes in the environment call for a change in IT at some future point, earlier choices may prevent the corporation from responding. Because dual focus firms are particularly open to the environment through their emphasis on customers and market issues, efforts to boost short-term IT support for the business strategy could possibly limit organizational flexibility and so prevent the firm from pursuing future business opportunities. While there is considerable scope for future research in this area, the prospects of an alignment paradox, especially if accompanied by turbulent conditions, is troubling for firms that consider strategic alignment a way to realize a greater return on their IT investments.

CONCLUSION

Although researchers have frequently argued that strategic alignment enables corporations to realize greater IT payoffs, there has been very little empirical research to confirm or deny this claim. In this paper, we use a model of the value chain to evaluate the link between strategic alignment and IT business value. We define strategic alignment as a bidirectional relationship between business and IT strategy. Specifically, strategic alignment reflects IT shortfall (the extent to which IT supports the business strategy) and IT underutilization (the extent to which business strategy capitalizes on IT). Strategic alignment is then modeled as an interaction or product term involving multiple process-level measures of business and IS strategy. To test the relationship between strategic alignment and payoffs from IT, we analyzed data from 63 firms. The results of this analysis confirm that strategic alignment is related to payoffs from IT at the process level. From this, we can conclude that firms that use IT to provide greater support for the business strategy will realize greater payoffs from IT. Despite this, our findings also point to the existence of an apparent alignment paradox—strategic alignment may lead to greater payoffs from IT, but this relationship is only valid up to a certain critical level of strategic alignment. Beyond this point, further strategic alignment leads to a decline in IT payoffs.

In the next phase of this research, we plan to explore different variables that might give rise to an alignment paradox. There is also a need to investigate the relationship between strategic alignment and organizational flexibility and to identify if management practices can reduce any of the negative consequences of strategic alignment. We encourage researchers to consider these important issues.

ACKNOWLEDGMENTS

This research has been supported by grants from the CISE/IIS/CSS Division of the U.S. National Science Foundation and the NSF Industry/University Cooperative Research Center (CISE/EEC) to the Center for Research on Information Technology and Organizations (CRITO) at the University of California, Irvine. Industry sponsors include ATL Products, the Boeing Company, Canon Information Systems, Conexant Systems, IBM, Nortel Networks, Microsoft, Seagate Technology, Sun Microsystems, and the Whirlpool Corporation.

ENDNOTES

[1] Decisions involving IT infrastructure may have long-term implications that restrict or limit a firm's ability to enact future changes in the business strategy. For example, in describing Dell's decision to reject SAP as a solution to Dell's integrated resource planning needs, Kraemer, Dedrick, and Yamashiro (2000) cite a leading Dell IT executive as saying, "SAP is like cement, flexible when poured but rigid once it hardens" (p. 14).

[2] Single segment corporations were chosen as a way to control for the differences between business strategy in each segment. For example, in a corporation like GE, business strategies can vary widely across segments.

[3] Average 1998 revenues for the 63 "complete" companies was $7.36 billion. Average revenues of incomplete companies (missing at most two surveys) were $5.49 billion, while non-responding companies (no survey received) had average revenues of $4.48 billion.

REFERENCES

Andrews, K. R. (1980). *The Concept of Corporate Strategy*. Homewood, IL: Dow Jones-Irwin.

Bakos, J. Y. &Kemerer, C.F. (1992). Recent Applications of Economic Theory in Information Technology Research, *Decision Support Systems*, 8 (5), . 365–386.

Bourgeois, L. J. III. (1985) Strategic Goals, Perceived Uncertainty, and Economic Performance in Volatile Environments, *Academy of Management Journal*, *28* (3), 548–573.

Broadbent, M. & Weill, P. (1993). Improving Business and Information Strategy Alignment: Learning from the Banking Industry, *IBM Systems Journal*, *32* (1), 162–179.

Chan, Y. E., Huff, S. L., Barclay, D. W., & Copeland, D. G. (1997). Business Strategy Orientation, Information Systems Orientation and Strategic Alignment, *Information Systems Research*, *8* (2), 125–150.

Computer Sciences Corporation (CSC). *Critical Issues in Information Systems Management*, Annual Survey, 2000.

Davis, G. & Olson, M. (1985). *Management Information Systems*. New York, NY: McGraw-Hill.

DeLone, W. H. & McLean, E. R. (1992). Information Systems Success: The Quest for the Dependent Variable, *Information Systems Research*, *3* (1), 60–95.

Henderson, J. C. & Venkatraman, N. (1993). Strategic Alignment: Leveraging Information Technology for Transforming Organizations, *IBM Systems Journal*, *32* (1), 4–16.

Jarvenpaa, S. L. & Ives, B. (1994). Organizational Fit and Flexibility: IT Design Principles for a Globally Competing Firm. In C. C. Snow (Ed.), *Strategy, Organization Design and Human Resource Management*. Vol. 3 pp. 1–39. Greenwich, Connecticut: JAI Press Inc.

Kearns, G. S. (1997). Alignment of Information Systems Strategy with Business Strategy: Impact on the Use of IS for Competitive Advantage. Unpublished doctoral dissertation, University of Kentucky.

Kraemer, K. L., Dedrick, J., & Yamashiro, S. (2000). Refining and Extending the Business Model with Information Technology: Dell Computer Corp., *The Information Society, 16* (1), 5–21.

McFarlan, W., McKenney, J. L., & Pyburn, P. (1983). The Information Archipelago – Plotting a Course, *Harvard Business Review, 83* (1), 145–156.

Mendelson, H. & Ziegler, J. (1999). *Survival of the Smartest: Managing Information for Rapid Action and World-Class Performance.* New York, NY: John Wiley & Sons.

Mintzberg, H. (1978). Patterns in Strategy Formation, *Management Science, 24* (9), 934–948.

Porter, M. E. (1985). *Competitive Advantage.* New York, NY: Free Press.

Porter, M. E. (1996). What is Strategy? *Harvard Business Review, 74* (6), 61–77.

Prairie, P. (1996). Benchmarking IT Strategic Alignment. In J. N. Luftman (Ed.), *Competing in the Information Age: Strategic Alignment in Practice.* pp. 242–290. New York: Oxford University Press.

Price Waterhouse (1996). *Information Technology Review 1995/96.* United Kingdom: Price Waterhouse.

Reich, B. Horner & Benbasat, I. (1996). Measuring the Linkage Between Business and Information Technology Objectives, *MIS Quarterly, 20* (1), 55–81.

Roach, S. S. (1991). Services Under Siege: The Restructuring Imperative. *Harvard Business Review, 69* (5), 82–91.

Rockart, J. F. & Flannery, L. S. (1983). The Management of End User Computing. *Communications of the ACM, 26*, 776-784.

Tallon, P. P., Kraemer, K. L., & Gurbaxani, V. (1998). *Fact or Fiction: The Reality Behind Executives' Perceptions of IT Business Value,* Working paper, CRITO, Graduate School of Management, University of California, Irvine.

Tallon, P. P., Kraemer, K. L., & Gurbaxani, V. (2000). Executives' Perceptions of the Contribution of Information Technology to Firm Performance: A Process-Oriented Approach, *Journal of Management Information Systems, 16* (4), 137–165.

Tallon, P. P., Kraemer, K. L., Gurbaxani, V., & Mooney, J. G. (1997) A Multidimensional Assessment of the Contribution of IT to Firm Performance. In Proceedings of the 5th European Conference on Information Systems. pp. 846–867. Cork, Ireland.

Venkatraman, N. (1989a). "Strategic Orientation of Business Enterprises: The Construct, Dimensionality, and Measurement," *Management Science*, 1989a, 35 (8), pp. 942–962.

Venkatraman, N. (1989b). The Concept of Fit in Strategy Research: Toward Verbal and Statistical Correspondence. *Academy of Management Review*, *14* (3), 423–444.

Venkatraman, N. & Ramanujam, V. (1987). Measurement of Business Economic Performance: An examination of Method Convergence. *Journal of Management*, *13* (1), 109–122.

Watson, R. T. (1990). Influences on the IS Manager's Perceptions of Key Issues: Information Scanning and the Relationship with the CEO. *MIS Quarterly*, *14* (2), 217–231.

Chapter II

Information-Induced Strategic Alignment: Toward a Semiological Analysis

Ra'ed M. Shams
University of Bahrain, Bahrain

Frederick P. Wheeler
University of Bradford, UK

The concept of strategic alignment between organizational policies for business and information systems (IS) has not been defined previously in informational terms. In this paper, we define informational aspects of organizational behavior in three semiological dimensions: pragmatics, semantics and syntactics. We also introduce dynamics as a fourth dimension to address time-related changes. We demonstrate the importance of these ideas in the analysis of strategic alignment by taking recent examples to show how informational attributes are often implicitly discussed in the literature. We believe that the precise definition of the informational aspects of alignment is a necessary prerequisite for the advancement of understanding in this important area.

INTRODUCTION

Undoubtedly, Information Technology (IT) is essential for capturing, processing, storing and transmitting data in large and small organizations. The effective deployment of IT enables organizations to sustain competitive advantage in the marketplace (Cash & Konsynski, 1985; Konsynski, 1993) and obliges them to consider the alignment of their IT and their businesses. Organizations that manage to align their IT with their organization's capabilities harvest better utilization of their IT investments (Sabherwal & Kirs, 1994) and have an overall better organizational performance (Chan, Huff, Copeland, & Barclay, 1997; Sabherwal & Kirs, 1994; Teo & King, 1999).

An organization could be in a certain state of alignment at any point of time. This state is achieved through complex processes based on actions taken by all strategic, tactical and/or operational levels in the organization to gain inter/intrasynergy between internal and external policies. Although alignment generally refers to arranging policies in different areas so that they relatively match or correspond with one another, the precise definition of alignment in terms of business/IS relationship context still needs further clarification. Henderson and Venkatraman (1993) differentiate in their capstone paper between "traditional views on linkage" and "strategic alignment." The former refers to the automation and support of business processes by IT; while strategic alignment implies a more fundamental and strategically important role for IT. They define (Henderson & Venkatraman, 1993, Table 1) strategic alignment as, "selecting appropriate *alignment* perspectives for achieving business objectives" (our emphasis). Similarly, Luftman's (2001) definition of alignment addresses the processes in which *alignment* can be achieved between IT and business departments. Consequently, the central concept of alignment is inadequately defined due to the recursive use of the term "alignment." Other researchers have restricted the notion of alignment to certain processes or attributes such as understanding and commitment (Reich & Benbasat, 2000), coordination of objectives and views (Burn & Szeto, 2000) and communication and management processes (Prairie, 1996). Therefore, there is a need for a comprehensive, multiattribute definition, when discussing alignment, because unthinking acquiescence to rhetorical exhortations to align IS with the business may result in unintended consequences.

Consider the results of research into decision making in complex environments. If alignment is interpreted as tight coupling of systems, the resulting "stiffness" in complex interacting organizational systems will increase the likelihood of failure (Perrow, 1984). But, this does not rule out the need for certain levels of tight coupling—to elevate the organization's efficiency while still allowing for innovation through change (Butler, Price, Coates, & Pike, 1998)—or creativity through differences (Stacey, 2000) by the loose coupling of the organizational systems. However, a business is more than a collection of decision-making processes and physical activities; it is also a network of relationships that attempt to drive decision making toward collective goals while attending to the diverse needs of individuals (Checkland, 1999; Checkland & Holwell, 1998). These aims may be at variance, and the increased importance of IT can amplify differences between business and IS specialists in terms of language, strategic expectations, and organizational needs.

BACKGROUND LITERATURE

As explained earlier, there is evidence of positive relationship between higher levels of integration and organizational performance (Chan et al., 1997; Sabherwal & Kirs, 1994; Teo & King, 1999). It is argued that integration should focus on business advantage rather than IT novelty (Doherty, Marples, & Suhaimi, 1999; King & Teo, 2000), which is of secondary importance. IT provides the medium and means of processing, refining and transmitting information—in some activities, IT has simply replaced the ancient technology of pen and paper—but it is information that is of primary interest (Clarke, 2000).

Research on the linkages between IS policies and business strategies goes back over two decades, since the work of King (1978). He proposed a one-way sequential integration and approach from business planning to IS planning. The discussion of integration/alignment has raised the question of whether business strategy should drive or be driven by developments in IT (Venkatraman, 1991). For example, in certain organizations corporate strategy pulls the development of information strategy along in support, but in organizations that are dependent on information technology to sustain their competitive advantage the pull linkage is expected to fail (Applegate, McFarlan, McKenney, & Cash, 1996). Probably the most well-known framework for discussing the alignment between IS and business departments is the Strategic Alignment Model (SAM) (Henderson & Venkatraman, 1993). This seminal model identifies the issues that need to be resolved between the domains of business strategy, IT strategy, organizational infrastructure and IS infrastructure. Table 1 compares the four alignment perspectives on, or dominant patterns of, strategic alignment identified from SAM (Venkatraman, 1991). Each perspective is a process anchored in one of the four domains for which an appropriate sequence of perspectives on strategic planning has been adopted. These perspectives are meant to allow strategic fit and functional integration to occur (Papp, 2001). Papp (2001) has added several other perspectives starting from other anchors in the model.

Table 1: Original Alignment Perspectives of the SAM [Adopted from Papp (2001) and Venkatraman (1991)]

	Competitive Potential	Technology Potential	Business Value / Strategy Execution	Service Level
Domain Anchor	Product-market Arena	IT arena	Organisational domain	IS products and services
Management Focus	Reengineer business processes	Adapting the IT platform	Transforming work and organisation	Redesigning IS portfolio
Analytical Frameworks	Competitive Strategy frameworks	Technology scan and forecasting scenarios	Business process analysis	Portfolio analysis of applications
Measures	Business measures relative to competitors	Measures of IT capability	Organisational efficiency	Service levels
Strongest Domain	IT strategy	Business strategy	Business strategy	IT strategy
Pivot	Business strategy	IT strategy	Business Infrastructure	IT Infrastructure
Impact	Business Infrastructure	IT Infrastructure	IT Infrastructure	Business Infrastructure

In complement to the above well-known model, strategic alignment has had different names and been researched from different angles. Luftman (2001) identified five levels of alignment maturity and their corresponding maturity criteria. Chorn (1991) argues that there should be alignment between competitive situations, strategy, organizational culture and leadership style. Alignment has been approached in different ways, from the point of business and IS alignment (Chorn, 1991; Henderson & Venkatraman, 1991), strategic fit (Chan, et al., 997; Goodhue & Thompson, 1995; Henderson & Venkatraman, 1994), cross-functional integration (Nelson, 2001), organizational fit (Earl, Oxford Institute of Information Management, & PA Consulting Group, 1996), the socio-technical approach (Mumford & Beekman, 1994), and the extent of integration between IT and business activities (Teo & King, 1997). Additionally, strategic alignment has been discussed in terms of strategy and structure (Chan, 1997, 1999; Chan, 2001; Henderson & Venkatraman, 1993, 1994; Segars & Grover, 1999; Teo & Ang, 1999), while other studies have focused on the social dimensions of alignment (Cooper, 1998; Horton, 1998; Reich & Benbasat, 2000). Horovitz (1984) discussed all three highly interlinked aspects: strategy, structure and social.

Although most studies have been concerned with material outcomes to improve the efficiency and performance of organizations, such as IT plans, structures, performance, and so on, information within IS also influence the organizational experiences of employees, their welfare and their quality of life. Thus, social aspects, such as the vagueness and ambiguity that often characterize human affairs, are usually blamed for the ineffective utilization of IT in businesses (Peppard & Ward, 1999). In addition to the lack of systemic definition of the concept of alignment, few studies tried to investigate its social aspects (Chan, 1997), but they either do not take a comprehensive view or were too broad to effectively generate a working frame (Caldow & Kirby, 1996). For instance, some research projects have attempted to identify the factors that affect alignment between IS and business departments (e.g., Chan, 1997; Luftman & Brier, 1999; Teo & Ang, 1999; Teo & King, 1997). Others have focused on specific alignment attributes, such as shared business vision between the IS department and the organization as a whole (Roepke, Agarwal, & Ferratt, 2000); what make IS plans useful (Teo & Ang, 2000); the alignment of expectations in IS projects (Cooper, 1998); the interlink between planning, organizational knowledge and communications (Nelson, 2001); events that influence the alignment process (Reich & Benbasat, 2000); the effect of shared knowledge between business and IS departments on the organization's performance (Nelson & Cooprider, 1996); and the advent of electronic commerce (Galliers, 1999), particularly when linked to business network redesign (Venkatraman, 1994).

However, current ways of approaching the alignment issue are at an early stage and focus on particular aspects of the problem, for example, by proposing different approaches or methods to achieve alignment (Henderson & Venkatraman, 1991, 1993; Kearns & Lederer, 2000; Luftman, 2001; Nelson, 2001) or focusing on specific alignment attributes as identified above. Thus, it is time to consider a systemic view of alignment and its detailed attributes. Hence, this research is an attempt to complement previous research studies rather than to compete with them; these studies have been invaluable in identifying the need for and nature of strategic alignment and have identified, through empirical evidence, that the nature of alignment depends upon the timeframe for analysis (Reich & Benbasat, 2000). The next two sections set the logical underpinnings for our proposed solution emerging from the fields of information and semiotics studies.

ALIGNMENT AND INFORMATION

Because goals of economic institutions and activities are embodied within the goals of the social networks and activities (Granovetter, 1985, 1992), decisions are made by groups of people who have different background values, assumptions, or objectives, and who explicitly and implicitly influence the creation of alignment. People interact with each other using different types of tacit and explicit information governed by a set of organizational procedures (Checkland & Holwell, 1998).

Thus, information is the core component of any IS, whether computerized with IT (CIS) or noncomputerized (Mingers, 1995, 1996; Stamper, 1973). It is information that connects these people, whether in personal relationships, leisure, learning or business. IS consists of information, people and procedures.

On the contrary, IT is meant to effectively and efficiently automate IS by reprocessing information mathematically and logically. CIS can be seen as a service system that serves those people who are taking actions (Checkland & Holwell, 1998). King, Grover, and Hulfnagel (1989) cited in Ghuloom (1997, p. 23) said that, "IT depreciates over time since its potential for adding value decreases as time goes by. In contrast, information appreciates as time passes. The new uses of information and better understanding of it causes this appreciation in worth."

But, there exists a major confusion between the material output of information as a commodity to make more money and information as the nervous system that creates or obfuscates understanding and makes or changes human relationships (Stamper, 2000). It is information that provides competitive advantage rather than IT per se (Clarke, 2000).

Stamper (1973) found the following:

Information ... is a process of creating, adjusting and maintaining relationships among the participants in a drama or real task. This is a totally different perspective from that of the technical computer specialist who thinks of information as a commodity to be stored, retrieved and processed by machinery. (p. 255).

SEMIOTICS AND ORGANIZATIONAL BEHAVIOR

Information is represented and transmitted in certain forms, collectively called signs, such as written alphanumeric characters, spoken words and actions. Signs gain specific sociably recognized interpretations (Mingers, 1995) through habitual learning from custom or convention, or generally from the social environment surrounding us (LaFollette, 2000). We found Stamper's (Stamper, 2000) definition of signs brief and precise: "A sign is anything that 'conveys' information because it stands for something else [such as intentions, meanings and/or actions] within a community of users."

Therefore, signs, in the form of information, have semiotic properties (Mingers, 1995, 1996; Stamper, 1973). They are generated within the organization or arise in its environment and are interpreted by the organization. It follows that semiotic attributes already are attributes of the organization or they are inherited or learned from its environment. Thus, an organization has semiotic properties, and the signs and messages its members use reflect the organizational state.

Figure 1: Logic of the Proposed Definition of Informational Alignment

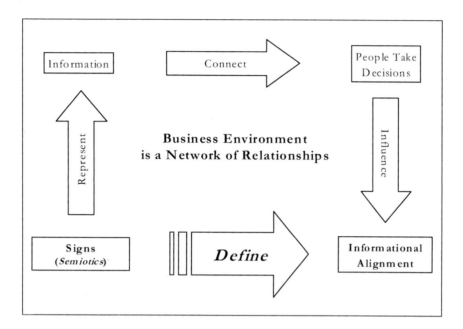

Linking the discussion in the previous section to the above argument, we propose that strategic informational alignment can be analyzed in terms of semiotic dimensions. Thus, the quest for strategic alignment leads to the properties of signs and suggests that the significant properties of IS are to be found in semiotics (Stamper, 1973, p. 255). Figure 1 illustrates our proposed links between informational alignment and semiotics.

Semiotics is the scientific study of signs,[3] and has three classical subdivisions: pragmatics, semantics, and syntactics (Morris, 1938). These dimensions are meant to apply pure semiotics to the study of human behaviors (sometimes called behavioristics) in a successful attempt to make empirically verifiable predictions about human behaviors (Morris, 1946). A fourth subdivision of semiotics, empirics, was defined by Stamper (1973) and is concerned with the statistical properties of information. This is largely a material rather than a human aspect of information and as such is not part of our present concern.

In the next sections, we will precisely define from the semiotics literature the above four dimensions and link them to their organizational behaviors, named hereafter as informational attributes, from the IS literature. Subsequently, a model will be discussed that combines all the four dimensions and its implications on informational alignment.

INFORMATIONAL DIMENSIONS OF ALIGNMENT

Following Morris (1946), we identify pragmatics with "the origin, uses and effects of signs within the behavior in which they occur." (p. 219) In a business context, pragmatics is concerned with the relationship of signs to the people who interpret them and those who may originate them.

"Semantics deals with the signification of signs in all modes of signifying," according to Morris (1946). By signification, Morris meant the (possibly implied) set of conditions to which a sign refers. For example, the standard European exit sign is a legal requirement in public buildings within the European Community. It signifies a way out of a building through a door or opening, possibly preceded or followed by stairs, to a safe level. It does not normally imply an exit by jumping through a tenth-story window. Most Europeans will understand the exit sign in this sense, although they may not have read the regulations that govern the use of the sign. Therefore, semantics deals with explicit and implicit significance, including the background of understanding in which signs are interpreted.

And Morris (1946) said, "Syntactics deals with combinations of signs without regard for their specific significations or their relation to the behavior in which they occur." Morris suggested that syntactics concerns the formal relations between signs. It is possible to place signs in particular sequences, or to follow rules for manipulating signs without specifying the semantic or pragmatic attributes of those signs. For example, a computer programmer gives written or verbal instructions for the completion of a business procedure to an automaton, ensuring that the sequence of signs conforms to specific rules. The automaton has no knowledge of the significance of the sign and the designer of the automaton will have interpreted the sign sequence beforehand, thereby anticipating the behavior the programmer intended to invoke. Thus, the syntactic properties of signs can be separated from semantic and pragmatic properties. Moreover, in a business context, the syntactic, semantic and pragmatic properties of signs are certainly human creations.

Morris's three dimensions give an analytically exhaustive subdivision only if their concepts are defined more broadly than they often are (Noth, 1990). Hence, it will help to identify correspondences between the three properties and organizational behaviors. We define the state of organizational behavior in three semiotic dimensions as follows. The pragmatic state of an organization is the structure of common or conflicting intentions and interests between its members. The semantic state represents the structure of tacit and explicit organizational understanding, which may be common or particular to certain individuals. The syntactic state consists of the structure of organizational procedures, routines, or recipes, which may be uniformly adopted or may be specific to the work of certain individuals or groups. These structures are embedded within social and moral structures, such as relationships involving trust and personal commitment.

Based on the latter definitions of semiological dimensions, it follows that each individual has his or her own *understanding* of the signs in the world around us. Groups of people may or may not share that understanding together. Hence, certain *intentions* are formed that will be translated into *purposeful actions* to try to realize the intentions that will recursively create new signs (Mingers, 1995) and affect the understanding of the world (Checkland & Holwell, 1998; Checkland & Scholes, 1990).

Informational aspects of alignment span through the other traditional aspects of alignment discussed above: strategy, structure and social. As we now illustrate, it is possible to identify examples of pragmatics, semantics and syntactics alignment in IS research.

Pragmatic Alignment

Pragmatic alignment consists of matching intentions and interests and leads to signs and messages that channel the influence of power (Horton, 1998) to achieve intentions, or that are aimed to produce a change of attitude leading to compliant behavior.

Intentions are the conceptions formed by, consciously or unconsciously, directing the mind, and hence, human actions toward an object, subject or action.[4]

Figure 2: Informational Attributes of the Pragmatics Dimension

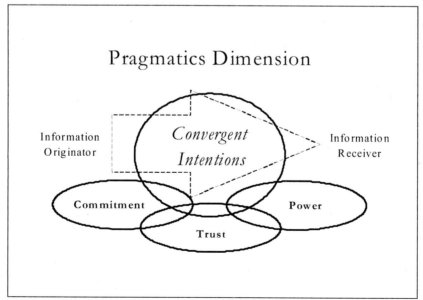

Observations of pragmatic alignment behaviors are recorded in several IS studies, in terms of the influence of power, commitment and trust (Figure 2). Information contents most probably enable convergences in intentions depending on the information originator and receiver.

Introducing a new IS in an organization is usually resisted when it is intended to alter the balance of power (Markus, 1994). An example of the influence of power to achieve a state of pragmatic alignment is illustrated by the often-stated need for support from senior executives if IS projects are to sustain business success (Broadbent & Weill, 1993). Therefore, in order for IS plans to be useful, they must be promoted to top management (Teo & Ang, 2000).

Sometimes IS managers may need the support of a senior executive, such as the CEO, to empower them. At other times, strong leadership by IS management (Luftman & Brier, 1999) can be used to neutralize the anticipated influence of line managers. IS managers can also secure support among users for IT projects by identifying appropriate business sponsors (Chan, 1997, 1999).

Not only is the budgetary and rhetorical support of top management influential in IS success, but top management must be committed to the strategic use of IT (Broadbent & Weill, 1993; Teo & Ang, 1999). Signs of this commitment, for example, include the allocation of suitable and sufficient resources to IS projects, and senior executives directing rather than restraining IS plans (Teo & Ang, 1999). Equally, it is known that the IS department must signal their commitment to the plans and goals of the business (Luftman & Brier, 1999), and they must show a sense of ownership toward the needs and problems of the business departments (Broadbent & Weill, 1993).

The credibility of the IS department is a key factor in improving the relationship between IS and business departments (Luftman & Brier, 1999). The converse behavior is also observed, at least for short-term alignment, where failures in IT implementation lower the level of commitment and, hence, reduce the level of trust (Reich & Benbasat, 2000). Trust is closely linked to power (Allen, Colligan, Finnie, & Kern, 2000), both of which influence and are influenced by reinforcing behavioral signals. The length of tenure of the CIO is a sign of commitment, which helps to build strong relationships between business and IS departments, and is reinforced when the CIO gains the respect of business departments through successful project outcomes (Chan, 1997, 1999). Users' trust in IS staff is built by recognizing and being responsive to their needs and by keeping up to date with new developments in IT (Teo & Ang, 1999). This competency in IT signifies that the IS department can provide business departments with strategic technical solutions to their needs and problems and may lead to IS management participating in business planning (Reich & Benbasat, 2000; Teo & Ang, 1999).

Semantic Alignment

Semantic alignment involves harmonizing the structure of tacit and explicit organizational knowledge, for example, by the shared understanding of business issues, the common interpretation of strategic vision, and shared expectations (Broadbent & Weill, 1993; Luftman & Brier, 1999). The business knowledge of IS managers has been found to be a critical factor for alignment (Luftman & Brier, 1999; Teo & Ang, 1999; Teo & King, 1997). Figure 3 shows the possible informational attributes that formulate the semantics dimension. Next, examples of each attribute are discussed.

Figure 3: Informational Attributes of the Semantics Dimension

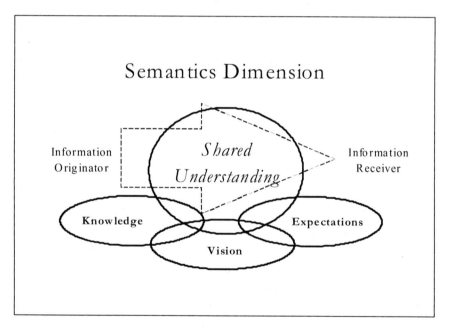

Successful deployment of IT requires that IS managers clearly understand business objectives and strategies (Teo & Ang, 1999, 2000; Teo & King, 1997). Where they have a high level of business and IS knowledge, they are more likely to become involved in the organization's strategy development (Luftman & Brier, 1999) and thereby influence the deployment of their own visions and plans (Teo & Ang, 1999). A high degree of shared domain knowledge among IS and business executives results in opening channels of communication between them (Reich & Benbasat, 2000).

On the other hand, a lack of business knowledge by the IS department will shake the confidence of business managers (Teo & Ang, 1999), and IS managers may be perceived as computer "geeks" who do not speak the same language as others. Teo and King (1997) advocate through their empirical work that the business knowledge of the IS manager is the main organizational factor that drives alignment. Likewise, any planning and control mechanisms, such as the IS steering committee, will fail if little or no shared knowledge exists between the participants (Reich & Benbasat, 2000). Strategic movement of personnel between the business and IS departments facilitates the sharing of knowledge (Chan, 1997, 1999). Similarly, user training is considered an important enabler to alignment (Broadbent & Weill, 1993; Chan, 1997, 1999).

When the IS department shares a vision with the rest of the organization, it is better positioned to offer useful technological solutions (Chan, 1997, 1999; Luftman & Brier, 1999; Roepke, Agarwal, & Ferratt, 2000). Vision as an emergent set of convergent ideas and actions in an organization (Mintzberg, 1994) is usually difficult to articulate (Reich & Benbasat, 2000) and, hence, difficult to communicate and share. Therefore, capturing corporate vision requires different sets of techniques (Avison, Eardley, & Powell, 1998), and most strategy models fail to address it sufficiently (Stacey, 1996). When worldviews are understood by all parties (Checkland & Scholes, 1990), the organization is expected to achieve greater alignment and business success (Allen et al., 2000; Broadbent & Weill, 1993; Newport, Dess, & Rasheed, 1991; Reich & Benbasat, 2000).

It is emphasized that organizations' new strategies should be aligned with their business culture (Caldow & Kirby, 1996). It is difficult to solve conflicts arising from such misalignment (Markus, 1994). The strategy must change, or the culture should be carefully changed to match the new strategy (Semler, 1997). Common goals and aligned objectives are considered of high importance especially in organizations with cross-functional teams, so that decisions are not made in ignorance of the consequences to stakeholders (Weir, Kochhar, LeBeau, & Edgeley, 2000).

As the organization converges toward shared knowledge and vision, the level of disparity of perceptions is reduced. Expectations set the limits and boundaries to perceptions of success and satisfaction. Business departments perceive the IS department to be successful and worthy of their trust (Chan, 1997, 1999) if and only if IS meets its commitments, in terms of project delivery and user support, to the expectations of the business departments (Teo & Ang, 1999). The degree to which expectations are achieved or exceeded induces a level of satisfaction with IT, and the level of satisfaction, in turn, influences the perceived level of success (Cooper, 1998). The management of user expectations is considered important in building the shared understanding (Allen et al., 2000; Cooper, 1998).

Syntactic Alignment

Syntactic alignment consists of synchronized work routines, timely planning procedures and management control procedures with formal and informal communications, reporting structures and coordinated meetings (Figure 4). IS researchers identified the need for effective interpersonal communication in order for IS to be in harmony with the business (Luftman & Brier, 1999; Newport, Dess, & Rasheed, 1991) and for social interaction to reduce semantic variance between groups (Allen et al., 2000; Nelson & Cooprider, 1996). A strong relationship between the IS manager and the top management is usually achieved through informal settings and less structured communications (Chan, 1997, 1999). Similarly, the generation gap between younger, high achievers and older, cost-oriented employees (Chan, 2001) could be reduced through social and informal communications.

Although that informal social communication reduces semantic variance between groups (Nelson & Cooprider, 1996), it is insufficient when developing strategic IS plans (Lederer & Mendelow, 1987), and this leads to the need for formal procedures and structured communications. Moreover, there seems to be a general agreement that some of the informational attributes, such as mutual influence, trust (Broadbent & Weill, 1993; Nelson & Cooprider, 1996), commitment (Broadbent & Weill, 1993), shared knowledge and shared vision (Broadbent & Weill, 1993; Nelson & Cooprider, 1996; Reich & Benbasat, 2000; Teo & Ang, 1999) are better realized through structured communication rather than informal communications. Structured, bi-directional, communication at all levels in the organization is important to achieving integration between functions and between people (Weir et al., 2000).

Figure 4: Informational Attributes of the Syntactics Dimension

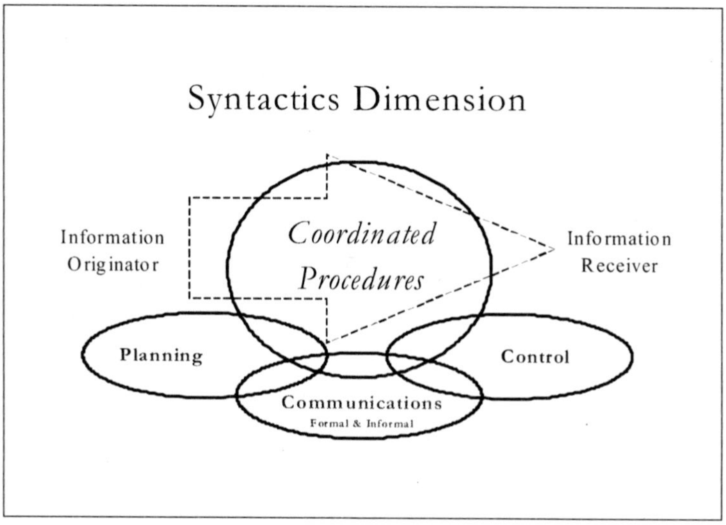

Corrective control procedures involve monitoring, feedback, learning and timely action. Thus, effective control procedures, in fast-changing IT environments, for example, must be two-sided processes, because control and empowerment must work simultaneously (Davies, 1999). IS control procedures aim to check the appropriateness of IS decisions in achieving organizational goals and to learn from the success or failure of IT projects (Ahituv, Zviran, & Glezer, 1999; Applegate et al., 1996).

Major cross-functional IT projects require syntactic alignment, because they involve coordinated processes and structures of human behavior (Newport, Dess, & Rasheed, 1991). It is crucial in such projects to involve business and IS managers (Davidson & Movizzo, 1996; Weir et al., 2000). Teo and Ang (1999) mentioned the importance of aligning planning horizons between business and IT. Similarly, Chan (1997, 1999), emphasized the need for close links between business and IS plans and the importance of an IS steering committee. Although plans are sets of rationalized, decomposed and articulated actions to achieve certain objectives (Mintzberg, 1994), flexibility must be maintained to serve emergent visions (Mintzberg, 1979; Stacey, 1996). This interaction between planning and vision is a clear example of the various possible interactions between the informational attributes of alignment.

Interactions between the Informational Attributes of Alignment

There is strong interplay between the syntactic, semantic and pragmatic dimensions of alignment, and the social environment of values, trust, and commitment. A few examples are explained below to show some possible interactions within and between the informational dimensions of alignment.

First, the credibility of the IS department is a key factor in improving the relationship between IS and business departments (Luftman & Brier, 1999). Trust is likely to be built by increasing semantic alignment: recognizing and being responsive to the needs of users and by keeping up-to-date with new developments in IT. Business departments perceive the IS department to be successful and worthy of their trust (Chan, 1997, 1999) if and only if the IS department meets its commitments, in terms of project delivery and user support, to the expectations of the business departments (Burn & Szeto, 2000; Teo & Ang, 1999).

Second, a formal reporting structure can be an enabler of pragmatic alignment (Luftman & Brier, 1999) if empowered cross-functional groups report to senior managers (Clarke, 2000; Luftman & Brier, 1999; Reich & Benbasat, 2000). Equally, syntactic alignment, in the form of effective formal communication, requires clear channels and explicit planning practices, and facilitates the semantic convergence of worldviews held by the different stakeholders (Broadbent & Weill, 1993;

Cooper, 1998; Filley Alan, House Robert, & Kerr, 1976; Nutt, 1989). In addition, timely meetings between the IS and business departments before and during the development and implementation of an IT project help to ensure that users' requirements are met (Teo & Ang, 1999).

Finally, communication is the medium to share vision and knowledge, leading to understanding between business and IS departments (Reich & Benbasat, 2000). If knowledge is not shared between the IS and business departments, planning practices are deemed to degrade or to be superficial (Reich & Benbasat, 2000), whereas the converse occurs if planning practices are well used (Broadbent & Weill, 1993). Structured communication procedures also improve semantic alignment by removing ambiguity and misunderstanding between the IS and business departments (Luftman & Brier, 1999).

Based on the discussion in the above section, it is possible to introduce:

PROPOSITION 1: Strategic informational alignment is the convergence of organizational behaviors, and hence, the convergence of informational attributes of those behaviors, in the space of three semiotic dimensions: pragmatics, semantics and syntactics.

Informational Dimensions of Alignment (IDA) Model

Several possible states of alignment are suggested by amalgamating the above three semiotics dimensions (Figure 5). An organization is aligned if there is convergence between the informational attributes of any of the main subsets in the Informational Dimensions of Alignment (IDA) Model. Furthermore, the intersections between the main subsets create additional states of alignment. The center of the diagram where all subsets intersect could be seen as the ideal state of alignment, but organizations are not expected to be in such state for long, because, according to the theory of dissipative structures, it needs high organizational energy to sustain this position (Stacey, 2000). Similarly, the absence of any convergences between the informational attributes leads to anarchy (Davenport, Eccles, & Prusak, 1992), which could be visualized as anywhere outside the three sets of the Venn diagram.

Davenport, Eccles, & Prusak (1992) identified several political organizational states based on different attributes. They introduced two attributes, commonality of vocabulary and access to information, which are related to the semantics and syntactics dimensions, respectively. For example, their notion of technocratic utopianism is based on the idea that IT, not information, is the creator and sustainer of the organization's competitive advantages. Technocratic utopianism depends on a level of commonality in procedures used for information sharing. This state can be visualized as residing at the bottom of Figure 5, within the subset that represents syntactic alignment alone. It is not positioned within the pragmatics alignment set due to the divergences in people's intentions and is also outside the semantics alignment set due to the high possibility of misunderstanding information created by IT without concomitant understanding or purpose.

Mintzberg (1983) identified several organizational "systems" that formulate the "internal coalition," or alignment, in organizations. The "system of authority," personal or organizational, and the "system of politics" fall under the discussion of power; while the "system of expertise" is associated with the semiotics dimension of alignment, including its informational attributes: shared knowledge, vision and

Figure 5: Informational Dimensions of Alignment (IDA)

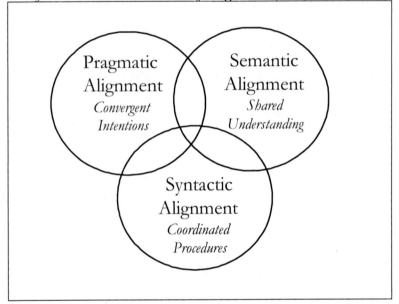

perceptions. Employees with different "ideologies" should be able to work together in harmony if they have shared trust based on respect of each other's beliefs and values.

This leads to the following:

PROPOSITION 2: There are different states of alignment, corresponding to different degrees of convergence, in each semiotic dimension.

But it is difficult to keep an organization's state of alignment static (Newport, Dess, & Rasheed, 1991). The dynamics dimension of alignment discussed below explains the reasons behind this changing nature.

The Dynamics of Alignment

An organization is a set of subsystems interacting together to achieve a certain goal (Checkland, 1999). It is considered a complex system (Checkland, 1999; Perrow, 1984; Thietart & Forgues, 1995) due to the high level of interactions between its different subsystems. Its performance is a function of how well the parts fit and work together as a whole. Hence, the processes of solving problems in organizations must be systemic (Checkland, 1999; Simon, 1976).

An example of the systemic nature of organizational behavior is the study by Sauer and Yetton (1994). They studied an organization that had two Enterprise Resource Planning (ERP) systems running concurrently. They were not merely IT systems but rather complex systems of people interacting together while making decisions to run the organization. One ERP system was dominant, while the other was recessive. When the dominant ERP system was apparently stable, the recessive ERP system was building momentum without being noticed until it contributed to the failure of the dominant system.

Because the issue of alignment arises from the impact of change on business, we introduce the notion of Organizational Dynamics, as a fourth dimension, to be able to represent the trajectory of organizational behavior over time. Hence, we define the alignment mode as the alignment state of the organization linked with the trajectory it is following. In this way, we encompass the effects of change, reversibility and irreversibility (Prigogine & Stengers, 1984, 1997).

Organizational dynamics denotes time-related organizational behaviors, often arising as delayed or unintended consequences of earlier decisions. Nowadays, the rapid developments in IT may lead organizations to change their business and IS strategies faster than they used to do two or three decades ago (Downes & Mui, 1998a, 1998b). Dynamics encompasses short-term change, which may be predictable (Stacey, 2000) and reversible, and long-term unpredictable (Stacey, 2000) and irreversible change (Prigogine & Stengers, 1984; Thietart & Forgues, 1995). A short-term, reversible change in IS policy could be the piloting of a new IT (represented by Scenario I in Figure 6 moving from A to Z then back to A). For example,[5] an IT project manager decided in an early stage of an IT project to halt its implementation when she realized the incapability of the system integrator to deliver a major phase. First, this decision would have been unattainable without the support and understanding of the business project manager and the rest of the project team. Second, because this phase of the project was meant to entirely reengineer the business processes of the company's human resources activities, the success of this phase was anticipated to be dependent on a new state of alignment: active involvement, strong commitment and shared understanding of all employees in the company. Therefore, if the project had not been halted in its early stages, the

Figure 6: Bifurcation of Decisions and Trajectories of Informational Alignment States

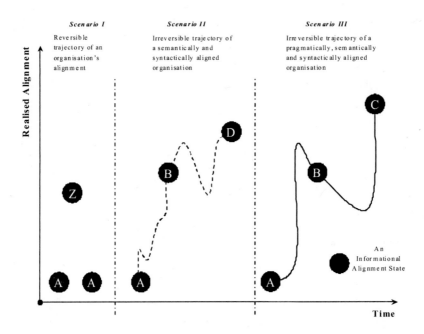

decision and its consequences would have been thorny in later stages. In contrast, irreversible change could be the reengineering of supply chains in the digitized economy (Negroponte, 1995) (represented by Scenario I and II in Figure 6). The empirical evidence shows clear differences between the nature of short-and-long-term alignment, without knowing the exact reasons causing it (Reich & Benbasat, 2000). Moreover, the trajectory of alignment between IS planning and business planning may determine the level of integration, namely, administrative, sequential, reciprocal or full integration (King & Teo, 1997, 2000).

The alignment state may change depending on certain internal or external conditions. Such change may be influenced by the changes in personnel, organizational policy, IT developments and the competitive marketplace. For instance, employees may follow certain rules and procedures to share information within the organization dictated by a newly appointed CEO or a powerful executive. These "monarchy" or "feudalism" states (Davenport, Eccles, & Prusak, 1992) of alignment lead the organization to be syntactically and semantically aligned (represented by the dashed line from A to B in Figure 6), but are pragmatically aligned only when intentions start to converge due to certain alliances between those powerful executives (represented by the straight line from A to B in Figure 6).

These active movements within the IDA Model (see figure 5) trace the organization's trajectory of alignment modes, which may be irreversible and unrepeatable. Organizations move from one dynamic state of alignment to another (Thietart & Forgues, 1995) and tend to follow a certain trajectory to optimize resources and create stability (Davenport, Eccles, & Prusak, 1992). Reversing such actions will not restore the original state of alignment, and the adoption of other organizations' best practices will not necessarily yield repeatable results (Thietart & Forgues, 1995). Similar organizational states may be reached in different ways (reaching to State B in Scenarios II and III), but due to organizational complexity and the dependence on previous states of alignment, the consequences of applying a particular policy could be totally different and sometimes disastrous.

Elaborating on the example discussed above, the monarch CEO could try to convince his managers to embark on a business process reengineering project (BPR) by developing trust and neutralizing the power in the organization. This includes giving away some of his or her own power privileges. Hence, the commitment level is expected to rise and the project to succeed when full alignment is allowed to form. This is demonstrated by Scenario III in Figure 6 as the organization's trajectory moved from A to B to C. In contrast, managers could be forced to participate in the BPR project by exerting extra power and exercising tight control procedures and strict planning. In this case, the policy will be expected to produce totally different results, which could seriously jeopardize the project and its success. This is demonstrated by scenario II in Figure 6, moving from A to B to D.

The discussion of trajectories could be seen in terms of moving within the semiotic space towards a peak of alignment, like climbing a mountain (Figure 7).

Figure 7: The Semiotic Topology of Alignment's Trajectory

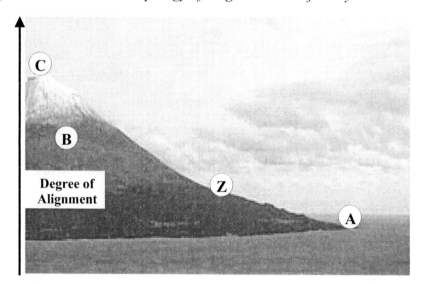

If you approach a particular point on the way up, you can get there by different routes, but you may not be able to go down by the same route, so the process is not reversible, necessarily. Point C is the peak of alignment, the center of the Venn diagram (Figure 5).

Peoples' behaviors change as they learn. This causes human systems to be indeterminate. Hence, the long-term role of managers is to steer their organizations between the different states of alignment rather than deterministically moving between different dynamic possibilities (Stacey, 2000). Nevertheless, predicting in advance the possible alignment states and modes should enlighten the way ahead for managers.

Finally, the above discussion leads to two more propositions that address the dynamics dimension of informational alignment:

PROPOSITION 3: Different modes of alignment are appropriate for particular strategic contexts.

PROPOSITION 4: The mode of alignment changes dynamically and may be reversible, irreversible, or liable to radical transformations.

CONCLUSION

The concept of strategic alignment between organizational policies between business and IS has not been defined previously in informational terms. Therefore, we defined the informational properties of organizational behavior by analogy, with the semiotic properties of signs, as a way of discussing the notion of alignment more precisely. We find that the issues of pragmatic, semantic and syntactic alignment are discussed repeatedly in recent research studies in strategic alignment, although evidently, the authors do not use the same terminology.

This chapter focused on the informational attributes of alignment within an organization but our definitions can be adapted in an obvious way to apply to strategic alignment between organizations. For example, strategic alignment between business partners involves the governance of IT and structures of authority for business decision rights, the structures of shared knowledge between partners and structures of coordinated business processes. These are, respectively, pragmatic, semantic and syntactic alignment issues. We have demarcated the scope of our discussion, focusing on information, without suggesting that we have produced an all-encompassing framework with which to analyze strategic alignment.

We suggest that analyzing alignment in terms of these informational dimensions will inform the effective deployment of an organization's human and IS resources.

The overall objective has been a more precise understanding of the nature of strategic alignment that will enable the exploration of questions such as whether absolute alignment is necessary, or even desirable. This should assist in improving performance and predicting outcomes of IS projects. Such questions are the subject of our ongoing research.

ENDNOTES

[1] Current address: Competition Commission, New Court, 48 Carey Street, London WC2A 2JT

[2] (Oxford University Press, Pearsall, Trumble, Soanes, Stevenson, & Elliott, 1999: p. 33)

[3] (Oxford University Press, Pearsall, Trumble, Soanes, Stevenson, & Elliott, 1999: p. 1303)

[4] (Oxford University Press, Pearsall, Trumble, Soanes, Stevenson, & Elliott, 1999: p. 736)

[5] This example is based on an interview that was conducted in a telecommunication company as part of this ongoing research.

REFERENCES

Ahituv, N., Zviran, M., & Glezer, C. (1999). Top Management Toolbox for Managing Corporate IT. *Communications of the ACM, 42*(4), 93–99.

Allen, D. K., Colligan, D., Finnie, A., & Kern, T. (2000). Trust, Power and Interorganizational Information Systems: The Case of the Electronic Trading Community Translease. *Information Systems Journal, 10*(1), 21–40.

Applegate, L. M., McFarlan, F. W., McKenney, J. L., & Cash, J. I. (1996). *Corporate Information Systems Management: Text and Cases* (4th Ed.). Chicago: Irwin.

Avison, D. E., Eardley, W. A., & Powell, P. (1998). Suggestions for Capturing Corporate Vision in Strategic Information Systems. *Omega, 26*(4), 443–459.

Broadbent, M. & Weill, P. (1993). Improving Business and Information Strategy Alignment: Learning from the Banking Industry. *IBM Systems Journal, 32*(1), 162–179.

Burn, J. M. & Szeto, C. (2000). A Comparison of the Views of Business and IT Management on Success Factors for Strategic Alignment. *Information and Management, 37*(4), 197–216.

Butler, R. J., Price, D. H. R., Coates, P. D., & Pike, R. H. (1998). Organizing for Innovation: Loose or Tight Control? *Long Range Planning, 31*(5), 775–782.

Caldow, J. C. & Kirby, J. B. (1996). Business Culture: The Key to Regaining Competitive Edge. In J. N. Luftman (Ed.), *Competing in the Information Age: Strategic Alignment in Practice* (Vol. 10, pp. 293–321). New York: Oxford University Press.

Cash, J. I., Jr. & Konsynski, B. R. (1985). IS Redraws Competitive Boundaries. *Harvard Business Review, 63*(2), 134–142.

Chan, Y. E. (1997). Aligning Business and Information Systems Strategy and Structure: Eight Case Studies. *Queens University Working Papers* (WP 97-07).

Chan, Y. E. (1999, August 13–15). *IS Strategic and Structural Alignment: Eight Case Studies.* Paper presented at the Fifth Americas Conference on Information Systems (AMCIS'99), Milwaukee, Wisconsin.

Chan, Y. E. (2001). Information Systems Strategy, Structure and Alignment. In R. Papp (Ed.), *Strategic Information Technology: Opportunities for Competitive Advantage* (Vol. IV, pp. 56-81). Hershey, PA: Idea Group Publishing.

Chan, Y. E., Huff, S., Copeland, D., & Barclay, D. (1997). Business Strategic Orientation, Information Systems Strategic Orientation, and Strategic Alignment. *Information Systems Research, 8*(2), 125–150.

Checkland, P. (1999). Systems Theory and Management Thinking. In P. Checkland (Ed.), *Systems Thinking, Systems Practice* (Appendix, pp. A45–A61). Chichester: John Wiley & Sons Ltd.

Checkland, P. & Holwell, S. (1998). *Information, Systems, and Information Systems: Making Sense of the Field.* Chichester; New York: Wiley.

Checkland, P. & Scholes, J. (1990). *Soft Systems Methodology in Action* (Reprinted as part of book available with Fred named: Soft Systems Methodology in Action ed.). Chichester: John Wiley & Sons Ltd.

Chorn, N. H. (1991). The "Alignment" Theory: Creating Strategic Fit. *Management Decision, 29*(1), 20–24.

Clarke, S. A. (2000). *Information Systems Strategic Management: An Integrated Approach.* New York: Routledge.

Cooper, A. (1998, 15–17 April 1998). *Managing Expectations: Aligning Perception & Reality.* Paper presented at the 3rd UKAIS Conference, University of Lincolnshire & Humberside.

Davenport, T. H., Eccles, R. G., & Prusak, L. (1992). Information Politics. *Sloan Management Review, 34*(1), 53–65.

Davidson, W. H. & Movizzo, J. F. (1996). Managing the Business Transformation Process. In J. N. Luftman (Ed.), *Competing in the Information Age: Strategic Alignment in Practice* (Vol. 11, pp. 322–358). New York: Oxford University Press.

Davies, A. (1999). *A Strategic Approach to Corporate Governance.* Aldershot: Gower.

Doherty, N. F., Marples, C. G., & Suhaimi, A. (1999). The Relative Success of Alternative Approaches to Strategic Information Systems Planning: An Empirical Analysis. *Journal of Strategic Information Systems, 8*(3), 263–283.

Downes, L., & Mui, C. (1998a). The End of Strategy. *Strategy & Leadership, 26*(5), 4–9.

Downes, L. & Mui, C. (1998b). *Unleashing the Killer App: Digital Strategies for Market Dominance.* Boston, MA.: Harvard Business School Press.

Earl, M. J., Oxford Institute of Information Management, & PA Consulting Group. (1996). *Information Management: The Organizational Dimension.* Oxford, UK; New York: Oxford University Press.

Filley Alan, C., House Robert, J., & Kerr, S. (1976). *Managerial Process and Organizational Behavior* (2nd Ed.). Glenview, IL.: Scott Foresman.

Galliers, B. (1999). Towards the Integration of E-Business, Knowledge Management and Policy Considerations within an Information Systems Strategy Framework. *Journal of Strategic Information Systems, 8*(3), 229–234.

Ghuloom, M. A. A. (1997). *An Empirical Investigation of Information Technology Adoption Behaviour in Banks in Bahrain.* Unpublished doctoral dissertation, University of Glasgow, Glasgow.

Goodhue, D. L. & Thompson, R. L. (1995). Task-Technology Fit and Individual Performance. *MIS Quarterly, 19*(2), 213–236.

Granovetter, M. (1985). Economic-Action and Social-Structure—the Problem of Embeddedness. *American Journal of Sociology, 91*(3), 481–510.

Granovetter, M. (1992). Economic Institutions as Social Constructions—a Framework for Analysis. *Acta Sociologica, 35*(1), 3–11.

Henderson, J. C. & Venkatraman, N. (1991). Understanding Strategic Alignment. *Business Quarterly, 55*(3), 72–78.

Henderson, J. C. & Venkatraman, N. (1993). Strategic Alignment: Leveraging Information Technology for Transforming Organizations. *IBM Systems Journal, 32*(1), 4–16.

Henderson, J. C. & Venkatraman, N. (1994). Strategic Alignment: A Model for Organizational Transformation via Information Technology. In T. J. Allen & M. S. Scott Morton (Eds.), *Information Technology and the Corporation of the 1990s: Research Studies* (Vol. 9, pp. 202–220). New York: Oxford University Press.

Horovitz, J. (1984). New Perspectives on Strategic Management. *Journal of Business Strategy, 4*(3), 19–33.

Horton, K. (1998, 15–17 April 1998). *Dynamics of Power in Information System Strategy*. Paper presented at the 3rd UKAIS Conference, University of Lincolnshire & Humberside.

Kearns, G. S. & Lederer, A. L. (2000). The Effect of Strategic Alignment on the Use of IS-Based Resources for Competitive Advantage. *The Journal of Strategic Information Systems, 9*(4), 265–293.

King, W. R. (1978). Strategic Planning for Management Information Systems. *MIS Quarterly, 2*(1), 27–37.

King, W. R., Grover, V., & Hulfnagel, E. H. (1989). Using Information and Information Technology for Sustainable Competitive Advantage: Some Empirical Evidence. *Information & Management, 17*(2), 87–93.

King, W. R. & Teo, T. S. H. (1997). Integration between Business Planning and Information Systems Planning: Validating a Stage Hypothesis. *Decision Sciences, 28*(2), 279–308.

King, W. R. & Teo, T. S. H. (2000). Assessing the Impact of Proactive Versus Reactive Modes of Strategic Information Systems Planning. *Omega, 28*(6), 667–679.

Konsynski, B. R. (1993). Strategic Control in the Extended Enterprise. *IBM Systems Journal, 32*(1), 111–142.

LaFollette, H. (2000). Pragmatic Ethics. In H. LaFollette (Ed.), *The Blackwell Guide to Ethical Theory*. Oxford: Blackwell Publishers.

Lederer, A. L. & Mendelow, A. L. (1987). Information Resource Planning: Overcoming Difficulties in Identifying Top Management's Objectives. *MIS Quarterly, 11*(3), 389–399.

Luftman, J. N. (2001). Assessing Business-IT Alignment Maturity. In R. Papp (Ed.), *Strategic Information Technology: Opportunities for Competitive Advantage* (Vol. VI, pp. 105–134). Hershey, PA.: Idea Group Publishing.

Luftman, J. N. & Brier, T. (1999). Achieving and Sustaining Business-IT Alignment. *California Management Review, 42*(1), 109–122.

Markus, M. L. (1994). Power, Politics and MIS Implementation. In R. Galliers & B. S. H. Baker (Eds.), *Strategic Information Management Challenges and Strategies in Managing Information Systems* (Vol. 14, pp. 297–328). Oxford: Butterworth-Heinemann.

Mingers, J. (1995). Information and Meaning—Foundations for an Intersubjective Account. *Information Systems Journal, 5*(4), 285–306.

Mingers, J. (1996). An Evaluation of Theories of Information with Regard to the Semantic and Pragmatic Aspects of Information Systems. *Systems Practice, 9*(3), 187–209.

Mintzberg, H. (1979). *The Structuring of Organizations: A Synthesis of the Research.* Englewood Cliffs, NJ: Prentice-Hall.

Mintzberg, H. (1983). *Power in and around Organizations.* Englewood Cliffs, NJ: Prentice-Hall.

Mintzberg, H. (1994). The Fall and Rise of Strategic-Planning. *Harvard Business Review, 72*(1), 107–114.

Morris, C. W. (1938). *Foundations of the Theory of Signs.* Chicago: The University of Chicago Press.

Morris, C. W. (1946). *Signs, Language and Behavior.* Englewood Cliff, NJ: Prentice-Hall.

Mumford, E. & Beekman, G. J. (1994). *Tools for Change and Processes: A Socio-Technical Approach to Business Process Re-Engineering.* Netherlands: C.S.G. Publications.

Negroponte, N. (1995). *Being Digital* (1st Ed.). New York: Knopf.

Nelson, K. M. & Cooprider, J. G. (1996). The Contribution of Shared Knowledge to IS Group Performance. *MIS Quarterly, 20*(4), 409–432.

Nelson, M. R. (2001). Alignment through Cross-Functional Integration. In R. Papp (Ed.), *Strategic Information Technology: Opportunities for Competitive Advantage* (Vol. III, pp. 40–55). Hershey, PA.: Idea Group Publishing.

Newport, S., Dess, G. G., & Rasheed, A. M. A. (1991). Nurturing Strategic Coherency. *Planning Review, 19*(6), 18–47.

Noth, W. (1990). *Handbook of Semiotics.* Bloomington, IN: Indiana University Press.

Nutt, P. C. (1989). *Making Tough Decisions: Tactics for Improving Managerial Decision Making.* San Francisco; London: Jossey-Bass.

Oxford University Press, Pearsall, J., Trumble, B., Soanes, C., Stevenson, A., & Elliott, J. (Eds.). (1999). *The Concise Oxford Dictionary* (10th Ed.). New York: Oxford University Press.

Papp, R. (2001). Introduction to Strategic Alignment. In R. Papp (Ed.), *Strategic Information Technology: Opportunities for Competitive Advantage* (Vol. IV, pp. 1–24). Hershey, PA.: Idea Group Publishing.

Peppard, J. & Ward, J. (1999). "Mind the Gap": Diagnosing the Relationship between the IT Organisation and the Rest of the Business. *Journal of Strategic Information Systems, 8*(1), 29–60.

Perrow, C. (1984). *Normal Accidents: Living with High-Risk Technologies.* New York: Basic Books.

Prairie, P. (1996). Benchmarking IT Strategic Alignment. In J. N. Luftman (Ed.), *Competing in the Information Age: Strategic Alignment in Practice* (pp. 242–290). New York: Oxford University Press.

Prigogine, I. & Stengers, I. (1984). *Order out of Chaos: Man's New Dialogue with Nature.* London: Heinemann.

Prigogine, I. & Stengers, I. (1997). *The End of Certainty: Time, Chaos, and the New Laws of Nature* (1st Free Press Ed.). New York: Free Press.

Reich, B. H. & Benbasat, I. (2000). Factors that Influence the Social Dimension of Alignment between Business and Information Technology Objectives. *MIS Quarterly, 24*(1), 81–113.

Roepke, R. P., Agarwal, R., & Ferratt, T. W. (2000). Aligning the IT Human Resource with Business Vision— the Leadership Initiative at 3M. *MIS Quarterly, 24*(2), 327–353.

Sabherwal, R. & Kirs, P. (1994). The Alignment between Organizational Critical Success Factor and Information Technology Capability in Academic Institutions. *Decision Sciences, 25*(2), 301–330.

Sauer, C. & Yetton, P. W. (1994, December 14–17). *The Dynamics of Fit and the Fit of Dynamics: Aligning IT in a Dynamic Organization.* Paper presented at the Fifteenth International Conference on Information Systems, Vancouver, British Columbia, Canada.

Segars, A. H. & Grover, V. (1999). Profiles of Strategic Information Systems Planning. *Information Systems Research, 10*(3), 199–232.

Semler, S. W. (1997). Systematic Agreement: A Theory of Organizational Alignment. *Human Resource Development Quarterly, 8*(1), 23–40.

Simon, H. A. (1976). *Administrative Behavior: A Study of Decision-Making Processes in Administrative Organization* (3rd Ed.). New York: Free Press.

Stacey, R. D. (1996). Emerging Strategies for a Chaotic Environment. *Long Range Planning, 29*(2), 182-189.

Stacey, R. D. (2000). *Strategic Management and Organisational Dynamics: The Challenge of Complexity* (3rd Ed.). Harlow, England: Financial Times.

Stamper, R. K. (1973). *Information in Business and Administrative Systems.* London: Batsford.

Stamper, R. K. (2000). Organisational Semiotics: Informatics without the Computer. In E. K. Liu, R. J. Clarke, R. K. Stamper, & P. B. Anderson (Eds.), *Organising Signs: Studies in Organisational Semiotics - 1.* London, New York: Kluwer.

Teo, T. S. H. & Ang, J. S. K. (1999). Critical Success Factors in the Alignment of IS Plans with Business Plans. *International Journal of Information Management, 19*(2), 173–185.

Teo, T. S. H. & Ang, J. S. K. (2000). How Useful are Strategic Plans for Information Systems? *Behaviour & Information Technology, 19*(4), 275–282.

Teo, T. S. H. & King, W. R. (1997). Integration between Business Planning and Information Systems Planning: An Evolutionary-Contingency Perspective. *Journal of Management Information Systems, 14*(1), 185–214.

Teo, T. S. H. & King, W. R. (1999). An Empirical Study of the Impacts of Integrating Business Planning and Information Systems Planning. *European Journal of Information Systems, 8*(3), 200–210.

Thietart, R. A. & Forgues, B. (1995). Chaos Theory and Organization. *Organization Science, 6*(1), 19–31.

Venkatraman, N. (1991). IT-Induced Business Reconfiguration. In S. Morton (Ed.), *The Corporation of the 1990s* (Vol. Strategic Options, Chapter 5, pp. 95–186). New York: Oxford University Press.

Venkatraman, N. (1994). IT-Enabled Business Transformation: From Automation to Business Scope Redefinition. *Sloan Management Review, 35*(2), 73–87.

Weir, K. A., Kochhar, A. K., LeBeau, S. A., & Edgeley, D. G. (2000). An Empirical Study of the Alignment between Manufacturing and Marketing Strategies. *Long Range Planning, 33*(6), 831–848.

Chapter III

Inventory Productivity Impacts of IT-Enabled Supply Chain Coordination in Manufacturing Environments

Kristina Setzekorn
Oakland University, USA

Arun Rai
Georgia State University, USA

Arlyn J. Melcher
Southern Illinois University at Carbondale, USA

This chapter describes an empirical analysis of the mediating effects of supply chain coordination strategy and manufacturing IT infrastructure on the relationship between business complexity and inventory turnover. Business complexity describes the diversity and volatility associated with a firm's product markets. To cope with this complexity, firms deploy inventory buffers. This deployment should decrease inventory turnover. An extensive manufacturing IT infrastructure can increase a firm's "sense and respond" capability, reducing the need for buffers, and can thereby improve inventory turnover. As this technology enables enhanced coordination, and as firms' efforts to reduce buffers within their own organizational boundaries earn diminishing marginal returns, firms attempt to optimize performance across organizational boundaries within the supply chain, i.e., adopt a cooperative supply chain coordination strategy. This supply chain coordination should improve inventory turnover.

INTRODUCTION

Problem Definition

Background and Relevance

The fundamental questions of whether and how information technology (IT) contributes to firm performance have been answered in different ways. Thus, IT Value research findings have been equivocal, with some studies finding negative performance impacts (Berndt & Morrison, 1995; Johansen, Karmarkar, Nanda, & Seidmann, 1996), some finding no overall effect (Barua, Kriebel, & Mukhopadhyay, 1995; Dos Santos, Peffers, & Mauer, 1993; Loveman, 1994; Strassman, 1985; Strassman, 1990), and some finding positive impacts (Brynjolfsson & Hitt, 1996; Brynjolfsson & Yang, 1997; Hitt & Brynjolfsson, 1996; Mukhopadhyay, Kekre, & Kalathur, 1995).

To reconcile these findings, several studies suggest that contextual factors associated with the firm and its environment mediate IT's performance effects (c.f., Banker, Kauffman, & Morey, 1990; Brynjolfsson & Yang, 1997; Scott-Morton, 1991; Venkatraman, 1991; Weill, 1992). Brynjolfsson and Hitt find that "firm effects" accounted for roughly half the productivity benefits attributed to IT. That is, firm capabilities (e.g., managerial expertise in matching business strategy with market context) may leverage investments in IT to enable sustained competitive advantage. They (Brynjolfsson & Hitt, 1995) suggest, "…an interesting extension would be to identify common characteristics of the highly productive firms and thereby examine some of the conventional wisdom regarding management best-practice" (p.12).

This chapter explores how business complexity, supply chain coordination strategy and manufacturing IT infrastructure interact to impact inventory turnover. Business complexity describes the degree of difficulty associated with a firm's supplier- and customer-facing processes due to volatility and diversity of its product-market. Manufacturing IT infrastructure describes the extent of IT deployment for manufacturing planning and control (MPC) functions. Coordination strategy describes the firm's attempts to coordinate processes across firm boundaries to optimize the entire supply chain's performance. Inventory turnover describes the firm's ratio of outputs to inputs.

Business complexity has become a crucial consideration, as global competition drives companies to seek strategic advantage through technology. These technologies include those associated with Internet- and intranet-enabled e-business, point-of-sale (POS) scanners, electronic data interchange (EDI), flexible manufacturing systems (FMS), automated warehousing and rapid logistics. Management strategies such as efficient customer response, mass customization, lean manufacturing and agile manufacturing similarly apply new technology to improve time performance and thus gain advantage (Fisher, 1997).

Such heightened competition has led firms to diversify their product offerings into product markets with which they have little experience, and at the same time, to compete on cost, quality, reliability and responsiveness. No longer can firms be satisfied to compete on a single performance dimension. They are attempting to maximize performance on all dimensions, while struggling to cope with product proliferation and heightened customer expectations in unfamiliar product markets.

The reduction of physical costs associated with production, transportation and inventory; and of market mediation costs associated with stock-outs and mark downs, has thus become a strategic necessity. To the extent that IT can be used to accurately forecast demand; efficiently plan, schedule and accomplish production; and purchase and manage inventory in the supply chain, it can improve performance.

As companies struggle to maintain ever-shrinking margins and higher levels of operational excellence within their organizational boundaries, their efforts earn diminishing marginal returns. Accordingly, organizations have begun to optimize performance across organizational boundaries in the supply chain. IT advances present opportunities to streamline and integrate key operations and processes by achieving superior coordination between distributed activities within and across a firm's boundaries. As IT reduces coordination costs, economic theory says that demand for coordination is increased. Shin (1997) says, "…IT can contribute to firm productivity by reducing coordination costs, thus facilitating a higher level of coordination" (p. 135). Consequently, schedules have been made more stable as firms within a supply chain coordinate product designs and demand forecasts and production among themselves.

Brynjolfsson and Yang (1997) have found that firms investing in complementary "intangibles," such as business process adjustments, training and interorganizational relationships, reap four times the return from their investment in IT as those not making these investments. To the extent that firms are able to leverage IT with cooperative interorganizational relationships, to coordinate and integrate their marketing, planning and production decisions, we posit that they improve performance.

Supply chains have thereby been able to reduce uncertainty and increase schedule stability. This increases production efficiency and reduces inventory buffers and their attendant physical costs (purchasing, production, transportation and storage) throughout the entire supply chain. This potentially confers competitive advantage, in that working capital tied up in inventory is substantially reduced, and thus available for other differentiating, value-adding opportunities.

Market mediation costs are also reduced. These include costs associated with lost sales and customer dissatisfaction due to stock outs, as well as lower profits due to product markdowns. In volatile industries, these costs can exceed the manufacturing cost (Fisher, 1997). Thus, enhancements to inventory turnover represent a strategic opportunity for firms.

Problem Statement

This chapter reports the results of our exploratory study of how business complexity, supply chain coordination strategy and manufacturing IT infrastructure interact to affect inventory turnover. Our research question asks, "How do manufacturing IT infrastructure and supply chain coordination strategy mediate the relationship between business complexity and inventory turnover?" Inventory turnover is measured as sales revenue/average value of total inventory. This measure is consistent with the typical productivity ratio, outputs/inputs, with outputs measured by sales revenue, and inputs measured by investment in, or cost of, that input.

As alluded to in the introduction, productivity is strategic in the current context of e-business, in that low cost has become an order qualifier, a strategic necessity in competing for orders. Scarce resources freed by enhanced productivity become available for other differentiating, value-adding applications. Productivity is thus one measure of a firm's management precision and operational excellence.

Alternatively, customer responsiveness is important in diverse, volatile markets, where many innovative, high-margin, rapidly obsolescing products are sold. In these product markets, efficiency is secondary to effective inventory positioning in the supply chain so as to minimize market mediation costs.

Previous empirical studies have generally attempted to measure generic IT dollar investments and their relationships to productivity or profitability, or to firm valuation. These studies have mostly relied upon highly aggregated data, from a broad spectrum of firms representing a variety of industries. None, of which we are aware, include complexity and coordination strategy in the study of manufacturing IT infrastructure and its affect on inventory turnover.

A few theoretical studies (Das, Zahra, & Warkentin, 1991; Holland & Lockett, 1997) proposed models that include complexity and/or coordination strategy with IT infrastructure and suggest that their fit is important for firm performance. Few of these relationships have been tested empirically, and we are not aware of any studies that have empirically tested the mediation effects of manufacturing IT infrastructure and supply chain coordination strategy on the relationship between business complexity and inventory turnover. Also, because our study controls for many confounding factors, and our partial least squares (PLS) method of analysis is more precise than first-generation multivariate methods, we are able to distinguish these mediation effects, where previous studies have not.

THEORETICAL BASIS OF RESEARCH

Theoretical Model and Conceptual Definitions

Our research model is represented in Figure 1. The path numbers refer to research hypotheses. The blocks refer to constructs explained below and identified in Table 1.

Business Complexity

Business complexity has been defined as the degree of difficulty associated with a firm's supplier-facing and customer-facing processes (Holland & Lockett, 1995). It incorporates diversity and volatility aspects. This is consistent with the transaction cost perspective in which uncertainty results from imperfect foresight and difficulty in solving problems containing multiple variables.

It drives management decisions regarding IT infrastructure and coordination strategy and may also impact inventory turnover. Although the construct does not directly measure external uncertainties, it reflects these, through the firm's reactions. While a firm can choose from an array of strategic and IT infrastructure alternatives

Figure 1: Research Model

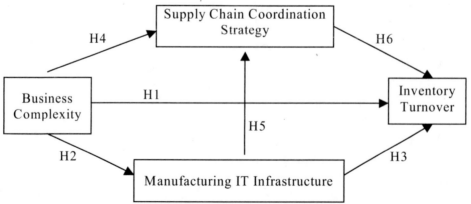

with respect to these environmental stimuli, its optimal responses are constrained by the marketplace. If the business context is volatile and competitors are responsive, the marketplace will punish inertial firms. Similarly, if customers award orders based on price, high-cost producers will be selected against. Business complexity thus reflects an environmentally limited array of managerial responses.

Manufacturing IT Infrastructure

Manufacturing IT infrastructure is conceptually defined as the enabling base of shared IT capabilities that "provides common services to a range of applications" (Broadbent et al., 1997, p.175), including "…information to efficiently manage the flow of materials, …coordinate internal activities with those of suppliers, and communicate with customers about market requirements" (Vollmann et al., 1992, p. 2). It is hypothesized to mediate business complexity's impact on inventory turnover. Its possible values are constrained by business complexity.

Supply Chain Coordination Strategy

Supply chain coordination strategy measures the extent to which the firm has integrated its activities with those in the larger business network so that efficiencies are maximized across the whole business network—not just the individual function or firm (Venkatraman, 1991). A less cooperative supply chain coordination strategy, i.e., one in which the firm's activities are not integrated with those of its suppliers and customers, is predicated on making the most efficient use of available resources. This translates to a zero-sum game in which nothing is left "on the table" for trading partners, and supply chain relationships are exploitive in nature. Because a gain by one partner is construed as a loss to another, firms do not voluntarily cooperate. Strategic advantage depends on achieving low total unit costs, above all else. As knowledge is considered power, firms hoard information. Personal and professional relationships are not relevant—cost minimization is the only consideration.

This contrasts with a more cooperative supply chain coordination strategy, in which firms and value chains are managed as interdependent, set to achieve ever-increasing returns. Managers see cooperative relationships as the means to synergy that enables innovation, decreased cycle times, decreased inventory, increased quality, increased responsiveness and reliability—and thereby a means to earn and leverage competitive advantage. They see these relationships as being so critical to their strategy, to changing joint pay-offs, as to justify leaving value "on the table" for their trading partners, so both may come away winners and thereby ensure that the relationship will remain a cooperative partnership into the future.

These partnerships are particularly strategic. They are inimitable to the extent that they are specific to the individual managers who craft the relationships incrementally over time, specific to the interplay of firms' cultures, and they exploit the distinctive capabilities of each firm, resulting in an effective symbiotic adaptation to the market context.

Inventory Turnover

Inventory turnover is the dependent variable, calculated as annual sales revenue/value of average total inventory (Vollmann, Berry, & Whybark, 1992). This is consistent with Brynjolfsson and Yang's (1997) calculation of productivity and is an accepted measure of the physical efficiency of a firm's supply chain (Fisher, 1997). There are several other performance measures, such as capacity utilization, unit manufacturing cost, etc., but inventory turnover is a key measure, as it addresses the physical movement of goods and how the efficiency of this process can be impacted by the enhanced coordination and information sharing capabilities of IT.

Though inventory turnover is partially an efficiency measure, it also reflects firms' effectiveness in responding to market context. Whether the market dictates responsiveness, or low-cost strategies, or both, annual sales revenue reflects success in meeting market demands, regardless of whether they are efficiency related or effectiveness related.

As will be elaborated in the next section, past research examined the impact of complexity on performance, IT on performance, IT investment and use to

Table 1: Conceptual Construct Definitions

Construct	Characteristics	Conceptual Definition
Business complexity	Independent construct	Degree of difficulty associated with buying and selling processes; incorporates diversity and volatility aspects
Manufacturing IT infrastructure	Mediating construct	Enabling base of shared manufacturing IT capabilities, which provide common services to a range of applications
Coordination strategy	Mediating construct	Extent to which the firm integrated its activities with those in the larger business network
Inventory turnover	Dependent construct	Physical efficiency of a firm's supply chain, measured as: sales/average inventory investment

counter business complexity, and use of coordination strategies to counter business complexity. Our choice to include these theoretical constructs in this study is motivated by their proposed relevance (detailed in the next section) and by the availability of their indicators in our secondary data set.

Relationships and Hypotheses

Business complexity is an independent construct, comprised of diversity and volatility aspects. This is consistent with the transaction cost perspective in which uncertainty results from imperfect foresight and difficulty in solving problems containing multiple variables. Aldrich (1979) similarly describes complexity as involving a high number, diversity and distribution of task-environment elements.

Business complexity should decrease inventory turnover, as the firm employs resources to buffer itself from uncertainty and as more product lines and individual products inflate inventory levels. Product and product line diversity also decrease forecast accuracy, as competitive environments containing multiple product markets are more difficult to understand and coordinate. It is difficult to intimately know many competitors' bases for competing or diverse assortments of customers and their order-winning and order-qualifying criteria. This decreased forecast accuracy results in inaccurate production planning, schedule instability and difficulty in inventory management and purchasing.

These cause firms to incur two kinds of costs. Physical costs are those associated with expediting production and transportation and with "just in case" inventory storage. Market mediation costs result from product markdowns or from opportunity costs and customer dissatisfaction connected with stock outs (Fisher, 1997). Uncertainty increases these costs. Bhaskaran (1998) says, "Failure to control schedule instability results in high average inventory levels in the system" (p.633). Evans and Wurster (2000) say, "Inventory and work-in-process are purely physical things, but if information were accurate and timely, factories could operate with a fraction of their current inventory. Inventory is merely the physical correlate of deficient information" (p. 10).

This excess inventory is added at every link and has immense efficiency and effectiveness implications for firms, industries and economies. Considerable inventory efficiencies could be realized with better information, as reduced holding costs and greater number of inventory turns result in working capital efficiencies, improved cash flows and time performance.

Lee, Padmanabhan, and Whang (1997) state the following:
Various industry studies found that the total supply chain, from when products leave the manufacturers' production lines to when they arrive on the retailers' shelves, has more than 100 days of inventory supply.

Distorted information has led every entity in the supply chain—the plant warehouse, a manufacturer's shuttle warehouse, a manufacturer's market warehouse, a distributor's central warehouse, the distributor's regional warehouse, and the retail store's storage space—to stockpile because of the high degree of demand uncertainties and variabilities. It's no wonder that the [Efficient Consumer Response] ECR reports estimated a potential $30 billion opportunity from streamlining the inefficiencies of the grocery supply chain. (pp.93-94)

This rationale motivates Hypothesis 1:

Hypothesis 1:   *Business complexity is negatively associated with inventory turnover.*

Holland (1995) suggested that interorganizational information systems (IOS) shifted the focus of strategic analysis from the level of the individual firm to that of the total supply chain. Firm competitiveness depends on efficiencies and effectiveness only possible through supply chain cooperation and coordination. To the extent that manufacturing planning and control (MPC) systems enable this cooperation and coordination, they should mediate business complexity's impact on inventory turnover. Holland and Lockett (1997) propose a research framework in which IOS (of which MPC is an instance) interact with the effects of business complexity, and they suggest that future research should consider implications for performance outcomes.

Ghemawat and Costa (1993) cast information architecture decisions in terms of the static-dynamic dichotomy, saying, "A key concern in defining decision rights is the trade-off between the information or knowledge problem and the control problem" (p.63). Extensive information capabilities can more effectively access idiosyncratic knowledge across the organization and the supply chain, and thereby enhance responsiveness. This knowledge access and responsiveness should differentially enhance performance in unstable, uncertain environments. Broadbent, Weill, O'Brien, and Neo (1996) link IT capability with business complexity, saying, "Greater IT infrastructure capability is required where firms need to respond more rapidly to changes in the market place" (p.175). Rai and Bajwa (1998) presented empirical evidence indicating that firms operating in complex environments were more likely to adopt executive information systems (EIS) for decision support.

Alternatively, Fisher (1997) suggests that companies selling diverse, high-contribution margin products in uncertain markets should manage processes to maximize responsiveness, rather than efficiency. He suggests that these outcomes are mutually exclusive, in that the former maximizes revenue using more expensive finished goods inventory, while the latter minimizes production and inventory cost using more raw material and WIP inventory. Thus, he suggests that MRP systems requiring long, frozen production schedules maximize efficiency but are not suitable for unstable, highly complex contexts requiring responsive processes.

We suggest that firms deploy more extensive manufacturing IT infrastructures in contexts characterized by high business complexity. This motivates our second hypothesis:

Hypothesis 2: *Business complexity is positively associated with a more extensive manufacturing IT infrastructure.*

"Productivity Paradox" is a term coined to describe the decline in productivity growth that began in the 1970s, just as IT investment began to dramatically increase. Labor productivity growth slowed from 2.5% per year from 1953 to 1968 to 0.7% per year from 1973 to 1979. Multifactor productivity growth also fell from 1.75% a year to 0.32% over this time frame. Concurrent with these declines, office computers and machines capital rose from 0.5% of all producers' durable equipment in the 1960s to 12% in 1993 (Brynjolfsson & Yang, 1996).

Berndt and Morrison (1995) reported a negative correlation between total factor productivity and high-tech capital formation between 1968–1986. Loveman (1994) found a gross margin close to zero for 60 manufacturers over a five-year period. Dos Santos, Peffers, and Mauer (1993), and Strassman (1985, 1990) found little direct correlation between IT spending and business profitability. Though Barua, Kriebel, and Mukhopadhyay (1995) found a positive relationship between IT investment and three intermediate variables, it was too small to affect final output in their manufacturing sample. Weill (1992), after disaggregating IT by type of use, found productivity to be positively associated with transactional IT use but negatively associated with strategic IT use and not associated with informational IT uses.

On the other hand, Brynjolfsson and Hitt (1996) and Hitt and Brynjolfsson (1996) found that IT has shown gross margin increases of 60% on a macroeconomic level but no profitability increase. Brynjolfsson and Yang (1997) found that a $1 increase in the quantity of installed computer capital is associated with a $10 increase in the firm's valuation by financial markets. This is about four times more than a dollar invested in such conventional physical assets as uninstalled computer capital on the open market. They suggest that this is due to firms' investment in complementary "intangibles," such as process reengineering, change management and employee training.

Many of these studies assess aggregate, tangible IT investments, whereas little has been done to develop and test theory about patterns of IT use and their impacts on key performance variables. Additionally, we are examining the mediating effects of IT use on the hypothesized negative performance impacts of business complexity and how these mediating IT effects are mediated by a firm's supply chain coordination strategy. Thus, because we suspect manufacturing IT infrastructure affects inventory turnover, as its attributes interact with business complexity and coordination strategy, we model it as a mediating construct.

Banker, Kauffman, and Morey's (1990) empirical study infers that the use of point of sale and order management IT in Hardee's restaurants differentially improved efficiency in stores having menus that were more complex. Vollmann, Berry, and Whybark (1992) cite several examples in which firms realized substantial benefits from their manufacturing IT infrastructures. Such benefits include reduced inventories, increased production rates, increased assembly efficiency, improved on-time delivery performance, increased gross margin, as well as improved inventory turnover. One European firm, Kumera, OY, increased its inventory turnover from 2.5 to 10 times after implementing an MPC system during a period of heavy competition. To the extent that IT can be used to accurately forecast demand; efficiently plan, schedule and accomplish production; and purchase and manage inventory in the supply chain, it should improve inventory turnover. This reasoning motivates our third hypothesis:

Hypothesis 3: *A more extensive manufacturing IT infrastructure is positively associated with inventory turnover.*

Bobbitt and Ford (1980) suggest that firms respond to volatile environments by diversifying their product markets, thereby further increasing business complexity. Decision makers respond to this complexity through divisionalization, which according to Keats and Hitts (1998), "…allows [the] development of specialized knowledge to deal with specific environmental elements and creates decentralized decision-making authority to take needed actions" (p. 574). This structural divisionalization can be conceptually extended to include outsourcing, strategic alliances and networked or virtual organization structures.

Emery and Trist (1965) link environmental uncertainty with coordination strategy. To maximize organizational performance in turbulent environments, they suggest the formation of an "organizational matrix [by]...dissimilar organizations whose fates are positively correlated....[to] maximize cooperation ..." (p.29). This organizational matrix describes a model in which cooperation is institutionalized—one in which firms' goals and destinies are coaligned. Such a model has been named a Value-Added Partnership (VAP) by Johnston and Lawrence (1988). In a VAP, each firm focuses on one link in the value-added chain in which it is distinctly competent. This focus translates to lower product-market complexity, thus lower uncertainty, lower diversity, lower overhead, lower bureaucracy and shorter response time. Firms may also share purchasing services, R&D resources, warehouses and information, allowing them to thereby accrue efficiencies of scale, scope and knowledge and information.

This strategic alliance model has become the norm in dynamic, high-tech markets, as first mover advantage and critical mass become paramount for survival. Thus, firms may decrease both dimensions of business complexity through a more cooperative supply coordination strategy:

Hypothesis 4: Business complexity is positively associated with a more cooperative supply chain coordination strategy.

Brynjolfsson and Yang (1997) and Clemons and Row (1992), among others, suggest that IT by itself cannot confer competitive advantage—that only by changing in concert organizational structure and strategy, can competitive advantage be won. Rockart and Short (1993) say, "…Until the right skills, attitudes, and systems are in place, an organization cannot exploit the potential opportunities in the environment that are enabled by IT" (p.191).

Similarly, Short, and Venkatraman (1992) examine the shifts Baxter made in order to exploit IT, in the form of its ASAP system, to gain strategic advantage. They say, "Attention, therefore, has shifted away from the technology itself to the interrelationships between the technology and the firm's ability to manage concordant changes in internal structure and work processes" (p. 8).

Davidow and Malone (1992) also suggest that firms need to change more than just technology to maximize firm performance.

> Many manufacturing companies that have invested heavily in flexible manufacturing systems in recent years have had trouble making the new technology achieve its potential. The culture and practices that support long production runs of standardized parts don't fit the new emphasis on wide product variety (p.99).

That is, new technology overlaid on an organization's unchanged strategy, management processes and individuals' roles is not optimally exploited (Venkatraman, 1991). Complementary "intangibles" (e.g., training, re-engineered business processes and interorganizational relationships) greatly leverage the performance of tangible IT investments (Brynjolfsson & Yang, 1997).

Malone, Yates, and Benjamin (1987) predict the emergence of electronic markets and electronic hierarchies due to enhanced IT integration capabilities. Electronic hierarchies entail few suppliers, as an intermediate step from hierarchical, ownership strategies toward electronic markets characterized by infinite numbers of competing suppliers, selling completely specifiable products. Clemons, Reddi, and Row (1993) predict a closer relationship with fewer suppliers, called a "move to the middle hypothesis," analogous to electronic hierarchies and VAPs. Bakos and Brynjolfsson (1993), Pine (1993) and Piore (1991) concur. Holland and Lockett (1997) call this a "mixed mode" network structure. The market-based or hierarchical structure is thus modified by IT-enhanced communication capability to enable the networked organization, virtual corporation or the value-added partnership. Brynjolfsson, Malone, Gurbaxani, and Kambil (1994) state:

> ...the current downsizing of firms, the popularity of outsourcing, and the rise of value-adding partnerships is not simply a management fad, but may have a technological and theoretical basis....it may be no accident that IT is often the catalyst for "re-engineering" projects that result in greater outsourcing and leaner internal staffing. (p.1642)

Milgrom and Roberts' (1990) model also predicts decreased vertical governance due to falling IT costs, and increased IT capability. They speculate that complementarities between technological, marketing and organizational variables cause discontinuities in the optimal adoption of strategies. For instance, it may not be optimal to adopt flexible manufacturing systems without also adjusting operations and marketing strategies.

Brynjolfsson (1994) predicts a similar result, using the Grossman–Hart–Moore framework for incomplete contracts, modified to account for ownership of information assets. He says that IT:

> . . . will result in reduced integration and smaller firms [i.e., more cooperative supply chain coordination strategy] to the extent that it leads to better informed workers who need incentives; enables more flexibility and less lock-in in the use of physical assets; and allows direct coordination among agents, reducing the need for centralized coordination. On the other hand, the framework suggests that more integration [i.e., a less cooperative supply chain coordination strategy] will result from IT where network externalities or informational economies of scale support the centralized ownership of assets and it facilitates the monitoring and thus contractibility of agent's actions. (p.1658)

That is, he would predict cooperative supply chain coordination strategies enabled with interorganizational information systems in markets characterized by such flexible assets as robotics, computer integrated manufacturing (CIM) and computer aided manufacturing (CAM); and by better informed or more skilled workers. Potential exists to integrate industry value chains by including a firm's suppliers and customers in the design, production and distribution functions.

Networking capabilities, MPC, CAD, CAM, shared databases, communications standards, standardized software and hardware and computer-based corporate memory have lowered barriers to entry for smaller firms and lowered the risk of opportunistic behavior from collaborators through decreased asset specificity and improved mutual monitoring. These effects have lowered transaction costs, i.e., the costs of contracting in the market, as opposed to producing in-house, and have thus enabled a shift to cooperative coordination strategies.

These technologies have also decoupled product life cycles from process life cycles (Noori, 1994; Milgrom & Roberts, 1990; deGroote, 1994), and have thereby caused economies of scale to be replaced with economies of scope and with economies of information (Davidow & Malone, 1992; Gurbaxani & Whang, 1991; Pine, 1993; Rotemberg & Saloner, 1991). The latter refers to network externalities in which the addition of another node to a network costs very little but affords the network members disproportional benefits. The value of IT is an increasing function of the connectivity it enables. Davidow and Malone (1992) say:

> The goal is to transform information into knowledge using human expertise. Therefore, the value of information results from its being shared across knowledge workers, nodes and networks. Value increases the more it is used.

Transaction cost economic theory prescribes vertical integration (less cooperative supply chain coordination strategy) when there are high search and contracting costs associated with dealing in the market. It also is prescribed when risk of opportunism by trading partners exists. Davidow and Malone (1992) say:

> ...the widely followed competitive model suggests that companies will lose bargaining power—and therefore the ability to control profits—as suppliers or customers gain strength....If a company perceives a trading partner as an adversary, it may ship shoddy materials, squeeze margins, delay payments, pirate employees, steal ideas, start price wars, or corner a critical resource—all practices that reveal a lack of concern for the supplier's or customer's well-being. The conventional solution is vertical integration. When organizations along the value chain are under one management, it is presumed that they can coordinate their activities and work toward a common purpose. (p.98)

Thus, to the extent that IT lowers search costs and controls opportunism risk by increasing monitoring capability, decreasing causal ambiguity and enabling an organizational memory, it lowers transaction costs. This shifts supply chain coordination strategy toward a more cooperative orientation, as opposed to a more opportunistic orientation. Also, as companies' use of manufacturing IT to maximize efficiency and effectiveness within their own organizational boundaries (a prerequisite for supply chain integration) earn diminishing marginal returns, they attempt to optimize performance across organizational boundaries in their supply chain using a more cooperative supply chain coordination strategy. The possibility also exists that less-powerful firms may be coerced by trading partners to deploy coordinative manufacturing IT. We hypothesize that:

Hypothesis 5: *A more extensive manufacturing IT infrastructure is positively associated with a more cooperative supply chain coordination strategy.*

Supply chain coordination strategy is comprised of the extent to which the firm uses integrated planning and capacity leasing, its number of suppliers and parts, and its production flexibility. Higher levels of these constituents (except number of suppliers and parts, which has a hypothesized negative relationship) encourage specialization and focus as firms develop and exploit economies of scale, scope and knowledge.

Keats and Hitt (1988) say that this enhanced focus can be considered an interorganizational analog to divisionalization, in that it "…allows [the] development of specialized knowledge to deal with specific environmental elements and creates decentralized decision-making authority to take needed actions" (p.574). This focus further decreases product market diversity and uncertainty.

Holland (1995) suggests that the focus of strategic analysis should be shifted from the level of the individual firm to that of the total supply chain. Firm competitiveness depends on efficiencies and effectiveness increasingly achieved through supply chain cooperation and coordination. Schedules are made more stable as firms within a supply chain coordinate product designs and demand forecasts and production. Bhaskaran (1998) suggests that this supply chain cooperation and coordination decrease uncertainty, which improves productivity. She says, "The need to optimize the performance of…the supply chain connecting raw material to finished product… is often overlooked….[and] results in high average inventory levels in the system" (p.633). Brynjolfsson and Yang (1997) found that firms investing in complementary "intangibles" (e.g., business process adjustments and interorganizational relationships) reap four times the return from their investment in IT. To the extent that firms are able to leverage IT with cooperative supply chain relationships, to coordinate their marketing, planning and production decisions, we suspect they improve performance:

Hypothesis 6: *A cooperative supply chain coordination strategy is positively associated with inventory turnover.*

EMPIRICAL STUDY

Measurement and Analytical Methods

One approach to model building uses current theory to develop and operationalize constructs and then postulate relationships between them. Survey instruments are developed, then primary data are gathered and analyzed and hypotheses are confirmed or disconfirmed, based on this data analysis.

A major difficulty associated with primary data collection is nonresponse. With so many researchers in quest of data with which to build theory, and relatively few cooperative Fortune 500 CEO and CIO respondents, low response rates raise the possibility of nonresponse bias, thereby limiting theory generalizability. This approach also entails risk, as it necessitates significant up-front investment of time and other resources without assurance of sufficient response to allow analysis or other meaningful output from the effort.

A second approach begins with secondary data and then attempts to draw meaning from them, using current theory to populate constructs with available data, then posit and test relationships. This use of secondary data can be problematic, to the extent that researchers are constrained in their construct operationalization to the use of available data that may have been gathered by unknown others to study an unrelated research question. Consequently, as these operationalizations may necessarily be forced or narrow, explanatory power may be low. The researcher also has no control over survey context, such as the survey questions, sampling frame or survey administration. For these reasons, research (including this study) using secondary data should be regarded as exploratory, and resulting generalizations should be drawn warily.

Sample

The Global Manufacturing Research Group (GMRG) data set was a collective effort containing general survey data gathered by different operations management researchers in several countries in 1994 and 1995. It addresses the general manufacturing context and MPC practices of two specific industries—companies

that manufacture small machine tools and those that manufacture nonfashion textiles
—and a catchall "other" category. There were 254 U.S. responses over all three
categories. Because the "other" category did not offer the desired control for
extraneous variables and the nonfashion textile industry did not provide a sufficiently
large sample ($N = 37$), the study was limited to the U.S. small machine tool
manufacturing industry. This sample included 96 responses, of which 93 were
usable. Because the data are specific to a single industry over two years in a low-
inflation economy, many extraneous variables are thereby controlled. Similarly, our
focus on MPC systems minimized problems associated with aggregating all IT
applications. We thus avoid the problem as pointed out by Mukhopadhyay, Kekre,
and Kalathur (1995) where "...the impacts of effective systems are neutralized by
ineffective systems" (p. 149).

Various sampling frames and collection methods were used. Generally, in the
U.S., small machine tool and nonfashion textile manufacturers listed in business
directories were selected by SIC code, and were then mailed a survey with cover
letter, some preceded by a phone call. The available response data for this
secondary data set are aggregated for the three industry categories, and we were
not provided a separate response rate for the manufacturers of small machine tools.
However, approximately 250 responses were received from about 1570 U.S.
surveys sent, yielding a 16% overall response rate (personal correspondence from
Gyula Vastag, August, 1998). As we do not have access to the mailing list or the
contact information for respondents, we are unable to test for nonresponse bias.
We thus characterize this study as exploratory. As shown in Table 2, most of the
respondents held responsible positions, and thus, we assume, were knowledgeable
or otherwise had access to the information requested in the survey instrument. The
sample profile is provided in Table 3.

The respondent firms employed an average of 114 workers, ranging from a
minimum of one to a maximum of 12,000 employees. They produced an average
of 4.5 product lines, ranging from a minimum of one to a maximum of 21. Their

Table 2: Respondents' Titles

Respondents' Titles	Frequency	%
Owner	13	14
President/CEO/Managing Director	32	36
V.P./Director	23	26
Department/Division Head	17	19
Group/Section Manager	3	3

Table 3: Sample Profile

	Range	Min	Max	Mean	St. Dev.
# Employees	1199	1	1200	114	181
# Lines	21	1	22	5	10.8
Annual Sales	$324M	$60K	$325M	$17.4M	39.5M
% Make to Order	100	0	100	71	33.6
% Jobshop Operation	100	0	100	70	36.9

annual sales averaged $17.43 million, ranging from $60,000 to $325 million. About 70% of responding firms used batch processing and make-to-order operations.

The operationalization of study variables is provided next. This will include enumeration of actual items used, their descriptive statistics, their transformations and a discussion of the factor analyses used to determine psychometric properties.

Study Variables

Independent Variable: Business Complexity

Business complexity is modeled with four indicators: product diversity, product line diversity, planning volatility and production volatility. Operational definitions are listed in Table 4, descriptive statistics are provided in Table 7 and measurement properties are listed in Table 9. Each indicator is operationally defined and statistically described next.

Product Diversity

Product diversity is measured as the mean number of products forecast and planned. These values were recoded to conform to a zero to five scale. Cronbach's alpha for this indicator was an acceptable 0.8701.

Product Line Diversity

Product line diversity is measured as the mean of the number of lines produced, the number of lines forecast, and the number of lines planned. These values were each recoded to conform to a zero to five scale. Cronbach's alpha for this indicator was 0.9257.

Planning Volatility

Planning volatility reflects dynamism and uncertainty in the market. The more volatile the market, the more responsive the firm's planning needs to be and the shorter the planning periods. In a stable market, the firm does not need to change its plans frequently and can utilize longer forecasting and planning horizons. Thus, the length of forecast and length of plan are reverse coded, as they are hypothesized to be negatively related to volatility. That is, the more dynamic the market, the shorter the forecasting and planning horizons. It is measured as the mean of the forecast period length and the length of production planning period, both trans-formed to a zero to five scale and reverse coded. Reverse coding is accomplished by subtracting the transformed score (0 to 5) from five for each observation. Cronbach's alpha for these items measured 0.6505—low, but still acceptable for exploratory research (Hair et al., 1992, p. 449).

Production Volatility

Production volatility reflects market volatility by measuring the firm's produc-tion schedule instability. Its indicators include the percentage of orders for which engineering changes occur after start of production, the percentage of orders for which customer schedule changes occur after start of production and the percent-age of incoming materials rejected. These indicators were transformed to a zero to five scale.

Mediating Variables

Manufacturing IT Infrastructure: Manufacturing IT infrastructure has six indicators. They include the extent of computer deployment for: sales forecasting, production planning, production scheduling, inventory management, purchasing and product design. These are each measured on a five-point Likert scale, with 1

Table 4: Business Complexity

Business complexity--Firm's response to the scale & difficulty of supplier- and customer-facing processes in the marketplace (Holland and Lockett, 1997). (Less Complex ↔ More Complex)

  A) Product diversity: Number of products. (Less Complex ↔ More Complex)
     1. Number of products for which sales forecasts are developed (Few ↔ Many)
     2. Number of products for which production plans are developed (Few↔Many)
  B) Product line diversity: Number of product lines. (Less Complex ↔ More Complex)
     1. Number of product lines produced (Few ↔ Many)
     2. Number of product lines forecast (Few ↔Many)
     3. Number of product lines in production plan (Few↔Many)
  C) Planning volatility: (Less Complex↔More Complex)
     1. Reverse of Months into future company's sales forecast extends (Few↔Many)
     2. Reverse of Months into future company's production plan extends (Few↔Many)
  D) Production volatility: (Less Complex ↔More Complex)
     1. % Orders for which customer schedule changes occur after the start of production (Low↔High)
     2. % Orders for which engineering or design changes occur after the start of production (Low↔High)
     3. % Incoming material rejected (Low↔High)

indicating no use and 5 indicating extensive use. These operational definitions are provided in Table 5, and their descriptive statistics are provided in Table 8.

Supply Chain Coordination Strategy: Supply chain coordination strategy has four indicators: integrated planning, capacity leasing, number of suppliers/part and production flexibility. These operational definitions are provided in Table 6, their descriptive statistics are provided in Table 8 and results of the factor analysis are detailed in Table 10.

Integrated Planning: This is is measured as the mean of seven items. They include the extent to which the company has invested resources (over the last two years) in just-in-time (JIT) programs, materials requirement planning (MRP) programs, supplier partnership programs and total quality management (TQM) programs; the extent to which the sales forecast is used for subcontracting decisions and the extent to which customers' future plans are considered in the development of the company's production plan. These are measured on a one to five Likert-type scale, where one means "never" and five means "very often."

Capacity Leasing: Capacity leasing is measured as the firm's propensity to lease temporary capacity when demand exceeds supply and to lease excess capacity to others when capacity exceeds demand. Capacity leasing is measured as the mean of two items, each measured on a five-point Likert scale, with one meaning "never" and five meaning "very often."

Table 5: IT Infrastructure

Manufacturing IT Infrastructure: The enabling base of shared IT capabilities, that, according to Broadbent et al. (1997) says, "provides common services to a range of applications" (p.175), including, as Vollmann et al. (1992) stated, "…information to efficiently manage the flow of materials, …coordinate internal activities with those of suppliers, and communicate with customers about market requirements" (p.2). (Less Extensive↔More Extensive)

Extent of IT Deployment for
   A. Sales forecasting (Low↔High)
   B. Production planning (Low↔High)
   C. Production scheduling (Low↔High)
   D. Inventory management (Low↔High)
   E. Purchasing (Low↔High)
   F. Product design (Low↔High)

Number of Suppliers/Part: This single item was transformed to a zero-to-five scale and subtracted from five. It is reverse coded, because it is theoretically inversely related to cooperative supply chain coordination.

Production Flexibility: This is measured by the extent to which setup time and setup cost determine the company's production lot sizes. It is measured as the mean of two items, each measured on a five-point Likert scale, with one indicating "not at all" and five meaning "to a great extent."

Research Methods

Descriptive Statistics

Means, standard deviations and ranges for the latent variables are reported in Tables 7 and 8. To compute these descriptive statistics, multiple-item scales were averaged and summed.

Table 6: Supply Chain Coordination Strategy

Supply Chain Coordination Strategy: "Choices made for coordinating economic activity with trading partners and includes… degree to which the relationship with trading partner …reflects a long-term commitment, a sense of mutual cooperation, shared risk and benefits, and other qualities consistent with concepts and theories of participatory decision making" (Henderson, 1990, p.8).
 (Less Cooperative ↔ More Cooperative)

　　　A. Integrated planning: (Low↔High)
　　　　　1. Extent to which firm invests in
　　　　　　JIT, MRP, TQM, and supplier partnership programs (Low↔High)
　　　　　2. Extent to which sales forecast is used for subcontracting
　　　　　decisions (Low↔High)
　　　　　3. Extent to which customers' future plans are considered in the
　　　　　development of the company's production plan (Low↔High)

　　　B. Capacity leasing: (Low↔High)
　　　How often company responds to capacity imbalance by
　　　　　1. leasing temporary capacity from others (Low↔High) or by
　　　　　2. leasing excess capacity to others (Low↔High)

　　　C. Reverse of Number of suppliers/part: (Low↔High)

　　　D. Production flexibility: (Low↔High)
　　　　　Extent to which the firm considers
　　　　　　1. setup time (Low↔High) and
　　　　　　2. setup cost (Low↔High)
　　　　　in determining the size of its production lots.

Measurement Properties of Multiple-Item Scales

To test for unidimensionality, the indicators were factor analyzed using principal components analysis, followed by a promax rotation. This oblique rotation method was selected, as our factors are likely correlated, and our results will be further analyzed using the partial least squares modeling package, PLSGraph, which does not assume independence of factors. Missing cases were replaced with the mean.

The resulting factors were then tested for reliability. Items shown to reduce reliability for the composite indicator were excluded. All variables' Cronbach's alphas exceed 0.60. While the minimum reliability is usually 0.70, lower reliabilities are acceptable for exploratory research (Hair et al., 1992, p. 449). Unidimensional, reliable variables were then formed by taking the mean of these items. These mean values were then standardized and used in partial least squares (PLSGraph, Version 2.91.03.04, 100 iterations) analyses.

The pattern matrices of these factors are provided in Tables 9 and 10, and the factor correlation matrix is shown in Table 11. Factor analysis results for business complexity show that nine items have excellent loadings (greater than 0.71), and one has very good loading (greater than 0.63) (Tabachnick & Fidell, 1989). Factors extracted in this analysis cumulatively explain 74.05% of the variance, which is more than satisfactory in social science research. Table 11 shows that the business complexity factors are not significantly correlated with one another, that they are in fact, four relatively distinct factors. Table 10 shows that only one manufacturing IT infrastructure factor was extracted. This single factor explained 53.63 % of the variance. In addition to the three composite indicators shown in Table 8, coordination strategy also has a single item indicator, number of suppliers/part, that did not load reliably with any of the other factors but was deemed theoretically relevant. As seen in Table 10, five coordination strategy items showed excellent loadings (greater than 0.71), three were good (greater than 0.55), and two were fair (greater than 0.45). These factors explained 61.76% of the variance, which is satisfactory for social science research (Hair et al., 1992). Table 11 shows that these factors are distinct.

Summary of Reliability and Validity Analyses

Our factor analyses yielded expected factor structures. This provides evidence of measurement validity and unidimensionality. All factors showed adequate reliability, with Cronbach's alpha values larger than 0.60. The intercorrelations between the independent, mediating and dependent variables are shown in Table 11.

Table 7: Descriptive Statistics for Independent Variables

Construct	Variables	Items	Min	Max	Mean	Std.Dev
Business Complexity	Product diversity		0.00	5.00	0.56	1.21
		Number of products for which sales forecasts are developed	0.00	5.00	0.53	1.27
		Number of products for which production plans are developed	0.00	5.00	0.57	1.14
	Product line diversity		0.00	5.00	1.08	0.99
		Number of product lines produced	0.23	5.00	1.02	0.91
		Number of product lines forecast	0.00	5.00	1.28	1.12
		Number of product lines in production plan	0.00	5.00	1.08	1.07
	Planning volatility		0.63	5.00	3.80	0.78
		Reverse of Months into future company's sales forecast extends	0.00	4.90	3.68	0.86
		Reverse of Months into future company's production plan extends	0.00	5.00	3.91	0.95
	Production volatility		0.00	4.83	1.01	0.93
		% Orders for which customer schedule changes occur after the start of production	0.00	5.00	1.12	1.50
		%Orders for which engineering or design changes occur after the start of production	0.00	4.75	0.88	0.95
		% Incoming material rejected	0.00	5.00	1.00	1.01

Table 8: Descriptive Statistics for Mediating and Dependent Variables

Construct	Variables	Items	Min	Max	Mean	Std.Dev.
Mfg. IT						
		Extent of computer use for sales forecasting	1.00	5.00	2.31	1.29
		Extent of computer use for production planning	1.00	5.00	3.12	1.44
		Extent of computer use for production scheduling	1.00	5.00	3.27	1.45
		Extent of computer use for inventory mgt.	1.00	5.00	3.63	1.47
		Extent of computer use for purchasing	1.00	5.00	3.46	1.40
		Extent of computer use for product design	1.00	5.00	3.71	1.39
S.C. Coord. Strategy						
	Integrated planning		1.00	5.00	2.97	0.79
		Extent to which firm invests in JIT	1.00	5.00	2.45	1.37
		Extent to which firm invests in MRP	1.00	5.00	3.13	1.22
		Extent to which firm invests in TQM	1.00	5.00	2.85	1.28
		Extent to which firm invests in supplier partnership programs	1.00	5.00	3.21	1.33
		Extent to which sales forecast is used for subcontracting decisions	1.00	5.00	3.03	1.14
		Extent to which customers' future plans are considered in the development of the company's production plan	1.00	5.00	3.14	1.27
	Capacity leasing		1.00	5.00	2.43	1.39
		How often company responds to capacity imbalance by leasing temporary capacity from others	1.00	5.00	3.33	1.35
		How often company responds to capacity imbalance by leasing excess capacity to others	1.00	5.00	2.59	1.62
	Reverse (# suppliers/part)		0.05	4.95	0.22	0.55
	Production flexibility		1.00	5.00	2.62	1.26
		Extent to which the firm considers setup time in determining the size of its production lots.	1.00	5.00	2.64	1.32
		Extent to which the firm considers setup cost in determining the size of its production lots.	1.00	5.00	2.60	1.31
Inventory Turnover		Annual sales/ investment in average total inventory	1.57	350	18.61	43.70

Table 9: Measurement Properties of Independent Variables' Multiple-Item Scales

Constructs	Variables	Items	Eigenvalue	Loading	Missing N	% Variance Explained	Cronbach's α
Business Complexity						74.05	
	Product diversity		1.658			15.47	0.8701
		Number of products for which sales forecasts are developed		0.867	36		
		Number of products for which production plans are developed		0.865	31		
	Product line diversity		2.421			24.78	0.9257
		Number of product lines produced		0.879	6		
		Number of product lines forecast		0.881	27		
		Number of product lines in production plan		0.845	32		
	Planning volatility		1.572			13.85	0.6505
		Reverse of Months into future company's sales forecast extends		0.835	1		
		Reverse of Months into future company's production plan extends		0.865	2		
	Production volatility		1.879			19.96	0.6553
		% Orders for which customer schedule changes occur after the start of production		0.799	4		
		% Orders for which engineering or design changes occur after the start of production		0.875	3		
		% Incoming material rejected		0.657	6		

Table 10: Measurement Properties of Mediating Variables' Multiple-Item Scales

Constructs	Variables	Items	Eigenvalue	Loading	Missing N	%Variance Explained	Cronbach's α
Mfg. IT			3.218			53.63	
		Extent of computer use for sales forecasting			0		
		Extent of computer use for production planning			0		
		Extent of computer use for production scheduling			1		
		Extent of computer use for inventory management			1		
		Extent of computer use for purchasing			1		
		Extent of computer use for product design			0		
S. C. Coord. Strategy						61.76	
	Integrated planning		2.304			23.79	0.8053
		Extent to which firm invests in JIT		0.628	1		
		Extent to which firm invests in MRP		0.782	1		
		Extent to which firm invests in TQM		0.486	2		
		Extent to which firm invests in supplier partnership programs		0.562	1		0.8715
		Extent to which sales forecast is used for subcontracting decisions		0.602	1		
		Extent to which customers' future plans are considered in the development of the company's production plan		0.586	1		
	Capacity leasing		1.825			16.96	0.9146
		How often company responds to capacity imbalance by leasing temporary capacity from others		0.929	0		
		How often company responds to capacity imbalance by leasing excess capacity to others		0.928	6		
	Production flexibility		2.106			21.01	
		Extent to which the firm considers setup time in determining the size of its production lots.		0.941	4		
		Extent to which the firm considers setup cost in determining the size of its production lots.		0.920	4		

Table 11: Indicators' Intercorrelations (**denotes p<. 01, * denotes p<. 05, using Spearman correlation coefficient, one-tailed test)

Variable (alpha)	Product diversity	Product line diversity	Planning volatility	Production volatility	Forecasting	Planning	Scheduling	Inventory mgt.	Purchasing	Product design	Integrated planning	Capacity leasing	Reverse # suppliers/part	Production flexibility
Product diversity (.8701)	1.000													
Product line diversity (.9257)	.048	1.000												
Planning volatility (.6505)	.068	-.236*	1.000											
Production volatility (.6553)	-.131	-.159	-.112	1.000										
Forecasting	.027	.259**	-.374**	-.065	1.000									
Planning	.230*	.419**	-.251**	-.003	.557**	1.000								
Scheduling	.163	.279**	-.259**	.119	.369**	.741**	1.000							
Inventory mgt.	.222*	.278**	-.290**	-.019	.355**	.590**	.602**	1.000						
Purchasing	.103	.170	-.098	.149	.313**	.535**	.528**	.585**	1.000					
Product design	-.221*	.058	-.005	.189*	.155	.114	.155	.128	.271**	1.000				
Integrated planning (.8053)	.022	.007	-.125	-.198*	.248**	.297**	.095	.169	.208**	-.057	1.000			
Capacity leasing	.127	-.042	-.102	.224*	.113	.199*	.241*	.167	.089	.005	-.004	1.000		
Reverse # Suppliers/part	-.051	.019	.090	-.106	-.152	.052	.037	.225*	.039	-.145	.002	-.059	1.000	
Production flexibility (.9146)	.248*	-.043	.209*	-.175	-.041	.015	-.003	.112	.015	-.142	-.073	.150	-.260**	1.000
Inventory Turnover	-.030	-.274**	.312**	-.132	-.240*	-.321**	-.314**	-.531**	-.177	.062	.077	-.099	-.125	-.032

Model Evaluation

Because PLS makes no assumptions regarding distribution in its parameter estimation, traditional parametric methods for assessing significance are not valid. Wold (1980) suggests that nonparametric prediction-oriented methods are more applicable for PLS. R^2 is used to assess predictiveness for dependent latent variables. The effect size f^2 measures the change in R^2 if a predictor latent variable is removed from the model. It is calculated as

$$f^2 = (R^2_{\ included} - R^2_{\ excluded})/ 1 - R^2_{\ included}$$

$R^2_{\ included}$ denotes the dependent latent variable's R^2 when the independent latent variable is included in the structural equation, and $R^2_{\ excluded}$ denotes the dependent latent variable's R^2 when the independent latent variable is omitted from the structural equation. Values of f^2 equal to 0.02, 0.15 and 0.35 gauge whether a predictor latent variable has a small, medium or large effect on the dependent latent variable, respectively (Chin, 1998, p.317).

All latent variables in our study, with the exception of inventory turnover, were modeled as formative, because their indicators were construed to "add up" to the latent variable's essence, with each measuring a subset of the total latent variable, rather than each being a different correlated measure of the same property. Measures are not necessarily correlated. Inventory turnover has a single indicator, so it is measured with a reflective indicator. Thus, our estimates' stabilities are examined using a jackknifing resampling procedure (Chin, 1998).

Model

Our PLS model is shown in Figure 2. The R^2 values listed beneath the dependent latent variables' labels show the amount of variance explained by the variable, and thus can assess the variables' predictiveness. The path coefficients show the degree of association between latent variables, while indicator weights show the extent to which items are related to the latent variable. One-tailed adjusted t tests were used to assess significance of the latent variables' indicators and the paths connecting them. A one-tailed test is used, as directionality is being hypothesized. That is, our hypotheses postulate positive and negative associations (for indicators' associations with latent variables, as well as latent variables' relationships to each other), based on theory.

Results

Explained variance and effect sizes for our PLS Model are listed in Table 12. The results indicate that 25.6% of the variance in manufacturing IT infrastructure, 13.8% of the variance in supply chain coordination strategy, and 21.1% of the

*Figure 2: Model * $p<.10$. ** $p<.05$, *** $p<.01$, one-tailed test*

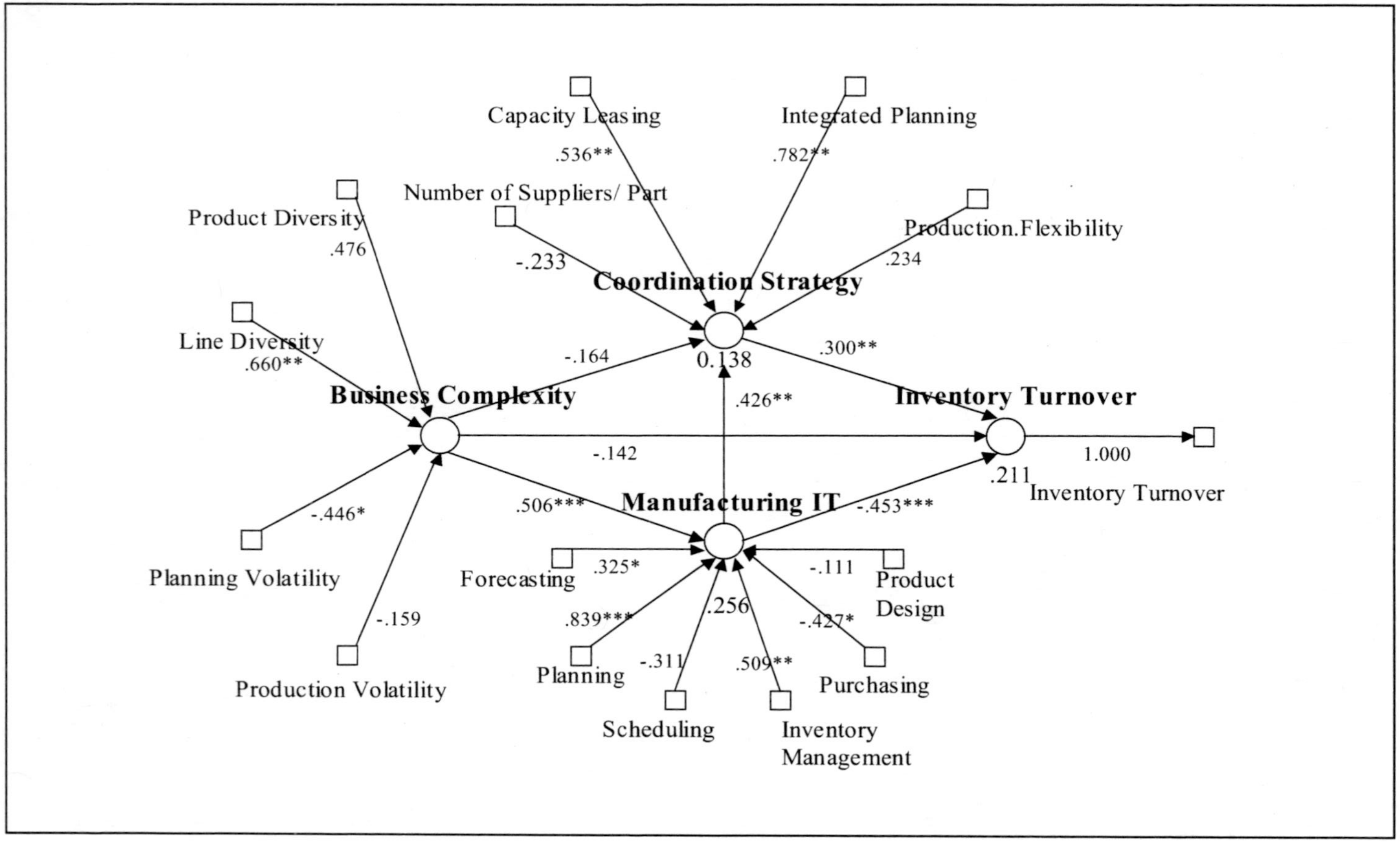

Table 12: Variables' R^2 and f^2

Variable	R^2	f^2
Business complexity		0.023 [i]
Manufacturing IT infrastructure	0.256	0.261 [ii]
Supply chain coordination strategy	0.138	0.062 [iii]
Inventory turnover	0.211	

[i] f^2 is calculated for business complexity as $(0.211 - 0.193) / (1 - 0.211) = 0.02$

[ii] f^2 is calculated for manufacturing IT infrastructure as $(0.211 - 0.005) / (1 - 0.211) = 0.26$

[iii] f^2 is calculated for coordination strategy as $(0.211 - 0.162) / (1 - 0.211) = .06$

variance in inventory turnover are explained by the full model. Our results indicate that business complexity and supply chain coordination strategy have small effects, while manufacturing IT infrastructure has a moderately large effect on inventory turnover.

The path coefficient relating business complexity with inventory turnover was not significant at even the 0.10 level. Thus, these results do not support Hypothesis 1, that business complexity is associated with decreased inventory turnover. Even when manufacturing IT and supply chain coordination strategy are removed from the model, the path between business complexity and inventory turnover is not significant. This may be an artifact of our data, and the narrow and forced way we operationalized business complexity. Perhaps there was not enough variance in our sample, because all respondents belonged to the same industry.

While product line diversity (significant at 0.01) and product diversity (not significant) are positively related to the business complexity variable, the planning volatility (significant at the 0.1 level) and production volatility (not significant) indicators are negatively related to the variable. We infer from these results that more product lines and longer forecasting and planning horizons are associated (though not significantly) with higher inventory turnover.

The path coefficient relating business complexity with manufacturing IT infrastructure was positive and significant at the 0.001 level. This supports Hypothesis 2. Weights for IT deployment for forecasting (significant at 0.1), planning (significant at 0.001), and inventory management (significant at 0.05) are positive, while those for scheduling (not significant), purchasing (significant at 0.1), and product design (not significant) are negative. From this information, we infer that firms with more product lines and longer forecasting and planning horizons deploy more IT for forecasting and inventory management and less for purchasing.

The path coefficient relating manufacturing IT infrastructure with inventory turnover was negative and significant at the 0.001 level. Hypothesis 3 was thus not supported. Based on these results, we infer that IT deployment for forecasting, planning and inventory management are associated with lower inventory turnover, and that IT deployment for purchasing is associated with higher inventory turnover.

Hypothesis 4 was not supported, as the path connecting business complexity with coordination strategy was not significant. This may again be due to our narrowly operationalized constructs, or it may reflect low variation in our sample.

The path coefficient relating manufacturing IT infrastructure with supply chain coordination strategy (significant at the 0.01 level) was positive, thus supporting Hypothesis 5. Weights for integrated planning (significant at 0.01) capacity leasing (significant at 0.05), production flexibility (not significant) and reverse of number of suppliers (not significant) are positive. We infer from this information that IT deployment for forecasting, planning, and inventory management is associated with higher levels of integrated planning and capacity leasing, while IT deployment for purchasing is associated with lower levels.

Hypothesis 6 was supported, as the path connecting supply chain coordination strategy with inventory turnover is positive and significant at the 0.05 level. We thus infer that integrated planning and capacity leasing are associated with higher inventory turnover.

DISCUSSION

Business complexity is not related to inventory turnover at even the 0.10 level of significance, in our study. Diminishing marginal returns from sales of unrelated successive product lines might not hold, as they would not require the same resources, other than those related to coordination and management. Economies of scale were also overlooked—raw material costs might not increase at the same rate for successive product lines due to volume purchasing or production improvements, though economies of scale may entail buying in larger quantity and holding more cycle inventory. If a corporation enjoys increasing returns and favorable economies of scale, business complexity could have a positive, nonzero impact on inventory productivity.

While planning volatility is negatively (though not significantly) related to inventory turnover as expected, product line diversity is positively (though not significantly) related to inventory turnover. This latter is an interesting result and does not support our original thinking. However, it does support Keats and Hitt (1988) who say that firms in challenging business contexts improve competitive performance by diversifying into multiple product markets. Fisher (1997) says this is successful, to the extent that firms are able to position inventory to maximize responsiveness.

He says that MRP systems are too inertial, requiring long frozen schedules, to support such a responsive strategy. His thinking is partially born out in this study, as IT deployment for sales forecasting, production planning, and inventory management is negatively related to inventory turnover if not coupled with a cooperative supply chain coordination strategy. IT deployment for forecasting, planning, and inventory management must not enhance sales or minimize the value of inventory without concurrent deployment of planning integration and capacity leasing. Perhaps these technologies are complementary with integrated planning and capacity leasing, so that without these, they confer no advantage. On the other hand, purchasing IT enhanced inventory turnover. Purchasing IT infrastructure probably decreased average inventory investment, without need of other complementary supply chain coordination.

Firms may thus deploy manufacturing IT for different purposes in response to different elements of business complexity. Its elements also differ in their requirements for complementary supply chain coordination strategies. Manufacturing IT is not generic, and perhaps is deployed in a targeted approach to deal with specific contextual elements. Perhaps manufacturing IT also needs to be studied in a similarly theoretically targeted way, considering its strategic complementarities.

When firms have short horizons and few product lines, they deploy more IT for purchasing. Having more product lines and longer planning horizons is positively related to IT deployment for forecasting, planning, and inventory management. Managers may deploy these systems to cope with product market diversity as they enable integrated planning and capacity leasing, even though the systems do not decrease average inventory. Cooperative supply chain coordination strategies probably entail longer-term perspectives, as cooperative supply chain strategies (requiring trust and communication) require time to develop.

Or, perhaps investments in these traditional technologies have succumbed to the law of diminishing marginal returns, and all potential efficiencies have been wrung from them. Without complementary investments, they may not be optimally leveraged. This relationship may also be an artifact of the time lags between IT deployment and improved inventory turn realization.

Integrated planning and capacity leasing are positively related to IT deployment for forecasting, planning, and inventory management but are negatively related to IT deployment for purchasing. Integrated planning and capacity leasing must require information processing capability provided by forecasting, planning, and inventory management technologies. Perhaps IT deployment for forecasting, planning, and inventory management decreases the cost of cooperative supply chain coordination, which increases its degree of use (Shin, 1997).

Besides decreasing the actual monetary costs of coordination, IT can also decrease the "transaction risk" component, i.e., the risk associated with trading partners' opportunism. IT can do this through enhanced monitoring capability that decreases causal ambiguity. These can contribute to an improved organizational memory that can record a trading partner's actions and increase likelihood of punishing opportunistic trading partners. Additionally, this threat of being found out may deter opportunism (Clemmons & Row, 1992).

Perhaps causality is bidirectional. That is, a firm's trading partners also may coerce it to support integrated planning and capacity leasing through IT deployment for forecasting, planning, and inventory management.

This complementarity between integrated planning, capacity leasing, and elements of manufacturing IT infrastructure probably enhances interorganizational "sense-and-respond capabilities" to improve performance, as evidenced by coordination strategy's positive relationship with inventory turnover at a 0.05 significance level.

Extensive manufacturing IT deployment for forecasting, planning, and inventory management may enable firms to adjust coordination strategy toward a more cooperative orientation (more integrated planning and capacity leasing), which showed improved inventory turnover. With concurrent adjustment toward a more cooperative supply chain coordination strategy, inventory efficiencies can be attained. This supports the previously discussed literature, reinforcing the idea that IT by itself does not confer advantage (i.e., inventory turnover); that only by adjusting organizational and interorganizational processes, strategies, and structures concurrently with IT changes, can performance be improved and perhaps strategic advantage won (c.f., Brynjolfsson & Yang, 1997; Clemons & Row, 1992; Davidow & Malone, 1992; Rockart & Short, 1989; Short & Venkatraman, 1992; Venkatraman, 1991).

Implications for Theory

This research was able to empirically test theoretical frameworks (c.f., Das et al., 1991; Holland & Lockett, 1997) suggesting that the degree of fit between an organization's complexity level, its supply chain coordination strategy, and its manufacturing IT infrastructure influence its performance. Firms with longer planning horizons and more product lines deployed more IT for forecasting, planning, and inventory management. This deployment, though associated with lower levels of inventory turnover, was associated with higher levels of integrated planning and capacity leasing, which were associated with higher inventory turnover.

It empirically supports the theorists who postulate that IT alone is insufficient to predict strategic success, that other factors, especially those that are tacit, i.e., intangible and inimitable, also need to be adjusted in order to reap IT's promised payoff. Our results also confirm Brynjolfsson and Yang's (1997) assertion that tangible IT investments must be leveraged by complementary investments in intangibles. It supports Bhaskaran's suggestion that this supply chain cooperation and coordination improve forecast accuracy and schedule stability, which improve productivity (1998).

Our study adds an additional theoretical dimension, as previous empirical IT value studies have generally measured highly aggregated IT dollar investments and their relationships to financial performance measures. We have instead measured IT deployment (which necessarily includes some investment and adoption decisions related to complementary "intangibles" such as training, change management, and process reengineering) for a particular use in a single industry over a two-year period. This focus has allowed us to control for many confounding factors, and our PLS method of analysis allowed us to distinguish the mediation effects of coordination strategy and manufacturing IT infrastructure, where previous studies may not have. Thus, our deployment measures have included some intangible elements and excluded some extraneous factors.

Implications for Practice

In this age of e-business, competition is so intense that managers cannot wait for unequivocal proof that technologies confer advantage. However, they must also beware of generalizing theoretical prescriptions. Managers must analyze IT deployment in terms of desired, sometimes conflicting, performance impacts; using relevant, sometimes nonfinancial, measures; and in terms of complementary investments, some of which are intangible. We found that firms with more product lines deployed more forecasting, planning, and inventory management IT, but without complementary deployment of integrated planning and capacity leasing, they experienced significantly lower inventory turnover. However, with these complementary investments, they reaped significantly better inventory turnover.

If inventory turnover is critical, deployment of these technologies must be coupled with cooperative coordination strategies. Managers must consider complementary investments and strategic adjustments in order for tangible IT investments to confer advantage. The ability to consider the total situation, to ask the correct questions, to measure the critical outcomes, as well as to apply the relevant technologies will confer competitive advantage.

Limitations

This study uses secondary data, collected by others, in 1994 and 1995. We relied upon GMRG members' generosity in providing the data. We do not know the companies contacted, those surveyed, or those that responded. We thus have no good way to check for nonresponse bias. Also, because the variable operationalizations are constrained to data available in the data set, explanatory power and generalizability of the results may be low, so we characterize this study as exploratory.

Future Research

We would like to extend the study to measure competitive advantage. We would like to study our model's effects on such performance measures as unit cost of manufacturing, product quality, throughput speed, delivery speed and reliability, flexibility and design time. This would be important in contexts where inventory efficiency is secondary to market responsiveness. We would also like to compare the data set's two maximally different industries (in terms of process and competitive criteria) with regard to the model. Finally, we would like to extend the study of these constructs to a more modern IT paradigm, that of B2B e-commerce, possibly in the auto industry, where supply chain coordination strategy and business complexity are paramount concerns.

ACKNOWLEDGMENTS

We wish to thank Greg White, Clay Whybark, Gyula Vastag, Linda Sprague, and other GMRG members for kindly providing us the data on whose analysis this chapter is based. We also appreciate Wynn Chin's providing us the PLSGraph software and advice in its use.

REFERENCES

Aldrich, H. E. (1979). *Organizations and environments.* Englewood Cliffs, NJ: Prentice-Hall.

Banker, R. D., Kauffman, R. J., & Morey, R. C. (1990). Measuring gains in operational efficiency from information technology. *Journal of Management Information Systems, 7* (2), 29–54.

Barclay, D., Higgins, C., & Thompson, R. (1995). The partial least squares (PLS) approach to causal modeling, personal computer adoption and use as an illustration. *Technology Studies, 2* (2), 285–324.

Barua, A., Kriebel, C., & Mukhopadhyay, T. (March 1995). Information technology and business value: An analytic and empirical investigation. *Information Systems Research, 6* (1), 1–24.

Berndt, E.R. & Morrison, C.J. (1995). High-tech Capital formation and economic performance in U.S. manufacturing industries: An exploratory analysis.

Journal of Econometrics, 65, 9–43. `

Bhaskaran, S. (Summer 1998). Simulation analysis of a manufacturing supply chain. *Decision Sciences, 29* (3), 633–657.

Bobbitt, H. R., Jr. & Ford, J. (1980). Decision maker choice as a determinant of organizational structure. *Academy of Management Review, 5,* 13–23.

Broadbent, M., Weill, P., O'Brien, T., & Neo, B. S. (1996). Firm context and patterns of IT infrastructure capability. In A. Srinivasan, S. Jarvenpaa, & J. I. DeGross (Eds.), *Proceedings of the 17th International Conference on Information Systems,* (pp. 174–194), Cleveland, OH.

Brynjolfsson, E. & Hitt, L. (1995). Information technology as a factor of production: The role of differences among firms. *Economics of Innovation and New Technology, 3* (4), 183–200.

Brynjolfsson, E. & Hitt, L. (1996). Paradox lost? Firm-level evidence on the returns to information systems spending. *Management Science, 42* (4), 541–558.

Brynjolfsson, E. & Yang, S. (1996). Information technology and productivity: A literature review. *Advances in Computers, 43,* 179–215.

Brynjolfsson, E. & Yang, S. (1997). The intangible benefits and costs of computer investments: Evidence from financial markets. In E. R. McLean, R. J. Welke & J.I. DeGross, (Eds.). *Proceedings of the 18th International Conference on Information Systems,* Atlanta, GA.

Brynjolfsson, E., Malone, T., Gurbaxani, V., & Kambil, A. (1994). Does information technology lead to smaller firms? *Management Science, 40* (12), 1628–1644.

Burns, T. & Stalker, G. M. (1961). *The management of innovation.* London: Tavistock.

Chin, W. (1998). The partial least squares approach to structural equation modeling. In Marcoulides, G. A., (Ed.), *Modern research methods.* Mahwah, NJ: Lawrence Erlbaum Associates, 295–336.

Chin, W., Marcolin, B., & Newsted, P. (1996). A partial least squares latent variable modeling approach. In S. Jarvenpaa, A. Srinivasan, & J. I. DeGross (Eds.), *Proceedings of the 17th International Conference on Information Systems,* Cleveland, OH.

Clemons, E. K., & Row, M.C. (1992). Information technology and industrial cooperation: The changing economics of coordination and ownership. *Journal of Management Information Systems, 9* (2), 9–28.

Clemons, E. K., Reddi, P. S., & Row, M.C. (Fall 1993). The impact of information technology on the organization of economic activity: The "move to the middle" hypothesis. *Journal of Management Information Systems, 10* (2), 9–35.

Das, S. R.,. Zahra, S. A, & Warkentin, M. E. (1991). Integrating the content and process of strategic MIS planning with competitive strategy. *Decision Sciences, 22,* 953–983.

Davidow, W. H., & Malone, M. S. (1992). *The virtual corporation,* New York: Harper Collins Publishers.

deGroote, Xavier. (July 1, 1994). Flexibility of production processes: A general framework. *Management Science, 40* (7), 933.

Dos Santos, B. L., Peffers K. G., & Mauer, D. C. (1993). The impact of information technology investment announcements on the market value of the firm. *Information Systems Research, 4* (1), 1–23.

Emery, F. E. & Trist, E. L. (1964). The causal texture of organizational environments, *Human Relations,* 21–31.

Evans, P., & Wurster, T. (2000). *Blown to bits: How the new economics of information transforms strategy.* Boston: Harvard Business School Press.

Fisher, M. (March–April 1997). What is the right supply chain for your product? *Harvard Business Review,* 105–116.

Ghemawat, P., & Ricart Costa, J. E. (1993). The organizational tension between static and dynamic efficiency. *Strategic Management Journal, 14,* 59–73.

Gurbaxani, V., & Whang, S. (January 1991). The impact of information systems on organizations and markets. *Communications of the ACM, 34* (1), 59–73.

Hair, J. F., Anderson, R. E., Tatham, R. L., & Black, W. C. (1992). *Multivariate data analysis with readings.* New York: Macmillan, Inc.

Henderson, J. (Spring 1990). Plugging into strategic partnerships: The critical IS connection. *Sloan Management Review,* 7–18.

Hitt, L. M. & Brynjolfsson, E. (June 1996). Productivity, business profitability, and consumer surplus: Three different measures of information technology value. *MIS Quarterly, 20* (2), 121–142.

Holland, C. (1995). Cooperative supply chain management: The impact of inter-organizational information systems. *Journal of Strategic Information Systems, 4,* (2), 117–133.

Holland, C. & Lockett, G. (September 1997). Mixed mode network structures: The strategic use of electronic communication by organizations. *Organization Science, 8* (5), 475–488.

Johansen, J., Karmarkar, U., Nanda, D., & Seidmann, A. (Spring 1996). Computer integrated manufacturing. *Journal of Management Information Systems, 12* (4), 59–82.

Johnston, R., & Lawrence, P. R. (July-August 1988). Beyond vertical integration—The rise of the value-adding partnership. *Harvard Business Review,* 94–101.

Keats, B. W., & Hitt, M. A. (1988). A causal model of linkages among environmental dimensions, macro organizational characteristics, and performance. *Academy of Management Journal, 31* (3), 570–598.

Lee, H. L., Padmanabhan, V. & Whang, S. (Spring 1997). The bullwhip effect in supply chains. *Sloan Management Review, 38* (3), 93–102.

Loveman, G. W. (1994). An assessment of the productivity impact of information technologies. In T.J. Allen & M. S. Scott Morton, (Eds.), *Information Technology and the Corporation of the 1990s: Research Studies*, (pp. 84–110). Oxford University Press.

Malone, T. W., Yates, J. & Benjamin, R. I. (1987). Electronic markets and electronic hierarchies. *Communications of the ACM, 30*, 484–497.

Melcher, A. (1976). *Structure and Process of Organizations*, Englewood Cliffs, NJ: Prentice-Hall, Inc.

Milgrom, P. & Roberts, J. (June 1990). The economics of modern manufacturing: Technology, strategy and organization. *The American Economic Review, 80* (3), 511–528.

Mukhopadhyay, T., Kekre, S. & Kalathur, S. (1995). Business value of information technology: A study of electronic data interchange. *MIS Quarterly, 19* (2) 137–156.

Noori, H. (1994). The decoupling of product and process life cycles. *International Journal of Production Research, 29* (9), 1853–1865.

Pine, B. J. (1993). *Mass Customization: The New Frontier in Business Competition.*

Piore, M. J. (1991). Corporate reform in American manufacturing and the challenge to economic theory. In M. S. Scott-Morton (Ed.), *The corporation of the 1990s.* (pp. 43–60). New York, NY: Oxford University Press.

Rai, A. & Bajwa, D. (Fall 1997). An empirical investigation into factors relating to the adoption of executive information systems: An analysis of EIS for collaboration and decision support. *Decision Sciences, 28* (4), 939–974.

Rockart, J. F. & Short, J. E. (Winter 1989). IT in the 1990s: Managing Organizational Interdependence. *Sloan Management Review*, 7-16.

Rotemberg, J., & Saloner, G. (1991). Inter-firm competition and collaboration. In M. S. Scott-Morton, (Ed.), *The corporation of the 1990s*, (pp. 95-121). New York: Oxford University Press.

Scott-Morton, M. (Ed.). (1991). *The corporation of the 1990's.* New York: Oxford University Press.

Shin, N. (1997). The impact of IT on coordination costs: Implications for firm productivity. In E. R. McLean, R. J. Welke & J.I. DeGross, (Eds.), *Proceedings of the 18th International Conference on Information Systems*, Atlanta, GA.

Short, J. E. & Venkatraman, N. (Fall 1992). Beyond business process redesign: Redefining Baxter's business network, *Sloan Management Review*, 7–21.

Strassmann, P. A. (1985). *Information Payoff: The Transformation of Work in the Electronic Age*. New York, NY: Free Press.

Strassmann, P. A. (1990). *The Business Value of Computers: An Executive's Guide*. New Canaan, CT: Information Economics Press.

Tabachnick, B. G. & Fidell, L. S. (1989). *Using Multivariate Statistics*. New York: Harper Collins Publishers, Inc.

Venkatraman, N. (1991). IT-induced business reconfiguration: The new strategic management challenge. In M. S. Scott-Morton (Ed.), *The corporation of the 1990s* (pp. 122–158). New York: Oxford University Press.

Vollmann, T. E., Berry, W., & Whybark, D. C. (1992). *Manufacturing Planning and control systems*, Boston: Richard D. Irwin, Inc.

Weill, P. (1992) The relationship between investment in information technology and firm performance: A study of the valve manufacturing sector, *Information Systems Research, 3* (4), 307–333.

Willliamson, O.E. (1991). Comparative economic organization: The analysis of discrete structural alternatives, in *Administrative Science Quarterly, 36* (1), 269–296.

Wold, H. (1980). Model construction and evaluation when theoretical knowledge is scarce: Theory and application of partial least squares. In J. Kmenta & J. B. Ramsey (Eds.), *Evaluation of Econometric Models*, (pp.47–74). New York: Academic Press.

Chapter IV

Information Technology Spending Association with Organizational Productivity and Performance: A Study of the Mexican Banking Industry, 1982–1992

Carlos J. Navarrete
California State Polytechnic University, USA

James B. Pick
University of Redlands, USA

This chapter examines the relationship between IT expenditure and bank profitability, efficiency, productivity, and performance for Mexican banks. The principal research method is correlation analysis between IT expenditure and four bank performance indices: a profitability index that combines bank profits, income, operational cost, and financial cost; a performance index that includes credit and bank income market share; a productivity index consisting of the number of employees, branches, and managers; and an efficiency index that includes banks' operational cost and income. The unit of analysis is the firm. The data are from the 18 banks comprising the Mexican banking industry from 1982–1992, when Mexico's banks were owned by the federal government. The study's interpretations are supported by interviews with four bank CIOs and a CEO, in office during the period. The main findings are that bank IT expenditure ratio is positively correlated to bank performance and productivity indices, whereas IT expenditure is not correlated with bank efficiency or profitability indices. There are fluctuations in the strength of correlation during the 11-year period, which are explained. The chapter results not only reject the productivity paradox but also provide insights to explain the paradox and IT contribution to the firm performance.

INTRODUCTION

In the early 1990s, the "productivity paradox" triggered a notable academic effort to study the impact of IT on national economies, industrial sectors, firms, and individuals. Taking advantage of the Mexican government's 11-year ownership of the banking industry, this chapter examines whether or not IT spending contributes to the productivity and performance of organizations. The federal government's ownership of Mexican commercial banks during the period from 1982 to 1992 offered an opportunity to empirically study the productivity paradox. During this eleven-year period, each bank in Mexico was required to present its information technology budget to the federal government's Finance and Planning Office. This policy requirement had the following implications:

·   Information about IT expenditures was available for all commercial banks.
·   Banks used the same IT definitions and budgetary practices and procedures.
·   The result was a consistent longitudinal data set on IT expenditures that was not available in Mexico before or since this era.

The chapter's objective is to present an empirical study of the association between IT spending and the productivity and performance of organizations. Specifically, the project conducts an empirical study:

·   Of the productivity paradox
·   With a homogeneous definition of IT
·   Using an ex-post ratio methodology
·   Regarding the productivity paradox for an industry in a developing country
·   Using longitudinal data for 11 years

BACKGROUND

In addition to introducing the relevant studies regarding the productivity paradox, this section presents three aspects relevant to this project: Historical facts of the Mexican banking industry from 1982 to 1992; Mexico's economic performance for this period; and IT spending in the banking industry according to several bank CEOs and CIOs, who where interviewed to find out the patterns and purposes of IT spending in their banks.

The Mexican Banking Industry and Its Period of Government Ownership (1982–1992)

The Mexican banking industry goes back to European origins in the 19th century. It developed and evolved during more than a century of great changes in the economy and society of Mexico. This chapter does not have space to discuss the full history of this industry, but rather this section emphasizes the relatively short period in the late 20th century of government ownership. There has been a huge debate about the government's 1982 takeover of Mexico's commercial banks. There is no agreement about the government action being legal, fair, or necessary. According to Tello (1984), the former Treasury Secretary, the following reasons triggered the government decision to nationalize the commercial banks.

· Banks had unfair advantages due to obsolete financial law and regulation.
· Thanks to government privileges, banks had disproportionate economic power vis-à-vis other industries and the federal government.
· As part of large industrial groups, banks failed in playing their economic role as financial intermediaries.
· Despite their profitability, banks were inefficient.
· Profit seeking by banks promoted speculation and other negative practices that unfairly hurt the economy.

In late 1982, the new De la Madrid administration took office and introduced an economic agenda with two main points: to adjust the economic system and to significantly reduce the government's corporate ownership.

Graphs 1 and 2 show how inflation and the Mexican gross domestic product (GDP) changed from 1978 to 1991. It is clear that due to the 1982 economic turmoil, the national economy shrunk almost 6 percentage points in 1983 (Aspe, 1993). As inflation lessened, GDP shifted to positive outcomes for the years 1984 and 1985. However, by 1986, inflation rose again, and the GDP turned down. During 1987, the economy reached an annual inflation rate of 159% (Aspe, 1993).

Graph 1: Mexico's Annual Inflation Rate, in Percent, 1978–1991

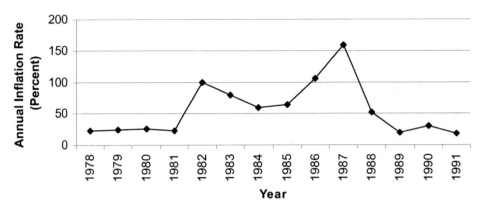

Graph 2: Mexico's Economic Growth, 1978–1991

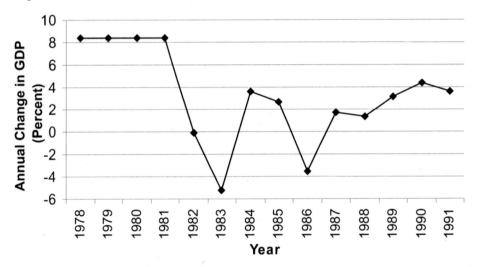

Under President Salinas's administration, which commenced in late 1988, the inflation rate steadily declined (Graph 1), fostering economic growth (Graph 2). In addition to economic improvement, the Salinas administration reduced the number of companies owned by the government. A privatization program reduced the number of government companies from 1155 in 1982 to 217 in 1992. Among the companies privatized were the 18 commercial banks that composed the banking industry. They were sold to investing groups in late 1991 and early 1992.

IT Spending in the Banking Industry

Another perspective on these 11 years of economic change and turmoil is that of executives in banks who made investment decisions during this period. Table 1

Table 1: Bank CEOs and CIOs Interviewed

Name	Position	Period of Bank Responsibility
Alfredo Capote	CIO	19791982
Alfonso Garcia Macias	CEO	1983-1988
Gerardo Garcia Noriega	CIO	1985-1988
Erasmo Marin	CIO	1988-1992
Roberto Chong	CIO	1985-1989

summarizes interviews with bank CEOs and CIOs that focused on their investment decisions (Navarrete, 2001). The objectives of these interviews were to validate the accuracy of IT spending data and to find out the IT spending practices of some of the Mexican banks during the nationalized period. This section presents the opinion of the banks' CIOs and CEOs regarding the IT spending during the nationalization period.

According to CIO Alfredo Capote (1999), the nationalized banks followed procedures to justify IT projects similar to those before the nationalization. These procedures divided IT projects into two groups. The first group included those projects with a cost-benefit justification in which the benefits had to offset the costs for the top management to approve the investments. The second group included those projects that called for less tangible justification, i.e., projects often related to the development of IT infrastructure.

This IT spending justification, based on intangible benefits, prevailed during the government ownership period of the banking industry. According to the interviews, the budgeting procedure in the banks was to present an annual spending plan with two sections: the operational and the development expenses. The IS budget was then evaluated by the top management according to the bank's strategy and availability of resources. Alfonso Garcia Macias, CEO of International Bank and BCH Bank during the government ownership period, pointed out that banks could not use the same evaluation procedure for all IT investments. The evaluation procedure was set according to the type of investment the firm desired. For some long-term investments, one could not expect a short-term impact on profits. For example, in the case of Internacional Bank, which absorbed other banks after the industry's nationalization, the justification for IT spending was to develop the systems and the IT architecture that allowed the bank to absorb other banks and still operate as an organization with a common business strategy. Here, IT spending had a long-term impact. On the other hand, in the case of BCH Bank, Garcia

Macias (1999) mentioned that there was no time or money for a long-term business and IT strategy when he took over as CEO. Rather, the IT spending decisions were oriented toward providing the bank with "leading edge" IT technology prior to the divestiture.

The banks did not base their strategies on bank profitability. Instead, they competed through gains in employee and branch productivity and market competition. Garcia Macias (1999) pointed out that they looked to enhance the bank's organizational efficiency and to give better services than their competitors. Similarly, Garcia Noriega (1999) stated that top management at his bank compared his bank with other banks mainly when they brought new products to the market. "You had to react; otherwise you would have lost your position in one or two years."

This orientation to the market conforms with Brynjolfsson's (1993) "Consumer Surplus and Profit Dilution" explanation of the productivity paradox. Garcia Macias (1999), for example, explained that his bank had to join the "RED" an automated teller machine (ATM) network promoted by medium- and small-size banks to offer ATM services to their customers. Through the "RED," these banks competed with large banks that were individually developing their own ATM network. Under the "RED" project, one small bank installed only two ATMs just to gain the image of being part of the "RED" network (Chong, 1999). Likewise, Garcia Macias's bank gained market image.

In the opinion of the CEOs and CIOs, the positive impact of the IT investments on the performance of the banks should have appeared in two years, on average. For example, Garcia Macias (1999) pointed out that after 1985, when Mexico's federal Telecommunications Law (Note 1) changed, each bank developed its wide-area networks (WAN), principally to establish online connection for all of its branches across the country. It took, however, some time between the initiation of the investments and the time that a WAN was up and running. At the Internacional Bank, this took two years.

Prior to the Mexican government takeover of the commercial banks in 1982, the IT infrastructure was generally suitable. However, following 1982, the IT infrastructure was too weak to support the banking industry's consolidation triggered by the nationalization process (Chong, 1999). The government invested in IT. However, by 1992, not all the banks were at the same IT level. Some banks, e.g., Atlantico, were not finished with their investment in the IT infrastructure, while others, e.g., Internacional, had a sound IT infrastructure with all their branches automated and linked "online" across the country. The transaction processing systems (checking, savings, universal accounts, etc.) of these two banks were optimally working (Garcia Noriega, 1999). Other banks were at the leading edge of IT banking. For example, at BCH bank, the top management invested in IT to make the bank more attractive to future investors and to sell it at a reasonable price

(Garcia Macias, 1999). Overall, the industry emphasized customer-oriented IT projects but largely ignored the "back office systems," which deterred the efficiency of the banks (Capote, 1999).

The level of IT spending was linked to the performance of the bank. If the bank had a good year, the bank could spend more on IT to fulfill its IS plan and strategy (Chong, 1999). Year after year, the banks increased their IT spending, rising from 2% of operational costs in 1982 to 9% in 1992, in average. However, top management could not spend more than the resources available to the bank at the time (Garcia Macias, 1999).

In summary, during the nationalized period, the banks competed by enhancing their banking infrastructure efficiency and their employees' productivity. IT spending was oriented toward providing better banking services regardless of the bank's profits or operational efficiency. IT spending was not approved through cost-benefit evaluations in all the cases. Often, bank strategies and intangible benefits were at the center of IT spending decisions. At the beginning of the nationalized period, the banks' strategies and IT investments were mostly oriented toward the organizational integration of banks. At the end of this period, IT spending was oriented toward preparing the banks for sale.

RESEARCH SUPPORTING AND REJECTING THE PRODUCTIVITY PARADOX

One way to look at prior research in this area is according to whether or not the results of the different studies support the productivity paradox. In addition, studies on either side of this question have used different levels of analysis. For instance, Ahituv and Giladi (1994) found that at the organizational level, there was no correlation between IT variables and profitability or productivity. At the industrial sector level, Loveman (1994) found that the contribution of IT capital to output was almost zero. Brynjolffson and Hitt (1996) demonstrated IT spending's positive impact at the firm level. A number of studies are supportive of the productivity paradox (Scott Morton, 1991; Weill, 1992; Strassman, 1990; among others), while other studies have rejected it (Harris & Katz, 1991; Dewan & Kreamer, 1998). Some studies have had mixed results depending on their particular submodels. For instance, Dos Santos et al. (1993), when evaluating the impact of IT investment announcements on firms' value, found that IT investments in general do not increase firm value, but innovative IT investments do. This body of studies does not come to a conclusion one way or the other regarding the validity of the productivity paradox. It would seem to depend on such factors as time, place, research model, and unit of analysis.

There is literature supporting and rejecting the paradox, but there is not space in this chapter to discuss it fully. Briefly, at the national level, all studies regarding the impact of IT investments on the United States economy show disappointing results (Strassman, 1990; Schrage, 1997). In contrast, Dewan and Kraemer (1998) report that developed countries (e.g., Germany), at the national level, have positive returns on IT investments.

Other firm level studies in the United States, such as Dos Santos et al. (1993) and Weill (1992), show mixed results. Dos Santos et al. report IT investments as having no impact on excess of return, but their study found that when the IT investment in an organization is related to an innovation, it increases the firm's value. Weill (1992) reports that when the investment decision is directed to transaction processing systems, the investment produces significant productivity gains. However, if the investing decision is oriented to other kinds of systems, there is no evidence of positive impact. It is also evident that none of these listed studies is from developing countries, which have a paucity of research projects in the IS field. Finally, another overall pattern one can see in studies rejecting the paradox is prevalence of the firm level. By contrast, projects supporting the paradox tend to be at the national and industrial levels.

METHODOLOGICAL APPROACHES TO STUDY THE PARADOX

Another way look at previous research in this field is to analyze different approaches and researchers' recommendations to enhance the quality of research and, thus, its results. This section presents researchers' recommendations regarding unit of analysis, data quality, measurement of variables, and conceptual research models.

Unit of Analysis, Constructs, and Performance Measures

In order to maximize the results of research on the value of information for organizations, researchers advise to carefully define the level of analysis of research projects. Banker et al. (1993) suggest that projects should address an individual, a work group, a business unit, a firm, groups of firms within an industry, or a national economy. Brynjolfsson and Hitt (1996) consider the firm level as the most appropriate for studying the impact of IT investments. The ideal situation, according to these authors, would be for researchers to have access to firm level variables that serve as obstacles for the tangible and intangible outputs of firms. Wehrs (1999) proposes a two-dimensional model combining time and level of analysis. For this author, research should take into account, in addition to the level of analysis, the moment of the evaluation (ex-ante or ex-post) related to the moment of the investment.

Another important element to consider when doing research regarding the productivity paradox is the construct definition. The construct definition allows or constrains the data collection and the data analysis. The construct definition usually faces two aspects: first, the IS/IT constructs or parameters, and second, the organizational measures the researcher wants to test or evaluate. In the case of IS/IT parameters, several researchers have selected IT expenditure to test IT impact on organization performance.

IT investment is a stronger construct than expenditure for testing the impact of IT on organizations; however, it has proved easier to collect data of IT spending. Several researchers (Harris & Katz, 1988; Alpar & Kim, 1990) used IT expenditure as a surrogate measure for IT investments.

The performance measures most frequently used are profits, sales, assets, number of employees (Ahituv et al,. 1999), sales growth, return on assets, and change in labor (Weill, 1992). Furthermore, based on Kaplan and Norton's (1992) balance-scorecard approach, Willcocks and Lester (1996) propose a set of performance measures such as profits/employee, purchases invoice/employee, or development efficiency.

Willcocks and Lester, like other researchers, propose to test the impact of IT investments on relevant units of the organization. For example, if the investment is related to a business process, there should be an evaluation of the impact of the investment in the new business process. Kauffman and Weill (1989) advise researchers to carefully compose a data set that properly measures relevant aspects of performance and IT investments. Data and measures are linked with the conceptual model the researcher uses to interpret or test the relationship between IT and benefits.

Conceptual Models

A variety of conceptual models have been used so far to study the productivity paradox. McKeen, Smith, and Parent (1999) show how conceptual models have evolved to characterize the impact of IT investments. In the "basic model," researchers try directly to find the relationship between IT and the organization performance. More elaborate models complement the "basic model" with other intervening variables that limit the benefits of IT in organizations. These include "conversion effectiveness" in the Weill (1992) model, "IT deployment" in the McKeen and Smith model, and "IT conversion" and "structural factors" in the Markus and Soh (1993) model. However, a conceptual model can only be operationalized if appropriate data are available.

IT SPENDING AND THE PERFORMANCE OF ORGANIZATIONS

The main limitations reported by researchers regarding evaluating the impact of IT investments and spending on organizations are data availability, a homogeneous definition of IT across companies, and access to consistent performance measures. The Mexican government ownership of the commercial banks offered an opportunity to test the relationship between IT spending and the banks' performance. The case of the Mexican banks may be unique, because it allowed:

·   Access to the IT spending of all the banks within the industry
·   A data set obtained under the same IT definition
·   A study based on an 11-year longitudinal data set

Despite the importance of the productivity paradox to the Information Systems (IS) field, there are few opportunities to empirically test this paradox because of data unavailability. Several researchers suggest changing the research direction in this area. Lucas (1999), for example, argues that researchers should stop studying the IT impact on organizational performance or value and start studying how to use computers in a productive way. However, the large stream of research studies described in the previous section argues for the importance of studying IT impact on value. Furthermore, the research opportunity that the Mexican banking industry and the availability of data offer fully justifies the project.

Another constraint for quantitative research on the productivity paradox arena is lack of a homogeneous IT definition. Ahituv and Giladi (1994), Wehrs (1999), and McKeen et al. (1999), among others, point out that without a proper definition of IT, sound research in the productivity paradox arena is impossible. McKeen et al. (1999) propose that IT expenditure should include computers, software, people, and communication technology. Unless we can establish a concrete IT definition across companies and company units, we will be unable to consistently measure IT impact on organizations. The present project takes advantage of the official definition of IT expenses that applied under Mexican law during the study period. Under this law, banks had to report, under the same format, IT expenses defined as hardware, software, computing services, and telecommunications. All Mexican banks observed this obligation during the nationalized period. This IT definition is close to the ones used in other studies concerning the impact of IT on organizations.

Another objective of the study is to investigate whether or not the productivity paradox is present in developing countries, and specifically, if it is present in Mexican organizations. There is no reported research from developing countries regarding the paradox that is based on data samples from companies or industries.

Thus, another objective of the present work is to study the presence or not of the productivity paradox in the banking industry of a developing nation.

The project seeks to show that ratio methodologies are suitable for analyzing the impact of IT investments. Several researchers (e.g., McKeen et al., 1999; Alpar and Kim, 1990) suggest that ratio studies, which follow a model that simply links IT investments with firm performance, fail at identifying the benefits of IT investments in organizations. The authors argue that ratio studies fail to discriminate among exogenous factors affecting firm performance. Alpar and Kim's (1990) objection, although pertinent, does not invalidate this project's objectives and means. On the contrary, because this project looks at 18 different firms (a whole industry) over the same period, the intraindustry factors are more fully accommodated. There are still exogenous factors outside the industry, for which Alpar and Kim's criticism applies. In any case, the whole banking industry would have been affected by the same external conditions. For example, up to 1985, the Telecommunications Law (an external factor for the banking industry) forbade any company from investing in wide area networks (WANs). By the end of 1986 when the government lifted this prohibition, all banks in Mexico simultaneously took advantage of the change and heavily invested in telecommunications systems to give online services to their customers.

The last objective of the research in the chapter is to pursue a longitudinal study of the relationship of IT investment and bank performance. This objective matches the recommendation of several researchers regarding the need to conduct empirical studies using longitudinal data. Brynjolfsson suggests there is a lag between the moment of the investment and the moment at which its impact shows up. Lags can be studied through longitudinal data. Keen (1991) advises to monitor performance measures over time to identify the impact of IT. McKeen et al. (1999) recommend performing longitudinal studies, because the impact of IT on the organization's performance should be evident in the course of longer time periods. There is no reported longitudinal research with data extending more than 5 years that assesses the impact of IT investments on industry performance.

RESEARCH QUESTIONS

The investigation in this chapter will test the following questions in the context of the Mexican banking industry at the firm level over the period 1982 to 1992:

1.   Is IT expenditure related to bank profitability?
2.   Is IT expenditure related to bank efficiency?
3.   Is IT expenditure related to bank productivity?
4.   Is IT expenditure related to bank performance?

Table 2: Research Hypotheses

Research Question		Hypothesis
1	1	Bank IT expenditure is positively correlated with the bank profitability index.
2	2	Bank IT expenditure is positively correlated with the bank efficiency index.
3	3	Bank IT expenditure is positively correlated with the bank productivity index.
4	4	Bank IT expenditure is positively correlated with the bank performance index.

These questions intend to identify the relationship between IT expenditure and the performance or productivity of the firm.

Researchers explaining the productivity paradox argue that IT benefits will not necessarily be reflected in a company's profitability. The benefits of the investments can end up allowing the company to keep its market share (Clemons, 1991), or to diminish profits but to increase the value to the final customer (Brynjolffson, 1993). Scott Morton (1991) reports that there is no evidence of improvement on profitability due to IT investments. Question 2 will evaluate the relationship between IT spending and the efficiency of the banks.

Question 3 will test the relationship between IT spending and banks' productivity. Loveman (1994) and Scott Morton (1991) report a lack of correlation between IT investments and the productivity of firms. The results for Question 3 will reveal whether the Mexican case presents similar results.

Research Hypotheses

Table 2 shows the research hypotheses and their correspondence with research questions.

Bank IT expenditure is the ratio of bank expenses on hardware, software, telecommunication equipment, and IT services to bank operational costs. Each of the four indices is a weighted average of two to four variables. The indices are explained in detail in the chapter section, "Data Indices." Each hypothesis is tested statistically by Pearson correlation for each of the 11 years of the study period, without a lag between bank IT expenditure and the particular bank index. Each hypothesis is also tested by Pearson correlation with 1- and 2-year lags between bank IT expenditure and the particular bank index. This is done over 10 years for 1-year lags and over 9 years for 2-year lags.

Research Model

The corresponding research model is shown in Figure 1.

The research model depicts the weighted indices that will be used to measure the performance of the banks. There is an index for bank profitability, efficiency, performance, and productivity. This corresponds to what McKeen et al. (1999)

Figure 1: Research Model

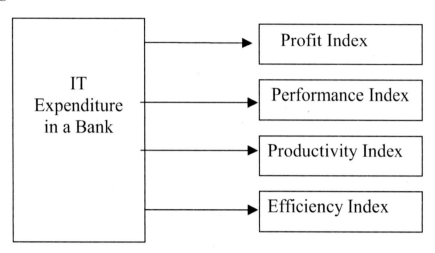

call the "basic" research mode, i.e., one that assumes a direct relationship between IT investments and organizational performance. The basic research mode was employed, because the historical data did not contain mediating factors inside the bank, and those factors could not be accurately determined at a later point. The research model of the present project is based on a ratio approach. The ratio approach, Wehrs (1999) points out, tests the relationship between an input represented by an IT investment ratio (i.e., IT investment divided by operational cost) and an "output" represented by a performance ratio (i.e., sales divided by assets). These studies are normally bivariate and tend to use cross-sectional data. In contrast, the present study uses longitudinal data, and the output measures are indices rather than a single variable.

Harris and Katz (1988) and Alpar and Kim (1990) utilize the ratio approach. Of special importance to this project is Harris and Katz's research, because they used an input ratio of IT expenses over noninterest operational expenses, a ratio similar to the one used in this project. Harris and Katz's output ratio is the ratio of noninterest operating expenses to premium income of insurance companies. Alpar and Kim's study is also relevant to this project, because they base their research on a data set of several banks. Alpar and Kim find no significant relationship between the ratio of IT investments and the performance ratios. However, they find a positive impact of IT investments on performance when they use a production function to test this relationship. Consequently, Alpar and Kim suggest that ratio studies are not suitable to study the impact of IT investments and the firms' performance. According to these authors, ratio studies leave out exogenous factors that affect the conversion of the investments into performance. As already pointed out, this objection is somewhat obviated with respect to exogenous factors external to banks, because this project is based on firms that constitute an entire banking industry. If it is true that external exogenous factors affect the conversion of investments into benefits, it can be assumed that these external exogenous factors would affect equally all the banks within the industry. However, the comments of Alpar and Kim are pertinent for the present study relative to exogenous factors internal to banks. Internal mediating data were not available for the study.

METHODOLOGY

This analysis tests, by correlation, the relationship between IT expenditure ratio and indices for bank: profitability, efficiency, performance, and productivity. For example, the IT spending relationship with the profitability index is tested through a bivariate correlation between the IT spending ratio (IT spending divided by operational cost) and a weighted average of the compounded index of profits, financial income, financial cost, and operational cost. The unit of analysis is the firm. A study using similar data but at the industry unit of analysis was reported by Navarrete and Pick (2002). A set of Pearson correlations were used to test the relationship between the IT spending ratio and the four indices. In these cases, the correlations are cross-sectional, as well as lagged longitudinally. That is to say, first, the associations of IT spending and each of the output indices are tested for the sample of banks in the same year. Then, the associations are tested for 1-year and 2-year lags. The correlations are tested at 0.05 and 0.01 levels of significance.

The Project's Data

This section discusses the sources of data for the research and data preparation, that is, adjustments and normalizing of the data prior to statistical analysis. The sources of data are important to discuss, because they were fairly unique, stemming from an unusual nationalized period. The data preparation is important, because the Mexican currency was not stable during this period, so currency adjustments had to be made. Also, size differences among the banks required normalizing. These support the paper's objective of performing empirical analysis to test hypotheses.

Data Sources

The two major sources of project data were the Mexican National Banking Commission (CNB, for its initials in Spanish), and Mexico's National Computing Programs Industry Association (ANIPCO, for its initials in Spanish). The CNB is the federal entity in charge of supervising banking operations, lending policies, economic interactions, and performance. Among other responsibilities, the CNB must report the banking financial statements quarterly and annually. This Commission has reported the financial statements since 1924. In 1992, the CNB published a special issue on the main characteristics and performance of the banking industry from 1982 to 1992 (Navarrete, 2001). Output ratios were calculated based on that report, as well as the CNB's annual financial statement reports, to test longitudinally the impact of IT expenditures. Similarly, ANIPCO collected the banks' IT expenditures based on the information that banks submitted annually to the government Finance and Planning Office, an office belonging to Instituto Nacional de Estadística, Geografía e Informática (INEGI). INEGI is the national statistical agency in charge of censuses, surveys, national cartography, and the country's IT infrastructure development, etc. Because the IT expenditure information was not collected directly from the banks, several interviews were done with the CEOs and CIOs of the banks to verify the accuracy of the data. Table 3 shows the IT expenditure of the banks from 1982 to 1992.

Data Preparation

Because the data were originally in current pesos, the data set had to be adjusted for analysis as follows:

1. Convert IT spending from current to real 1992 dollars, based on Mexico's price index and GDP.
2. Convert the financial statements of the 18 banks for the 11 years from current pesos to real 1992 dollars, as in Step 1.
3. Normalize the data. Because two banks accounted for almost half of the total industry market, while at the same time, six banks took up a tiny percentage of the market, it was necessary to normalize the data sample as recommended by Ahituv and Giladi (1994), dividing IT expenditure by the operational costs for each bank at each annual data point. Further, each output measure that did not already represent a ratio (e.g., market share) was divided by the bank's assets for that year.

Data Indices

To test the relationship between IT spending and organizational performance, four indices were developed for profitability, efficiency, performance, and productivity. In developing these indices, two approaches were followed.

First, several indices were developed based on a set of intercorrelated variables. This approach to develop the indexes is based on the development of indices for factor analysis (Newbold, 1990). According to Newbold an index can represent a set of variables if these variables have significant intercorrelations.

Two market share variables are significantly correlated, and hence were used to construct the bank performance index. These were as follows: the credit market

Table 3[1]: Mexican Banks' IT Spending (Current Dollars)

BANK	ITE1982*	ITE1983	ITE1984	ITE1985	ITE1986	ITE1987	ITE1988	ITE1989	ITE1990	ITE1991	ITE1992
Bank R	17.38	21.44	35.54	53.86	60.21	67.20	74.77	69.75	74.90	99.93	142.50
Bank P	18.87	14.39	21.32	32.11	37.44	56.89	61.23	70.90	79.62	113.79	150.60
Bank A	11.08	8.32	10.39	15.20	17.20	23.35	14.62	31.31	55.68	68.56	71.20
Bank D	6.74	4.80	5.47	8.12	9.61	11.18	11.50	14.16	25.04	35.64	41.00
Bank O	7.04	3.10	3.83	6.03	6.32	7.70	7.91	13.70	25.70	36.05	39.00
Bank I	5.39	3.67	4.51	5.90	5.31	6.83	6.95	7.83	15.92	22.72	27.60
Bank J	3.89	2.68	3.28	5.11	4.81	6.21	6.59	7.37	12.30	22.19	24.40
Bank S	2.40	1.83	2.60	3.67	3.54	4.47	4.07	4.37	6.81	13.55	17.60
Bank K	1.35	1.27	2.32	3.15	2.66	2.98	3.24	3.68	6.59	10.52	14.20
Bank Q	2.25	1.83	2.32	3.28	3.42	4.10	4.19	5.29	8.79	13.96	15.30
Bank F	0.60	0.56	0.82	1.31	1.64	2.73	3.35	2.99	4.39	8.34	10.10
Bank C	0.90	0.85	1.50	2.23	2.40	3.11	3.35	4.14	5.82	12.82	13.70
Bank M	1.20	0.99	1.50	2.36	2.15	2.86	2.76	3.45	5.60	12.19	14.90
Bank B	1.35	1.27	1.78	2.36	2.40	3.23	3.24	4.26	6.81	12.50	16.20
Bank N	1.20	1.13	1.78	2.49	2.40	2.73	2.76	2.42	4.06	9.38	9.80
Bank H	1.50	1.55	2.05	3.01	2.53	2.61	1.68	3.57	5.05	9.69	14.10
Bank L	0.90	1.27	1.78	2.36	2.28	2.36	2.16	3.34	9.55	7.82	9.10
Bank E	0.30	0.14	0.27	0.52	0.63	0.75	0.72	0.81	1.32	2.50	3.20

* ITE = IT expenditure

share (amount of money that each bank lent divided by the total money lent in the industry) and the direct income market share (amount of money each bank obtained from the market through different services like savings and checking accounts).

Similarly, the productivity index comprised three bank dimensions: number of nonmanagerial employees, number of managers, and number of branches. In the case of the bank productivity index, because the number of employees (the result of adding nonmanagerial employees and the number of managerial employees), the number of branches, and the IT spending ratio are significantly intercorrelated, the three measures were used to construct the productivity index.

A second approach was followed to construct the indices for profitability and efficiency. Because there were no significant intercorrelations between the different variables associated with banks' profits and efficiency, the parameter selection responded to the results of the set of interviews with CIOs and CEOs of the banks (Navarrete, 2001). According to these interviews, the banks oriented their IT spending toward enhancing customer services, without improving their "back office" systems. IT spending, consequently, should have increased the direct income, expanding the potential for profits. Operational cost and financial cost should lead to decreased profits. Following this reasoning, operational cost, financial cost, and direct income, together with bank's profits, comprised the profitability index. Last, the efficiency index was devised by including all the components of the operational efficiency ratio, as perceived by CIOs and CEOs: operational cost, total income, services income, and other income.

The weighted indices are calculated according to the following equation:

$$\text{Index}(j) = \Sigma\ (P(i)/AVG(P(i)))\ /\ \Sigma\ (1/AVG(P(i)))$$

where
    j = 1,2,3, and 4
    P = A variable
    i = Number of parameters in the index
    AVGP = Average value of a variable for the 11-year period

Table 4 presents the equations of the four indices, while Table 5 summarizes the measures involved for the input ratio and the four output ratios. It is important that the productivity index be defined as an inverse value of the weighted index. This responds to the fact that the correlations between the IT spending ratio and the employee ratio and branch ratio are negative. Using the inverse values will generate a positive correlation where

Table 4: Index Equations

Index	Description
Profitability	$\dfrac{(Pro(1/avgPro)+Inc(1/avgInc))-(OC(1/avgOC)-FC(1/avgFC))}{(1/avgPro+1/avgInc+1/avgOC+1/avgFC)}$
Efficiency	$\dfrac{(OC/avgOC+Inc/avgInc+FI/avgFI+OI/avgOI)}{(1/avgOC+1/avgInc+1/avgFI+1/avgOI)}$
Performance	$\dfrac{(CrMktSh(1/avgCrMktSh)+IncMktSh(1/avgIncMktSh))}{(1/avgCrMktSh+1/avgIncMktSh)}$
Productivity	$\dfrac{(1/avgEmp)+(1/avgBra)+(1/avgMgr)}{Emp(1/avgEmp)+Bra(1/avgBra)+Mgr(1/avgMgr)}$

Pro = Profits
Inc = Direct income
OC = Operational costs
FC = Financial costs
FI = Financial income
OI = Other income
CrMktSh = Credit market share
IncMktSh = Direct income market share
Emp = Number of employees
Bra = Number of branches
Mgr = Number of managers
avg X = Average of each variable

In summary, the case of the Mexican banking industry offered an opportunity to test the impact of IT on the performance of organizations. The 11-year government ownership allowed this project to have access to all banks' IT expenditures, a common IT definition across the banking industry, and use of a longitudinal data set on IT expenditure. The methodological approach is based on a correlation model, with the output measures consisting of weighted-average indices.

Table 5: Data Indices

Index Measure	Description
IT expenditure	Ratio of annual banks' expenses on hardware, software, telecommunication equipment, and IT services normalized by operational costs
Profitability Index	Weighted average index result of two profitability variables
Efficiency Index	Weighted average index result of four efficiency variables
Performance Index	Weighted average index result of two market share variables
Productivity index	Weighted average index result of the inverses of four size variables

IT SPENDING ASSOCIATION WITH BANKS' PERFORMANCE AND PRODUCTIVITY

Before looking at the results for the research questions, it is useful to examine the trends in IT spending by Mexican banks over the 1982–92 period. This can give greater insight into the environment of IT spending decisions relative to banking and the economy. This section discusses IT spending as a proportion of operational costs for large, medium, and small banks, the impact of the structure of banking on IT spending, and the impact of economic cycles on IT spending.

IT Spending in the Banking Industry

During the 11-year study period, IT spending as a proportion of operational cost as evidenced in Graph 3, shows a consistent pattern across large, medium, and small banks. As seen in Graph 3, IT spending behavior, as measured by the group averages, can be classified into six stages:

1. From 1982 to 1983, IT spending declined from 2%+ to 2% for all three groups.
2. A growth period of IT spending started in 1984 and ended in 1987. Large banks' IT spending proportion expanded from 2.1 to 6.2%, while small and medium size banks grew from 2% to 5.8 and 5.5% respectively.
3. IT spending experienced a contraction across the industry from 1987 to 1988. Large banks reduced IT spending by 30%, while medium and small banks decreased their spending by 23 and 27%.
4. IT spending rebounded the next two years; by 1990, large banks spent an average of almost 7% of their operational cost, while medium and small banks spent 5.7 and 6.3% respectively.
5. From 1990 to 1991, the industry's IT spending maintained its growth trend. However, a shift took place in the IT spending patterns by size groups. Medium-size banks that spent on average less than the other two groups in the nine previous years, rose to over 9%, outspending small and large banks. Small banks also proportionally outspent large banks.
6. For the last year, 1992, IT spending grew moderately across the industry. Medium-size banks spent more than 9%, small banks almost 9%, and large banks slightly more than 8% of their operational costs.

It is important to consider external shocks that affected IT spending. During the nationalized period, two important externalities that affected IT spending were economic growth and industry structure. First, the Mexican inflation rate and economic growth varied a lot during the 11-year period (see Graphs 1 and 2). The annual percent change in gross domestic product (GDP) matched the IT spending behavior of the banks grouped by size. Both graphs show two contractions caused by the economic crises in 1982 and 1987. Both graphs also show the two growth periods from 1984 to 1987 and from 1988 to 1990. In 1982, the Mexican economy contracted from a –0.6% annual growth to –5.2%. Similarly, IT spending of the banks grouped by size decreased from 2.5, 2.4, and 2.3% for large-, small-, and medium-size banks, respectively to 2.0%. Following this decline, positive economic growth periods were associated with substantial IT spending for all three groups of banks. It is worth pointing out that large banks showed greater sensitivity to changes in the economic environment of the country. During both economic crises in 1982 and 1987, the large banks' IT spending contraction exceeded the contractions of the other two size groups.

The second externality affecting IT spending behavior is the industry structure. In the 11-year period, there were two major changes in bank ownership. First, in 1982, the government took over control of the banks; and, second, from 1991 to 1992, the government sold back the banks to investor groups. The banking industry's nationalization is regarded as part of the Mexican economic crisis of 1982. Subsequently, the IT spending contraction of 1983 might be the result of a combination of the two factors. First, the economic crisis triggered annual inflation of up to 98%. Second, changes in the banks' top and middle management, alteration of business strategies, and changes in the organizational structure upset long-term IT spending.

Graph 3: Average Banks' IT Expenditure Grouped by Size

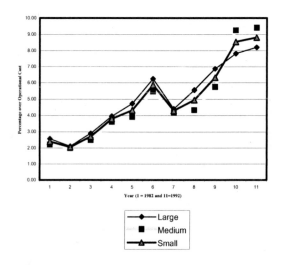

In the 1992 divestiture process, on the other hand, IT spending grew, because the federal government tried to "fix up" the banks for sale. In order to secure a higher price for small and medium banks, the government invested proportionally more in IT for small- and medium-size banks than in large ones (Garcia Macias, 1999).

The IT literature provides limited coverage on this topic. Theoretically, Kauffman and Weill (1989) advise that economic externalities affect IT spending in different industries unevenly. The case of the Mexican banks shows how sensitive to economic externalities IT spending can be. Two economic crises and two industry-wide changes in ownership triggered six different spending behaviors in an 11-year period.

FINDINGS: IT SPENDING AND THE PERFORMANCE INDICES

This chapter section summarizes the correlation findings. The findings on the correlations between the IT expenditure ratio and the respective performance index are grouped by research questions into four tables: the profitability index (Table 6), the efficiency index (Table 7), the productivity index (Table 8), and the performance index (Table 9). As pointed out in the methodology section, correlations are shown cross-sectionally for the current year and also for lags of 1 and 2 years between IT spending and the performance indices.

According to these tables, there is no positive correlation between the banks' IT spending and the profitability and the efficiency indices in the 11-year period. For the 1-year lagged results, there is no positive correlation between IT spending and the profitability and efficiency indices. For the 2-year lags, there is no positive correlation, and, in fact, there is an inverse correlation for the last time point, i.e., between IT spending in 1990 and the efficiency index in 1992.

For the productivity index, shown in Table 8, there are three scattered years out of 11 with a positive correlation between the IT ratio and the productivity index. Similar to the performance index, the last two years have an inverse correlation. It is interesting that the association between the two variables is stronger after 1- and 2-year lags, in particular, 4 or 5 years out of 10 have positive associations.

There is a positive correlation between the IT spending and the performance index for the middle period of 1984-1989, but two negative correlations for 1991 and 1992 (Table 9).

In summary, Hypothesis 1 is not supported, because there is no significant positive correlation between IT spending and the profitability index. Similarly, Hypothesis 2 is not supported, because there is no correlation between IT spending and the efficiency index for the entire period of the study. On the other hand,

Hypothesis 3 is partially accepted, because the correlations mostly support the hypotheses. Last, Hypothesis 4 is partially supported, because there are six periods out of 11 with positive and significant association between the IT spending ratios and the performance index.

Table 6: Correlation between IT Expenditure and the Profitability Index

Year	82	83	84	85	86	87	88	89	90	91	92
	-0.415	-0.388	-0.338	-0.210	-0.234	-0.396	-0.231	-0.380	-0.072	0.284	0.250
	0.087	0.112	0.171	0.402	0.349	0.104	0.356	0.120	0.775	0.253	0.316
1-year lag		-0.480	-0.312	-0.378	-0.205	-0.243	-0.410	-0.214	-0.395	0.176	0.314
		0.093	0.207	0.122	0.415	0.330	0.091	0.393	0.105	0.484	0.204
2-year lag			-0.490*	-0.390	-0.365	-0.206	-0.265	-0.384	-0.233	-0.242	0.218
			0.039	0.110	0.136	0.412	0.287	0.115	0.353	0.333	0.385

Note: * 0.05 confidence level.
          ** 0.01 confidence level.

Table 7: Correlation between IT Expenditure and the Efficiency Index

Year	82	83	84	85	86	87	88	89	90	91	92
	0.091	0.003	-0.329	0.103	-0.163	-0.086	-0.128	-0.027	0.434	-0.089	0.112
	0.712	0.911	0.325	0.674	0.504	0.726	0.601	0.912	0.063	0.718	0.647
1-year lag		-0.021	-0.152	-0.307	-0.159	-0.016	-0.045	-0.298	0.167	0.101	-0.148
		0.931	0.535	0.880	0.516	0.948	0.855	0.215	0.494	0.681	0.546
2-year lag			0.453	-0.130	-0.308	-0.057	-0.010	-0.355	0.200	0.048	-.653**
			0.051	0.596	0.199	0.815	0.968	0.136	0.413	0.844	0.002

Note: * 0.05 confidence level.
          ** 0.01 confidence level.

Table 8: Correlation between IT Expenditure and the Productivity Index

Year	82	83	84	85	86	87	88	89	90	91	92
	0.423	0.506*	0.307	0.242	0.465	0.534*	0.282	.629**	0.449	-0.460	-0.514*
	0.080	0.032	0.215	0.333	0.052	0.022	0.257	0.005	0.062	0.055	0.029
1-year lag		0.427	0.581*	0.282	0.229	0.511*	0.536*	0.225	.486*	0.470*	-0.390
		0.077	0.011	0.256	0.362	0.030	0.022	0.369	0.041	0.049	0.055
2-year lag			0.267	0.583*	0.300	0.323	0.528*	0.536*	0.041	0.482*	0.379
			0.283	0.011	0.226	0.191	0.024	0.022	0.873	0.043	0.121

Note: * 0.05 confidence level.
          ** 0.01 confidence level.

Table 9: Correlation between IT Expenditure and the Performance Index

Year	82	83	84	85	86	87	88	89	90	91	92
	0.307	0.421	.708**	0.537*	.719**	.784**	.614**	0.700*	-0.023	-.692**	-0.504*
	0.215	0.082	0.001	0.022	0.001	0.000	0.007	0.001	0.927	0.001	0.033
1-year lag		0.277	0.453	.669**	0.553*	.717**	0.777*	0.564*	.648**	-0.020	-.685**
		0.366	0.059	0.002	0.017	0.001	0.000	0.015	0.004	0.937	0.002
2-year lag			0.237	0.423	.692**	0.560*	.667**	0.769*	0.457	0.667*	-0.059
			0.345	0.080	0.001	0.016	0.003	0.000	0.057	0.003	0.816

Note: * 0.05 confidence level.
          ** 0.01 confidence level.

DISCUSSION OF RESULTS OF IT SPENDING AND ORGANIZATION'S PERFORMANCE

The correlation findings only partially support the hypotheses. This section discusses and attempts to explain the mixed empirical results in terms of banking industry during the study period, IT spending orientation, and impact of change of ownership.

Explanation of Empirical Findings: The Banking Industry during the Study Period

The government nationalized the commercial banks in 1982, because it perceived them as overly profitable by conducting bad and unfair banking practices and, also, as quite inefficient. After the nationalization, banking strategies altered to limit excess profits. The banks spent on IT to compete through better services (Garcia Noriega, 1999) and productivity (Garcia Macias, 1999). During the nationalized period, their IT spending was never oriented toward improving the banks' profits. Our research finding of lack of positive correlation between IT spending and profits is consistent with the banks' shift, starting in 1982, in spending orientation.

The nationalization of banks during the study period also explains the efficiency findings. One would have expected the government to improve efficiency during its ownership period. However, there is no evidence that the banks invested to improve organizational efficiency during the period of government ownership. On the contrary, the banks kept the same policy toward spending for IT efficiency that they had before the nationalization. The banks invested and developed an efficient "front end" to support banking services for their customers, but they delayed investing in "back office" systems, which overall hurt their efficiency as organizations (Capote, 1999). The present empirical findings are consistent with this banking behavior.

Explanation of Empirical Findings: IT Spending Orientation

The banks' orientation, during the nationalized period, to improve services and productivity, explains the partial support for Hypotheses 3 and 4. This subsection draws on interviews with two bank CIOs at the time. Some banks waited for a year to deploy their IT plans (Chong, 1999). These plans sought to have the requisite IT to keep the banks competitive (Garcia Noriega, 1999). The banks spent more on IT, while they kept their number of employees and branches (i.e., inverse indicators of productivity) almost constant.

The findings show that correlations between IT expenditure and productivity became stronger with a 1-year lag. This corroborates the CIOs' expectations regarding the time it takes for an IT investment to become productive. Most of the CIOs interviewed estimated that it took between 1 and 2 years for an IT project to become productive.

The correlations between IT spending and the performance index are also aligned to the spending behavior of the banking industry. This occurred mainly because the spending was oriented toward improving customer services, to catch up with competing banks when they started a new service, and to adopt technologies, e.g., automatic teller machines, that potentially impacted customers' behavior. Garcia Noriega (1999), for example, points out that the IT spending budget was treated like marketing spending in that IT spending reflected growth plans and market expectations.

Explanation of Emprical Findings: Impact of Change of Ownership

This section focuses on explaining why the empirical correlation findings are weaker at the start and finish of the study period. The major changes in ownership at both ends of the study period appear to have had a huge impact on the relationship between IT spending and the performance and productivity indices. After the nationalization in 1982, the federal government sought to fuse banks together, reducing the number of banks to 18. At the end of the period, the government prepared the banks for their private sale. The two changes in ownership explain the following three questions: 1) why, at the beginning of the period, there are few positive correlations for the indices; 2) why there are 6 years of positive correlations in mid-period for the performance index and some for the productivity index; and 3) why at the end of the period, the correlations with the indices tend to show no positive correlation or an inverse significant correlation in the cases of the performance and productivity indices.

In the 1982–1983 adjustment period to nationalization, the government and its policies adjusted to supervising and operating the banking system. In 1982, the new top management of the banks first had to consolidate the industry, to redefine the banks' processes to comply with the new banking regulations, and to set the banks' strategies to succeed in the new environment. Also in this adjustment period, several larger banks took over smaller banks. This time of flux and change explains the lack of correlation between IT spending and the bank indices for years 1982 and 1983.

In the second period, 1984 to 1989, under new policies and a consolidated banking industry, the banks developed and grew in their range and quality of services and in the productivity of employees and branches. During this period, the correlations between IT expenditure and performance and productivity are consistently significant and positive.

At the start of the third period from 1989 to 1992, the federal administration announced its intention to reprivatize the banking industry. In many respects, the changes in bank performance from 1989 through 1992 were needed or promoted by the Mexican government, in order to be able to sell the banks back to industrial groups. In particular, the government spent on IT to make them look more attractive to potential buyers. Furthermore, medium-size and small banks spent proportionally more in IT than larger banks, contrary to the opposite spending pattern by bank size in the prior 5 years. This "cosmetic" aspect of the divestiture process explains the lack of correlation between IT spending, which was high, and the indices of performance and productivity. IT spending occurred for "good appearances," rather than being focused on service and productivity growth.

THE PRESENT STUDY'S EMPIRICAL FINDINGS COMPARED TO PREVIOUS RESEARCH

This chapter section compares the empirical findings to prior research literature. The lack of positive correlations between IT expenditures and the bank profitability index for 11 years is aligned with the literature on the productivity paradox. For instance, Dos Santos et al. (1993) and Scott Morton (1991) report no evidence of IT expenditure/ and investment improving profitability.

Previous research reports somewhat similar results to the ones found in the Mexican banking case for profitability and efficiency. For example, Kauffman and Weill (1989) concluded there is no evidence of a positive impact on the IT investments; and Shrage (1997) and Ahituv and Giladi (1994) concluded that IT does not have a positive impact on the success or value of organizations.

Our study's positive correlations for the performance and productivity indices are not aligned with the productivity paradox, suggesting a positive association between IT spending and the organizations' performance and productivity. In particular, the present positive correlations with the performance index concur with the market explanation to the productivity paradox (Clemons & Row, 1989). Under this explanation, researchers suggest that investing/ and spending in IT obeys a competitive necessity, where the investment/ and spending area directed to assure a given level of service to the organizations' customers, allowing the organization to retain its market share (Clemons & Row, 1989). This explanation is supported by the present project's significant findings on the association between IT investments and the present performance index, which is based on market share variables.

Another study that rejected the productivity paradox pointed to the market explanation, as well as three other causes not in the present model (Brynjolfsson, 1993). In the current case, the Mexican banks' performance increased during the study period, because in the midst of an almost constant numbers of employees and branches, there were growing markets, numbers of transactions, customers, and services.

CHAPTER SUMMARY

The research objective was to empirically study the impact of IT investments on the performance and value of organizations. Specifically, the project conducted an empirical study:

· Of the productivity paradox
· At the firm level of analysis
· With an homogeneous definition of IT
· For an industry in a developing country

The research has mixed results, with the productivity paradox supported for the outcomes of profitability and efficiency but rejected for the outcomes of productivity and performance. Table 10 summarizes the results of testing the projects hypotheses.

At the firm level of analysis, the historical aspects of the industry, the IT spending orientation, and the impact of change of ownership explain the lack of correlations with the profitability and the efficiency indice. There are positive and significant correlations with the performance index for most years and with the productivity index for about half the years. These positive associations turned out to be present generally in those years not affected by the two changes of ownership of the industry.

The Mexican banking case shows how sensitive to externalities a banking industry can be. Two economic crises and two changes in bank ownership triggered six different spending behaviors in an 11-year period. The analysis of this behavior by groups of banks reflects that large banks were more sensitive to bank externalities. Large banks' IT spending behavior changed more due to the economic crisis and changes in bank ownership, while these behaviors were less apparent among small- and medium-size banks.

It is interesting that in another study with the same data, but analyzing data longitudinally at the industry level of analysis, IT industry spending and was associated with total industry profits (Navarrete and Pick, 2002).

Table 10: Summary of Results

Research Question	Hypothesis	Description	Partially Supported	Not Supported
1	1	IT expenditure is positively correlated with the profitability index.		✔
2	2	IT expenditure is positively correlated with the efficiency index.		✔
3	3	IT expenditure is positively correlated with the productivity index.	✔	
4	4	IT expenditure is positively correlated with the performance index.	✔	

The project's results have the following implications for practitioners:

· Economic and industry externalities affect organization performance and might inhibit the translation of IT spending/investment into organizational benefits.

· The benefits of IT can be associated with market share and employee and infrastructure productivity.

· When external factors do not limit the impact of IT spending/ and investment, the variable related to that spending/ and investment should be the main factor for finding out whether or not the technology is producing the desired output.

Discussion of Results and Future Trends

This section first discusses the soundness of the project's methodology and its limitations. The second part summarizes the project's implications for practitioners and researchers, and the third part offers ideas for future research in this field.

Evaluation of Methodological Approach

The project methodology consisted of an ex-post ratio study using longitudinal data that includes all the players in a given industry. According to Wehrs (1999), research design should make clear the moment of the evaluation. Ex-post studies, like this one, evaluate the impact of IT after the investment/ and expenditure took place. In this case, the project tested the impact of IT after 11 years of bank IT spending. Through a ratio study, the project tested the correlation between this IT spending and four indices: productivity, performance, efficiency, profitability.

Ratio studies statistically test the relationship between a ratio representing IT input and a ratio representing organizational performance. The project tested the correlation between the ratio of IT expenditure/operational cost and indices of output ratios. Researchers report two weaknesses of ratio studies. First, ratios are too simple to really capture the impact of IT on organizations; they correspond to a "basic model" (McKeen Smith, & Parent, 1999), which does not take into account other factors inhibiting or promoting organizational performance or productivity.

The present research results support that ratio studies are appropriate in finding IT impact on organizations. It turns out that IT impact on organizations is quite diverse and elusive, because IT can enhance some parameters or none at all. For example, the results of this project confirm the association of IT spending with the performance of the banks, based on a positive relationship between the IT ratio and the performance index of the banks. However, the IT ratio failed to correlate with the profitability index. The results of this project demonstrate that ratio studies are suitable for studying IT impact on organizations. In practice, however, ratio studies can become weak if there is not a wide range of firm outcome parameters with which to discover the impacts of the IT spending.

The second complaint about ratio studies is that they fail to account for other factors that inhibit performance. More evolved conceptual models try to reduce this problem. For example, the Weill (1992) model includes another construct, conversion effectiveness; the Lucas (1993) model includes design of technology, sound use and "other variables"; the Markus and Soh (1993) research proposes conversion effectiveness and structural factors. Furthermore, the results of this project confirm other factors influencing the impact of IT. For example, it is clear that industry and economic externalities diluted the IT spending benefits for Mexican banks. However, the influence of other factors and the measure of their impact on the conversion of IT into benefits poses a challenge even greater than the one represented for the productivity paradox. For example, McKeen et al. (1999) criticize the conversion effectiveness concept, because so far, there is no way to measure it. Moreover, even if it can be measured, the way to measure it varies from firm to firm.

Overall, despite the above noted concerns, ratio studies appeared to be the most feasible, if not the best, approach to test for positive impacts in the present study. The results can be enhanced if there is more information regarding firm strategies; if the data sample is longitudinal; and if the data sample has several organizational economic variables to test for productivity, performance, and/or efficiency gains.

Project Limitations

One limitation of this project, due to data unavailability, was the unfeasibility of calculating the marginal contribution of IT to firm output variables. Through a production function, other studies have measured how much an output variable increases due to an increase of IT capital. Lack of access to IT labor data and non-IT labor data in Mexican commercial banks precluded the use of a production function to estimate the contribution of IT to different bank outputs.

Using information from only one industry in a developing country limits the generalization of the project's findings. It would be an error to extrapolate the findings of this project to other settings, such as other industries, other periods, other countries, or countries of different development levels.

Implications for Practitioners

The project results lend credence to the argument that IT contributes to some aspects of firm performance, and, at the same time, helps explain the reasons why the productivity paradox appears in some research studies. The project's results must be taken cautiously, due to the limited and particular sample. With this caution, banking practitioners should be aware of the following:

1.   Economic and industry externalities that affect organizations and inhibit the translation of IT spending into organizational benefits
2.   IT spending that protects or increases market share
3.   IT spending that enhances employee and infrastructure productivity

The limited sample of this study suggests that practitioners should not expect IT investments/ and expenditures to have a homogeneous effect on organizations. The potential effect of these investments may be heterogeneous on performance, productivity, profitability, and efficiency. For example, in the first stage of the 11-year period in the Mexican banks, the change in ownership led to the consolidation of the industry, down to 18 banks. The new consolidated banks oriented their strategies toward the projects needed to integrate the newly merged banks. This priority reduced the likelihood of good banking performance. Later, in 1990–1992, the divestiture process affected the IT spending patterns. In this stage, the performance was not the only concern of the top management. They were also worried about preparing the banks for the selling process. Major events for the industry, the nationalization and the divestiture, deeply altered the spending decisions and bank performance.

The present study suggests that when external factors do not limit the impact of IT spending or investment, the variables directly related to the results of that investment/ and spending should be the main factors for finding out whether or not the technology is producing the desired output. Lucas (1999) even proposes to measure the system's use as an outcome indicator of IT investment. Further, Brynjolfsson and Hitt (1997) propose that aligning IS/IT strategy to customer needs will stimulate the IT impact on the firm's value.

The limited sample of this study indicates that one important contribution to firm value is to increase or protect market share. Clemons (1991) points out that when all players in a market have access to IT, investing can become a strategic necessity to protect market share. This argument is directly related to Brynjolfsson's explanation of the productivity paradox (1993). Consumers benefit from firms' IT investments.

Another finding of this project is that IT is related to the organizational productivity index. Based on Jurison's (1995) concept of productivity, this project tested an index based on the number of bank employees, branches, and managers. Jurison points out that because productivity measures the relationship between output (products or services) and the resources needed to produce them, there are two ways to improve productivity: to produce more with the same amount of resources or to produce the same with fewer resources. The Mexican banking experience belongs to the first case, because banks kept almost constant the number of employees and branches, while they stimulated more customers, services, and banking transactions during the period of the study. The correlation between IT spending and the productivity index points toward a positive association between the IT and the productivity of employees and branches. This result is aligned with the idea of IT's contributing to labor savings (Brynjolffson & Hitt, 1996).

It is worth mentioning, however, that the results suggest a productivity gain in employee and branch productivity, which is not the same as overall bank productivity. However, this result can only be extrapolated cautiously, due to the limited sample. To have an impact on the overall bank productivity, the gains for employee and branch productivity would have to be higher than the IT spending that promoted those gains. To illustrate, let us say that a bank spends one million dollars on IT in a given year, and thanks to this spending, there is a productivity gain in employees and branches that promotes a surplus of a half million dollars. Then, the IT spending contributes to employees' and branches' productivity. However, because the gains in employee and branch productivity gains do not offset the IT spending, this spending does not promote the bank's overall productivity gain. In the case of the Mexican banks, the information at hand does not let us verify if the IT spending impact on employee and branch productivity is translated into banks' gains in productivity.

Implications for Researchers

The results of the project have several implications for researchers studying the value of IT investment and the productivity paradox. At the firm level, researchers should consider the following factors:

- Common definition of IT across the organizational samples
- Homogeneity regarding size in the data sample
- IS/IT spending as a surrogate for IS/IT investments
- Use of a longitudinal data sample
- A range of constructs to represent an organization's productivity, performance, and efficiency
- Externalities that affect performance

As pointed out by several researchers, an IT definition that is consistently and commonly applied to all cases is fundamental for studying the impact of IT on firms' performance. Without such a common definition, any kind of testing procedure will show little or no impact of IT on organizations. The IT definition may not need to be as thorough as the one used by Callopy et al. (1994) for expenditure. Those authors define IT expenditures as ones concerning mainframes, minicomputers, microcomputers, data entry systems, data communication equipment, software, services, supplies, and overhead. It is more important to conduct a study with an adequate but common definition than a complete definition.

A data sample consisting of organizations of different size distorts the relationship between IT investments and firm performance. In the present data sample, three out of 18 banks accounted for more than 75% of the banking market. A normalization process allowed for the statistical analysis. Otherwise, the differences in size would have been large enough to distort the statistical results. The operational cost of the banks helped in normalizing the IT spending measure, while assets were used to normalize the performance measures.

Another implication for researchers is that, even though IT investments are a stronger construct to test the impact of IT, IT expenditure is a good surrogate measurement for IT investments. Several projects, like this one, have used IT expenses as a surrogate for IT investment. Furthermore, it has proven to be easier to collect the data of IT spending than to have access to IT investment information.

Access to a longitudinal sample was a fortuitous happening in this research. Studies with longitudinal data should be encouraged. Because IT expenditure generates different types of return, researchers need to analyze several economic periods to identify the potential benefits of the expenditure. Without a sample extending over several periods, external factors affecting the conversion into benefits can mislead the research results. A longitudinal data sample allows testing whether or not IT spending converts into additional firm value. If the present data sample had covered only the first or last four years, it would likely have been confronted with inconsistent results. Similarly, having only a data sample of the middle, 6-year "stable" industry period would have led to an unrealistic conclusion, i.e., that IT expenditure is always positively correlated with firm market share. Having access to a longitudinal data set allows testing of the impact of different externalities in the association of IT investment/ and spending with the performance of organizations.

Given the different forms of IT value, researchers should look for positive benefits in several firm variables, e.g., productivity, performance, profits, and efficiency. Profits should not be the only variable to test for positive relationships between the IT investments and the firm's productivity. In retrospective studies, like this one, the researcher should look for benefits in as many firm parameters as possible.

Relevant to the present research is the conversion effectiveness concept proposed by Weill (1992) and Markus and Soh (1993). According to these authors, the firm's conversion effectiveness accounts for external factors, such as organizational structure, managerial process, or economic trends, among others, that inhibit or facilitate the contributions of IT. In order to take into account these external factors, a set of interviews is useful for discovering the potential external factors affecting the translation of IT investments into organizational benefits or value. The present project's CEO and the CIO interviews helped in understanding the translation of IT investments into firm performance or value. The CEO is a key person to interview, because CEOs know the firms strategy and overall resources, they are key. They can point out the way IT was linked to their firm's strategy and what benefits were considered for investing in IT. The CIO can state the following: how IT investments were justified, when projects were successfully accomplished, what benefits—tangible and intangible—the IT projects brought to the firm and how long it took for a projects to fulfill their goals.

Future Research

The research agenda regarding the productivity paradox and the value of information is far-reaching. The diffusion of e-commerce and the Internet has further triggered projects in the organizational, industrial, and economic settings never before seen. This section offers ideas for several future research studies regarding the value of information and the Mexican banking industry.

1) *A follow-up study of the impact of IT on the survival of the Mexican banks.* After the now 10 years of private ownership of the Mexican banking industry, only six out of the 18 banks that were privatized in 1992 remain in business. The other 12 have joined other banks, been bought by other banks, or gone bankrupt. The objectives of this project would be to find out the bank's IT strategy after privatization; the contribution of IT, if any, to bank survival; and the IT impact on performance, size dimensions, and efficiency.

2) *Comparative study that measures the value of specific IT applications in the banking industries of developed and developing countries:* Following a current research trend of investigating how to make technology productive instead of trying to find the positive impact of technology, the purpose of this project would be to identify a set of information technologies actually in use or adopted by banks in developed and developing countries. The objective would be to measure their contribution to value, performance, or bank productivity, and to assess results comparatively across countries at different levels of economic development.

3) *IT spending behavior and IT investment justification procedures in the banking industry.* The purpose of this project would be to interview CIOs and CEOs of the private banks to find out whether or not private banks have different approaches to evaluating and justifying IT investments.

4) *Linking ex-post IT studies with ex-ante IT studies through balanced scored cards.* Another current trend in studying the value of IT for organizations is to link the benefits of the technology with its use. Willcocks and Lester propose using Norton's balanced scorecard to measure the value of IT based on its use or the motivating factors of the IT investments. The balanced scorecard also model can be used for linking ex-ante and ex-post IT impact studies. This linkage could follow the following steps: 1) identify ex-ante the IT investments drivers, that is, those mechanisms that translate the objectives of the IT investments into measurable outputs; 2) monitor the impact of the IT investments once the project or projects are implemented; 3) identify the relationship of the measurable outputs with firm's performance variables; and 4) monitor the firms' performance variables ex- post to track down the impacts if any are due to the IT project or projects.

END NOTES

[1]   Before 1985, all telecommunications equipment installed in the country belonged to the government and was operated by the government. The new telecomm law allowed the installation and operation of private networks.

REFERENCES

Ahituv, N. & Giladi, R. (1994). Business Success and Information Technology: Are They Really Related? *Proceedings of the Seventh Annual Conference of Management IS*, Tel Aviv University.

Ahituv, N., Lipovetsky, S., & Tishler, A. (1999). The Relationship Between Firm's Information Systems Policy and Business Performance: A Multivariate Analysis. In M. A. Mahmood and E. J. Szewczak (Eds.), *Measuring Information Technology Investment Payoff: Contemporary Approaches* (pp. 62–82). Hershey, PA: Idea Group Publishing.

Alpar, P. & Kim, M. (1990). A Microeconomic Approach to the Measurements of Information Technology Value. *Journal of Management Information Systems*, 7(3), 55-69.

Aspe, P. (1993). *Economic Transformation the Mexican Way.* Cambridge, MA: The MIT Press.

Banker, R. D., Kauffman, R. J., & Mahmood, M. A., (1993). *Strategic Information Technology Management: Perspectives on Organizational Growth and Competitive Advantage.* Hershey, PA: Idea Group Publishing.

Brynjolfsson, E. (1993). The Productivity Paradox of Information Technology, *Communications of the ACM, 36*(12), 67.

Brynjolfsson, E. & Hitt, L., (1996). Paradox Lost? Firm-Level Evidence on the Returns to Information Systems Spending, *Management Science, 42*(4), 541–559.

Brynjolfsson, E. & Hitt, L. (1997). MIT Analysis: Breaking Boundaries, *Informationweek,* Sep. 22, 54–61.

Callopy, F., Adya, M., & Armstrong, J. S. (1994). Principles for Examining Predictive Validity: The Case of Information Systems Spending, *Information Systems Research, 5*(2), 170–179.

Capote, A. (1999). *Interview with Alfredo Capote,* President and CEO of IBM de Mexico, February 3, 1999. Mexico D.F. Mexico. In Navarrete, C. J. (2001). *Information Technology Expenditure Relationship with Organization's Value and Performance.* Unpublished doctoral dissertation, Claremont Graduate University, Claremont, CA.

Chong, R. (1999). *Interview with Roberto Chong,* CIO of Atlantico Bank, March 13, 1999, Mexico D.F. Mexico. In Navarrete, C. J. (2001). *Information Technology Expenditure Relationship with Organization's Value and Performance.* Unpublished doctoral dissertation, Claremont Graduate University, Claremont, CA.

Clemons, E. K. (1991). Evaluation of Strategic Investments in Information Technology, *Communications of the ACM, 34*(1), 22–36.

Clemons, E. K. & Row M. C. (1989). Information Technology and Economic Reorganization. *Proceedings of the Tenth International Conference on Information Systems.* (pp. 341–351). December, Boston, MA.

Dewan, S. & Kraemer, K. L. (1998). International Dimensions of the Productivity Paradox. *Communications of the ACM, 41*(8), 56–62.

Dos Santos, B. L., Peffers, K., & Mauer D. C. (1993). The Impact of Information Technology Investment. Announcements on the Market Value of the Firm, *Information Systems Research, 1*(4), 1–22.

Garcia Macias, A. (1999). *Interview with Alfonso Garcia Macias,* CEO of Internacional and BCH Banks, Febrary 5, 1999, Mexico D. F., Mexico. In Navarrete, C. J. (2001). *Information Technology Expenditure Relationship with Organization's Value and Performance.* Unpublished doctoral dissertation, Claremont Graduate University, Claremont, CA.

Garcia Noriega, G. (1999). *Interview with Gerardo Garcia Noriega*, CIO of International Bank, April 21, 2000, Mexico D. F., Mexico. In Navarrete, C. J. (2001). *Information Technology Expenditure Relationship with Organization's Value and Performance.* Unpublished doctoral dissertation, Claremont Graduate University, Claremont, CA.

Harris, S. E. & Katz, J. L. (1988). Profitability and Information Capital Intensity in the Insurance Industry. *Proceedings of the 21st Annual Hawaii Conference on Systems Sciences* (124-130). Hawaii, U.S.

Harris, S. E. & Katz, J. L. (1991). Organizational Performance and Information Technology Investments Intensity in the Insurance Industry, *Organization Science, 2*(3), 263–295.

Jurison, J. (1995). Defining and Measuring Productivity. In P. Gray and J. Jurison, *Productivity in the Office and the Factory.* Danvers, MA: Boyd & Fraser.

Kaplan, R. S. & Norton, D. P. (1992). The Balanced Scorecard—Measures That Drive Performance, *Harvard Business Review, 70*(1), 71–80.

Kauffman, R. J. & Weill, P. (1989). An Evaluative Framework for Research on the Performance Effects of Information Technology Investments. *Proceedings of the 10th International Conference on Information Systems* (pp. 377-388). Boston, MA.

Keen, P. G. W. (1991). *Shaping the Future: Business Design Through Information Technology.* Boston, MA: Harvard Business School Press.

Loveman, G. W. (1994). An Assessment of the Productivity Impact of Information Technologies. In Allen T. J. & Scott Morton, M. S. *Information Technologies and the Corporation of the 1990's.* New York, NY: Oxford University Press.

Lucas, H. C. (1999). *Information Technology and the Productivity Paradox: Assessing the Value of Investing in IT.* New York: Oxford: Oxford University Press.

Lucas, H. C., Jr. (1975). The Use of an Accounting Information System, Action and Organizational Performance, *The Accounting Review, 50*(4), 735–746.

Markus, M. L. & Soh, C., (1993). Banking on Information Technology: Converting IT Spending into Firm Performance, Chapter 19. In R. Banker et al. (Eds.). *Strategic Information Technology Management: Perspectives on Organizational Growth and Competitive Advantage* (pp. 375–403). Harrisburg, PA: Idea Group Publishing.

McKeen, J. E., Smith, H. A., & Parent, M., (1999). An Integrative Research Approach to Assess the Business Value of Information Technology. In M. A. Mahmood and E. J. Szewczak, *Measuring Information Technology Investment Payoff: Contemporary Approaches* (pp. 5–23). Hershey, PA: Idea Group Publishing.

Navarrete, C. J. (2001). Information Technology Expenditure Relationship with Organization's Value and Performance. Unpublished doctoral dissertation, Claremont Graduate University, Claremont, CA.

Navarrete, C. J. & Pick, J. B. (2002). Information Technology Expenditure and Industry Performance: The Case of the Mexican Banking Industry, *Journal of Global Information Technology Management, 5*(2), 7–28.

Newbold, P. (1991). *Statistics for Business and Economics.* (3rd ed.) New Jersey: Prentice Hall, Inc.

Schrage, M. (1997). The real problem with computers, *Harvard Business Review, 75*(5), 178–188.

Scott Morton, M. S. (1991). *The Corporations of the 1990s Information Technology and Organizational Transformation.* Oxford University Press.

Strassman, P. A. (1990). *The Business Value of Computers: An Executive's Guide.* New Canaan, CT: Information Economic Press.

Tello, C. (1984). *La Nacionalizacion de la Banca en Mexico.* [The Mexican Banking Industry Nationalization]. Mexico, D. F., Mexico: Siglo XXI Editores, S.A.

Wehrs, W.E. (1999). A Road Map for IS/IT Evaluation. In M. A. Mahmood and E. J. Szewczak, (Eds.), *Measuring Information Technology Investment Payoff: Contemporary Approaches,* 5–23. Hershey, PA: Idea Group Publishing.

Weill, P. (1992). The Relationship Between Investment in Information Technology and Firm Performance: A Study of the Value Manufacturing Sector, *Information Systems Research, 3*(4), 307–332.

Willcocks, L. P. & Lester, S. (1996). Beyond the IT Productivity Paradox, *European Management Journal, 14*(3), 279–291.

Chapter V

An Empirical Analysis of Productivity Gains from Information Technology's Reduction of Coordination Costs[1]

Namchul Shin
Pace University, USA

Most information systems (IS) research has examined the impact of information technology (IT) on the organization of economic activities by starting from the theoretical speculation that IT reduces coordination costs and improves coordination of economic activities. This theoretical speculation, however, has not been empirically analyzed in the IS field. The value of IT for reducing coordination costs has also not been considered in the studies on IT productivity gains. This study empirically examines the relationship between IT and coordination costs, and the relationship between IT and firm productivity by considering coordination as a factor of production. The results indicate that IT is strongly associated with a decline in coordination costs and that IT and coordination make a substantial and statistically significant contribution to firm output. The results show that IT contributes to firm output by reducing coordination costs and improving coordination; that is, by making a higher level of coordination more efficient.

INTRODUCTION

Information technology (IT) has profoundly changed the way that business is conducted. With the use of IT, organizations can radically redesign their business processes. IT is also radically restructuring the market by altering customer–supplier relationships. These changes have occurred because IT enables better information processing, sharing, and faster responsiveness, thereby improving coordination of economic activities between separate units of an organization and across organizations. Most information systems (IS) research (Bakos and Brynjolfsson, 1993; Brynjolfsson et al., 1994; Clemons & Reddi, 1992; Gurbaxani & Whang, 1991; Malone et al., 1987, 1989) has examined the impact of IT on the organization of economic activities by starting from the theoretical speculation that IT reduces coordination costs and improves coordination of the economic activities critical to the best use of resources and the delivery of goods and services. This theoretical speculation, however, has not been empirically analyzed in the IS field.

Most previous studies on IT productivity gains have considered only the value derived from IT that improves capital and labor efficiency (Brynjolfsson & Hitt, 1993, 1996; Lichtenberg, 1993; Loveman, 1994). The value derived from IT that improves coordination of economic activities has not been considered in the studies. But, the ability of IT to reduce coordination costs and improve coordination of economic activities can contribute to firm productivity. Since coordination is necessary for a given level of firm output, and a higher level of coordination can contribute to an increase in firm output, IT contributes to firm productivity by reducing coordination costs and improving coordination of economic activities – that is, by making a higher level of coordination more efficient. Thus, the value derived from IT's reduction of coordination costs and its improvement of coordination among economic activities should be considered when examining the relationship between IT and firm productivity.

This paper provides an empirical analysis of the relationship between IT and coordination costs, based on the previous IS research. This paper also uses the information processing theory (Galbraith, 1973, 1977) to provide an empirical analysis of the impact of IT on firm productivity by considering coordination (costs) as a factor of production. Using the microeconomic production theory, an equation model is derived for the empirical analysis of IT impact on firm productivity.

THEORETICAL BACKGROUND

IT and Coordination Costs

Organizations need to process information in order to coordinate various economic activities. In today's complex and uncertain environment, the costs of information processing and sharing are enormous. According to previous studies (Gurbaxani & Whang, 1991; Malone et al., 1987, 1989), IT greatly reduces information processing costs by providing better means of information gathering and processing, monitoring, negotiating, and enforcing contracts.

Coordination costs refer to all the information processing costs necessary to integrate the various economic activities of separate units of an organization and between separate organizations. Coordination costs incurred within an organization include the costs involved in acquiring and processing information for decision making, accounting, planning, monitoring, and control processes. Coordination costs incurred in a market include the costs of searching and selecting suppliers and negotiating and enforcing contracts (Gurbaxani & Whang, 1991; Malone et al., 1987, 1989).

According to Malone et al. (1987), IT is widely used for coordinating economic activities and decreases the unit costs of coordination through the following three effects:

1.   Electronic communication effect: IT decreases information processing costs by allowing more information to be communicated in the same amount of time or by allowing the same amount of information to be communicated in less time.
2.   Electronic brokerage effect: IT decreases the costs of the product selection process by increasing the number of alternatives and by increasing the quality of alternatives selected.
3.   Electronic integration effect: IT reduces inventory holding costs by linking the supplier's and the buyer's inventory management processes and making the supplier's just-in-time delivery possible.

Gurbaxani and Whang (1991) also argue that IT can affect the underlying cost structure of a firm since this cost structure is closely related to the acquisition of information. According to them, IT reduces transaction-processing costs, including order-processing and inventory-related costs. IT also reduces costs related to control by providing cost-effective monitoring and performance evaluation devices. IT decreases the costs of documentation and communication and reduces decision-making costs by providing cost-effective means of acquiring and processing relevant information.

IT, Coordination, and Firm Output

The relationship between coordination and organizational performance has been reviewed by organizational researchers (Cheng, 1983, 1984; Hage, 1980; Lawrence & Lorsch, 1967). These researchers regard coordination as a necessary condition for effective organizational performance. Viewing the organization as an information-processing system, Galbraith (1973, 1977) argues that the primary function of an organization is to process the information for decision-making needed for a given level of performance. Egelhoff (1982) also considers information processing an important aspect of organizational performance.

Coordination refers to all the information processing necessary to integrate various economic activities. Such integration of various economic activities needs to be done between separate units of an organization and also between separate organizations when the organizations have some degree of interdependency for achieving their goals. From an information-processing perspective, Cheng (1984) argues that coordination is associated with a given level of organizational output performance: the higher the level of coordination, the better the organization can synthesize information into the organizational knowledge needed for better organizational output performance. According to Lawrence and Lorsch (1967), coordination also aims to achieve unity of effort among various subsystems in the accomplishment of the organization's task, which is a complete input–transformation–output cycle involving at least the design, production, and distribution of some goods and services.

The above organizational research agrees that a higher level of coordination can improve organizational output performance since coordination is a necessary condition for a given level of firm output performance. Since a higher level of coordination requires large coordination expenses, and since coordination can be achieved efficiently if coordination costs are reduced, IT can contribute to firm productivity by reducing coordination costs, thus facilitating a higher level of coordination. Production enhancement can also be achieved by IT applications that automate production processes and improve the capabilities of existing machinery. IT, however, is most often used to reduce coordination costs within and between organizations. Organizations can produce more if they cooperate, each specializing in its own productive activities and then interacting with one another to acquire the goods and services they need (Milgrom & Roberts, 1992). When organizations are specialized producers that need to trade, their decisions and actions need to be coordinated to achieve these gains. A key problem in achieving coordination is that the information needed to determine the best use of resources is not freely available. By providing better means of communication, information processing, and searching, IT reduces coordination costs, improves the coordination cost efficiency, and contributes to firm productivity.

The microeconomic theory of production considers the firm as a producer of goods and services. The production process requires a set of inputs, such as capital, labor, and materials in order to produce output. The theory of production assumes that a competitive firm will adopt the most productive bundle of inputs by substituting more productive inputs for less productive inputs. The most efficient economic output is produced by combining inputs in the most efficient manner over time. From this perspective, IT can be regarded as an input equivalent to capital, labor, or other production factors. As an input, IT contributes to an increase in firm output by improving the cost efficiencies of labor and capital. As mentioned above, productivity gains, however, can be achieved by coordination cost efficiency, as well as production cost efficiency. Thus, coordination (costs) will be considered as an important factor in the analysis of the impact of IT on firm productivity.

ECONOMETRIC APPROACH

The approach taken in this paper is to use an economy-wide U.S. firm-level data set to directly examine the relationship between IT and coordination costs and the relationship between IT and firm productivity. Thus, the unit of analysis in this study is the firm. The data are divided into six sectors: durable goods manufacturing; nondurable goods manufacturing; transportation and utilities; wholesale and retail trade; finance, insurance, and real estate; and services. Several regressions are run on this data to identify the direction and magnitude of the relationship between IT and coordination costs, controlling for firm-specific factors, such as research and development (R&D), advertising activities, and industry and year effects. Other regressions are also run on the same data to identify the direction and magnitude of the relationship between IT and firm output, while controlling for coordination and other production factors that contribute to firm output. Following a microeconomic theory of production, production factors such as total capital, labor, and R&D are considered in addition to coordination. A control for industry and year is also performed.

Data Sources and Variable Construction

Two data sources are used: (1) a data set on IS spending by large U.S. firms compiled by International Data Group (IDG) and (2) the Compustat database, a database of historical financial statement information. The data set on IS spending was collected annually in a survey of IS executives from Fortune 500 and other selected firms. IS spending data collected from 1988 to 1992 are used. The data set includes data on the market value of central processors used by each firm (mainframes, minicomputers, and supercomputers), the total central IS budget, the percentage of the IS budget devoted to labor expenses, the number of PCs and terminals in use, and a variety of other financial and IT-related information.

The total central IS budget figure reported in the survey includes labor expenses, materials, purchased services and software, and capital spending for the central IS department. The total central IS budget is used as a measure of IT spending. The market value of central processors is not used as a measure of IT spending since it is narrowly defined and does not include significant costs that could be counted as IT spending, such as personal computers, communication networks, file servers, and software.

The Compustat database is used to obtain the data for total capital spending, labor expenses, R&D expenses, advertising expenses, total sales, the number of employees, and the data needed for constructing the measures for coordination costs and value added. Selling and general administrative expenses are used to construct a measure of coordination costs. Selling expenses are referred to as "order-getting" and "order-filling" costs. They include such items as salaries and commissions of sales personnel, advertising, warehousing, customer service, and shipping. The first two items are examples of order-getting costs; the last three are order-filling costs. General administrative expenses include the costs of integrating the various activities of the organization. Examples of general administrative expenses are top executive salaries, legal fees, general accounting, and research and development (Hansen, 1990). Since coordination costs include costs involved in managerial decision-making, accounting, planning, and control processes (coordination costs incurred in an organization), and the costs of searching and selecting suppliers, negotiating and enforcing contracts (coordination costs incurred in a market), these costs must be included in selling and general administrative expenses, which are operating expenses (nonmanufacturing expenses for the manufacturing firms and nonservice expenses for the service firms).

Data are collected about the firms whose names match the firm names in the IDG data. The Compustat database provides the data for selling and general administrative expenses (the item name is *selling, general, and administrative expenses*). Since this item includes other expenses, which are not included in coordination costs, such as expenses for R&D, advertising, software, bad debt, and pension and retirement, the data for such items are obtained in order to construct a measure of coordination costs. For manufacturing industries, a measure of coordination costs is constructed by subtracting expenses for advertising, R&D, software, bad debt, and pension and retirement from selling, general, and administrative expenses. According to the definition used here, such expenses are not included in coordination costs. For nonmanufacturing industries whose R&D expenses are small, a measure of coordination costs is constructed by subtracting the expenses for advertising, bad debt, and pension and retirement from selling, general, and administrative expenses. For finance industries, a measure of coordination costs is constructed by subtracting only advertising expenses and pension and retirement expenses from selling, general, and administrative expenses since the other items are not applicable to the financial institutions.

Two measures of firm output are considered: (1) total firm sales and (2) value added. Total firm sales can be obtained by taking total sales from the Compustat database. Value added is defined as the value of the finished goods minus the value of raw materials and other suppliers. It is derived by subtracting the costs of raw materials from the value of production. The value of production is derived by subtracting the beginning inventory from the sum of the ending inventory and total sales. The Compustat database is also used to obtain the data for constructing the measure of value added. The data are collected for the firms whose names match the firm names in the IDG data. Since the data on the costs of raw materials are not available from the data source, a measure is constructed for the costs of raw materials by subtracting labor and overhead expenses from the costs of goods sold. The data items obtained from the Compustat database to construct the value added are as follows: total sales, the costs of goods sold, the ending inventory in finished goods and work-in-process, beginning inventory, labor and related expenses, depreciation and amortization, interest expenses, and rental expenses.

Table 1: Inputs as a Percentage of Total Sales (Five-Year Averages)

	Manufacturing	Service	Full Sample with R&D	Full Sample without R&D
IT (IS Budget)	2.13%	2.53%	2.25%	2.22%
Coordination Costs	10.98%	16.88%	11.81%	12.27%
SGA Expenses	16.68%	20.76%	17.56%	17.58%
Capital Spending	45.22%	54.19%	47.19%	47.19%
Labor Expenses	19.56%	17.84%	19.69%	19.19%
R&D Expenses	2.27%	N/A	2.41%	N/A
Number of firms	425	115	447	540
Average Firm Sales	$ 8,019 million	$ 8,335 million	$ 8,413 million	$ 8,086 million

Table 2: Inputs as a Percentage of Value-Added (Five-Year Averages)

	Manufacturing	Service	Full Sample with R&D	Full Sample without R&D
IT (IS Budget)	3.67%	4.22%	3.84%	3.80%
Coordination Costs	17.91%	26.13%	18.76%	19.85%
SGA Expenses	27.13%	32.27%	27.91%	28.34%
Capital Spending	76.53%	77.14%	75.63%	76.67%
Labor Expenses	32.40%	27.13%	31.75%	31.15%
R&D Expenses	3.81%	N/A	4.01%	N/A
Number of firms	361	110	379	471
Average Firm Value-Added	$ 5,145 million	$ 5,210 million	$ 5,521 million	$ 5,160 million

The series for all the variables used in the empirical analysis are also converted to constant 1987 dollars using appropriate deflators—an aggregate of deflators used to derive constant-dollar Gross Domestic Product (GDP) estimates. Most are based on price indexes published in *Bureau of Economic Analysis* (1993) and *Economic Report of the President* (1994). By dividing each series of variables by its associated deflators, nominal values are converted into constant-dollar or real values.

In order to control for the industry- and year-specific effects, dummy variables are included for each industry or sector categorized by the standard industrial classification (SIC) code. Summary statistics for the sample are presented in Tables 1 and 2. The sample includes 540 observations over 5 years on approximately 232 different companies.

Analysis of the Relationship between IT and Coordination Costs

Methodology

For analyzing the relationship between IT and coordination costs, an analysis of the combined data set for all five years is performed. Two different techniques are used: an ordinary least-squares (OLS) regression and a two-stage least-squares (TSLS) regression, while controlling for other explanatory variables such as advertising and R&D expenses.

Since it is difficult to apply time-series models and complete lag structures to the residuals due to the short data period, TSLS regression is used to correct potential biases caused by the simultaneity problem. To derive consistent estimates, 1-year lagged variables of IT, R&D, and advertising expenses are employed as instrumental variables, because they cannot be affected by the dependent variable in the following year. Advertising expenses and R&D expenses are used as control variables, because it is assumed that firms spending a large amount on R&D and advertising must be spending a large amount on coordination costs. ₂

In order to control for firm-size effect, the firm size is adjusted by dividing coordination costs by total sales and by dividing IT spending, advertising expenses and R&D expenses by the number of employees. Since large organizations are likely to spend more money on IT and the coordination of economic activities, the relationship between IT spending per employee and coordination costs per total sales; that is, the coordination cost efficiency is empirically examined. Error terms are also investigated by looking at the distribution of the residuals for each sector, and the research finds that the residuals for all the sectors are normally distributed. Thus, the data are not transformed.

The Model

The model measures the relationship between the level of IT spending and coordination costs for a given sector in a given year, while controlling for R&D expenses, advertising expenses, and industry- and year-specific effects. The basic model is as follows:

$$COOR_{it} = \beta_0 + \beta_1 IT_{it} + \beta_2 R\&D_{it} + \beta_3 AD_{it} + \beta_4 INDUSTRY_{it} + \beta_5 YEAR_{it} + \varepsilon$$

where

$COOR_{it}$	=	Coordination costs per total sales (the coordination cost efficiency) of the ith firm in year t
IT_{it}	=	IT spending per employee for the ith firm in year t
$R\&D_{it}$	=	R&D expenditure per employee for the ith firm in year t
AD_{it}	=	Advertising expenses per employee for the ith firm in year t
$INDUSTRY_{it}$	=	A dummy for each sector or industry where the ith firm is operating in year t
$YEAR_{it}$	=	A dummy for year for the ith firm.
ε	=	An error term with zero mean

The model is estimated for the full sample both with and without R&D, since the R&D variable is not applicable for most firms in sectors other than the manufacturing sector. The model is also estimated for each sector separately in order to see if the impact of IT differs across sectors.

The model for the relationship between IT and coordination costs basically tests a hypothesis: IT reduces coordination costs. According to this hypothesis, it is expected that the coefficient of IT spending in all the equations will be negative. The coefficients of R&D expenses and advertising expenses are expected to be positive.

Results and Discussion

From the analysis of the OLS regression, it was found that IT spending is strongly associated with a decline in coordination costs ($p < .01$) for the full sample and for each individual sector, except for the transportation and utilities sector (Table 3). The estimates are consistent with the hypothesis that IT reduces coordination costs. The t-statistics for the estimates of IT spending for the full sample both with and without R&D, the manufacturing, and the trade industry, are 8.304, 6.819, 2.864, and 2.693, respectively. Thus, the null hypothesis of zero effect of IT at the .01 (two-tailed) confidence level can be rejected for the full sample and for both individual industries.$_3$ The estimate of IT spending for the transportation and utilities sector is negative, as expected, but not significant. This may indicate that the effect of IT on coordination costs might be less significant in the transportation and utilities sector than in the manufacturing and trade sectors. The sample size for the transportation and utility industry, however, might affect the magnitude of the coefficient of IT spending. R&D expenses and advertising expenses also have significant positive relationships with coordination costs as expected ($p < .01$). The analysis using TSLS regression shows similar results (Table 4).

The results show that IT spending is strongly associated with lower coordination costs 4. While the results suggest that a 1% increase in IT spending per employee is associated with .0085% decrease in coordination costs per sales for the full sample with R&D, these results should only be used to draw conclusions about the direction of the impact, not the magnitude, since the measures used only capture some components of IT spending and coordination costs. Although these components can be expected to have a high correlation with overall costs, no implications about the magnitude of change should be drawn from the analysis.

The results imply that IT improves coordination cost efficiency and facilitates a higher level of coordination by reducing coordination costs for a given level of sales. Since coordination of economic activities can contribute to firm output, IT can contribute to firm output by improving coordination cost efficiency. Therefore, it is reasonable to assume that IT enhances firm productivity by improving both coordination cost efficiency and production cost efficiency, such as capital and labor efficiency. In the following section, an empirical examination is done on the relationship between IT and firm productivity, considering coordination (costs) as a factor of production.

Table 3: OLS Regression: Dependent Variable—Coordination Costs/Sales

	Manufacturing	Transportation and Utilities	Trade	Full Sample	Full Sample
IT/EMP	-.0036*** (2.864)[a]	-.0031 (1.319)	-.0039*** (2.693)	-.0085*** (8.304)	-.0063*** (6.819)
R&D/EMP	.0052*** (4.774)	N/A	N/A	.0072*** (8.248)	Not Included
AD/EMP	.0013** (2.032)	-.0039 (.605)	.0334*** (6.617)	.0034*** (6.455)	.0040*** (7.407)
Dummy	Industry and Year	Industry and Year	Industry and Year	Sector and Year	Sector and Year
R^2	43.8%	62.8%	73.8%	28.8%	17.6%
N(total)	437	35	68	459	549
DW[b]	2.00	1.93	1.93	1.81	1.54

Key: ***($p < 0.01$), **($p < 0.05$), *($p < 0.1$).
[a] T Statistics in parentheses.
[b] If the Durbin Watson (DW) statistic is close to 2, it indicates no serial correlation. If DW is greater than 2 or less than 2, it indicates high serial correlation. This suggests that the point estimates are correctly estimated, but that the standard error estimates may be biased upward or downward.

Analysis of the Relationship between IT and Firm Productivity

Methodology and Model

For analyzing the combined data of cross section and time series, OLS and TSLS regression estimates of the correlation between IT and firm output are also used, while controlling for other explanatory variables, industry- and year-specific effects. The model is based on the microeconomic theory of production. The research considers IT spending an input equivalent to capital and labor. It also incorporates R&D expenses and coordination costs as input factors that might affect the level of output. Output is defined as the number of units produced times their unit value.

Productivity is defined as the ratio of the level of output to a given level of input. The Cobb–Douglas model for production specification is adopted, since the Cobb–Douglas specification for the studies of IT productivity is widely supported in the literature (Brynjolfsson & Hitt, 1993; 1996; Hitt & Brynjolfsson, 1994;

Table 4: TSLS Regression[a]: Dependent Variable—Coordination Costs/Sales

	Manufacturing	Transportation and Utilities	Trade	Full Sample	Full Sample
IT/EMP	-.0040** (2.061)[b]	.0034 (.878)	-0.0090* (1.743)	-.0092*** (6.991)	-.0073*** (5.445)
R&D/EMP	.0045*** (3.195)	N/A	N/A	.0069*** (6.272)	Not Included
AD/EMP	.0017* (1.781)	-.0018 (.204)	.0257*** (3.201)	.0037*** (5.113)	.0047*** (6.072)
Dummy	Industry and Year	Industry and Year	Industry and Year	Sector and Year	Sector and Year
R^2	38.9%	52.0%	78.8%	26.7%	16.0%
N(total)[c]	272	23	36	287	336

Key: ***($p < 0.01$), **($p < 0.05$), *($p < 0.01$)

[a] Instrument variables : once lagged independent variables (IT spending, R&D, and AD).

[b] T Statistics in the parentheses.

[c] N(total) of TSLS is lower because each observation requires data for the current period and the previous period; this eliminates observations for all of 1988 and some in other years.

Lichtenberg, 1995; Loveman, 1994;). The Cobb-Douglas specification for the model is as follows:

$$OUTPUT = e^{\beta_0} IT^{\beta_1} CAPITAL^{\beta_2} LABOR^{\beta_3} R\&D^{\beta_4} COOR^{\beta_5}$$

In this specification, β_1 and β_5 are the output elasticity of IT and coordination, respectively.[6] From the Cobb–Douglas specification, a model for a linear regression can be derived by taking the natural logarithm, including industry and year dummies, as follows:

$$LnOUTPUT_{it} = \beta_0 + \beta_1 LnIT_{it} + \beta_2 LnCAPITAL_{it} + \beta_3 LnLABOR_{it} + \beta_4 LnR\&D_{it} +$$
$$\beta_5 LnCOOR_{it} + \beta_6 INDUSTRY_{it} + \beta_7 YEAR_{it} + \varepsilon$$

where

$LnOUTPUT_{it}$	=	Total sales or value added of the ith firm in year t
$LnIT_{it}$	=	IT spending of the ith firm in year t
$LnCAPITAL_{it}$	=	Total capital spending of the ith firm in year t

$LnLABOR_{it}$	=	Labor expenses of the ith firm in year t
$LnR\&D_{it}$	=	R&D expenditure of the ith firm in year t
$LnCOOR_{it}$	=	Coordination costs of the ith firm in year t.
$INDUSTRY_{it}$	=	A dummy for each sector or industry where the ith firm is operating in year t
$YEAR_{it}$	=	A dummy for year for the ith firm.
ε	=	An error term with zero mean

The model is estimated for the full sample both with and without R&D since the R&D variable is not applicable for most firms in the service industry. The model is also estimated for both the manufacturing industry and service industry separately in order to see if the productivity impact of IT is different in these industries.

The model is also estimated after dividing all the variables by the number of employees in order to examine the impact of IT spending per employee on output per employee since a firm can produce a higher level of output with a higher level of inputs. The use of a different specification increases the robustness of the results. For further robustness, the model is also estimated without the natural logarithm of coordination costs, by assuming that coordination costs are not a factor of production but still affect productivity.

The model for the relationship between IT and firm output tests two hypothesis: (1) IT contributes to an increase in firm output, and (2) coordination contributes to an increase in firm output. According to the hypothesis that IT and coordination contribute to firm output, it is expected that the coefficients on IT spending and coordination in all the equations will be positive. The coefficients of other variables, such as total capital spending, labor, and R&D expenses, are expected to be positive.

The Results

From the analysis of the full sample, controlled for year-specific effects, the research found that IT spending is strongly associated with increases in both firm sales ($p < 0.01$) (Table 5) and value added ($p < 0.05$) (Table 6). As shown in Column 7 of Table 5, the estimate of IT spending indicates that the elasticity of output (sales) for IT spending is 0.1894 when all other inputs are held constant. Because IT spending accounts for average of 2.22% of the value of output each year, this implies that the gross marginal product for IT spending is approximately 853% per year.[7] In other words, an additional dollar of IT spending is associated with an increase in output (sales) of 8.53 dollars per year on the margin. As expected, the estimate of coordination costs is positive and significant ($p < 0.01$). The output elasticity for coordination is 0.0818. This implies that each dollar spent on coordination is associated with a marginal increase in output (sales) of 67 cents.[8]

The above estimates are consistent with the hypotheses that the contributions of both IT and coordination are positive. The t-statistics for the estimates of the output (sales) elasticity of IT spending and coordination are 9.664 and 3.704 respectively (column 7 of Table 5). Thus the null hypotheses of zero contributions of both IT and coordination can be rejected at a .01 (two-tailed) confidence level.

Table 5: OLS Regression: Dependent Variable—LnSales

	Manufacturing		Service		Full Sample with R&D		Full Sample without R&D	
LnIT	.0780*** (3.963)[a]	.0955*** (4.705)	.1563*** (4.002)	.1200*** (3.172)	.1489*** (7.993)	.1406*** (7.457)	.1894*** (9.664)	.1820*** (9.461)
LnCOOR	.1594*** (7.595)		.2871*** (3.478)		.1686*** (8.231)		.0818*** (3.704)	
COOR		.00007*** (4.504)		.0001*** (5.241)		.0001*** (8.050)		.00008*** (5.835)
LnCAPITAL	.3507*** (12.830)	.3264*** (11.539)	.1101 (1.645)	.2080*** (3.147)	.4119*** (23.226)	.4311*** (23.971)	.3276*** (16.797)	.3397*** (17.697)
LnLABOR	.3320*** (10.780)	.3918*** (12.880)	.2850*** (3.053)	.2583*** (3.191)	.2621*** (8.861)	.3009*** (10.716)	.2963*** (9.946)	.2887*** (10.470)
LnR&D	.0087 (.471)	.0315* (1.664)	N/A	N/A	-.0334** (2.279)	-.0277* (1.900)		
Dummy	Industry and Year		Industry and Year		Sector and Year		Sector and Year	
R^2	95.0%	94.6%	78.6%	81.3%	93.6%	93.5%	88.5%	88.9%
N(total)	425		115		447		540	
DW[b]	2.11	2.06	2.03	1.95	1.72	1.64	1.57	1.51

Key : ***(p<.01), **(p<.05), *(p<.1)

[a]T Statistics in parentheses.

[b]If the Durbin Watson (DW) statistic is close to 2, it indicates no serial correlation. If DW is greater than 2 or less than 2, it indicates high serial correlation. This suggests that the point estimates are correctly estimated but that the standard error estimates may be biased upward or downward.

The results also show that capital spending and labor expenses are highly associated with an increase in firm output ($p < .01$). Interestingly, R&D expenses are highly associated with an increase in value-added, but with a decline in firm sales. It was also found that the contribution of IT and coordination to firm output – both sales and value-added – are positive and significant in both industries (Table 5 and 6). The signs of the estimates of other variables are also similar for both the manufacturing industry and service industry. However, R&D is strongly associated with an increase in value-added, but not with an increase in firm sales.

The results of the analysis without the natural logarithm of coordination costs are similar to the results of the analysis with the natural logarithm of coordination

Table 6: OLS Regression: Dependent Variable—LnValue-Added

	Manufacturing		Service		Full Sample with R&D		Full Sample without R&D	
LnIT	.0103 (.815)[a]	.0337** (2.367)	.0504** (2.531)	.0628*** (2.655)	.0052 (.407)	.0322** (2.010)	.0484*** (4.199)	.0769*** (5.425)
LnCOOR	.1780*** (12.750)		.2800*** (8.102)		.2272*** (17.530)		.2401*** (19.686)	
COOR		.00008*** (6.622)		.00006*** (4.745)		.00007*** (7.236)		.00009*** (9.458)
LnCAPITAL	.2226*** (12.227)	.1906*** (9.277)	.1397*** (5.061)	.1720*** (5.004)	.2392*** (20.395)	.2384*** (15.950)	.2194*** (19.892)	.2309*** (16.802)
LnLABOR	.5230*** (26.157)	.5852*** (26.662)	.4279*** (11.085)	.5144*** (12.196)	.4907*** (26.151)	.5672*** (24.579)	.4800*** (29.214)	.5579*** (28.404)
LnR&D	.0742*** (6.006)	.1072*** (7.819)	N/A	N/A	.0520*** (5.474)	.0697*** (5.802)		
Dummy	Industry and Year		Industry and Year		Sector and Year		Sector and Year	
R^2	98.0%	97.4%	97.8%	97.0%	97.5%	96.0%	96.7%	94.9%
N(total)	361		110		379		471	
DW^2	2.09	2.07	2.43	2.59	1.77	1.85	1.79	1.81

Key : ***($p<.01$), **($p<.05$), *($p<.1$)

[a]T Statistics in parentheses.

[b]If the Durbin Watson (DW) statistic is close to 2, it indicates no serial correlation. If DW is greater than 2 or less than 2, it indicates high serial correlation. This suggests that the point estimates are correctly estimated but that the standard error estimates may be biased upward or downward.

costs. IT spending, coordination costs, and other variables are strongly associated with increases in both firm sales ($p<.01$) and value-added ($p<.05$). The impacts of IT on firm output (both sales and value-added) are similar across both the manufacturing and service industries. Similarly, the coefficient of R&D is positive and significant for the analysis with value-added, but not for the analysis with firm sales. The results are shown in the even columns in Tables 5 and 6.

The analysis adjusting all the variables with the number of employees shows similar results.[9] The results of the TSLS regression analysis are also comparable to the results of the above OLS regression analysis. The standard errors of the coefficient estimates of the independent variables are substantially larger since instrumental variables are used. This reduces the significance levels of the coefficient estimates of the variables. The results of TSLS regression analysis are provided in Tables 7 and 8.

Table 7: TSLS Regression[a]: Dependent Variable—LnSales

	Manufacturing		Service		Full Sample with R&D		Full Sample without R&D	
LnIT	.0685* (1.738)[b]	.0699 (1.617)	.0925* (1.739)	.0652 (1.293)	.1717*** (6.131)	.1600*** (5.421)	.1664*** (5.887)	.1608*** (5.771)
LnCOOR	.1348*** (3.014)		.1682 (.733)		.2237*** (6.508)		.0759** (2.114)	
COOR		.00004 (1.378)		.00009** (2.224)		.0001*** (6.066)		.00007*** (4.043)
LnCAPITAL	.2447*** (4.774)	.2099*** (4.067)	-0548 (.387)	.0718 (.503)	.3787*** (16.021)	.3968*** (15.685)	.3016*** (11.505)	.3154*** (12.055)
LnLABOR	.5429*** (5.613)	.6518*** (7.617)	.6601** (2.222)	.5304** (2.605)	.2705*** (4.474)	.3678*** (6.896)	.3728*** (6.686)	.3582*** (7.590)
LnR&D	-.0434 (1.639)	.0288 (1.010)	N/A	N/A	-.0712*** (3.705)	-.0701*** (3.467)		
Dummy	Industry and Year		Industry and Year		Sector and Year		Sector and Year	
R^2	94.1%	93.0%	78.0%	81.5%	93.5%	92.9%	88.4%	88.8%
N(total)[c]	265		65		280		330	

Key: ***($p < .01$), **($p < .05$), *($p < .1$)

[a] Instrument variables: once lagged independent variables (IT spending, coordination, total capital, labor, and R&D).

[b] T Statistics in parentheses.

[c] N(total) of TSLS is lower because each observation requires data for the current period and the previous period; this eliminates observations for all of 1988 and some observations in other years.

Table 8: TSLS Regression[a]: Dependent Variable—LnValue Added

	Manufacturing		Service		Full Sample with R&D		Full Sample without R&D	
LnIT	.0577*** (2.909)[b]	.0656*** (2.610)	-.0116 (.478)	.0059 (.189)	.0369** (2.088)	.0554** (2.228)	.0428*** (2.973)	.0618*** (3.102)
LnCOOR	.2536*** (10.760)		.2221** (2.681)		.2918*** (15.576)		.2807*** (17.408)	
COOR		.00009*** (4.950)		.00002 (.886)		.00007*** (5.962)		.00008*** (7.120)
LnCAPITAL	.2392*** (8.918)	.1810*** (5.667)	.0866* (1.747)	.0607 (.870)	.2242*** (16.413)	.2238*** (11.632)	.2086*** (16.888)	.2191*** (12.629)
LnLABOR	.4089*** (8.913)	.5694*** (11.415)	.6331*** (6.026)	.7878*** (7.675)	.4115*** (13.029)	.5627*** (14.192)	.4592*** (18.675)	.5991*** (19.494)
LnR&D	.0433*** (2.969)	.0836*** (4.749)	N/A	N/A	.0345*** (3.228)	.0443*** (2.947)		
Dummy	Industry and Year		Industry and Year		Sector and Year		Sector and Year	
R²	98.3%	97.3%	98.5%	97.3%	98.0%	96.0%	97.8%	95.3%
N(total)[c]	224		61		236		285	

Key: ***(p < .01), **(p < .05), *(p < .1)

[a] Instrument variables: once lagged independent variables (IT spending, coordination, total capital, labor, and R&D).

[b] T Statistics in parentheses.

[c] N(total) of TSLS is lower, because each observation requires data for the current period and the previous period; this eliminates observations for all of 1988 and some observations in other years.

Overall, the results indicate that IT and coordination contribute to an increase in firm output measured by total sales and value added. In the previous section, it is found that IT spending is highly correlated with a decline in coordination costs. This indicates that IT spending reduces coordination costs for a given level of firm output: that is, IT improves coordination cost efficiency. Based on the findings obtained from the previous and current sections, it can be inferred that IT contributes to firm output by enhancing coordination cost efficiency, and thus, by facilitating a higher level of coordination.[10]

CONCLUSION AND DISCUSSION

This paper has conducted an empirical examination of the relationship between IT and coordination costs using the firm-level data. The results clearly show a significant negative relationship between IT spending and coordination costs for the five years from 1988 to 1992. These results strongly support the hypothesis that IT reduces coordination costs. By developing a measure for coordination costs, empirical evidence could be provided for supporting the theoretical speculation that IT reduces coordination costs.

An empirical examination of the relationship between IT and firm productivity using firm-level data was also conducted. The study tested a broad variety of specifications based on both the microeconomic theory of production that previous IS researchers used as their theoretical basis, and the information processing theory of organization that previous organizational researchers used as their theoretical basis. The study also examined subsamples such as the manufacturing industry and the service industry. Overall, it was found that IT and coordination are highly associated with an increase in firm output.

The main contribution of this study is to provide a theoretical explanation and empirical evidence for how IT improves firm productivity, which has been incompletely addressed in previous research on IT productivity gains. The study was done by focusing on one of the most salient features of IT: its reduction of coordination costs. The main argument is that IT reduces coordination costs for a given level of firm output and makes a higher level of coordination more efficient, thereby contributing to firm output. The empirical analysis of the relationship between IT and firm output is done by considering coordination (costs) as a factor of production on par with capital spending, labor expenses, and R&D expenses. Based on the findings obtained from the analysis of the relationship between IT and coordination cost, and the relationship between IT and firm output in, the study argues that IT contributes to firm output; that is, it improves firm productivity by enhancing coordination cost efficiency. The results provide empirical evidence that strongly supports the hypothesis that IT contributes to firm output by reducing coordination costs, thereby enhancing coordination cost efficiency.

ENDNOTES

[1] The earlier (shorter) version of this paper appears in *the Proceedings of the 18th International Conference on Information Systems* (December 1997) under the title, "The Impact of Information Technology on Coordination Costs: Implications for Firm Productivity."

[2] According to transaction cost economics (Williamson, 1975), high market transaction (external coordination) costs arise when transactions are supported by transaction-specific assets. Human assets are transaction specific when new products and technologies are developed by a particular research team and advertising is made by a particular advertising team.

[3] Muticollinearity is probably present in the analysis, but the estimates are still unbiased and statistically significant even though the possible presence of multicollinearity increases the standard errors of the estimates.

[4] To increase robustness, the model that divides coordination costs by the number of employees and IT spending, advertising expenses, and R&D expenses by total sales is analyzed. This analysis shows similar results.

[5] The amount of output that can be produced for a given unit of a given input is often measured as the marginal product of input, which can be interpreted as a rate of return—increase in output per input (Berndt, 1991; Brynjolfsson & Hitt, 1996).

[6] The output elasticity of IT, E_{IT}, is defined as: $E_{IT} = (\partial \text{Output}/\partial \text{IT})(\text{IT}/\text{Output})$. From the production specification, this reduces to:

$$E_{IT} = \beta 1\, e^{\beta 0}IT^{\beta 1-1}CAPITAL^{\beta 2}LABOR^{\beta 3}R\&D^{\beta 4}COOR^{\beta 5}(IT/\, e^{\beta 0}IT^{\beta 1}CAPITAL^{\beta 2}LABOR^{\beta 3}R\&D^{\beta 4}COOR^{\beta 5}) = \beta 1$$

The marginal product for IT is simply the output elasticity multiplied by the ratio of output to IT input (Brynjolfsson & Hitt, 1996):

$$MP_{IT} = \partial\, \text{Output}/\, \partial\, \text{IT} = E_{IT}(\text{Output}/IT)$$

[7] The earlier study done by Brynjolfsson and Hitt (1996) reported that the marginal product for IT was 81%. This study, however, used IS budget (flow) as a measure of IT, compared to Brynjolfsson and Hitt's study, which used computer capital (stock) as a measure of IT. This makes a difference in the magnitude of the marginal product.

[8] The marginal product of value added for IT spending is approximately 127% per year. The marginal product of value added for coordination is approximately 121% per year. The marginal products of both sales and value added for coordination indicate that coordination makes more contribution to value added than to sales.

[9] The tables are available from the author upon request.

[10] For a better understanding of the results, consider the following example: Suppose a firm is currently spending $1,200 for coordination and achieves sales of $10,000 and value-added of $6,000. With the use of IT, the firm can achieve better coordination cost efficiency and lower costs for coordination—say $1,000 for coordination—and can achieve the same level of sales, $10,000. Thus, the firm can increase sales from $10,000 to $10,134 (the marginal product of sales for coordination: 67%) and value-added from

$6,000 to $6,242 (the marginal product of value-added for coordination: 121%) by spending $1,200 for coordination as before. Since IT reduces coordination costs for a given level of firm output, firms can achieve higher levels of coordination more efficiently and can increase their output such as total sales and value-added. Thus, the findings imply that IT contributes to an increase in firm output by making coordination of various economic activities more efficient.

REFERENCES

Bakos, J. Y. & Brynjolfsson, E. (1995). Information Technology, Incentives and the Optimal Number of Suppliers, *Journal of Management Information Systems,* September.

Berndt, E. (1991). *The Practice of Econometrics: Classic and Contemporary*, Reading, MA, Addison-Wesley.

Brynjolfsson, E. & Hitt, L. (1993). Is Information Systems Spending Productive? New Evidence and New Results. In *Proceedings of 14th International Conference on Information Systems,* pp. 47–64. J.I. DeGross, R.P. Bostrom, & D. Robey (eds.), Orlando, FL.

Brynjolfsson, E. & Hitt. L. (1996). Paradox Lost? Firm Level Evidence on the Returns to Information Systems Spending, *Management Science,* April. 541–558.

Brynjolfsson, E., Malone, T. W., Gurbaxani, V., & Kambil, A. (December 1994) Does Information Technology Lead to Smaller Firms, *Management Science* (40:12), 1628–1644.

Bureau of Economic Analysis: Survey of Current Business. (1993). U.S. Department of Commerce, U.S. Government Printing Office, Washington, DC.

Cheng, J. L. C. (1983). Interdependence and Coordination in Organizations: A Role-System Analysis. *Academy of Management Journal,* (26) 156–162.

Cheng, J. L. C. (1984). "Organizational Coordination, Uncertainty, and Performance: An Integrative Study," *Human Relations,* (37:10). 829–851.

Clemons, E. K. & Reddi, S. P. (1992) The Impact of Information Technology on the Organization of Economic Activity: The Move to the Middle Hypothesis, Working paper, The Wharton School, University of Pennsylvania. 1992.

Economic Report of President. (1994). U.S. Government Printing Office, Washington DC.

Egelhoff, W. G. (1982). "Strategy and Structure in Multinational Corporation: An Information Processing Approach," *Administrative Science Quarterly* (27), 435–458.

Galbraith, J. R. (1973). *Designing Complex Organizations*. Addison-Wesley. Reading, MA.

Galbraith, J. R. (1977). *Organization Design*, Reading, MA: Addison-Wesley.

Gurbaxani, V., and Whang, S. "The Impact of Information Systems on Organizations and Markets," *Communications of the ACM* (34:1), January 1991, pp. 60-73.

Hage, J. (1980). *Theories of Organizations*, New York: Wiley.

Hansen, D. R. (1990), *Management Accounting*, Boston MA: PWS-Kent Publishing Co.

Hitt, L. & Brynjolfsson, E. (December 1994). The Three Faces of IT Value: Theory and Evidence in *Proceedings of the 15th International Conference on Information Systems*, 263–276. J.I. DeGross, S.L., Huff, & M.C. Munro (Eds.), Vancouver, British Columbia.

Lawrence, P. R. & Lorsch, J. W. (1967). Differentiation and Integration in Complex Organizations, *Administrative Science Quarterly* (12), 1–47.

Lichtenberg, F. R. (November 1993). The Output Contributions of Computer Equipment and Personnel: A Firm Level Analysis, National Bureau of Economic Research Working paper no. 4540, Cambridge, Ma.

Loveman, G. W. (1994). Assessing the Productivity Impact of Information Technologies in *Information Technology and the Corporation of the 1990s,* T. J. Allen & M. Scott-Morton, (Eds.), New York: Oxford University Press.

Malone, T. W., Yates, J., & Benjamin, R. I. (1987, June). Electronic Markets and Electronic Hierarchies. *Communications of the ACM,* 484–497.

Malone, T. W., Yates, J., and Benjamin, R. I. (1989, May/June). "The logic of electronic markets," *Harvard Business Review*, 166–170.

Milgrom, P. & Roberts, J. (1992). *Economics, Organization and Management*, Englewood Cliffs, NJ: Prentice Hall.

Williamson, O.E. (1975). *Markets and Hierarchies: Analysis and Antitrust Implications*, New York: Free Press.

Chapter VI

Information Technology Spending and the Value of the Firm: The Case of Mexican Banks

Carlos J. Navarrete
California State Polytechnic University, USA

James B. Pick
University of Redlands, USA

This paper analyzes the relationship between IT expenditure and the monetary value of organizations. Based on the case of the Mexican banking industry from 1982–1992, the paper's hypotheses test the relationship between IT expenditure and the real and perceived market values of banks. Correlations are performed between annual IT expenditures for a 10 year period —when Mexico's commercial banks were owned by the federal government— and bank selling prices, when the industry divestiture took place in 1992. The main findings are that IT spending has a positive impact on the value of the firm, when the value of the firm reflects the change of ownership or the control of the firm. Second, firms spending more on IT do not tend to reach higher selling prices. Other findings are presented. The model and its results are discussed in terms of the literature about value of investment and the productivity paradox.

INTRODUCTION

The contribution of information technology (IT) to nations' or organizations' productivity, performance, and value has been strongly questioned. Even today, when we face a transition into an "e-world" with an electronic alternative for activities such as e-banking, e-learning, e-government, etc., the value of IT and its contributions generate mixed opinions. On one side, to some economists, for example, the robust U.S. economy in the late 1990s was linked to information technology. On the other hand, doubts were reinforced when successful e-businesses, like Amazon.com, showed small or no profits on their financial statements. In the early 1990s, the productivity paradox triggered a notable academic effort to study the impact of IT on national economies, industrial sectors, firms, and individuals. There have been a number of research studies using different levels of analysis (Strassman, 1990; Scott Morton, 1991; Harris & Katz, 1991; Weill, 1992; Ahituv & Giladi, 1994; Loveman, 1994; Nault & Dexter, 1994; Dewan & Kreamer, 1998). The present researchers have investigated the productivity paradox in Mexico at the both the firm and industry levels (for the latter, see Navarrete and Pick, 2002).

The overall body of studies does not come to a conclusion regarding the validity of the productivity paradox. The issue would seem to depend upon such factors as the time, place, research model, and unit of analysis. Taking advantage of the 11-year Mexican government ownership of the banking industry and its divestiture process, this chapter studies whether or not IT spending contributes to the monetary value of organizations.

The federal government ownership of the Mexican commercial banks during the period from 1982 to 1992 offered an opportunity to empirically study the productivity paradox. During this 11-year period, each bank in Mexico was required to present its information technology budget to the federal government's Finance and Planning Office. This policy requirement had the following implications:

- Information about IT expenditures was available for all commercial banks.
- Banks used the same IT definitions and budgetary practices and procedures.
- A consistent longitudinal data set on banks' IT investment was available that had not existed before or since.

Between 1991 and 1992, the government sold back the commercial banks to investing groups through a divestiture process. In this process, the government first assessed the value of each bank through several normative approaches. Then, the divestiture committee used these values to set a minimum price for each bank, which later was used as a starting point for the bidding stage of the selling process. Several groups took part in the bidding stage, each group giving an offer to obtain control of the bank. Lastly, the divestiture committee gave the control of each bank to the group with the highest bid (Aspe, 1993).

LITERATURE REVIEW

IS/IT practitioners and many researchers support the notion of IT investments enhancing business capabilities, performance, and value. Furthermore, even though all technologies generate benefits—tangible and intangible—to firms, different technologies seem to create different types of returns (Lucas, 1999, among others). However, having these returns does not necessarily mean that firms are more valuable or become successful. In order to succeed, firms not only have to invest in IT, but they have to address many other factors (Brynjolffsson & Hitt, 1996). For example, they need to recognize that IT investments generate different types of returns, and that IT is only one of many issues contributing to firms' success. These aspects are only two of the many that researchers have used to explain why IT often seems to have no value for organizations.

Table 1 summarizes some aspects of the value that practitioners, academicians, and IT vendors claim firms will realize from investing in IT. This list of IT values and benefits has been growing in length and complexity. The benefits noted in the 1980s were clear and direct: reduction of work, return on time, competitive edge (Keen & Woodman, 1984), and increased return on investments (Parker & Benson, 1988). At present, even though some benefits continue to be cited, researchers are naming new and more complex benefits of IT: Enabling different organizational process structures (Brynjolfsson et al., 1997), allowing organizational flexibility (Kumar, 1999), and decreasing communication and coordination costs (Malone, 1997). This trend toward more complex benefits of IT has fostered measurement problems reported in almost all research projects in this area.

A further aspect of the measurement problem now evident is that IT projects need to be conjoint with other firm actions to become successful. IT cost reductions and IT's growing integration capabilities together with higher competition fosters business process reengineering (BPR) projects (Brynjolfsson et al., 1997). However, these authors also report that many BPR projects fail to fulfill their objectives. Several factors, such as the right technology, the right product mix, sound strategy, and proper change management, should be in place to let a BPR project accomplish its expected goals (Bashein et al., 1994). Another example of IT success depending upon other factors is reported by Malone (1997), who points out that IT-induced cost reduction permits decentralization, because it changes the economics of organizational decision making. However, Malone argues that if this decentralization is to bring positive results, it should be accompanied by proper balance

Table 1: Studies of the Value of IT

Author	Year	IT value
Keen and Woodman	1984	Eliminates work. Reduces return on time. Improves decision-making. Generates competitive edge. Increases quality of work life.
Parker and Benson	1988	Augments return on investments. Brings competitive advantage. Permits competitive response. Allows strategic IS architectures.
Clemons and Row	1991	Becomes a strategic tool. Can lead to sustainable advantage.
Venkatraman	1991	Permits analytic planning processes. Enhances competitive advantages. Permits getting an edge over competitors.
Yates and Banjamin	1991	Facilitates coordination of business tasks. Reduces costs. Increases functionality.
Bakos and Brynjolfsson	1993	Transforms the suppliers' relationship. Reduces coordination costs.
Malone et al.	1994	Modifies the value chain.
Malone	1997	Reduces communication and coordination costs.
Brynjolfsson et al.	1997	Permits different organizational process structures.
Brynjolfsson and Hitt	1997	Improves customer services. Allows targeting new customers. Improves quality. Gives executives more control. Fosters IT infrastructure. Improves production flexibility. Improves management information.
Kumar	1999	Gives organizational flexibility.

between top-down control and bottom-up empowerment. Finally, in the case of IT promoting competitive advantage, Hitt and Brynjolfsson (1996) point out that we do not know if the investment will generate such competitive advantage. If all firms have access to technology, investing in technology can become a strategic necessity (Clemons, 1991). The dynamics of competition suggests that no player can gain high profitability without facing strong competition. This strong competition leads to price reduction, diminishing companies' profits. Furthermore, to allow firms to gain competitiveness through IT investments, firms need to have IT capabilities to properly manage IT costs, to develop systems that fulfill organization's needs, and to use IT to support business goals (Rockart et al., 1996).

To summarize, defendants of the value of IT in organizations explain that two factors, measurement problems and the multidimensionality of conditions for IT to have a positive impact, inhibit IT benefits. In contrast, supporters of the tenet that investment in IT fails to produce positive outcomes, i.e., adherents to the productivity paradox, reject these explanations and call instead for new forms of IT deployment and management.

Another way to look at prior research in this area is to review it according to whether or not the results of the different studies support or reject the productivity paradox. Tables 2 and 3 list research studies supporting and rejecting the paradox.

Table 2: Research Supporting the Productivity Paradox

Author (Year)	Purpose of the Study	Results
Scott Morton (1991)	Find the impact of IT on organizations.	There is no evidence of improvement on productivity or profitability.
Weill (1992)	Find the relationship between IT investments and firms' performance.	No significant gains occur in systems other than transaction processing systems.
Dos Santos et al. (1993)	Evaluate the impact of IT investment announcements on the firms' value.	There is no impact (excess on return) of IT investments.
Loveman (1994)	Measure the impact of IT investments on firm's productivity.	IT impact on productivity is minimal or non-existent.
Strassman (1997)	Find the impact of IT spending and profitability.	There is no correlation between IT spending and industry profitability.
Shrage (1997)	Analyze the impact of computers.	The idea of computers having positive impact is just not true.
Strassman (1999)	Find the impact of IT spending on US bank productivity.	IT is not delivering the cost reductions that IT supporters claim.

Table 3: Research Rejecting the Productivity Paradox

Author (Year)	Purpose of the Study	Results
Panko (1991)	Is office productivity stagnant and is it caused by IT?	Industries with strict measure criteria (e.g., commercial banks) show substantial productivity growth due to IT.
Harris and Katz (1991)	Is there a relationship between firms' performance and IT investment intensity?	Firms' performance is linked to the level of IT investment intensity.
Dos Santos et al. (1993)	Evaluate the impact of IT investment announcements on the firms' value	Innovative IT investments increase firms' value.
Ahituv et al. (1999)	Is there a relationship between firms' information policy and business performance?	There is a positive relationship between IS attributes and firms' economic variables, when firms are classified into homogeneous groups.
Nault and Dexter (1995)	Find value added to firms due to IT.	The produced gain due to IT reaches 5-12% of full retail price.
Dewan and Kreamer (1998)	Study the productivity paradox in developed countries.	Developed countries receive positive and significant returns on their IT investments.

The current project's research model is influenced by Ahituv's (1989) value types. Ahituv identifies three different types of information value: normative, perceived, and realistic. A normative value is always the result of the application of a model——the better the model's representation of value, the more accurate the value will be. Unfortunately, the intangible nature of many IT benefits makes it very difficult to build a model that accurately depicts its benefits. The perceived value of information, according to Ahituv, relates to the user's "willingness" to pay for the information. The real value represents the cost involved in generating or actually paying for the information. All three value types are tested in the present project.

RESEARCH METHODOLOGY

In order to answer this study's research question and to test the corresponding hypotheses listed below, we statistically prove the relationship between IT input (in this case IT expenses) and banks' real and perceived value. Navarrete and Pick (2002) and Cron and Sobol (1983) used similar studies of input and performance to analyze the impact of IT on organizations. As seen in Figure 1, we test the correlation between the ratio of IT expenses to operational expenses and the banks' value.

Research Question 1. Does IT expenditure affect the market value of the banks?

Question	Hypotheses	
1	H1a	IT expenditure is positively correlated with real market value of the bank.
	H1b	IT expenditure is positively correlated with perceived market value of the bank.
	H1c	Cumulative (two, three, and five years) IT expenditure is positively correlated with real market value of the bank.
	H1d	Cumulative (two, three, and five years) IT expenditure is positively correlated with perceived market value of the bank.
	H1e	IT expenditure intensity is positively correlated with banks' value.

Figure 1: Research Model

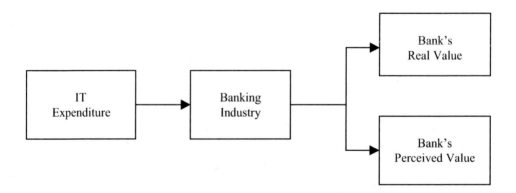

The methodology used to test the contribution of IT spending to the bank value has three parts. First, a bivariate correlation shows whether or not there is a relationship between IT expenditure and real and perceived value as measured by banks' market price and bidding offers. Second, a correlation between two, three, and five-year averages of IT expenditure and the banks' market price and bidding offers shows the impact of cumulative IT spending on firms' value. Lastly, a Spearman rank order correlation between IT expenditure and bank value shows whether or not banks with high IT expenditure obtain a higher selling price or higher offers than those banks spending less.

The Project's Data

The data used in this project come from three major sources: the Mexican National Banking Commission (CNB, for its abbreviation in Spanish), Mexico's National Computing Programs Industry Association (ANIPCO, for its initials in Spanish), and the banking divestiture process report (Aspe, 1993). The CNB is the federal entity in charge of supervising banking operations, lending policies, economic interactions, and performance. Among other responsibilities, the CNB must report banking financial statements quarterly and annually. This Commission has reported the financial statements since 1924, including the period when the banks were owned by the Mexican government. In 1992, the CNB published a special issue on the characteristics and performance of the banking industry from 1982 to 1992. Similarly to the CNB, ANIPCO collected banks' IT expenditures based on the information that banks submitted annually to the government Finance and Planning Office, an office belonging to Instituto Nacional de Estadistica, Geografia, e Informatica. Table 4 shows the IT expenditure of the banks from 1982 to 1992.

Since the IT expenditure information was not provided directly by the banks, we carried out several interviews with current and former CEOs and CIOs of the sample to verify the accuracy of the data. In total, we carried out six interviews, for example an interview with Alfredo Capote, formerly Marketing Director and presently President and CEO of IBM Mexico. According to these interviews, the ANIPCO data set accurately reflects the banks' expenditures during this period (hardware, software, telecommunications, and IT services).

Since the data were originally in current Mexican pesos, we had to adjust the data set for analysis as follows:

1)   Convert current to real values—Using price index and GDP time series, we translated current pesos and dollars into real dollars (1992).
2)   Normalize the data. Since two banks accounted for almost half of the total industry market, while at the same time, six banks took up a very tiny percentage of the market, we found it necessary to normalize the data sample

Table 4: IT Expenditure, 1992 Real Dollars (Millions)

BANK	ITE1982	ITE1983	ITE1984	ITE1985	ITE1986	ITE1987	ITE1988	ITE1989	ITE1990	ITE1991	ITE1992
Bank R	17.38	21.44	35.54	53.86	60.21	67.20	74.77	69.75	74.90	99.93	142.50
Bank P	18.87	14.39	21.32	32.11	37.44	56.89	61.23	70.90	79.62	113.79	150.60
Bank A	11.08	8.32	10.39	15.20	17.20	23.35	14.62	31.31	55.68	68.56	71.20
Bank D	6.74	4.80	5.47	8.12	9.61	11.18	11.50	14.16	25.04	35.64	41.00
Bank O	7.04	3.10	3.83	6.03	6.32	7.70	7.91	13.70	25.70	36.05	39.00
Bank I	5.39	3.67	4.51	5.90	5.31	6.83	6.95	7.83	15.92	22.72	27.60
Bank J	3.89	2.68	3.28	5.11	4.81	6.21	6.59	7.37	12.30	22.19	24.40
Bank S	2.40	1.83	2.60	3.67	3.54	4.47	4.07	4.37	6.81	13.55	17.60
Bank K	1.35	1.27	2.32	3.15	2.66	2.98	3.24	3.68	6.59	10.52	14.20
Bank Q	2.25	1.83	2.32	3.28	3.42	4.10	4.19	5.29	8.79	13.96	15.30
Bank F	0.60	0.56	0.82	1.31	1.64	2.73	3.35	2.99	4.39	8.34	10.10
Bank C	0.90	0.85	1.50	2.23	2.40	3.11	3.35	4.14	5.82	12.82	13.70
Bank M	1.20	0.99	1.50	2.36	2.15	2.86	2.76	3.45	5.60	12.19	14.90
Bank B	1.35	1.27	1.78	2.36	2.40	3.23	3.24	4.26	6.81	12.50	16.20
Bank N	1.20	1.13	1.78	2.49	2.40	2.73	2.76	2.42	4.06	9.38	9.80
Bank H	1.50	1.55	2.05	3.01	2.53	2.61	1.68	3.57	5.05	9.69	14.10
Bank L	0.90	1.27	1.78	2.36	2.28	2.36	2.16	3.34	9.55	7.82	9.10
Bank E	0.30	0.14	0.27	0.52	0.63	0.75	0.72	0.81	1.32	2.50	3.20

as recommended by Ahituv and Giladi (1994). In particular, we divided IT expenditure by the total operational expenditure of each bank for all annual data points.

FINDINGS

The literature review section cited that several researchers report IT provides value to organizations. Among the postulated benefits, they report that IT facilitates business task coordination, reduces coordination costs, increases functionality, increases operational efficiency, creates lower production cost, improves customer services, and increases productivity and profitability, among other things. However, research empirically testing such benefits has generated mixed results. For example, Ahituv and Giladi (1994) found that there is no correlation between IS and business success, Dos Santos et al. (1993) concluded there is no excess return of IT investments, and Kauffman and Weill (1989) stated that there is no evidence of positive impact of IT investments. This paper's results show the impact of IT expenditures on the market value of banks, answering the research question, Does IT expenditure affect the market value of the banks?

The results for the hypotheses are summarized as follows:

Question	Hypothesis		Result
1	H1a	IT expenditure is positively correlated with real market value of the bank.	Supported
	H1b	IT expenditure is positively correlated with perceived market value of the bank.	Supported
	H1c	Cumulative (two, three, and five years) IT expenditure is positively correlated with real market value of the bank.	Supported
	H1d	Cumulative (two, three, and five years) IT expenditure is positively correlated with perceived market value of the bank.	Supported
	H1e	IT expenditure intensity is positively correlated with bank value.	Not supported

Table 5 presents the Pearson correlation results between IT expenditures and the real value of the banks, as well as the correlation between the cumulative (two, three, and five years) IT expenditure and the real value of the banks. It is important to point out that the real value of the banks corresponds to the amount of money paid by new owners for acquiring control of the banks in 1992. During the nationalized period of 1981 to 1992, there are no data available on banks' real value.

Table 5: Correlation Between IT Expenditure and Real Value

Q1	H1a			IT expenditure is positively correlated with real market value of the bank.						

Correlation	Year 1	Year 2	Year 3	Year 4	Year 5	Year 6	Year 7	Year 8	Year 9	Year 10
Real value.	.128	.483*	.525*	.520*	.613**	.633**	.697**	.595**	-.132	-.516*
Sig (2tail)	.613	.042	.025	.027	.007	.005	.001	.009	.601	.028

Q1	H1c			Cumulative (two, three, and five years) IT expenditure is positively correlated with real market value of the bank.						

Correlation	Year 1	Year 2	Year 3	Year 4	Year 5	Year 6	Year 7	Year 8	Year 9	Year 10
Real value.		.382	.545*	.534*	.584*	.656**	.710**	.713**	.061	-.330
Sig (2tail)		.118	.023	.023	.011	.003	.001	.001	.808	.182

Correlation	Year 1	Year 2	Year 3	Year 4	Year 5	Year 6	Year 7	Year 8	Year 9	Year 10
Real value.			.526*	.562*	.582*	.655**	.706**	.701**	.216	-.161
Sig (2tail)			.025	.015	.011	.003	.001	.001	.389	.524

Correlation	Year 1	Year 2	Year 3	Year 4	Year 5	Year 6	Year 7	Year 8	Year 9	Year 10
Real value.					.617**	.666**	.700**	.713**	.381	.075
Sig (2tail)					.006	.003	.001	.001	.119	.767

** Correlation is significant at the .01 level (2-tailed).
* Correlation is significant at the .05 level (2-tailed).

Likewise, Table 6 shows the correlations between IT expenditure and the perceived value of the banks, as well as the correlations between the cumulative value of IT expenses and banks' perceived value. Here, perceived value represents the average of the amount of money offered by all the bank's potential buyers to purchase the bank.

Table 6: Correlation Between IT Expenditure and Perceived Value

Q1	H1b			IT expenditure is positively correlated with perceived market value of the bank.						

Correlation	Year 1	Year 2	Year 3	Year 4	Year 5	Year 6	Year 7	Year 8	Year 9	Year 10
Perc. Value	.124	.461	.500*	.499*	.602*	.624**	.687**	.587*	-.129	-.523*
Sig (2tail)	.637	.062	.041	.041	.011	.007	.002	.013	.623	.031

Q1	H1d			Cumulative (two, three, and five years) IT expenditure is positively correlated with perceived market value of the bank.						

Correlation	Year 1	Year 2	Year 3	Year 4	Year 5	Year 6	Year 7	Year 8	Year 9	Year 10
Perc. Value.		.366	.519*	.510*	.568*	.645**	.700**	.704**	.061	-.329
Sig (2tail)		.149	.033	.037	.017	.005	.002	.002	.816	.197

Correlation	Year 1	Year 2	Year 3	Year 4	Year 5	Year 6	Year 7	Year 8	Year 9	Year 10
Perc. Value.			.502*	.537*	.560*	.639**	.694**	.692**	.213	-.163
Sig (2tail)			.040	.026	.019	.006	.002	.002	.412	.533

Correlation	Year 1	Year 2	Year 3	Year 4	Year 5	Year 6	Year 7	Year 8	Year 9	Year 10
Perc. Value.					.592*	.646**	.683**	.700**	.374	.069
Sig (2tail)					.012	.005	.003	.002	.139	.791

** Correlation is significant at the .01 level (2-tailed).
* Correlation is significant at the .05 level (2-tailed).

Table 5 depicts three stages of correlation strength: in Year 1, there is no significant correlation between the expenditures of IT in that year and the real value of the banks. However, the correlations become significant in the second stage consisting of Years 2 through 8. Significance reaches the 0.001 level for year 5,6,7, and 8. The third stage, consisting of Year 9, has no positive correlation, and Year 10 has a negative correlation.

This pattern of three stages, no correlation, correlation, and no correlation, is also present for associations of cumulative IT expenditure and the real value of the banks (Table 5). For 2-year cumulative averages, period two (average of year one and two) has no correlation, while periods 3 through 8 demonstrate positive correlations. Periods 9 and 10 again show no correlation. Also in Table 5 it can be seen that averaged three 3-year periods and 5-year periods have positive correlation for almost all the years except for Years 9 and 10.

Quite similar to these results for the correlations between IT expenditure and the real value of the banks are the results for IT expenditure and perceived value of the banks (Table 6). Again, three stages are present: one for the averaged first two years that reveals no correlation; a second 6 year period with positive correlations; and the averaged two years at the end without correlations. Likewise, the cumulative IT expenditure for periods of two, three, and five years is correlated with banks' perceived value. The staged pattern of results resembles closely that noted for the real value of banks.

Having consistently positive correlations between IT expenditure and the value of the banks raises another question: Do banks spending more on IT register higher selling or bidding prices? Hypothesis H1e (IT expenditure intensity is positively correlated with banks value) answers this complementary question. Hypothesis 1e is tested by applying Spearman correlations between 5-year cumulative IT expenditure and real and perceived value of the banks. Table 7 shows the Spearman correlations between three periods of 5-year cumulative IT expenditures and the real value of the banks, while Table 8 shows Spearman correlations

Table 7: Spearman Correlation, IT Expenditure Intensity, and Bank Real Value

Period		Bank Real Value	Bank Book Value
Years 4-8	Correlation Coefficient	.201	-.329
	Sig. (1-tailed)	.212	.091
	N	18	18
Years 5-9	Correlation Coefficient	.226	-.463
	Sig. (1-tailed)	.184	.026
	N	18	18
Years 6-10	Correlation Coefficient	-.110	-.261
	Sig. (1-tailed)	.331	.148
	N	18	18

** Correlation is significant at the .01 level (1-tailed).
* Correlation is significant at the .05 level (1-tailed).

Table 8: Spearman Correlation, IT Expenditure and Bank Perceived Value

Period		Bank Real Value	Bank Book Value
Years 4-8	Correlation Coefficient Sig. (1-tailed) N	.172 .510 18	-.250 .333 18
Years 5-9	Correlation Coefficient Sig. (1-tailed) N	.150 .567 18	-.368 .147 18
Years 6-10	Correlation Coefficient Sig. (1-tailed) N	-.145 .580 18	-.218 .400 18

* Correlation is significant at the .05 level (1-tailed).
** Correlation is significant at the .01 level (1-tailed).

for the same cumulative values and the perceived value of the banks. The Spearman correlations are consistently insignificant for real and perceived value of banks in terms of real value and book value, rejecting the idea that banks spending more on IT attain higher real or perceived values.

DISCUSSION

The history of the Mexican banking industry may explain the absence of correlations at the early and late stages of the study period. Both were transitional stages; the first one involved the government nationalization of the industry. The second one included the government decision to re-privatize all the banks. As a result, perceived and real value reveal the same positive correlations in the middle, stable period, during which the industry was free of external government decisions, while they show contradictory results for the beginning and end transition periods. These results are quite encouraging if we contrast them against the literature review.

The literature review identified the most closely related studies regarding the value of the firm and IT investments (see Table 9). For all of them, the productivity paradox was confirmed. In particular, companies spent on IT but realized either no positive impact or slight impact. In none of these or other studies regarding the productivity paradox, however, did a researcher test the impact of the IT expenditures or investments on the value of the firm, during a period in which the control of the company changed. The present study reflects the impact of IT expenditure in such a period. The results of testing Hypotheses H1a, H1b, H1c, and H1d suggest that there was no positive impact of IT expenditure during the industry's transition periods, i.e., when the banks were in a consolidation stage, and when they were in preparation for divestiture. On the other hand, during the stability stage (1984 through 1990), the expenditure on IT was positively associated with the real and perceived value of the banks.

Table 9: IT Investments and Firms' Value

Varun (1998)	IT investments fail to improve perceived productivity.
Ahituv and Giladi (1994)	There is no correlation between IS variables and business success.
Dos Santos et al. (1993)	There is no impact (excess on return) of IT investments.
Weill (1992)	No significant gains in systems different to transaction processing systems.
Scott Morton (1991)	There is no evidence of improvement on productivity or profitability.
Kauffman and Weill (1989)	There is no evidence of positive impact of IT investments.
Lucas (1999)	Usage is a better indicator of performance than IT investments. IT investments do not increase the value of the firm.

Here two questions emerge. First, if IT expenditure is positively related to real as well as perceived value of the banks, why did Dos Santos et al. (1993) find no correlation between IT investments and the market value of the firm? Second, why was this impact not homogeneous over the entire period studied?

To begin with, Dos Santos et al. used an event-study methodology to analyze impacts of the information technology investments on company stock. Their conclusion is that there is no impact, i.e., excess of return on the stock market, due to IT investments. That is to say, investors did not react to investments in IT, and IT investments did not change the firms' value. However, for the present study of Mexican commercial banks, there is a positive correlation between IT investment and value. The explanation to this apparent contrast is that in the present study, the investors were buying the control of the bank, while for Dos Santos et al., investors were buying shares, short of control of the companies. This suggests an ordering of firms' value that starts at the bottom with the book value of the firm, and proceeds to shareholder value, perceived value of the firm, sale perceived value, and the sale value of the company. Tables 10 and 11 compare the correlations between the IT expenditures and the real, perceived, and book values of the banks. It is evident that there is no positive correlation for book value, but positive correlations exist for perceived value. On the average, these are smaller than for the real value. Several authors consider book value a bad proxy for firm's value (Higgins, 1992), because the book value does not properly take into account the value of different firms' assets such as trademarks, patents, and we would add, information technology. Shareholders did not react to IT investments (Dos Santos et al., 1993), but when the control of the company is at play, IT investments/expenditures have an impact on the value of the firms.

Table 10: Correlation between IT Expenditure and Real Value (Book Value Shown for Comparison)

Q1	H1a	IT expenditure is positively correlated with real market value of the bank.

Correlation	Year 1	Year 2	Year 3	Year 4	Year 5	Year 6	Year 7	Year 8	Year 9	Year 10
Real value.	.128	.483*	.525*	.520*	.613**	.633**	.697**	.595**	-.132	-.516*
Sig (2tail)	.613	.042	.025	.027	.007	.005	.001	.009	.601	.028
Real BV.	.035	-.424	-.283	-.358	-.420	-.343	-.032	-.328	-.387	.065
Sig. (2tail)	.892	.079	.255	.144	.083	.163	.900	.183	.113	.797

Note: BV = Book Value

Q1	H1c	Cumulative (two, three, and five years) IT expenditure is positively correlated with real market value of the bank.

Correlation	Year 1	Year 2	Year 3	Year 4	Year 5	Year 6	Year 7	Year 8	Year 9	Year 10
Real value.		.382	.545*	.534*	.584*	.656**	.710**	.713**	.061	-.330
Sig (2tail)		.118	.023	.023	.011	.003	.001	.001	.808	.182
Real BV.		-.198	-.349	-.300	-.394	-.363*	-.203	-.210	-.408	-.293
Sig. (2tail)		.432	.155	.226	.106	.138	.420	.403	.093	.238

Correlation	Year 1	Year 2	Year 3	Year 4	Year 5	Year 6	Year 7	Year 8	Year 9	Year 10
Real value.			.526*	.562*	.582*	.655**	.706**	.701**	.216	-.161
Sig (2tail)			.025	.015	.011	.003	.001	.001	.389	.524
Real BV.			-.278	-.330	-.320	-.362	-.255	-.260	-.384	-.344
Sig. (2tail)			.2363	.181	.195	.139	.308	.297	.115	.162

Correlation	Year 1	Year 2	Year 3	Year 4	Year 5	Year 6	Year 7	Year 8	Year 9	Year 10
Real value.					.617**	.666**	.700**	.713**	.381	.075
Sig (2tail)					.006	.003	.001	.001	.119	.767
Real BV.					-.296	-.302	-.248	-.292	-.413	-.381
Sig. (2tail)					.233	.223	.320	.240	.088	.119

Note: BV = Book Value

The second question that emerges from the findings is: Why are the correlations between the IT expenditure and the value of the banks not consistent over the entire 11-year study period? The explanation to the differences in the findings found in the three stages present in Tables 10 and 11 lies in the series of policies adopted by the Mexican government to consolidate the industry, to develop it in a noncompetitive environment, and finally to sell it back to private investors.

CONCLUSIONS

Even though banks are classified as a delivery sector, where they depend on IT to deliver their services, several studies show no positive impact of IT on the value

Table 11: Correlation between IT Expenditure and Perceived Value (Book Value Shown for Comparison)

Q1	H1b	IT expenditure is positively correlated with perceived market value of the bank.								

Correlation	Year 1	Year 2	Year 3	Year 4	Year 5	Year 6	Year 7	Year 8	Year 9	Year 10
Perc. Value	.124	.461	.500*	.499*	.602*	.624**	.687**	.587*	-.129	-.523*
Sig (2tail)	.637	.062	.041	.041	.011	.007	.002	.013	.623	.031
Perc.l BV.	-.065	-.393	-.253	-.327	-.341	-.287	-.033	-.265	-.359	-.148
Sig. (2tail)	.805	.118	.327	.201	.180	.264	.901	.303	.158	.571

Note: BV = Book Value

Q1	H1d	Cumulative (two, three, and five years) IT expenditure is positively correlated with perceived market value of the bank.								

Correlation	Year 1	Year 2	Year 3	Year 4	Year 5	Year 6	Year 7	Year 8	Year 9	Year 10
Perc. Value.		.366	.519*	.510*	.568*	.645**	.700**	.704**	.061	-.329
Sig (2tail)		.149	.033	.037	.017	.005	.002	.002	.816	.197
Perc. BV.		-.241	-.319	-.272	-.340	-.299	-.171	-.170	-.365	-.309
Sig. (2tail)		.352	.212	.291	.182	.243	.511	.513	.149	.227

Correlation	Year 1	Year 2	Year 3	Year 4	Year 5	Year 6	Year 7	Year 8	Year 9	Year 10
Perc. Value.			.502*	.537*	.560*	.639**	.694**	.692**	.213	-.163
Sig (2tail)			.040	.026	.019	.006	.002	.002	.412	.533
Perc. BV.			-.288	-.304	-.282	-.308	-.213	-.214	-.345	-.340
Sig. (2tail)			.263	.235	.272	.230	.412	.410	.175	.182

Correlation	Year 1	Year 2	Year 3	Year 4	Year 5	Year 6	Year 7	Year 8	Year 9	Year 10
Perc. Value.					.592*	.646**	.683**	.700**	.374	.069
Sig (2tail)					.012	.005	.003	.002	.139	.791
Perc. BV.					-.286	-.267	-.216	-.244	-.362	.363
Sig. (2tail)					.266	.301	.405	.345	.154	.153

Note: BV = Book Value

of the banks. The research in this chapter examined impacts at different levels of bank value: book value, perceived value, and real value. IT investments have no impact or very small impact on the book value of the firms. On the other hand, IT investments have a positive impact on the real value of the firm, when the value of the firm reflects the transfer of ownership or the control of the firm. These results agree with the financial managers' observations about the difference between companies share ownership and the control of the company. The sale value of the Mexican banks, for example, was 2.5 to 3.5 times their book value. The large fluctuations in value when the control of the organization is at stake explains the lack of positive impacts in those studies, using market share values to test the impact of IT on the value of organizations.

This finding is also consistent with the phenomenon of dot-com failure. Dot-com companies, which did not make profits at all, received huge amounts of investments and appreciated at the peak to astronomic selling prices. The buying or investing companies decided the amount of money they paid not based on the expected profits but on the number of customers, the size of their customer database, or their market share. In spite of the dot com burst, some economists argue these dot-com companies will generate profits in the long term. For example, Amazon.com posted profits for the first time in 2002.

Even though the findings of this project cannot be extrapolated to other banking industries, other time periods, industries, or countries, the findings are important to researchers and practitioners. From the practitioners' perspective, the results suggest that, contrary to most other research results, spending on IT does enhance the value of the firm, and that this value is not always reflected in the share value of the organization.

To researchers, the project results have several implications. First, as evident by some other research projects, the present research is made feasible thanks to the consistent IT definition used by all the firms in the study. Second, as recommended by Ahituv et al. (1999), researchers need to avoid working with a data sample having widely varied firm sizes. Size differences introduce intervening factors and dilute the evidence of IT impact on organizations. Third, longitudinal data helps in analyzing the impacts of IT on organizations. Fourth, externalities both from industry and the economy hide, dilute, or even inhibit positive impacts of IT on firms. Lastly, value is a subjective measure that depends on how it is measured: by a normative procedure, a personal perception, or an economic transaction. The subjective nature of value has two implications in the IS field: first, that book value is not a good proxy to study the impact of IT on the value of organizations, and second, that IT firms, with dot-coms as a contemporary example, can reach high selling valuations, at times, even though they do not have profits.

REFERENCES

Ahituv, N. (1989). Assessing the value of information: Problems and approaches. *Proceedings of the 10th International Conference on Information Systems*, pp. 315-326. Boston, MA.

Ahituv, N. & Giladi, R. (1994). Business success and information technology: Are they really related? *Proceedings of the 7th Annual Conference of Management IS*, Tel Aviv University.

Ahituv, N., Lipovetsky, S., & Tishler, A. (1999). The relationship between firm's information systems policy and business performance: A multivariate analysis. In M. A. Mahmood & E. J. Szewczak, (Eds), *Measuring Information Technology Investment Payoff: Contemporary Approaches*. pp. 62–82. Hershey, PA: Idea Group Publishing.

Aspe, P. (1993). *Economic transformation: The Mexican Way.* Cambridge Massachusetts: The MIT Press.

Bakos, J. Y., & Brynjolfsson, E. (1993). Information Technology, Incentives, and the Optimal Number of Suppliers. *Journal of Management Information Systems,* 10(2), 37–42.

Bashein, B. J., Markus, M. L., & Riley, P. (1994). Preconditions for BPR success: And how to prevent failures, *Information Systems Management*, 11(2), 7–13.

Brynjolfsson E., & Hitt L.(1997). MIT analysis: Breaking Boundaries. *Informationweek*, (649), 54–61.

Brynjolfsson, E., Renshaw, A. A., & Van Alstyne, M. (1997). The Matrix of change, *Sloan Management Review*, 38(2), 37–54.

Clemons, E. K. (1991). Evaluation of strategic investments in information technology, *Communications of the ACM,* 34(1), 22–36.

Clemons, E. K. & Row, M. C. (1991). Sustaining IT advantage: The role of structural differences. *MIS Quarterly*, 15(3), 275–292.

Cron, W. L., & Sobol, M.G. (1983). The Relationship between Computarization and Performance: A Strategy for Maximizing the Economic Benefits of Computarization, *Information and Management*, 6, 171–181.

Dewan, S., & Kraemer K. L. (1998). International dimensions of the productivity paradox. *Communications of the ACM*, 41(8), 56–62.

Dos Santos, B.L., Peffers, K., & Mauer, D.C. (1993). The impact of information technology investment announcements on the market value of the firm. *Information Systems Research*, 4(1), 1–23.

Harris, S.E., & Katz, J. L. (1991). Organizational performance and information technology investments intensity in the insurance industry. *Organization Science*, 2(3), 263–295.

Hitt, L. & Brynjolfsson, E. (1996). Productivity, Business Profitability, and Consumer Surplus: Three Different Measures of Information Technology Value, *MIS Quarterly,* 20(2), 121–142.

Kauffman, R.J., & Weill, P. (1989). An evaluative framework for research on the performance effects of information technology investments. *Proceedings of the 10th International Conference on Information Systems*, Boston, MA, 377–388.

Keen, P. G. W., & Woddman L. A. (1984). What to do with all those micros, *Harvard Business Review,* 62(5), 142–150.

Kumar, R.L. (1999). Understanding the business value of information systems: A flexibility-base perspective. In M. A. Mahmood and E. Szewczak, *Measuring Information Technology Investment Payoff: Contemporary Approaches.* pp. 301–320. Hershey, PA: Idea Group Publishing.

Loveman, G. W., (1994). An Assessment of the Productivity Impact of Information Technologies. In T. J. Allen; M. S. Scott Morton *Information Technologies and the Corporation of the 1990's.* NY, New York: Oxford University Press.

Lucas, H. C. (1999). *Information technology and the productivity paradox: Assessing the value of investing in IT.* New York, Oxford: Oxford University Press.

Malone, T. W. (1997). Is Empowerment just a fad? Control, decision making, and IT. *Sloan Management Review*, 38(2) 23–35.

Malone, T., Yates, J., & Benajamin, R. (1994). Electronic Markets and Electronic Hierarchies. Chapter 3. In *Information Technology and the Corporation of the 1990s: Research Studies*, T. J. Allen and M.S. Scott-Morton (Eds), New York: Oxford University Press.

Navarrete, C. J., & Pick, J.B. (2002). Information technology expenditure and industry performance: The case of the Mexican banking industry, *Journal of Global Information Technology Management*, 5(2), 7–28.

Navarrete, C. J. & Pick, J.B. (2003). Information technology spending association with organizational productivity and performance: A study of the Mexican banking industry, 1982–1992, Chapter 4. in *Creating Business Value with Information Technology: Challenges and Solutions*, N. Shin (ed.), Hershey, PA, Idea Press.

Panko, R. R. (1991). Is the office productivity stagnant?, *MIS Quarterly,* 15(2), 191–203.

Parker, M.M., & Benson, R. J. (1988). *Information economics: Linking business performance to information technology.* Englewood Cliffs, NJ: Prentice-Hall, Inc.

Rockart, J. F., Earl, M., & Ross, J. W. (1996). Eight imperatives for the new IT organization, *Sloan Management Review*, Cambridge, 38(1), 43–55.

Schrage, M. (1997). The real problem with computers. *Harvard Business Review*, 75(5), 178–188.

Scott Morton, M. S. (1991). *The corporation of the 90s: Information technology and organizational transformation*, New York: Oxford University Press.

Strassman, P. A. (1990). *The business value of computers: An executive's guide*. 1990, New Canaan, CT: Information Economic Press.

Strassmann, P.A. (1997). Computers have yet to make companies more productive. *Computerworld*, September 15, 1997.

Strassmann, P.A. (1999). *Information productivity*. New Canaan, Connecticut: Information Economics Press.

Venkatraman, N. (1991*).* IT-Induced Business Reconfiguration. Chapter 5. In M. Scott Morton (Ed.) *The Corporation of the 1990s: Information Technology and Organizational Transformation.* pp 122–158. New York: Oxford University Press.

Weill, P. (1992). The Relationship between Investment in Information Technology and Firm Performance: A Study of the Valve Manufacturing Sector, *Information Systems Research* 3(4), 307–332.

Yates, J., & Banjamin, R.I. (1991). The past and present as a window on the future. Chapter 3. In M. Scott Morton (Ed*.) The Corporation of the 1990s: Information Technology and Organizational Transformation.* pp 61–92. New York: Oxford University Press.

Chapter VII

Creating Business Value through E-Commerce

Jatinder N. D. Gupta
University of Alabama in Huntsville, USA

Sushil K. Sharma
Ball State University, USA

Electronic commerce (E-Commerce) has been the world's fastest growing industry and has made a big impact on businesses. The impact of e-commerce on industry, businesses and firms' competitive advantage has been phenomenal. Various business models have evolved in last few years. But, despite of this, the business value returned by e-business environment is being viewed with increasing skepticism by researchers and practitioners. How does e-commerce framework enhance business value? What are the different factors where business value can be measured? These are the kinds of questions addressed in our chapter.

INTRODUCTION

E-commerce and the Internet's growth are bringing fundamental changes to government, societies, and economies. The Web is fast emerging as a major player in the relationships between producers and consumers. Business and IT environments are in a constant state of flux. Businesses are constantly reinventing themselves in response to new market opportunities. Internet-enabled business information systems have great impact on the business value chains. Information technology assimilation is regarded as an important outcome in the efforts of firms to leverage the potential of information technologies in their business activities and strategies.

Many types of electronic markets have evolved to offer various kinds of traditional and innovative products and services. Electronic commerce appears to be an entirely new channel, not just a new mechanism for ordering, advertising, or providing customer support, and requires different strategies than traditional ones. Today, for high demand of services, e-commerce can increase revenue through increased productivity, reduced expenditures, and a better level of service with fewer resources. E-commerce tools can improve skills and change users' behavior. E-commerce tools can create a better understanding of the business and improve decision making.

The advancement of information and communication technologies such as the Internet and other networks help organizations to reach across the global markets. These technologies of e-commerce in the form of electronic networks are increasingly becoming a highly strategic part of commerce for buying and selling products, services, and information in global markets (Weston, 1999). The emergence of a knowledge economy has given a new identity to the power of the e-commerce, and we see the evolution of a new business paradigm. E-commerce has provided a number of opportunities for the betterment of the customers as well as for other business players.

Organizations are exploring new markets, new services, and new products in response to forces such as advances in information and communication technologies, business strategies such as mass customization, globalization, and shorter production cycles (Ada, 1999). E-commerce has not only improved the profits but has also increased anticipated rate of growth of transactions, market capitalization, customer reach, geographic growth, and product service scope. In fact, e-commerce has impacted efficiency, effectiveness, productivity, and quality in terms of expense reduction, increased revenue, and return on investment (ROI). In a way, e-commerce—buying and selling products, services, and information in multiple countries—is rapidly changing the business paradigm to business value. In the e-business environment, organizations are expected to achieve greater profit, reduce overhead, and have flexible workflow processes by collaborating business information, partners, and physical resources in a more effective manner. E-business environments should reduce internal operations costs and the costs of interacting with customers and suppliers. Several business models have evolved, few claiming to be successful in accomplishing these goals.

In this chapter, we discuss the manner in which the e-commerce framework enhances the business value for an organization. Our framework focuses on how the e-commerce framework affects critical business activities such as production, logistics, customer service, sales, and marketing in the context of their value chain.

The rest of the chapter is organized as follows. After describing our e-commerce framework and its components, we focus on how e-commerce framework creates business value. Since the impact of e-commerce framework and the measurement of business value may be different at the industry and the firm levels, we discuss these separately. This is followed by a discussion about the emergence of new intelligent enterprises and learning organizations that are made possible by the widespread adaptation of e-commerce framework. Finally, we conclude the chapter with a summary of our framework and some directions for future research.

E-COMMERCE FRAMEWORK

Internet driven e-commerce has not only changed our lifestyles but has also radically transformed businesses. In simple words, **electronic commerce** can be defined as doing business electronically or buying and selling information, products, and services via computer networks or Internet. E-commerce framework helps to streamline interactions of businesses with customers and suppliers, innovation in products, and integration of business processes. E-commerce is providing opportunity for organizations to conduct business through varieties of new business models. E-commerce is helping businesses for

· 	Globalization of markets
· 	Helping in innovations of products and services
· 	Helping to create buyer-oriented markets
· 	Facilitating business through cooperation, alliances, mergers, and acquisitions
· 	Helping to create virtual enterprises—New form of organizations
· 	Creating new business models for revenue streams

The new electronic business models created by e-commerce framework are helping organizations to generate huge revenues by integrating businesses with suppliers, trading partners, and others to facilitate various business processes. These electronic business models, broadly categorized as business-to-consumer (B2C), business-to-business (B2B), and consumer-to-consumer (C2C) allow businesses not only to sell their products and services online to consumers but also help the integration of business processes with its' suppliers and partners. Electronic business models help to improve market awareness, create new sales channels, and customize marketing. Businesses are able to speed up production, increase efficiency of processes, share information, and generate new information-based products. The integration of various business processes with business partners in the B2B business models form is helping to manage supply chains more efficiently, helping to reduce transaction expenses and even creating more efficient dynamic virtual organizations. Figure 1 summarizes the values created by B2B at the customer, business, and business partner levels. These models, in the form of electronic markets, bring multiple buyers and sellers together in a virtually centralized marketplace, where buyers and sellers can buy and sell at dynamic prices. E-commerce framework is facilitating organizations for global reach, one-stop shopping, reducing transaction costs and for offering more efficient pricing.

Figure 1: Electronic Business Models and Value Addition

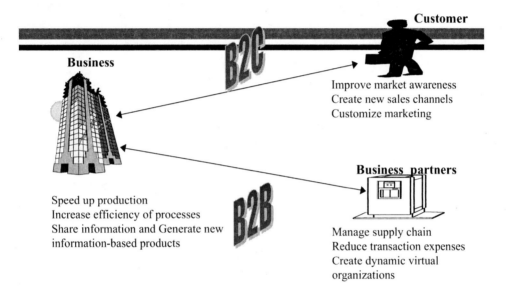

It is becoming clear that traditional business models are no longer sufficient to tackle fierce global competition. For their survival in global competition, organizations need different business methodologies that can help them to cut costs, improve quality of products and services, and create value for the businesses and e-commerce is providing that. E-commerce has changed the entire business para-

Table 1: Comparing Traditional and New Business Paradigms

Traditional Business Paradigm	New Business Paradigm
Focus on mass marketing	Targeting one to one
Focus on mass production	Focus on mass customizations
Supply-Side thinking for business	Demand-Side thinking for business
Customer as target	Customer as partner
Focus on generalization	Focus on specialization and value orientation

digm. Table 1 highlights how traditional business paradigm has changed to the present one (Sharma and Gupta, 2001a).

E-commerce framework is not just a Web site. It has many components of business that are integrated. First and the foremost, it has technology infrastructure to support electronic business. Technology infrastructure is integrated with many organizational infrastructures and systems such as partners, competitors, and associates. Technology infrastructure supports both internal and external business processes and helps to create new form of business models. Business models would interact with common business services infrastructure that is meant to support electronic payments and authentication. Also, business models may work in coordination with other business partners or third-party alliances (Turban et al., 2001). These and other related components of e-commerce framework are shown in Figures 2 and 3. Major components are discussed below.

Figure 2: E-Commerce Framework

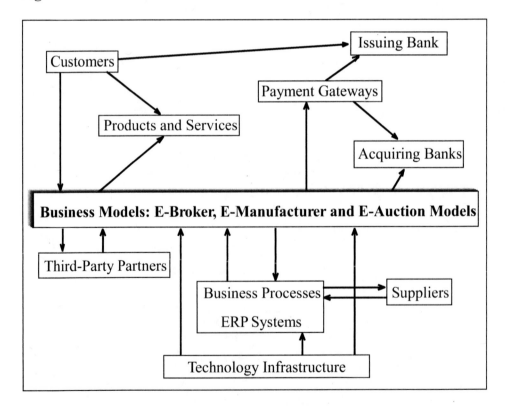

Figure 3: The E-Commerce Components and Activities

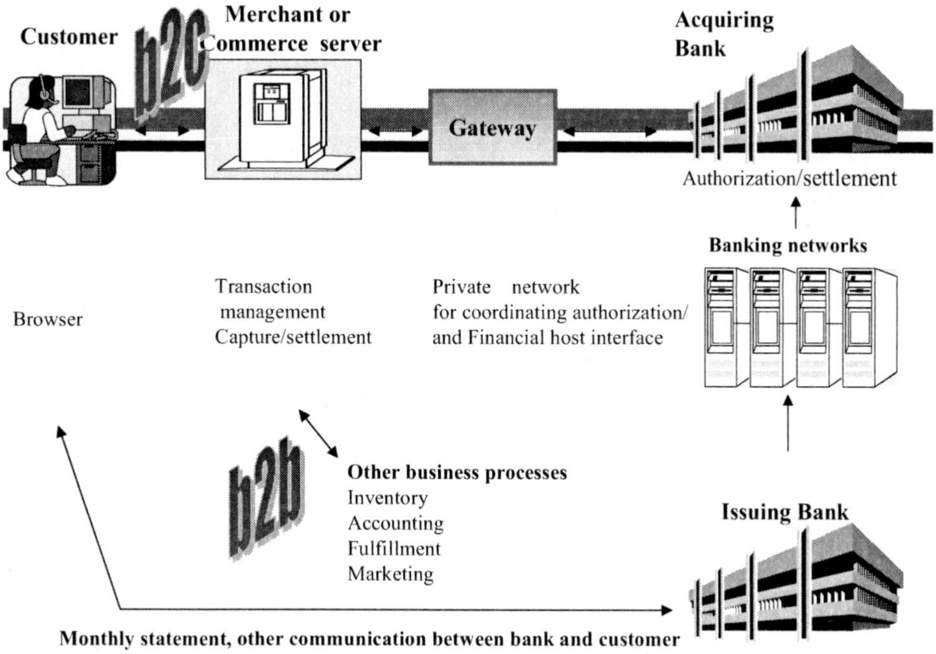

Technology Infrastructure

E-commerce uses the Internet as a main medium Web infrastructure as technology infrastructure. Internet architecture supports multimedia online interactions on a real-time basis. Internet infrastructure is made available to users through various Internet service providers (ISPs), and having an Internet connection, users can connect themselves to any merchants' Web server for buying online products and services. Technology infrastructure has to be strong to bear the capacity and take care of security concerns. There are already technologies such as firewall, encryption standards, etc., that could be used for protecting data from unauthorized access and misuse. The Web is fast emerging as a major player in the relationships between producers and consumers. Channels can be of different types, ranging from advertising channels, and order-processing channels, to customer support channels (Choudhury et al., 2001). Technology infrastructure includes network infrastructure inform of telecom, cable TV, wireless, Internet, LAN, WAN, Intranet and extranet. Publishing technologies such as HTML, Java, World Wide Web, VRML, and databases along with messaging and information distribution infrastructure such as EDI, e-mail, and hypertext transfer protocol. Technology infrastructure comprises many technical standards for documents, security, payments and network protocols (Turban et al., 2001).

Buyers (Customers) and Sellers (Merchants)

Buyers and sellers both use Web infrastructure for offering and receiving products and services online. Sellers create their Web sites or virtual storefronts to offer products and services. The Merchants use well-protected database servers to store the information about products and services, transactions, and various business rules. Buyers and sellers may interact directly or through various intermediaries for products and services.

Common Business Services Infrastructure for Payment Mechanism Integration

For realizing payments electronically, businesses need common business services infrastructure such as credit cards, smart cards, or any other form of electronic payment fully integrated with various financial institution and banks. Cyber cash, digicash, Paypal, Millicent, and Mondex are some of the major electronic payment methods used as electronic payments. Many businesses plan to offer their own payment gateways that can coordinate the payments between merchants' and customers' banks. The security and authentications are prime concerns for electronic payments for which businesses need a support of public key infrastructure agencies that can allocate the digital certificates to merchants, payment gateways and customers for digital transaction.

Organizational Infrastructures and Systems Support

E-commerce framework requires organizational infrastructure to support partners, competitors, associations, and collaboration with third party partners. It requires systems support of various regulatory bodies to control keys, tax structure, and systems to handle legal and privacy issues. E-commerce framework provides an opportunity for organizations to create new innovative products and services, enter into new global markets, align with trading partners, and have effective delivery mechanisms and business strategies.

IMPACT OF E-COMMERCE

E-commerce revolution has changed business models, revenue streams, customer base, and supply chains. E-commerce is helping to integrate the business processes across the suppliers and partners and has created profound effects on organizations' business strategies. Few value chain activities and sources of business value impacted by e-commerce are shown in Figure 4.

The potential value improvement from e-commerce framework can be seen at multiple levels ranging from the market level to the individual user in a business process context. E-commerce can help organizations to discover solutions for

Figure 4: Sources of Business Value

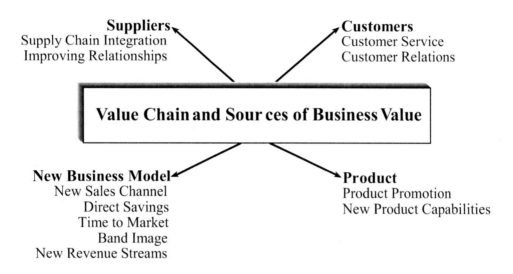

Suppliers
Supply Chain Integration
Improving Relationships

Customers
Customer Service
Customer Relations

Value Chain and Sour ces of Business Value

New Business Model
New Sales Channel
Direct Savings
Time to Market
Band Image
New Revenue Streams

Product
Product Promotion
New Product Capabilities

previously undiscovered business problems or opportunities (Davern & Kauffman, 2000). E-commerce helps an organization to extend its boundaries closer to customers. Business can be conducted directly through customers' premises by offering many self-service products and services. E-commerce also improves an organization's relationships with its customers, partners, and suppliers. In addition, e-commerce offers an opportunity for companies to sell their products all around the globe, and thus, helps to access distant markets in form of electronic markets.

From an operational perspective, e-commerce may help users to accomplish the task differently. It may change the daily workflow and may result into completion of task with higher speeds and comforts. E-commerce has made dramatic improvements on business processes. Improvements in task procedures, productivity, decision-making ability, labor savings, training, quality of work, learning curve, and change management costs are examples of improvements in business value (Ryan & Harrison, 2000).

E-commerce helps to create business value at many performance measures such as financial, customer, internal operations, and employee learning and innovation. The effects of e-commerce have traditionally been focused on financial and technological measures. E-commerce provides both tangible and intangible benefits, but many times researchers only highlight tangible benefits for measuring business value (Chircu & Kauffman, 2000). Like quality improvements from the end customer perspective, where quality in terms of the reduction of defects or the creation of a more substantial, usefulness of product, is never highlighted, although these are important factors to create business value. Another intangible benefit could be improved decision-making ability, either in the timeliness or accuracy of choices made. Productivity improvement, information access improvements, effectiveness and efficiency improvements, are some of the many factors that remain in the background and never get highlighted for business value improvements. Often, business value improvements, through e-commerce in the area of productivity, quality of work, and change management, are underreported (Gabler, 2001).

The impact of e-commerce can be measured by looking at the business value offered through e-commerce on that industry. Business value is derived through the following four ways

Improving Existing Processes

Marketing, manufacturing, and pricing are a few of the business processes that make the impact of e-commerce evident. For example; improving product promotion through mass-customization, one-to-one marketing, offering new direct sales channels for existing products, reducing the cost of some processes (e.g., information distribution), reducing the time to market, improving customer service through automated service, round-the-clock operation, and finally, improving the brand image, by offering electronic access to customers.

Offering Mass Customization

E-commerce has helped organizations collect detailed preferences and buying habits of customers and then customize the products and services accordingly to target them with specific offers, and generally deal with them in a personalized one-to-one way. Many products and services are offered using an interactive Web environment for a variety of self-service offerings.

Reducing Cost

E-commerce certainly helps organizations to reduce cost, because the e-commerce framework may help organizations to reduce workforce size for any given process or task. E-commerce also makes an impact on lifetime customer value improvements arising out of a marketing automation program, improved customer satisfaction from Web self-service, or an improved call center experience.

Offering New Products and Services

Using e-commerce infrastructures allows companies to fundamentally change the ways products are conceived, marketed, delivered, and supported. Further, e-commerce has improved business value at customer, supplier, product and business processes levels.

MEASURING BUSINESS VALUE OF E-COMMERCE

In a more dynamic commercial environment created by e-commerce, quantifying the business value of e-commerce framework is not that easy, as the real value delivered is not captured in typical IT metrics like response time and hardware utilization. Real value is expressed in business terms and improving value chains. There has been a real impact on efficiency, effectiveness, productivity, and quality in terms of expense reduction, increased revenue, and return on investment (ROI), but not all of the impact can be measured in quantitative values (Gabler, 2001). Also, at times, the impact may be instead on the rate and quality of transactions. For example, Amazon was considered a company with long-term high value. One-third of the capitalization value includes future perspective of products and services. The remaining two-thirds is assessed in terms of the value of existing customers, the value of customer and product growth, the potential value of advertising, and the value of corporate charges such as tax and working capital (James, 1999).

As discussed earlier, e-commerce enforces new rules by initiating improvements in both operational processes and management systems. Using Porter's framework, let us examine the business value created by the e-commerce framework.

Porter (1998) suggests that organizations focus on two key business objectives, operational effectiveness (efficiency and effectiveness) and strategic positioning (reach and structure). "Operational effectiveness means you're running the same race faster, ., but strategy is choosing to run a different race because it's the one you've set yourself up to win" (Porter, 1998, 2001). Thus, operational effectiveness entails performing similar activities better than rivals, while strategic positioning entails performing different activities or performing similar activities but in strategically different ways. Practices like benchmarking, TQM, and lean manufacturing are all necessary and valuable routes to improving operational effectiveness. For strategic repositioning, companies need to position themselves differently from their competitors. They need to do so by figuring out where the opportunities in the industry lie.

Efficiency is achieved by using e-commerce infrastructure to reduce operating costs or to improve productivity, while effectiveness comes from using e-commerce infrastructure to foster greater flexibility and responsiveness to changing market needs. Whereas for strategic positioning, each involves using e-commerce infrastructure to extend geographic reach or customer access, structure involves using e-commerce infrastructure to change industry or market practices (Ada, 1999). For example; for some top-performing organizations, however, electronic procurement is creating opportunities for time and expense savings. In fact, e-procurement is enabling them to gain both efficiencies and operational effectiveness across the enterprise, as staffs are able to invest more in value-adding components (Roth, 2001). Availing e-procurement, companies are able to reduce the number of suppliers, implement strategic sourcing, and merge purchasing and payments into a single process. For example, online catalogs and purchase orders not only reduce cycle time but also cut administrative costs and maverick purchases. And, by linking procurement with other departments and to back-end applications, leading companies are reducing total costs and improving internal controls.

Integration of suppliers and customers will also enable procurement areas to concentrate on paring expenses and improving strategic value. Companies that have implemented e-procurement and have some level of integration with the purchasing and payables applications have realized productivity gains ranging from 25 to 60% (Roth, 2001). E-commerce framework has improved company's value chain, ranging from customer service to relationships with suppliers.

It can be argued that while Porter's model uses the terms *value creation and competitive advantage* synonymously, there is a difference between these two terms. Thus, while e-commerce may create or enhance value, it may fail to provide any competitive advantage. Further, DeTienne and Jackson (2001) argue that knowing customers, suppliers, and their employees better and coordinating their activities efficiently through customer relationship management systems or knowledge management systems may increase organizational competitiveness. Thus, e-commerce may create competitive advantage through *social cohesion,* a factor not explicitly considered in Porter's competitive advantage model. While these issues are important research topics, they do not affect the discussion of the e-commerce framework proposed in this chapter, since our goal is to discuss the business value of e-commerce.

In this section, we discuss the business value of e-commerce at three different levels in the supply chain. At the aggregate level, industry as a whole may derive some value from the e-commerce framework. In addition, the company and its supplier may also gain value from the use of e-commerce practices.

Business Value of the Industry Level

E-commerce has a profound affect on the business industry. Some players are disappearing, new players are emerging, and the current actors are changing in order to survive.

E-commerce has a great effect on both customers and businesses:

·   Customers are affected greatly, as e-commerce provides them a convenient way to access information, low prices for products, and customized or personalized products and services. The new advances in technology mostly concern the consumer's direct access to information, through computer networks. Rather than keeping the information proprietary and accessing it through a specialized infrastructure, consumers can access any information of their interest any time from anywhere 24 hours, 7 days a week.

· Businesses are affected due to the integration of their various business processes. They have more control over their expenses, can offer dynamic pricing, and can create efficiency through cooperation and collaboration. Due to advances in workflow systems, businesses have opportunities to redesign their management processes and support them with automated tools for high outputs.

To understand this type of impact, we can use Michael Porter's framework of competitive advantage (Porter, 1985, 1998, 2001).

Supporting a Cost Advantage Strategy

E-commerce is helping to promote products in a cheaper and more interactive way. Through the use of multimedia information (sound, image, video), customers are able to get products with more options. Organizations are also saving money in advertising, handling sales through multiple channels and delivering products through a third party at lesser costs.

Supporting a Product Leadership Strategy

E-commerce offers opportunities for new products and/or new actors. E-commerce has definitely enhanced product attributes. An example of new product attributes could be knowledge databases accessible online and providing information to consumers for their purchases. Before making choices for a specific product or service, consumers could see the reviews of other consumers. For example, Amazon.com provide views, experiences, and opinions of other customers for the same product and could review their recommendations. E-commerce offering companies also support e-mail exchanges between consumers to create a virtual community of buyers and sellers. Electronic commerce is adding to the convenience of getting information about products and purchasing, for instance, by freeing customers from time or place constraints.

Supporting a Customer Focused Strategy

E-commerce is helping organizations maintain and enhance relations with their customers, for instance, memorizing their preferences and anticipating their needs or targeting them with specific offers. Mass-customization is another avenue of help, offering products especially targeted to customer needs, by integrating sub-products from different suppliers and repackaging them in one offer.

Disintermediation

E-commerce infrastructure is improving the diffusion of information to everyone, thereby reducing the power of existing intermediaries. Suppliers use direct electronic contact to target customers directly, thereby suppressing the need for intermediaries. The e-commerce infrastructure helps provide many value-added services along with products and services.

Value-Chain Coordination

E-commerce has helped organizations integrate various organizational components such as warehouses, plants, marketing outlets, franchises, and partners located at many geographical distant places. This has improved business, and many organizations are outsourcing the expertise and adding business value where they find that their own processes are inefficient. Another important component of the supply chain is ordering where an e-commerce framework offers significant value. E-commerce framework allows users to place an order online in the form of electronic ordering. Electronic ordering helps eliminate a middleman, or dealers who are involved in supply chain in traditional business models. With the disintermediation of various distributors, dealers, etc, the cost of products offered to customers could be low. Although skeptics mention that there are still many security and trust issues involved that prevent users to order online. However, the online ordering process helps customers to order with no time and space constraints. Customer support is the final link in the chain between the businesses and the consumer. It adds value to products and services and is an integral part of a successful business. Today, customers demand comparison shopping, 3-D images, personalization, auctions, easy ordering and returns, advanced search mechanisms, real-time voice-enabled customer service links, and nanosecond response time. And this all is not possible without e-commerce framework (Schneider, 2000). E-commerce can lead to brand awareness and an increase in consumer loyalty. Companies can possibly improve the business value if they offer e-commerce.

The use of an e-commerce framework to create self-service or to allow customers to support each other will not only help customer support and relationships, but will also take a considerable load off the company's support staff. At the same time, by bringing customers, businesses, and other partners together in the form of a virtual community, it may help to build strong bonds and may build loyalty for brand names while promoting collaboration among its customers.

Strategic Alliances

E-commerce framework is helping for strategic alliances. Alliances have become necessary due to increasing competition and the desire to reach global markets. Through alliances, companies can have better economies of scale and can perform the same business functions for a substantially lower cost. Alliances provide an opportunity for one partner to internalize the skills of the other, improving its position both within and outside the alliance

Improving Relationships

E-commerce is helping to greatly in improving relationships with customers, employees, and suppliers to business partners and shareholders. Companies realize that building relationships is tomorrow's competitive corporate asset and that e-commerce is helping organizations in this direction. There are many virtual communities who share their ideas, opinions, and experiences with each other. This all is helping organizations to be competitive. The e-commerce framework is fast emerging as a major player in the relationships between producers and consumers. These relationships can be described in terms of channels, or the paths that products or services take as they move from source to destination.

Companies create their web sites to advertise the products and services they offer. Web sites also provide an element of interactivity for ordering products and services online. This front end of companies that help companies to interface with customers and receive online orders or other forms of interactions is called "virtual store-front" applications (Chaudhury, et al., 2001). E-commerce through its technological infrastructure plays a significant role for customer support, customer services and after-sales support since most of these services are primarily information-based (Chaudhury, et al., 2001).

E-commerce framework offers the Web as an advertising channel to market products and services. The Web, as compared to other advertisement channels such as newspapers, radio, television, junk mail, and so forth, offer many advantage to both consumers and companies. The web is interactive in nature and so it gets the customers more involved with the media and provides more empowerment to customers for their choices and preferences. The web is also a much more focused medium in contrast to television or newspaper. It helps target one-to-one marketing and helps capture the buying habits of the customer. The web offers a participatory tool for online interactions and helps to create virtual communities. Virtual communities can help to bring many people around the globe to come closer, socialize and share their own experiences or opinions on different topics, which may help to better understand each other sociologically.

Business Value at the Company Level

Electronic commerce strategies are helping in finding new sources of value addition, in a world where information is increasingly a commodity. Organizations have multiple roles: information brokers to pass information from product suppliers to customers, transaction processors to forward money, and advisors to provide added-value information to their customers, assisting them in their choices of specific products and services. The first two of these roles are increasingly taken over by e-commerce technology by reaching to the customers directly and providing them free information and processing their transaction needs at consumers' preferences and choices. For the third role, E-commerce helps organizations to target their suppliers and customers and build long-term relationships through continuous Internet-based interactions. Many organizations have customer relationship management implemented for catering to the needs of customers, and some offer many self-service products and services.

Organizations have started integrating their systems with their suppliers and partners and helping them for the selection of technologies to implement, to redesign internal business processes, and to benchmark themselves against the best practices in the industry, etc. Electronic commerce technology is used to increase convenience (*product leadership*) in buying, reduce transaction costs, and improve the service delivered to individual users (*customer focus*).

E-commerce allows companies to offer products and services at low prices. Today, customers don't have to travel long distances to get products from a store, long wait times, they don't have to wait or shuffle through paper catalogs. In fact, these are all problems that are taken care of by having an Internet connection at home and purchasing products and services online. Depending on the state of broadband communications infrastructure, most of the information could be delivered to a home PC or television. The *experience* of shopping is probably the only thing that electronic media will never be able to fully replicate and should therefore be fully exploited in the real world. The open nature of the Internet can reduce barriers for small and medium enterprises to exploit opportunities. For example, through a sophisticated Web-based intranet, BMW of North America has achieved maximum control over its pipeline and empowered its national and regional corporate layer with easily accessible, detailed intelligence on which to base business decisions (Toy, 2001).

Companies also have opportunities to partner themselves with many other companies to market their products and services, which will act as an additional channel for sale. Many of these partnerships will be free or involve very little cost. For instance, a travel company can have a partnership with search engines such as Yahoo, Excite, and Infoseek, which attract millions of visitors each month for travel related information and transactions. By partnering with such Web sites, travel companies can ideally get their brand out to customers as they research a purchase. A good example of this strategy is seen in one of the first and biggest travel partnerships on the Internet. In October 1997, Preview Travel paid America Online $32 million to become the primary provider of travel services on AOL for the next five years. The deal accomplished two goals for Preview: Creating revenue from transactions and advertisements, and more importantly getting the Preview brand in front of AOL's growing base of paying customers.

Business Value at the Suppliers Level

E-commerce framework has helped suppliers sell directly to customers, in order to reduce the large distribution costs encountered today. This has helped not only in reducing the cost of products but also in offering added benefits to customers directly. Product suppliers such as airline companies, hotel chains, or destinations will try to leverage electronic commerce as new distribution channels, reducing the cost of their promotion, and improving their reach. The key here is to find a differentiating factor from the competition, as most of these online marketing efforts appear similar. Being part of a larger construct, with good advertising and a strong brand name, should be key to driving online traffic and ultimately sales. The issue for these product suppliers is to maintain their sense of identity online and keep access to their customer data. More and more, the precise knowledge of customer profiles, the details of their buying processes, and the linked products they buy are key to successful marketing.

EMERGING TECHNOLOGIES AND ORGANIZATIONS

E-commerce and the related technologies are rapidly changing the organizational forms and the nature of commerce. The exponential growth in technology enables the emergence of knowledge-based and learning organizations. It also paves the way for the next major shift in e-commerce toward wireless and mobile commerce.

M-Commerce

M-commerce is the continuation of e-commerce with the Palm handheld, wireless laptops, and a new generation of Web-enabled digital phones already on the market. Their effectiveness and range of applications today is limited by a lack of bandwidth, but that bottleneck is being removed, albeit in a piece-meal and fragmented way. M-commerce is not a new distribution channel, a mobile Internet or a substitute for PCs. Rather, it is a new aspect of consumerism and a much more powerful way to speak with consumers (Noharia & Leestma, 2001). M-commerce will enable mobilized sales and service people to process orders on the road, and allow consumers to purchase product whenever and wherever it suits them. Using wireless technologies, mobile commerce would enable consumers and business people to shop, bank, close business deals, and even pay for vending machine goods with portable Internet devices (Cassano, 2000). M-commerce implementation is inevitable.

Attracting and retaining customer relationships by providing mobile communications is the next wave, as e-businesses scramble to gain or retain the competitive advantage (Lewis, 2000). IDC predicts the value of United States m-commerce revenue will jump from US$29 million in 2000 to US$20.8 billion in 2004 (Lewis, 2000). One reason for the growth of m-commerce will be the growth of mobile users. The number of wireless Internet subscribers in 2004 will reach 29 million in the US and 47 million in Europe, according to IDC (Lewis, 2000).

There are quite a few technologies coming up to support m-commerce. WAP, General Packet Radio Service (GPRS), and Bluetooth, are all the various forms of wireless technologies, that will make m-commerce possible. Wireless Application Protocol (WAP) is a standard to bring the wireless Web to mobile phones and personal digital assistants (Keen, 2001). GPRS is the 2.5G bit/sec. broadband wireless capability that fills the gap between first-generation digital phones and the massive, planned - and much delayed - third-generation wireless services (Keen, 2001). Bluetooth is a computing, networking and telecommunications industry specification that describes how mobile phones, computers, and other electronic devices can talk with each other using a short range, low-cost radio connection. Bluetooth's m-commerce role will likely be facilitating micro payment transactions, such as with vending machines and in-store purchases, where more-expensive wireless Internet connections are less practical (Cassano, 2000).

Learning and Intelligent Organizations

The technological, competitive, marketplace, social, economic, political, and highly uncertain business conditions of the 21st century need different kinds of organizations. Until organizations think of inventing new tools, technologies, and methods to operate and manage, they will find it difficult to sustain their competitiveness with the present form of systems (Rowden, 2001; Levine, 2001). The learning organization model is emerging to help firms plan and execute significant organizational change amid rapidly changing business conditions. Learning organizations are generally described as those that continuously acquire, process, and disseminate knowledge about markets, products, technologies, and business processes (Sharma & Gupta, 2001b). This knowledge is often based on experience, experimentation, and information provided by customers, suppliers, competitors, and other sources. Continuous learning is essential for surviving-let alone prospering-in dynamic and competitive environments. Learning is at the heart of a company's ability to adapt to a rapidly changing environment (Popper & Lipshitz, 2000). The learning organization as proposed by Senge will be crucial to attaining a competitive advantage in a dynamic, rapidly changing market. Organizations that fail to learn and develop their people will not be competitive beyond 2005 (Thorne & Smith, 2000).

The organizations of the future must focus on integrating their people with technological tools to derive the maximum benefits (King, 2001). The customer will be incorporated into the organization as a partner in the business and as an extension of the organizational culture. Future learning organizations may have to integrate suppliers into the organizational structure to add value to the organization's customers. Customers and suppliers will work together and form interorganizational teams to improve the value chain (Thorne & Smith, 2000). Even the workforce for many organizations will be decentralized and even home-based via interactive networks. The successful organization's focus will shift from a control-based to a trust-based system through dedicated, trustworthy, and loyal employees. The innovations of the future will enable the virtual workplace to become a reality. The technology of the future will enable organizations to be cheaper, faster, flexible, and more competitive. Organizations that are able to align the collective productive and creative energies of their people through teams will be able to maintain and expand their competitive advantage (Thorne & Smith, 2000). Organizations need to be tightly focused and highly specialized. Organizational purpose will be more than just increasing profit or market share; it will reflect an ongoing commitment to adding value to employees, customers, and the wider community. Organizations need to be intelligent. Intelligent organizations would be those enterprises where organizations would use knowledge management and other business intelligence solutions for variety of analytical capabilities. These analytical capabilities may offer enterprises the opportunity to improve customer services and partner relationships, and to create marketable knowledge products from an enterprise's own internal data (Sharma & Gupta, 2001b). Vickers argues that 21st century organizations should seek to achieve learning capacities in an intelligent manner. He suggests that organizational learning will become an important process for the survival of the enterprises (Vickers, 2000).

CONCLUSIONS

Globalization, rapid technological change, and the importance of knowledge in gaining and sustaining the competitive advantage characterize 21st century organizations. The past decade has seen the exponential growth of e-commerce. The environment of e-commerce and knowledge management has changed the busines—consumer relationship paradigm. In the electronic world of knowledge-based economy, competitive advantage will be with those organizations that have strong social cohesion with their customers, clear understanding of their expectations, and a capacity to deliver fast. Social cohesion means knowing customers, suppliers, and their employees better and coordinating their activities efficiently through customer relationship management systems or knowledge management systems. Organizations have information about products, services, processes stored in various systems such as databases, file servers, Web pages, emails, and enterprise resource planning (ERP). If all of this information is stored centrally and is available and accessible to all of the employees and stakeholders (customers, suppliers) in the form of knowledge, it will not only reduce the time wasted on searching for particular data and allowing better business decisions to be made throughout the enterprise but also provide decision makers with more time for innovation and creativity. Knowledge has become central to the organizational strategy in increasing organizational competitiveness. It is used in organizations to gain competitive advantage in the new century. Companies are taking steps toward better harnessing and utilizing corporate knowledge. The collective knowledge of a company is almost unmeasurable and certainly priceless.

E-commerce framework facilitates increased competition through globalization and through deregulation (competitors coming from other industries), changing customer demands (different lifestyles, different demographics), and increasing expectations (more convenience and value, getting used to the customization of offerings). Although it is difficult to measure or quantify every benefit e-commerce provides to enhance business value, the e-commerce framework has been creating long-term business value for customers as well as businesses. E-commerce provides the customers with choices, information, convenience, time, and savings with improvements in business value and provides opportunities for businesses to improve their marketing methods for various products and services through innovative ways. E-commerce has already changed the way traditional business transactions are conducted. It has fundamentally changed the ways products are conceived, marketed, delivered, and supported to create improved business value.

To realize the full range of business values of e-commerce, future research needs to focus on the development of knowledge management and acquisition, identification of the changes required in the principles and practices of supply chain management, and the creation and maintenance of adaptive and learning organizations.

REFERENCES

Ada, S. (1999). The impact of electronic commerce on the publishing industry: Towards a business value complementarily framework of electronic publishing. *Journal of Information Science*. 25.2, 133–145.

Cassano, D. (2000). E-business unplugged. *Communications News*. 37.11, 54–55.

Chaudhury, A., Mallick, D.N., & Rao, H.R. (2001). Web channels in e-commerce. *Association for Computing Machinery. Communications of the ACM.* 44.1, 99–104.

Chircu, A.M. & Kauffman, R.J. (2000). Limits to value in electronic commerce-related IT investment. *Journal of Management Information Systems.* 17.2, 59–80.

Davern, M.J. & Kauffman, R.J. (2000). Discovering potential and realizing value from information technology investments. *Journal of Management Information Systems.* 16.4, 121–143.

DeTienne, K.B. & Jackson, L. (2001). Knowledge management: Understanding theory and developing strategy. *Competitiveness Review.* 11.1, 1–11.

Gabler, J.M. (2001). Linking business value to IT investments. *Health Management Technology.* 22.2, 75–76.

Hammond, C. (2001). The intelligent enterprise. *InfoWorld.* 23.6, 45–46.

Hatch, J. & Zweig, J. (2001). Strategic flexibility: The key to growth. *Ivey Business Journal.* 65.4, 44-47.

James, D. (1999). Accounting for the Net: Beyond the balance sheet. *Australian CPA.* 69.11, 22–23.

Keen, P.G.W. (2001) Go mobile—now, *Computer World.* 35.24, 36.

King, W.R. (2001). Strategies for creating a learning organization. *Information Systems Management.* vol 18, Issue 1, 12–20.

Levine, L. (2001). Integrating knowledge and processes in a learning organization. *Information Systems Management.* 18.1, 21–33.

Lewis, S. (2000). M-commerce: Relationships on the move. *Asian Business.* 36.12, 55.

Noharia, N. & Leestma, M. (2001). A moving target: The mobile-commerce customer. *MIT Sloan Management Review.* 42.3, 104.

Popper, M. & Lipshitz, R. (2000) Organizational learning: Mechanisms, culture, and feasibility. *Management Learning.* 31.2, 181–196.

Porter, M. (1985). *Competitive. Advantage.* New York: Free Press.

Porter, M. (1998). Clusters and the New Economics of Competition, *The Harvard Business Review,* 76(6) November-December, 77—90.

Porter, M.E. (2001). Strategy and the Internet. *Harvard Business Review.* 79.3, 62–78.

Roth, R.T. (2001). eProcurement: Cutting costs, adding value. *Financial Executive.* 17.7, 62–63.

Rowden, R.W. (2001). The learning organization and strategic change. *S.A.M. Advanced Management Journal.* 66.3, 11–16.

Ryan, S.D & Harrison, D.A. (2000). Considering social subsystem costs and benefits in information technology investment decisions: A view from the field on anticipated payoffs. *Journal of Management Information Systems*. 16.4, 11–40.

Schneider, P. (2000). Internet winners—Fundamentals first. *CIO*. 13.18, 100–06.

Sharma, S.K. & Gupta, J.N.D. (2001a). E-Commerce opportunities and challenges. In *E-commerce Diffusion: Strategies and Challenges*, M. Singh & T. Teo (Eds), Heidelberg Press, Heildeberg, Victoria, Australia.

Sharma, S.K. & Gupta, J.N.D. (2001b) A Framework for Building Learning organizations. *Working paper*. Department of Management, Ball State University.

Thorne, K. & Smith, M. (2000). Competitive advantage in world class organizations. *Management Accounting*. 78.3, 22–26.

Tov, S.B. (2001). Using IT for competitive advantage: A case study. *Information Strategy*. 17.4, 24–28.

Turban, E., Lee, J., King, D. & Chung, H.M. (2001). *Electronic Commerce—A managerial Perspective*. Upper Saddle River, New Jersey: Prentice Hall.

Vickers, M. (2000). Clever versus intelligent organizations: Cases from Australia. *The Academy of Management Executive*. 14.3, 135–136.

Weston, R. (1999). Value chains go global. *Informationweek*. 717. 125.

Chapter VIII

The Moral and Business Value of Information Technology: What to do in Case of a Conflict?

Bernd C. Stahl
University College Dublin, Ireland

This chapter explores the question of the value of information technology from a wider angle than the usual financial perspective. The central thesis is that value is always more than just a financial notion, that it always includes a moral or ethical dimension. From this starting point, the paper investigates the different types of values that play a role in information technology. Due to the multitude of values that determine our dealing with information technology, it is clear that there can be conflicts between them. The paper, therefore, proceeds to introduce a framework that allows the conciliation of competing values by introducing values of a higher order, so-called option values and legacy values. It is then demonstrated that this framework can help solve the problem of value conflicts in IT.

INTRODUCTION

The question of this chapter is how the use of IT in business and the resulting gain of business value can be interpreted from an ethical perspective. Of central interest is whether there is a conflict between the business value and the moral value of IT and what to do in that case.

The starting point of the analysis will be the term "value." Value is, among other things, a moral notion. But of course, value does not have to be understood in terms of morality and ethics. If someone talks of the value of their car or house, then economic considerations are the first to come to mind. Talking about the business value of IT therefore seems to be based on an unclear notion. What sort of value are we talking about here? The title of the book clearly points in a certain direction. "Creating business value with IT" implies that there is something that can unequivocally be recognized as business value. Furthermore, this value can be created; it is thus an object of intentional action by (economic) actors. Finally, the creation of business value can be achieved in whatever way by the use of information technology. My argument is that all of the just-mentioned concepts can be ethically relevant. If this is so, then one can ask what the relationship between business and moral value is. If a conflict between them is conceivable, then the next question will be: according to what rules can managers decide between the two?

THE NOTION OF VALUE

Most readers of this book probably have a very clear idea about what they expect from it and therefore what the business value of IT might be. Presumably, this idea has something to do with the supposition that business value is about money and profits, and that IT is a tool that can be used to increase this value.

Financial Value

More generally and in the language of economists, a first definition of the notion of value could be that every economic actor wants to maximize his or her profits. Value, in this case understood as financial value, can be created by increasing profits. Therefore, creating business value of IT can be measured by increases in profits. This model contains two problems: first, it confines the notion of value more closely than necessary. Second, it is unrealistic. Because I will elaborate on the first point in greater length later on, let me start with the second, with the lack of realism. Maximization of profit is simply impossible to achieve by a real-life economic actor. In order to achieve it the actor would have to fulfil the conditions of the "economic man," and would have to be completely rational, decide according to preference and maximizes personal utility. Real persons are not able to act this way and it is doubtful whether it is even desirable that they could (cf., Homann, 1997, p. 19).

This is not to say that profits are of no value in business or that they do not play an important role in making decisions. My point is merely that profits are not the only reason for actions in business. However, financial value has one big advantage: its unambiguousness. Everybody knows what profits are. Unfortunately, even this point is not as clear as it seems at first sight. It is one of the classical problems of the introduction of information systems in businesses that their influence on economic performance is unknown in advance and often not even measurable in hindsight. This is caused by the fact that information technology has a multitude of tangible and intangible results, and that it intensively interacts with other features of an enterprise such as its organizational structure.

Moral Value

The definition of value as financial value is simply too narrow to be of value. This little pun points in the direction I want to argue. In our daily life value means more than just money. If we look at empirical studies of values that people esteem then we find things like family, love, happiness, health, security, etc. The concept of value that I want to suggest is that of moral value. The interesting thing in the context of this book is that all values have a moral component. Speaking of moral value obviously comprises much more than just money. On the other hand, the term "moral value" is even less clear than "business value." How can one define (moral) value? For a tentative definition, I recommend a look at German moral philosophy. The German word for value is *Wert*. *Wert*, however, does not only stand for value. If you retranslate it and you find next to "value" such words as "amount," "deserving," "price," and also the word "worth." Some German philosophers have therefore suggested the definition of a value as something that is worth the effort (cf. Walther, 1992). In my mind, this is a good starting point for the reflection of value. A company, for example, will only install an information system if the deciders think it is worth the effort.

Ethics and Morality

Ethics and morality are ancient notions that have been systematically discussed at least since the times of the ancient Greeks. Because I started the overview over the moral definition of value with the German term, I will continue with German moral philosophy. In this "German tradition," ethics and morality are often distinguished along the lines of theory and practice. Morality in this tradition consists of the factual norms of a given society. It has the purpose of facilitating human coexistence, solving conflicts, enabling peace, etc. Ethics, on the other hand, is the theory of morality. It can be seen as a mere description of morality. More often, it is understood to be the justification, the revision, the check for inconsistencies. In other words: morality is something one has, whereas ethics is something one knows. This kind of distinction is common in German business ethics and is advocated by many of its protagonists such as Steinmann and Löhr (1994, p. 10), Homann and Blome-Drees (1992, p. 16), Lenk (1997, p. 6), or Ulrich (1997, p. 43). It is useful because it helps avoid confusion between what we do and what we should do. Every society or group needs some kind of morality. The philosophically more interesting term is that of ethics, because the discussion about morality starts here.

For our topic, for the question of values, the distinction between ethics and morality is also important. Values can be moral as well as ethical, and the status and purpose of values depends on this level of abstraction.

Ethics, Morality, and Value

Values have a connection to ethics and morality. Social and moral values can change, which leads to a change in ethical systems. Some ethical theories rely explicitly on values as a foundation. According to Maritain (1960, p. 43) Plato's ethics are an example for that. In Plato's case, the dignity and the aesthetics of values are what touches the soul and gives validity to ethics. Other authors see value as a precondition of ethics. For Jonas (1984, p. 102) a theory of values or a theory of value in general is necessary in order to determine what ought to be. A similar argument is put forward by Hausman and McPherson (1996) when they say (in the case of consequentialism), "Questions of intrinsic value are not necessarily the most important moral questions, but they must be answered first because everything else depends on their answers" (p. 101).

If we follow the distinction between ethics and morality, then we can say that values are one possible basis for morality. On the other hand, any given morality will generally produce values. An example of the values of IT in business could be code of conduct or an acceptable use policy. This is based on (moral) values such as the respect for the needs of employees or the importance of service to customers. Once these values become part of corporate morality, then they can be reflected in value decisions concerning IT, such as the acquisition of an e-mail system that allows for privacy protection. Values are also related to ethics in that they tend to be deduced from an ethical framework and that they need ethical theories to be justified. If, for example, the privacy of employees is considered an important value, then management must be able to defend this choice of value, and for that purpose, an ethical theory is necessary.

How can these ideas be applied with regard to the business value of IT? The entire system development and design process of IT, for example, is based on values. The same is true for all decisions in an organization, such as the decision to buy a new information system. While one might argue that the final value is always the maximization of profits, there are a multitude of values that managers, designers, and analysts have to take into account. Candidates for these values might be speed of processing, input or output, user friendliness, use of technical resources and knowledge, customer satisfaction, etc.

Value Conflicts

Any decision based on value consideration has to deal with the problem that there is a virtual infinity of values to choose from. Usually, the decider will consider more than just one value. A manager making decisions about the acquisition of IS may consider the financial questions but will also recur (often subconsciously) to values learned during socialization, such as human dignity, social welfare, charity, etc. Whenever more than one value is considered, there is the danger of a conflict between them. An example that everybody knows who has ever bought a home computer is the conflict between the values speed and price. It is impossible to satisfy both to a maximum.

If one admits all sorts of values, then the problem becomes worse due to the multitude of possible values. This is a classical problem of moral philosophy, where the conflict of values is also a frequently discussed problem. In democratic societies, we usually recognize the pluralism of values and concede everybody's right to choose their own values. The problem with this seems to be that it leads straight to moral relativism and arbitrariness. How can we organize social life if everybody can choose the values they prefer? One answer to this question was developed by Hubig (1995), who suggests that the right to choose values, that pluralism itself, is a value of its own right. He tries to reconstruct nonrelativistic values from the fact of relativism. If we value pluralism, then protecting it is a value higher than the individual values that constitute pluralism in the first place. From this idea, he deduces values that are of a higher order than our normal values. They are the values that guarantee the plurality of values. These he calls option values and legacy values (*Optionswerte, Vermächtniswerte*). Option values are those values that leave open the option for individuals to choose their values. Legacy values are values that enable individuals to form their own personality and thus allow them to choose their values. These two sorts of values are not concrete moral values. In our terminology, they are ethical rather than moral values. They fulfil their purpose in cases in which moral values are in conflict. This is the idea whose application to value problems of IT is the center of this paper. If (moral and financial) values clash because of the use of IT, then there are higher-level values that managers can consider when they try to find a solution.

This is the quintessence of the paper. Nonfinancial values are important in business, and they can clash with other, financial or nonfinancial, values. In that case, an ethical theory of values can help determine which decision to make. The rest of the paper will take a more detailed look at some of the issues raised by this argument.

BUSINESS VALUE

The business value of IT depends on the definition of all three of the terms involved, on business, value, and IT. I will limit the definition of business to organizations that are active in a market environment such as we find it in our Western democratic states. Businesses tend to be privately owned, and in order to survive in their markets, they have to adhere to some rules. Most notably, they have to make profit. At least they cannot afford to make losses over a lengthy period of time. There are two different perspectives on business that are embodied in the two academic disciplines of economics and business studies. The first perspective is concerned with the national or political economy, while the second takes a look at the practical problems of people or organizations acting within this setting. While these are analytically different perspectives, they influence each other in practice. The business value of IT for any given company is strongly dependent on the macroeconomic settings and environment. Even the best business model for e-commerce that might generate huge amounts of profits is doomed to failure if it is realized in an economy in which the minimum preconditions for e-commerce are not realized. When looking at the relationship of value and business, we will therefore have to keep both perspectives covered.

(Moral) Value in Business

The first question concerning the relationship of values and business might be what the role of values in business is. Apart from the obvious importance of financial values, one answer one can hear to this question is that business does not really have anything to do with values, that it is free of moral values. This is what De George calls the "Myth of Amoral Business" (De George, 1999, p. 11). In this view, the economic system is seen to be the neutral ground where the economic actors meet to negotiate, trade, or produce. Morals and ethics do not enter the equation, because everybody seeks his or her own advantage. However, this point of view is neither theoretically nor practically viable. From the very beginning, economic theory was founded on moral theories. The marketplace, even when understood as amoral, has always had the purpose of producing morally desirable outcomes such as wealth, freedom, equality, etc. This perception has changed, but it is still true that economic theories have a strong relationship with morality. According to Helgesson (1998), there are two ways in which economic theory can have ethical implications. "Firstly, there may be explicit or implicit value assumptions within the theory. [...] Secondly, the theory may have a social impact and affect how people think and act." (Helgesson, 1998, 53) Apart from the theoretical objections to the idea of amoral business there is also a strong practical argument against it, which says that this view does not correspond in to the way any economic system works (p. 16).

Financial Value

Classically, money is seen as the central value in the economic system. This does not contradict our definition of value. Money is what makes it worth the effort to work in a business. However, the exclusive concentration on money, on financial value in business produces other questions such as the problem of measurement. For example, what is the financial value of our natural environment? Then, there are some areas where we might easily determine the money value of a good but where we do not want to recognize it as valid. An example is illegal substances such as drugs. It is easy to find out the street value of drugs, but our societies are doing everything they can to change it. Then there is the question of the value of human beings. Again, this may be measurable from the economist's point of view, but most managers would be loath to do so. This is a serious problem for safety-critical information systems. How do we compare the financial value of increased safety with the value of the human life that is protected? The conclusion we should draw from this paragraph is that not all values are commensurable, and that it is a categorical mistake to try to reduce them all to financial value.

This is pertinent for the question of the business value of IT, because it should keep us from trying to simply add all expected financial values of a certain technology. If a new information system leads to an expected increase in profit of, say, $10 million, but at the same time, leads to the unemployment of 150 people or worse working conditions in an organization, then we may make the decision to acquire it anyway. We should not justify that by weighing expected profits against expected losses, because these may simply not be comparable, at least not on a financial scale.

Another problem with the exclusive use of money as value in business is the theorem of maximization. We tend to teach our business students that the final end of all business actors is profit maximization. Profit maximization would, for example, mean that companies endanger the lives of their employees or customers if the expected compensation they have to pay for that is less than the expected gain.[1] There are enough examples for this kind of behavior, but only very few people would admit that they act according to this maxim. Profit maximization is a clear example for a conflict between financial and moral values, because it categorically decides against all nonfinancial considerations..

The next problem with profit maximization is that it leads to epistemological problems. How can we know that we maximize profits by certain behavior? To answer this, we would have to know the outcomes of alternative actions, which by definition is impossible. Also, there are different time frames for maximization that result in different, maybe even contradictory, action. Maximizing profit for the next quarter will certainly have different outcomes than maximizing profit for the next century.

We can summarize this section by saying that money cannot be viewed as the sole value in business. I am not suggesting the abolition of money, and I do not condemn it as intrinsically immoral. My point is that the exclusive concentration on money and profit in business is neither theoretically nor practically feasible. By concentrating on financial questions, businesses reduce complexity in such a manner that they may not be able to react to changes and challenges adequately. This will then lead to a decreasing financial value. Put another way, concentrating too much on money may make a business lose it.

This then leads to the last point concerning financial value. In the extreme, making money or failing to do so is a question of the survival of a firm. A firm going bankrupt affects many parties, most notably, the employees. Sending employees into unemployment is clearly a moral problem. But most other decisions having to do with money are also at least of a partly moral nature. A company that makes money can invest and expand the business interest. It is also in a position to participate to the community. Customers and suppliers may be able to make better deals with it. Finally, companies making money are the basis of a functioning market economy, which, in turn, is the basis for democracy, freedom, and well-being. This shows that despite all of the potential contradiction between financial and moral values, financial values are at the same time moral values. So, every disagreement between money and morality, between financial and moral values, is in fact at the same time also a dispute between two kinds of moral value.

VALUE AND IT

Information technology can be defined as "the tangible means by which information is manipulated and carried to its ultimate users" (Mason et al., 1995, p. 80). This wide definition leaves space for most of the artifacts that affect our daily lives and maybe even more, our business life.

Similar to the case of the economy, one can hear the argument that technology is ethically neutral. Technology, or so the argument goes, is a tool, and, as such, only its use can determine its ethical content. Analogous to the myth of a-moral business,

De George (1998, p. 45) calls the "myth of a-moral computer programming and information processing." For a long time, scientists and technicians were not perceived as responsible for the use of technology that they developed (Lenk, 1994, p. 43). That means that good use of technology is morally good and only bad use can make it morally bad. This argument has been severely discredited by the developments of the 20th century, starting with World Wars I and II and the technological catastrophes at the end of the century associated with names like Chernobyl, Bhopal, Seveso, etc.

The ethical relevance of information technology is obvious. Changes in IT lead to differences in how we interact and how we perceive other human beings and reality itself. Values thus play an important role in IT. At the most basic level the decision to buy an information system, for example, needs to be based on values. The decision maker has to believe that the system is worth being acquired, that it has value. The design of IT, for example, necessarily has to rely on value assumptions (Huff and Martin, 1995, p. 82). For the discussion of the value of IT, I will again distinguish between moral and financial value. Doing so, I will demonstrate again that even from the profit point of view, moral values of IT are not to be neglected.

The Moral Value of IT

According to a definition by the Association of German Engineers (VDI), the purpose of technological systems is to enhance human possibilities for action (VDI, 1991). This in itself is already a moral value, and it can even be seen as a second-order value, as an option value. The use of IT can be helpful in achieving moral objectives such as communication, freedom, and emancipation.

Information technology is designed to convey information. This delivery of information is an important part of communication. Communication in turn is a necessary condition for morality and ethics. There are philosophical theories that concentrate exclusively on communication in the analysis of ethics such as the German discourse ethics (cf., Apel, 1988; Habermas, 1983, 1991). But, even those ethical concepts that do not put communication in the centre of attention have to rely on the assumption of functioning communication. This is not to say that communication is always of moral value. However, without communication, there is no morality and an increase in communication always offers the chance of improved morality.

Another substantial moral value that can be furthered by IT is freedom. The relationship between ethics and freedom is close, but the discussion of this relationship is hampered by the ambiguity of the concept of freedom. In the context of IT, freedom can mean the unhindered access to information and a resulting increase of possibilities. Translated into everyday life, this can mean the emancipation from traditional structures and forces. Again, this can be viewed as an option value. In general one can state that communication and morality are closely linked and that therefore, IT as a means of communication and values as an expression of morality are also linked.

However, there is also a downside to IT with respect to values. IT can be said to produce accidental and necessary moral problems. Accidental are those problems that happen because of the use of IT but are not necessarily linked to it. On the other hand, there are moral problems of IT that are intrinsically related to IT. Among the accidental moral problems of IT, we find the usual objects of computer and information ethics. These are questions of access, accountability, power and its distribution, etc. On the other hand, we have the problems that are inherent in IT. Most of those are based on anthropological or metaphysical assumptions that are rarely mentioned. The most important ones of these problems are those that contort or rule out communication. One important point is the invisibility of the other. When we communicate with IT, we usually do not see the other, and in many cases, we have no idea who it is. This leads to a natural tendency to no longer see him as another person but as just some kind of abstraction. The result is the loss of necessity to treat him morally.[2] Another problem is the loss of some important parts of communication. The nonverbal part of communication is systematically omitted in some kinds of technological communication. Other moral problems such as the invasion of privacy, lack of trust, information overload, technostress, etc., are also based on faulty anthropological assumptions in IT.

We can thus conclude that the value of IT is ambiguous with respect to morality. What remains to be seen is the business value of IT.

The Business Value of IT

The Association of German Engineers offers a list of values that are decisive in technology (VDI, 1991). On this list, there are two values that are clearly of an economic nature. One is economic efficiency on the microlevel of the firm, and the other is economic welfare on the macrolevel of society. Those two are, of course, related. If every company works efficiently, then it stands to reason that the economy will produce wealth. This general argument about technology is certainly true for information technology. IT can rationalize organizations, cut cost, and increase profits. The benefits of IT for the economy surpass the simple accumulation of many benefits on the microlevel. IT creates network effects. According to Metcalfe's law the utility of networks equals the square of the number of users (Pitt, 1999, p. 119f). This means that the individual efforts of increasing financial value lead to an increasing rate of value production in the economy.

On the other hand, IT does not necessarily increase the profit of an organization. First, there are the costs of introducing IT. Second, IT requires maintenance and updating, the price of which is less obvious. Third, IT can produce a range of intangible costs that may be impossible to measure but are still relevant for the success of the enterprise. These intangible costs can range from disaffection of employees and customers to problems with the core business tasks. Most important are probably the effects on the organization, as they often result from the introduction of IT.

We see that even in the hard-core business area of profits and financial value, information technology is ambiguous. It is often not clear whether IT produces financial value. The increasing use of IT in most sorts of businesses, however, is a good estimator for a general feeling that it does. Again, the financial value of IT cannot be clearly divided from its moral value. If IT helps improve business processes, it can lead to more success of the company and to new jobs. That would also be a moral value. If a worker can communicate better or work is alleviated, then these are also moral values.

Conflict between Business and Moral Value of IT

It is easy to imagine a situation where the business value of IT seems to conflict with moral values. A less expensive system may make economic sense but be ergonomically not optimal, which could be a moral problem. Higher security standards may be morally desirable but economically not viable.

However, a closer look will reveal that these value conflicts are rarely clearly money against morality but usually contain conflicts among moral or among financial values. An ergonomically bad system could save money in acquisition but lead to less satisfied employees with corresponding decrease in productivity. Higher investments in security may be costly, but they can also help build a good reputation of a company and thus increase the flow of orders. Most if not all values have a moral side. Therefore, value conflicts are rarely between money and morality but usually between different values of the same kind. It is therefore impossible to give a simple answer to the question: what to do in case of a value conflict. A statement of the sort: "always do what is moral" does not help, because almost every possible action can help some moral cause and be based on some moral value. On the other hand, value conflicts are frequent, and managers or other decision makers need some kind of guideline in helping them make good decisions.

This is where the moral theory of higher-order values discussed earlier can be helpful. In the case of the conflict of values, management should determine which choice would allow the realization of option values and legacy values. Which decision leaves more space to further development and future options and which decision allows the affected human beings a better development of their personality?

This may sound a little bit abstract at first sight, but a few examples may help in understanding the concept. If a company decides it needs to store its data electronically, then it may have several options. It can, for example, write its own program or acquire a commercial database. The value conflict may be between financial values and the value of using your own IT department or having a highly specific data structure. In this case, option values can help. Management should ask: which decision will leave open the most and the most important future options. This question may help decide the problem.

Another example could be whether to monitor employee e-mail. This is a classical example for a conflict between predominantly moral and financial values. Management could argue that it needs to know what employees are doing during their work hours. The moral side would be that privacy is a highly esteemed moral value. In this case, the legacy value would be helpful. Management should ask which choice would allow the affected parties or people to best develop their personality (which, in turn, would probably financially benefit the company). The answer would be that privacy is part of our personality development, and without privacy, people may not live up to their potential. The decision would probably go in favor of privacy and against monitoring.

Many real life problems will be more complex than the two examples. The question of surveillance may additionally have a legal aspect, the liability of the company. The choice of software may additionally depend on the in-house knowledge of information systems or on the directives of the parent company. Nevertheless, most decisions have to take into account several dimensions that can be described as values, as being worth the effort. Whenever these values come in conflict, be it between different types of values such as financial and moral or between similar values, deciders need some sort of criterion to help them make the decision. These criteria can be higher-order values, and with option and legacy values, we have two tools to offer that can help in making decisions and which, at the same time, are ethically sound.

CONCLUSION

Decisions are based on values, and decisions concerning IT are no exception to this rule. Values can concern everything that a person or an organization believes to be worth the effort. The most prominent value in business is money or financial value. However, even in business decisions, many values apart from money play a role, and indeed, even financial value can usually be interpreted to have a moral side to it. The same can be said for IT. Design and use of IT are deeply dependent on underlying values, which again can be of a financial or moral or any other nature. It can be said that the different values are translatable to a certain degree.

The difficulty concerning decisions based on values appears when there are several values that have to be considered, but these values do not lead to the same conclusion, that is when values come in conflict. One typical case of conflict is that between financial and moral values. However, we have seen that it is rarely the case that moral and financial values clash unequivocally. Usually, these conflicts can be described as conflicts among moral or among financial values as well.

The difficulty for managers and deciders in the case of a value conflict is to find out according to what value a decision should be made. In this paper I introduced a moral theory of values that rests on the assumption that there are values of a higher order that come into play in the case of value conflicts. These values were called option values and legacy values. Option values are those that allow the affected parties the maximum of future values, whereas legacy values allow the personal development of the parties affected. If there is a clash between values, deciders should make a decision that realizes a maximum of these two, of options and of potential for development.

It was shown that this theory is applicable to value conflicts in IT. It can help management make the right decisions. Incorporating higher-order values into decision processes can then again have a positive feedback on the underlying values. Because the theory is a part of moral philosophy and is based on ethical ideas, it stands to reason that it leads to morally superior solutions. But at the same time, it is also plausible that it is good for the financial side. A company that keeps open a maximum number of options will be able to react flexibly in the future. A company that allows its employees to develop their personalities to an optimum will have high intellectual and social capital. Even though this thesis would have to be subject to empirical research, I believe that adhering to the value model introduced in this chapter would not only be the good thing to do but would also lead to high profitability of an organization.

ENDNOTES

[1] This is what Ford did in the Pinto case, where management decided not to install passive safety measures, because it was thought that the compensation for the expected additionally killed people was going to be less than the additional profit. This has made the "Pinto case" a standard example in all textbooks on business ethics. It stands to reason that it was not only a morally doubtful thing to do but also a serious blow to Ford's reputation.

[2] The question of the other in ethics has been intensively discussed in French ethics of the 20th century and is linked to names like Sartre, Levinas, or Ricoeur. I will leave it with this short hint at the problem. If ethics is based on direct contact with the other, on the countenance, or on the perceived equal, then the invisibility of the other will affect it.

REFERENCES

Apel, K. O. (1988). *Diskurs und Verantwortung: das Problem des Übergangs zur postkonventionellen Moral.* 3rd edition 1997 Frankfurt a. M.: Suhrkamp.

Berger, R. (1996). Ethik der Technik: Gestaltungskunst von Entscheidungen. In: *Ethik und Sozialwissenschaften,* 7(2/3). Opladen: Westdeutscher Verlag.

Collste, G. (1998). Value Assumptions in Economic Theory. In Grenholm, C. H. & Helgesson, G. (Eds.), *Value Assumptions in Economic Theory,* (pp. 9–17). Uppsala: Uppsala University.

De George, R. T. (1999): *Business Ethics.* 5th edition Upper Saddle River, NJ: Prentice Hall

De George, R. T. (1998). Computers, Ethics, and Business. In *Philosophic Exchange* 1997–1998 (45–55).

Donaldson, Thomas & Preston, L. E. (1995). The Stakeholder Theory of the Corporation: Concepts, Evidence, and Implications. *Academy of Management Review, 20*(1), 65–91.

Emcke, C. & Schwarz, U. (1999). Tanz ums goldene Kalb. *Der Spiegel,* 51(99), 50.

Habermas, J. (1998). *Faktizität und Geltung: Beiträge zur Diskurstheorie des Rechts und des demokratischen Rechtsstaats.* Frankfurt a. M.: Suhrkamp.

Habermas, J. (1991). *Erläuterungen zur Diskursethik.* Frankfurt a. M.

Habermas, J. (1983). *Moralbewußtsein und kommunikatives Handeln.* Frankfurt a. M.: Suhrkamp.

Hausman, D. M. & McPherson, M. S. (1996). *Economic Analysis and Moral Philosophy.* Cambridge, MA: Cambridge University Press.

Helgesson, G. (1998). Ethical Preconditions in Economic Theory—A First Inventory. In Grenholm, C. H. & Helgesson, G. (Eds.) *Ethics, Economics and Feminism,* (pp. 51–82). Uppsala: Uppsala University.

Homann, K. (1997). Individualisierung: Verfall der Moral? Zum ökonomischen Fundament aller Moral. In: Aus Politik und Zeitgeschehen - Beilage zur Wochenzeitung *Das Parlament* - B21/97 16.Mai 1997. Bonn: Bundeszentrale für politische Bildung.

Homann, K. & Blome-Drees, F. (1992). *Wirtschafts- und Unternehmensethik.* Göttingen: Vandenhoek & Ruprecht.

Hubig, C. (1995). *Technik- und Wissenschaftsethik*. 2nd edition, Berlin, Heidelberg, New York: Springer Verlag.

Huff, C. & Martin, C. D. (1995). Computing Consequences: A Framework for Teaching Ethical Computing. *Communications of the ACM*, 38(12), 75–84

Jonas, H. (1987). *Technik, Medizin und Ethik. Zur Praxis des Prinzips Verantwortung*. 2nd edition, Frankfurt a. M.: Insel Verlag.

Jonas, H. (1984). *Das Prinzip Verantwortung*. 1984 Frankfurt a. M.: Suhrkamp

Lehner, F. & Schmidt-Bleek, F. (1999). *Die Wachstumsmschine—Der ökonomische Charme der Ökologie*. München: Droemer Verlag

Lenk, H. (1997). *Einführung in die angewandte Ethik*. Stuttgart Berlin Köln: Kohlhammer.

Lenk, H. (1994). *Macht und Machbarkeit der Technik*. Stuttgart: Reclam.

Lenk, H. (ed.) (1991). *Wissenschaft und Ethik*. Stuttgart: Reclam.

Lenoir, R. (1991). Entretien avec René Lenoir. In Lenoir, Frédéric (Ed.) (1991): *Le temps de la responsabilité - Entretiens sur l'éthique*, (pp. 7–118). Paris: Fayard.

Lübbe, H. (1993). Sicherheit. Risikowahrnehmung im Zivilisationsprozeß. In: Bayerische Rück (Hg.), (1993): *Risiko ist ein Konstrukt. Wahrnehmungen zur Risikowahrnehmung*, (pp. 23–42). München: Knesebeck.

Lübbe, H. (1990). *Der Lebenssinn der Industriegesellschaft—über die moralische Verfassung der wissenschaftlich-technischen Zivilisation*. Berlin et al: Springer Verlag.

Maritain, J. (1960). *La philosophie morale—Examen historique et critque des grands systèmes*. Pairs: Librarie Gallimard.

Marx, K. (1998). *Das Kapital—Kritik der politischen Ökonomie*, 3 Bd, Band 1, MEW Bd 23. 16. Auflage Berlin: Dietz Verlag.

Mason, R. O., Mason, F., & Culnan, M. J. (1995). *Ethics of Information Management*. Thousand Oaks, London, New Delhi: Sage Publishing.

Pitt, L. (1999). Strategy in the Digital Age—Five New Forces. In Liebl, Franz (Ed.). *E-conomy—Management und Ökonomie in digitalen Kontexten*, (pp. 117–124). Marburg: Metropolis Verlag.

Priddat, B. P. (1998). *Moralischer Konsum - 13 Lektionen über die Käuflichkeit*. Stuttgart Leipzig: Hirzel Verlag.

Ropohl, G. (1994). Ein paar Gewißheiten unter Unsicherheit. In *Ethik und Sozialwissenschaften*, 5(1).

Schwartz, P. & Gibb, B. (1999). *When Good Companies Do Bad Things: Responsibility and Risk in an Age of Globalization*. New York: John Wiley & Sons.

Steinmann & Löhr (1994). *Grundlagen der Unternehmensethik.* 2nd edition, Stuttgart: Schäffer Poeschel.

Ulrich, P. (1998). *Wofür sind Unternehmen verantwortlich?* St. Gallen: Institut für Wirtschaftsethik, Uni St. Gallen.

Ulrich, P. (1997). *Integrative Wirtschaftsethik—Grundlagen einer lebensdienlichen Ökonomie.* Bern, Stuttgart, Wien: Haupt.

VDI-Ausschuß Grundlagen der Technikbewertung (1991). *Richtlinie VDI 3780 Technikbewertung:* Begriffe und Grundlagen.

Walther, C. (1992). *Ethik und Technik Grundfragen-Meinungen-Kontroversen.* Berlin, New York: de Gruyter.

Weizsäcker, C. C. von (1999). Globalisierung: Garantie für Freiheit und Wohlstand oder Ende der Politik und Abschied vom Staat? Aus ökonmischer Sicht. In Mangold, H. von & Weizsäcker, C. C. von (1999). *Globalisierung - Bedeutung für Staat und Wirtschaft* (pp. 9–51). Köln: Wirtschaftsverlag Bachem.

Zimmerli, W. Ch. (1998). Ethik in der Technik - überfällig oder überflüssig?. In Zimmerli, W. Ch. (1998). *Ethik in der Praxis - Wege zur Realisierung einer Technikethik* (Mensch - Natur - Technik; Bd. 6). Hannover: Lutherisches Verlagshaus.

Zimmerli, W. Ch. (1994). Unternehmenskultur - neues Denken in alten Begriffen. Verantwortung, Technologie und Wirtschaft an der Schwelle zum dritten Jahrtausend. In Zimmerli, W. Ch. & Brennecke, V. M. (Eds.), *Technikverantwortung in der Unternehmenskultur—Von theoretischen Konzepten zur praktischen Umsetzung.* Stuttgart: Schäffer—Poeschel Verlag.

Chapter IX

Establishing the Business Value of Network Security Using Analytical Hierarchy Process

Susan J. Chinburg, Ramesh Sharda, and Mark Weiser
Oklahoma State University, USA

Information technology (IT) has become a critical functionality for business today. Choosing the appropriate network security that will protect IT functions and meet business needs can be a bewildering but necessary process. The problem is deciding what and how much to do. The objective of this paper is to propose a new process that will facilitate the mapping of network security to the business's priorities using well-known classification schemes and decision support systems. Establishing a relationship between such diverse functions requires that the two areas be described in terms that can be related. Network security is described in terms of services and mechanisms that provide the functionality using the Open System Interconnection (OSI) Security Architecture classification. Business value and activities are described using Michael Porter's business value chain. First, the classification schemes for each area are subjectively related to establish an initial functionality/business value relationship. Second, a decision support tool called analytic hierarchy process (AHP) is used to establish an analytical and more objective relationship between the two classification schemes. The result of this work is a prioritized list of security services related to business needs instead of just being driven by technological criteria. An example that illustrates this concept is described in the paper. To the best of the authors knowledge, this is the first application of using AHP in the decision-making process of choosing network security in relationship to business needs.

INTRODUCTION

Information technology (IT) has become a critical functionality of business today. Securing business assets related to network functionality in a manner that justifies cost has become critical to the business process. Choosing the appropriate network security for the business can be bewildering at best. It is well agreed that network security must be addressed, but the problem is deciding what to do and how much to do (Schneier, 2000). There is not a "one-size-fits-all" solution. For example, deciding how much security is needed to protect cash resources depends upon the perspective of the business. The hot dog vendor and the large bank on the same street corner both need to secure cash, but the level of need is very different for each business, as well as the resources available to implement the security solution. In today's business environment, where IT investments are subject to increasing cost-benefit analysis and justification (Lewis, 2001), the IT professional must be able to relate IT investments to business needs. The business professional must be able to relate the business needs to the IT investments. Therefore, a business value justification is needed to answer the question of what and how much.

Network security is an oxymoron. Networking means to share and connect, while security usually refers to shutting and locking the door. Establishing a relationship between these two opposing concepts provides a challenge within itself. To compound the difficulty for the business, the language that surrounds network security is usually shrouded with technical terms that are not well understood by the business community. In this paper, a proposal is made to map network security to business needs so that technical security experts are able to more readily understand how security issues fit the business needs and so that business experts can understand which technical security concepts will fit their business needs. The goal is to allow the security technical professional a way to implement a security solution that fits the needs of that business.

This paper is organized as follows. First, two classifications schemes are related to each other to establish an initial subjective mapping. Network security is described in terms of the OSI security architecture, and business activities are described using Porter's (1985) business value chain. Second, using a decision support tool, called analytic hierarchy process (AHP) (Saaty & Vargas, 2001), an initial analytical effort is examined that establishes priorities for security services that have been mapped to business needs. To the best understanding of the authors of this paper, this is the first time this methodology of using these two well-known classification schemes and AHP, a decision support tool, to relate them has been proposed. Last, future research plans are outlined. The end goal of this research is to establish a methodology that will allow the identification of network security that is needed and directly mapped to business value. Thus, the business professional would be able to define from a process level the business security needs; and the security engineer could then translate these process level descriptions into actionable steps.

BACKGROUND AND METHODS

How should businesses evaluate their individual security situations? Are all aspects of network security needed throughout all businesses, and are the levels of security needed at each part of the business the same? Should the needs of the most critical or important activities drive the network security design for the entire company? How should the resources available for network security be deployed so that the business is realizing the best value for its investment? These are questions that network security research needs to answer in relation to business activities. The first step in answering these questions is to establish a relationship between network security and business functions. Developing this relationship requires using generalized classification schemes for both network security and business that can be related to each other.

OSI Security Architecture, Services, and Mechanisms

Technological advances usually drive network security research, and the development of new technology is usually an ad hoc reaction to security problems. These processes are not usually driven by the need to relate security plans to business needs. To effectively develop a security plan that meets business needs, network security will have to be described in terms that are not dependent on technology or the occurrence of problems. The OSI security architecture provides such a generalized classification scheme. It describes five classes of security service and 13 different mechanisms to operationalize the services (Oppliger, 1998a; ISO, 1989), as listed in Tables 1 and 2. Open System Interconnect (OSI) is a well-accepted model developed by the International Standards Organization (ISO) to establish standards for the technical fields of computers, networking, and communications. ISO is a voluntary, nongovernment organization founded in 1947 with current membership from the national standards organizations of most countries in the world today (ISO, 2001). The ISO issues standards from those that cover detailed components, such as nuts and bolts, to high-level process concepts, such as the OSI Reference model that establishes communication processes between different network/communication systems. As part of that effort, a network security architecture was defined that described security services and the mechanisms to implement the services. Each service type has a unique conceptual definition. However, the actual functionality of each group overlaps, and each service is actualized by more than one mechanism (Table 3). The OSI network security architecture classification scheme presented in this paper allows organization in this field of study without bringing in the actual technology or product to implement the service. By grouping security services and mechanisms, disjoint and unrelated techniques and topics become part of a framework of understanding. It is beyond the scope of this paper to review in detail the ISO OSI Security Architecture. Interested readers are referred to Oppliger, (1998a) ISO, (1989) and ISO (2001).

Table 1: Classes of OSI Security Services (ISO, 1989; Oppliger, 1998a) with Selected Relevant Literature

Classes of OSI Security Services		
Services	**Definition**	**Selected Relevant Literature**
Authentication	Provide verification of the source of the communication	Feldmeir & Karn, 1990; Gong, 1993, 1990; Oppliger, 1996
Access Control	Provide protection against unauthorized use, used to enforce the rights granted to individuals or entities to access the system	Feldmeir & Karn, 1990; Morris & Thompson, 1979; Gong, et al., 1993; Bertino, Ferrari & Alturi, 1999
Confidentiality	Protect the ability to make information unavailable or undisclosed to unauthorized access by people, entities, or processes	Stubblebine, Syverson, & Goldschlag, 1999
Integrity	Provide protection so that data integrity is preserved, meaning that the data will not be altered in any unauthorized manner	Oppliger, 1998; Stallings, 2000; Chin, 1999; Jonsson et al., 1998; Falk & Trommer, 1998
Non-repudiation	Set up mechanisms to preclude one of the parties involved in a communication from later denying being involved in the communication	Oppliger, 1998; Stallings, 2000; Bowman, 2000

Table 2: OSI Security Mechanisms (ISO, 1989 & Oppliger, 1998a) with Selected Relevant Literature

OSI SPECIFIC Security Mechanisms		
Mechanism	**Definition**	**Selected relevant literature**
Encipherment	Also called encryption uses cryptographic techniques to protect the confidentiality of data units and traffic flow information	Stallings, 2000, Jerichow, et.al., 1998, Abadi and Needham, 1996, Garfinkel, 1996, , Blaze, et.al., 1996, Scheier, 1996, Diffie and Hellman, 1976
Digital signature	Appends data to a data unit that allows the receiver to prove the source and the integrity of the data unit and protect against forgery by the receiver	Birch, 1998, Oppliger, 1995, Bowman, 2000
Access control	Determine 'who and what' will access data, Allow access or deny access depending upon the rules previously established	Gong, et.al, 1993, Oppliger, 1997
Data integrity	Protect data units, selected fields within a data unit, or sequences of data units and fields within a communication	Oppliger, 1998a, Stallings, 2000, Fabian, 1998, Ahmed and Vrbsky, 1998
Authentication exchange	Allow the verification of the identities of the sender and receiver	Reiter and Stubblebine, 1999, Oppliger, 1996, Halevi and Krawczyk, 1998
Traffic padding	Protect against traffic analysis attacks	Oppliger, 1998a
Routing control	Techniques that determine the path of how a given data unit will reach its destination	Hauser, Przygiendo, and Tsudik, 1999
Notarization	Provides assurances of certain properties of data units. Trusted third party (TTP) provides the assurance in a testifiable manner	Oppliger, 1998a
OSI PERVASIVE Security Mechanisms		
Trusted functionality	General concept that can be used to extend the scope or to establish the effectiveness of other security mechanisms	Jacobs, 1999, Myerson, 1999, Scheider, 2000
Security labels	Associated with system resources and will indicate sensitivity levels required to maintain security of the data	Oppliger, 1998a
Event detection	Processes that enable the owner to know when violations occur	Messmer, 1999, Spatscheck and Peterson, 1999, Lane and Brodley, 1998
Security audit trail	Compiles records of system activities to ensure compliance with policy and procedures	Schneier and Kelsey, 1999, Kienzle and Wulf, 1997
Security recovery	Procedures to recover from an event	Stephenson, 2000

Authentication services provide verification of the source of the communication. Access control services provide protection against unauthorized use of the communication system and can be used to enforce system access rights. Confidentiality services are used to provide protection of the communication against unauthorized use. Authentication, access control, and confidentiality services are all well covered in the literature and represent areas that have been extensively researched. Integrity services provide protection so that the communication will not be altered in an unauthorized manner. Nonrepudiation services are those that set up mechanisms to preclude one of the parties involved in a communication from later denying being involved in the communication. Integrity and nonrepudiation services with the boom in e-commerce are in greater demand but have not been the subject of as much individual research (Table 1).

Much research has focused on the mechanisms that actually provide the security service (see Table 2). There are two broad categories of mechanisms, specific and pervasive, that put the above-mentioned services into operation. Specific mechanisms are those that describe a specific technique or process; whereas pervasive mechanisms describe a general process that applies to the overall communication system. Table 2 lists the specific mechanisms described by the OSI security architecture and definitions for each mechanism.

Relationship of Security Mechanisms to Security Services

Security services' functionalities overlap and are provided by many of the same mechanisms as illustrated by Table 3. For example, the mechanism of encipherment (encryption) is actually a broad classification of processes that can be used or needed by all of the security services to accomplish the purposes of each service. This contrasts with traffic padding, as it is a mechanism that is usually only invoked when confidentiality is needed.

Generally, most security services can use a multitude of mechanisms, depending upon the actual implementation of the service. The specific mechanisms chosen to actually implement the service will depend on the importance of the service to the business and how the service will be deployed.

Business Value Chain

Business value chain as defined by Porter (1985) provides an excellent classification mechanism (Figure 1) for identifying the business activities that should be used in setting priorities for network security. Porter's value chain breaks a business into its strategically relevant activities. The relevant activities can then be used to define the core competencies of any business or the source of differentiation between businesses. Inbound logistics are those activities associated with receiv-

Table 3: Relationship of Security Mechanisms to Security Services (Oppliger, 1998a). A "✓" in the Box Indicates that the Mechanism is Used or Needed by the Security Service.)

	Authentication	Access Control	Confidentiality	Integrity	Nonrepudiation
Encipherment	✓	✓	✓	✓	✓
Digital signature	✓	✓		✓	✓
Access control	✓	✓	✓		✓
Data integrity	✓				
Authentication exchange	✓			✓	✓
Traffic padding			✓		
Routing control		✓			
Notarization				✓	✓
Trusted functionality	✓	✓	✓	✓	✓
Security labels	✓	✓	✓	✓	✓
Event detection			✓	✓	
Security audit trail	✓		✓	✓	
Security recovery			✓	✓	

ing, storing, and disseminating inputs to product. Operations activities are associated with the transformation of input into final product. Outbound logistics, on the other hand, are associated with collecting, storing, and physically distributing product. Marketing and sales provides the means by which the buyer can purchase the product and induces them to purchase the product. Service activities provide service to enhance or maintain the value of the product. In any business these primary activities are supplemented by several support activities. Firm infrastructure is the general management, planning, finance, accounting, legal, governmental affairs, and quality management, cuttings across all primary activities. Human resource management activities are involved with recruiting, hiring, training, development, and compensation and support both primary and support activities of the business. Technology development activities are those efforts that improve the product and the process related to the product and its features. They can support the entire chain but can be associated with a particular primary or support activity. Procurement is the function of purchasing inputs used in the value chain. Interested readers are referred to Porter (1985) for a detailed discussion of this model.

Figure 1: Business Value Chain as Defined by Porter (1985)

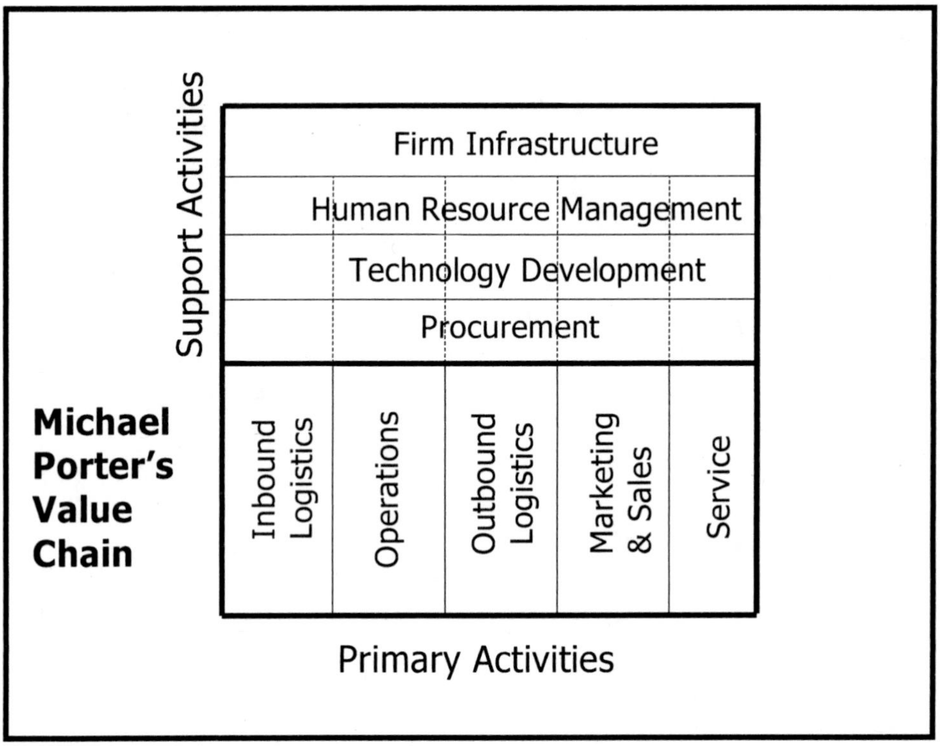

Comparison of Business Value Chain Activities and Security Services

An initial comparison of business chain primary and support activities with security services (Table 4) indicates that nearly all services are important at some level for almost all of the business activities.

Those activities focused outside the company, such as inbound and outbound logistics, seem to require a greater number of security services, as well as a higher level of services. Conversely, those activities associated primarily with internal business functions, operations, and possible service, seem to require fewer services and not as high a level of security. Certain internal business activities can require more services. For example, technology development, usually associated with

Table 4: Initial Pairing of Primary Business Value Chain Activities and Security Services. Low (L) indicates minimum need, Moderate (M) indicates that this service is needed to some level. High (H) means that this services is needed at the highest level.

Primary Activities	Inbound	Operations	Outbound	Marketing & Sales	Service
Authentication	M+	M	M+	M	M
Access Control	M+	M	M+	M	M
Confidentiality	M+	L	M+	M	M-
Integrity	M+	M	M+	M	L
Nonrepudiation	M+		M+	M	

Support Activities	Firm Infrastructure	Human Resource Management	Technology Development	Procurement
Authentication	M	M	M	M
Access Control	M-H	M-H	M-H	M
Confidentiality	L	M	M	M
Integrity	L	L	L	M
Nonrepudiation		L		

competitive advantage for the business, might require greater levels of confidentiality than other activities. In general, nonrepudiation security services are required for those activities associated with the exchange of product, money, and some human resource activities. However, arguments could also be made that all activities would require every service, perhaps with a different level of emphasis.

This initial evaluation of subjectively relating services to activities showed very similar results to that of relating services and mechanisms; most business activities could use most services. While providing a subjective comparison, this method proved to be insufficient to recommend or evaluate the type and level of security needed. Therefore, the next step is to analytically establish the priority of security services for each business activity, since from the subjective comparison, there was no clear distinguishable relationship.

Analytic Hierarchy Process (AHP)

A process that will analytically evaluate the priority of each security service to the different activities of the business to determine value is needed. To determine these priorities, we decided to examine the applicability of using a decision support process such as AHP. This section briefly reviews the AHP process and describes the initial attempt to use AHP to determine priorities.

AHP is a hierarchy process that involves both rational and intuitive input to recommend a solution from alternatives evaluated with respect to several criteria (Saaty & Vargas, 2001). In AHP, pairwise comparisons are made between criteria or alternatives to develop overall priorities for ranking decision alternatives. The reader is referred to Saaty and Vargas (2001) for a complete discussion of AHP. This process can be supported by one of many software packages, such as Expert Choice (1994), that have been created to automate the calculation of priorities from user-entered preferences.

Using AHP to Evaluate Priorities for Security Services

In the AHP hierarchy, the objective or goal is at the top, the criteria are on the next level, and the options or alternatives fall on the subsequent levels. The hierarchy used in this study (Figure 2) is a simple three-level hierarchy (Saaty & Vargas, 2001). On the top level, the goal of the decision was the question, "Which security services to select?" The second level consists of the business activities defined in the business value chain. Finally, security services are defined in the third level as the alternatives.

Usually, when using AHP, a series of alternatives or projects are defined. The goal is to facilitate a priority ranking of the alternatives. Each alternative is different with unique characteristics. In this application of AHP, the third-level alternatives are the same for each second-level activity, because the goal of this AHP application is to establish a ranking or priority for the same five security service alternatives for the entire business and each activity. The simple AHP model in Figure 2 can be presented to an organization to develop a preference profile of security services related to the business value chain activities (criteria). Next, the importance of the security services with respect to each value chain activity (alternatives) will be determined. Decision makers in an organization would be presented with options to perform pairwise comparisons among the services with respect to each activity. Individual preferences can then be aggregated into group preferences.

To illustrate the applicability of AHP to this problem, a pairwise comparison of the activities and services with respect to each activity separately was performed. The results for this initial AHP pairwise comparison of security services for inbound

Figure 2: AHP Hierarchy for Selecting Priority of Security Services for Each Activity of the Business Chain. (For each activity on the second level of the chart the third level of the five security services will be repeated.)

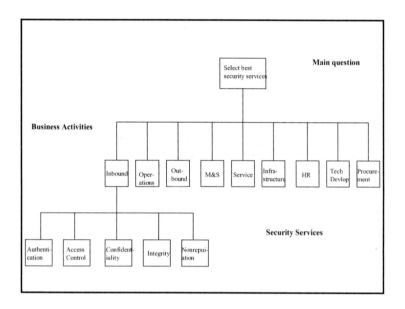

Table 5: Initial Pairwise Comparison of Security Services for the Inbound Business Activities Using the AHP Methodology. The top number indicates the rating for the service in the left column when compared to the service in the vertical column. For example, access control was rated as 2/1 when compared to confidentiality but a 1/ 2 when compared to integrity. Access control is twice as important than confidentiality for inbound activities.

INBOUND					
	Authentication	Access control	Confidentiality	Integrity	Non-repudiation
Authentication	1	1 / 1	1.5 / 1	1 / 1	1.3 / 1
Access control	1 / 1	1	2 / 1	1 / 2	2 / 1
Confidentiality	1 / 1.5	1 / 2	1	1 / 2	1 / 1.5
Integrity	1	2 / 1	2 / 1	1	1 / 1.5
Non-repudiation	1 / 1.3	1 / 2	1 / 1	1.5 / 1	1
Priority values	0.213	0.227	0.12	0.245	0.195

business activities are presented in Table 5. The rating of 1/1 means that the two items were considered of equal importance for that activity. A 2/1 rating means that the service in the left-hand column is considered twice as important as the service in the horizontal row. For example, access control was rated as 2/1 when compared to confidentiality, and as 1/2 when compared to integrity. Therefore access control was considered twice as important as confidentiality but only half as important as integrity.

Using this matrix (Table 5), priority values of the security services were calculated using the eigen values of the matrix. In the last row of Table 5 are the priority values for security services as related to inbound activities. For inbound activities, integrity has the highest priority value of .245, while confidentiality has the lowest of 0.12. The calculated priorities for each security service for each business activity are presented in Figure 3.

RESULTS OF THE AHP ANALYSIS

Using AHP and a three-level hierarchy (Figure 2) a pairwise comparison was done to establish the priority of the five security services for each business activity (Figure 3). In this evaluation for the business in general, authentication had the highest priority, whereas nonrepudiation had the lowest. Authentication was the highest priority for six out of nine activities; but for marketing and sales, nonrepudiation

Figure 3: Priorities for Security Services for the Primary and Support Activities of the Business Value Chain as Calculated by AHP Using the Initial Pairwise Comparisons

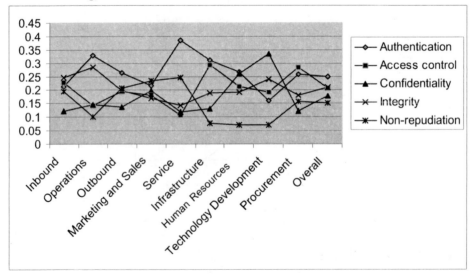

was rated as the highest priority. Nonrepudiation was the lowest for four other services. Confidentiality was the highest priority for technology development but was the lowest or second lowest for the other business activities. For the business in general, authentication has the highest priority with access control and integrity tied for second. Nonrepudiation services are the least important overall but the most important in marketing and sales.

Using this information, the technology professional can now design a security plan that fits the overall business needs. The plan could be customized for certain activities. For those functions that support marketing and sales, nonrepudiation services could be implemented, but other activities would not have to be burdened with nonrepudiation. Every activity would need authentication services, whereas technology development activities could benefit from greater confidentiality services.

SUMMARY

The main purpose of this paper was to define a process that would customize the security needs of an individual organization in a manner that is driven by the business activities of the organization. Two approaches were examined. First, by using a subjective comparison of two classification schemes, we showed that each part of the business might need or benefit from each security service on some level. The security service needed and level of service depends upon situation. For example, outside business activities require more services than those business activities focused within the organization.

Next, a process that would establish priorities was needed. Therefore, an analysis using AHP, a decision support tool, was conducted. Applying the AHP process to this problem allowed a set of priorities, driven by business needs, to be determined. Security service priorities for the entire business as well as for each business activity were then determined. Network security professionals can use this information to determine the appropriate network security services for each business activity and the overall organization.

Network security as a research discipline is in infancy stages (Kurose, 1999). There has been a lack of a cohesive, encompassing security solution (or set of common terms) that can be deployed in a widespread manner. This paper proposes a new approach to addressing this issue. Two well-known and accepted models, the OSI security architecture and Porter's Business Value Chain, establish a communication channel between the two disciplines. AHP creates a prioritization of the security services related to the business needs. While actual security implementation will still be done by those with the technological knowledge, this implementation will be closely tied to the business goals and should provide greater value to the business.

However, there are some limitations to this process that will need to be addressed in future research. By nature, this type of evaluation is very subjective and suffers from the bias of the decision maker. A respondent is asked to give an opinion about the importance of a security service. However, their response will be influenced by the individual's situation. Input should be gathered from several sources throughout the business so that an overall perspective can be gained.

A potential confusion that could be caused by this methodology relates back to the example of the hot dog vendor and large institutional banks that need to provide security for their cash assets. Both businesses could potentially establish identical priority ratings for the security services. However, the implementation of the security services for each business would be different. Security also has to be implemented within the budgetary constraints for each business.

Finally, the difference between internal and external security should be examined. Many experts contend that the greater security threat is from within the organization (Hurley, 1999). If that is the case, perhaps the level of services affecting internal activities should be higher than initially proposed.

CONCLUSIONS AND FUTURE RESEARCH

This methodology has shown that relating generalized classification schemes using a decision support tool can provide an effective way of determining network security needs that will create the best business value. Future plans for this research will first focus on expanding and developing the AHP hierarchy with a fourth layer, the security mechanisms. Second, this methodology will need to be validated by developing a case study. Third, the study should be expanded and generalized by a series of security projects that would include technological details. Last, while the initial intent of this research is to develop an a priori process to define network security needed by a business, this method could be expanded to a post-hoc technique for security auditing to identify missed or neglected security needs.

REFERENCES

Abadi, M. & Needham, R. (1996). Prudent engineering practice for cryptographic protocols, *IEEE Transactions on Software Engineering*, 22, 1, 96–15

Ahmed, Q. N. & Vrbsky, S. V. (1998). Issues in security for real-time databases. In *Proceedings of the ACM SE Conference*, 4, 297–299

Bertino, E., Ferrari, E. & Alturi, V. (1999). The specification and enforcement of authorization constraints in workflow management systems, *ACM Transactions on Information and Systems Security*, 2, 1, 65–104.

Birch, D. (1998) Smart solutions for net security, *Telecommunications, International Edition,* 32, 4, 53–56.

Blaze, M., Diffe, W., Rivest, R. L., Schneier, B., Shimomura, T., Thompson, E., & Wiener, M. (1996). Minimal key lengths for symmetric ciphers to provide adequate commercial security. Retrieved April 21, 1999 from the World Wide Web: http:/www.coutnerpane.com/keylength.html.

Bowman, L. M. (2000). E-signatures: signed, sealed, delivered, *ZDNet News*, Retrieved September 29, 2000 from the World Wide Web: http://www.zdnetnews.com/stories/news/0,4586,2634368,00.html.

Chin, S. K. (1999). High-confidence design for security, *Communications of the ACM*, 42, 7, 33–37.

Diffee, W., & Hellman, D. E. (1976). New directions in cryptography, *IEEE Transactions on Information Theory*, 22, 6, 644–654.

Dowd, P. W. & McHenry, J. T. (1998). Network Security: It's time to take is seriously, *IEEE Computer,* 9, 24–28.

Expert Choice Software. (1994). *Expert Choice Inc.*, Pittsburgh, PA.

Fabian, W. (1998). Beyond cryptography: Threats before and after. In *Proceedings Security Technology, 1998, 32nd Annual International Carnahan Conference*. 97–107. L.D. Sanson. ed. IEEE.

Falk, R., & Trommer, M. (1998). Managing network security—a pragmatic approach. In *Proceedings Reliable Distributed Systems, 17th Annual IEEE Symposium*. 398–402. IEEE.

Feldmeir, D. C. & Karn, P. R. (1990). UNIX password security—ten years later. In *Proceedings of CRYPTO '89*, 44–63.

Garfinkel, S. I., Public key cryptography, *Computer*, 6, 101–104.

Gong, L. (1990). Verifiable-test attacks in cryptographic protocols. In *Proceedings INFOCOM '90, 9th annual Joint Conference on the Computer and Communication Societies, the Multiple Facets of Integration*, 686–693. IEEE, 2.

Gong, L. (1993). Increasing availability and security of an authentication service, *IEEE Journal on Selected areas in Communications*, 11, 5, 657–662.

Gong, L., Lomas, M. A., Needham, R. A., & Saltzer, J. (1993). Protecting poorly chosen secrets from guessing attacks, *IEEE Journal on Selected Areas in Communications,* 11, 5, 648–656.

Halevi, S. & Krawczyk, H. (1998). Public-key cryptography and password protocols. In Proceedings of 5th Conference on Computer & Communications Security, San Francisco, CA, ACM. 122–131.

Hauser, R., Przygienda, T., & Tsudik, G. (1999). Lowering security overhead in link state routing, *Computer Networks*, 31, 8, 885–894.

Hurley, Hanna. (1999). Fear thyself, *Telephony,* 236, 25, 30.

ISO. (1989). ISO/IEC 7498–2, Information processing systems—*Open Systems Interconnection Reference Model - Part 2: Security Architecture.*

ISO. (2001). Referenced in (Nov, 2001), http://www.iso.org/iso/en/aboutiso/introduction/whatisISO.html.

Jacobs, S. (1999). Tactical network security. In *Proceedings Military Communications Conference, MILCOM 1999,* pp. 651–655. IEEE, 1.

Jerichow, A., Muller, J., Pfitzmann, A., Pfitzmann, B., & Waidner, M. (1998). Real-time mixes: a bandwidths-efficient anonymity protocol, *IEEE Journal on Selected Areas in Communications,* 16, 4, 495–509.

Jonsson, E., Stromberg, L., & Lindskog, S. (1999). On the functional relations between security and dependability impairments. In *Proceedings from the 1999 New security Paradigm Workshop, Sept, 1999,* pp. 104-111. Ontario, Canada, ACM.

Kienzle, D., & Wulf, W. A. (1997). A practical approach to security assessment, in *proceedings New Security Paradigms Workshop, Langdale, Cumbria,* pp. 5-16. UK, ACM.

Lane, T., & Brodley, C. E. (1998). Temporal sequence learning and data reduction for anomaly detection. In *Proceedings for the 5th Conference on Computer & Communications Security.* pp. 150-158. San Francisco, CA, ACM.

Lewis, D.(2001). Top execs rein in CIOs, Retrieved July 20, 2001 from the World Wide Web: www.internetweek.com/newslead01/lead071301.htm.

Messmer, E. (1999). Network intruders, *Network World,* 16, 40, 67–68.

Morris, R. & Thompson, K. (1979). Password security: a case history, *Communications of the ACM,* 22, 594–597

Myerson, J. (1999). Risk management, *International Journal of Network Management,* 9, 305–308.

Nerurkar, U. (2000). Security analysis and design, *Dr. Dobb's Journal,* 11, pp. 50–56.

Nichols, R. K., Ryan, D. J., & Ryan, J. J. C. H. (2000). *Defending your digital assets against hackers, crackers, spies, and thieves,* New York: McGraw-Hill

Oppliger, R., (1999a). *Security Technologies for the World Wide Web,* Norwood, MA: Artech House.

Oppliger, R. (1999b). Shaping the research agenda for security in e-commerce. In *Proceedings Database and Expert Systems Applications, 1999, 10th International Workshop.* pp. 810-814. IEEE

Oppliger, R. (1995). Internet security enters the middle ages, *Computer,* October, 10, 100-101.

Oppliger, R. (1996). *Authentication Systems for Secure Networks,* Norwood, MA: Artech House.

Oppliger, R. (1997). Internet Security: Firewalls and Beyond, *Communications of the ACM,* 40, 5, 92–102.

Oppliger, R. (1998a). *Internet and Intranet Security,* Norwood, MA: Artech House.

Oppliger, R. (1998b). Security at the Internet Layer, *IEEE,* 9. 43-47

Porter, M. (1985). *Competitive advantage, creating and sustaining superior performance,* New York: The Free Press, Macmillan, Inc.

Reiter, M. K. & Stubblebine, S. G. (1999). Authentication metric analysis and design, *ACM Transactions on Information and System Security,* 2, 138–158

Saaty, T. L. & Vargas, L. G. (2001) *Models, methods, concepts and applications of the analytic hierarchy process,* Norwell, MA: Kluwer Academic Publishers

Scheider, F. B. (2000). Enforceable Security Policies, *ACM Transactions on Information and System Security,* 3, 1, 30–50.

Schneier, B. (1999). Risks of relying on cryptography, *Communications of the ACM,* 42, 10, 144.

Schneier, B. (2000). *Secrets & Lies: Digital Security in a Networked World,* New York: John Wiley & Sons

Schneier, B. & Kelsey, J. (1999). Secure audit logs to support computer forensics, *ACM Transactions on Information and System Security,* 2, 2, 159–176.

Spatscheck, O. & Peterson, L. L. (1999). Defending against denial of service attacks in SCOUT. In *Proceedings USENIX Association, 3rd Symposium on Operating Systems Design and Implementation (OSDI '99),* pp. 59–72.

Stallings, W. (2000). *Network security essentials: applications and standards,* Upper Saddle River: Prentice-Hall.

Stephenson, P. (2000). *Investigating Computer-Related Crime,* Boca Raton, FL: CRC Press.

Stubblebine, S. G., Syverson, P. F., & Goldschlag, D. (1999). Unlinkable serial transactions: protocols and applications, *ACM Transactions on Information and System Security,* 2, 4, 354–389.

Chapter X

Increasing Business Value of Communications Infrastructure: The Case of Internet-Based Virtual Private Networks

Bongsik Shin
San Diego State University, USA

Daniel C. Kinsella, Jr.
Deloitte & Touch LLP, USA

An Internet-based Virtual Private Network (IVPN) is a system and service that enables secure communication within a controlled user group across the Internet public infrastructure. For the last few years, the Internet-based VPN has been available, providing organizational use for meaningful applications. The paper empirically investigates the value of IVPNs in managing communications among distributed business entities. For this, we conducted two case studies based on the information gathered from two companies. Then, a general decision model of the IVPN is proposed, which could be used for the assessment of its strategic value as well as for the design of virtual telecommunication networks at other organizations.

INTRODUCTION

In today's information age, companies are realizing that in order to retain a competitive advantage, they must capitalize on advanced data communication capabilities. Efficient, reliable, and secure communications among business partners, suppliers, customers, and investors are vital for a company to obtain increased productivity and business competency. Rapid increase in virtual processing at business organizations further highlights the importance of quality communication networks (Chesbrough & Teece, 1996; Davenport & Pearlson, 1998; Davidow & Malone, 1992).

The spread of virtual processing is taking place in both intra- and interorganizational relationships as a measure to remain competitive and resilient in the marketplace. Omnipresence of virtual offices (i.e., telework, mobile work), diffusion of distributed enterprise resource planning and work-flow management, and the emergence of network corporation represent intraorganizational virtual processes. Electronic data interchange (EDI), extranets, and integrated supply-chain/procurement management represent interorganizational virtual process. Maintaining a communication network that effectively connects virtual components becomes a key business success factor.

In order to conduct high quality communications and virtual process management, many businesses have traditionally purchased or leased private lines between the company headquarters and their branches. Others utilize conventional dial-up resources to maintain connectivity and/or remote access both within the United States and overseas. As a third alternative, businesses increasingly use the Internet for communications, marketing, and for conducting transactions with customers and suppliers. Nonetheless, one of the main obstacles that prevents companies from jumping onboard the Internet is a lack of confidence in the security and quality of transmissions. Considering that the Internet is the largest Wide Area Network (WAN) in the known universe, and that secure and stable network capability is critical for business transactions, technologies have been developed to improve the integrity of data transmissions over the Internet. This is known as the Internet-based Virtual Private Network (IVPN). It is a system and service that enables secure communication within a controlled user group, across the Internet.

The paper investigates the business value of IVPNs on organizational communication. First, we review existing literature to discuss primary technical issues and potential business benefits and risks of the technology. Second, two case studies are conducted to illustrate implications in managing communications among distributed business entities. Information was gathered from two companies through interviews and the review of documentation. Lastly, we present a decision model of the IVPN, which could be used for the assessment of its strategic value and for the design of virtual telecommunication networks in organizations.

LITERATURE REVIEW

Internet-Based VPN

VPNs are well-established wide area network (WAN) services that have been available through privately owned service networks (i.e., ISDN, Frame Relay, and ATM) since the early 1990s. For years, despite several benefits such as the real-time availability of billing and accounting information and increased security, the main disadvantage of private VPN services has been their high cost. With the growth of the Internet; however, a very different form of VPN has emerged. The IVPN has attained industry attention because of its cost effectiveness and flexibility for supporting distributive, mobile, and virtual networks in a scalable manner.

In the IVPN, "virtual" implies that the network is created in a dynamic manner, with connections set up according to organizational needs. Unlike those on leased-lines links, the IVPN does not maintain permanent connections between the endpoints that make up the corporate network. Instead, a connection is created between two sites when it is needed. When the connection is no longer needed, it is torn down, making bandwidth and other network resources available for other uses. "Virtual" also means that the logical structure of the network is comprised of the network devices, regardless of the physical structure of the underlying network (the Internet in this case).

Hiding the Internet Service Provider and Internet infrastructure from IVPN applications is made possible by a concept called tunneling (Garrison, 1998). Tunneling, the packaging one of network packet (the tunneled packet) inside another (the transport), is at the heart of all IVPN implementations. Tunneling allows streams of data and associated user information to be transmitted over a shared network within a virtual pipe. This pipe makes the routed network totally transparent to users. To create a tunnel, the source end encapsulates its packets in IP packets for transit across the Internet. The encapsulation may include encrypting the original packet and adding a new IP header. At the receiving end, the gateway removes the IP header and decrypts the packet if necessary, forwarding the original packet to its destination.

Tunnels can consist of two types of endpoints, either an individual computer or a LAN with a security gateway, which might be a router or a firewall. Only two combinations of these endpoints are usually considered in designing IVPNs. In the first case, *LAN-to-LAN* tunneling, a security gateway at each endpoint, serves as the interface between the tunnel and the private LAN. All the traffic on each LAN is unchanged. Once traffic passes through the IVPN device on the edge of the LAN, it is encrypted and tunneled to a similar device at the second site. At that point, it is decrypted and put onto the LAN in native format. The second case, that of *client-to-LAN*, is the type usually set up for a mobile user who wants to connect to the corporate LAN. The client initiates the creation of the tunnel on his/her end in order to exchange traffic with the corporate network. To do so the client runs special client software on his/her computer to communicate with the gateway protecting the destination LAN. In this scenario, the devices at each end of the connection must handle the establishment of the tunnels and encrypt and decrypt the data passed between the two points.

IVPN solutions can be mostly applied into three types of internet-working scenarios: Intranet IVPN, remote access IVPN, and extranet IVPN (Kovac, 1999). Intranet IVPN involves connectivity between a corporation and its branch offices over the Internet. Normally, both ends (branch offices) of the IVPN are considered safe and reliable; therefore, these LAN-to-LAN connections are assumed to have minimal security risk. This allows the IVPN solution to focus on improving speed and performance more than encryption or authentication.

Remote Access IVPNs are designed to support corporations who have traveling employees who must transmit information back to the branch offices or to the headquarters building. Many companies are realizing that leased lines and dial-up access are expensive and difficult to manage for mobile workers. Remote access IVPNs let traveling employees make use of the worldwide Internet as a backbone for reaching back to their office. Remote Access IVPNs are easier to implement and maintain than more traditional modem pools or faxing approaches.

Extranet IVPNs are also referred to as "business-to-business" VPNs. While intranets are somewhat isolated and involve trusted endpoints, extranets are intended to reach business partners, customers, and suppliers. These models require an enhanced hierarchy of security so that well-defined access to specific resources can be granted to consultants or trading partners. Extranet IVPNs must be interoperable with a variety of applications (including legacy), platforms, and protocols that reside in the destination's computing environment.

Strategic Benefits

The primary driver toward IVPN technologies is cost savings. It is said that IVPNs decrease costs related with communications system equipments, administration, maintenance, network management, and communication itself (Brown, 1999; Kosiur, 1998; Yuan, 1999). In many enterprises today, users are communicating across wide areas over leased lines or via traditional remote access from a long-distance carrier network. While these technologies can provide sufficient access control and protection of data, they come at a large cost. Leasing costs and long-distance carrier charges far exceed the cost of monthly Internet service packages (Aventail, 1999; Becker & Machler, 2000). When a company has many mobile workers or many branch offices globally, cost savings from IVPN usage become more significant, because the Internet is typically priced based upon access speed (Kosiur, 1998). However, there could be hidden costs and technical obstacles that limit IVPN success (King, 1999).

Table 1 summarizes existing literature that compared between IVPN services and others in terms of monthly operational cost. Cost-savings show a great deal of

Table 1: Monthly Cost Effects of an IVPN, RAS: remote access services, FR: frame relay service, Network scope: S - number of sites, U—number of users.

Cost $ (thousand/year)		Cost	Network	
Private Lines	IVPN	Savings	Scope	Assumptions
9.3 (T-1)	3.8	59%	3 (S)	- 3 sites are Boston, NYC, and DC - Single leased line, not meshed -Exclude local loops and support personnel costs
71 (T-1)	17	76%	10 (S)	- Connects SF, Denver, Chicago, NYC, LA, Salt Lake, Dallas, Minneapolis, DC, and Boston - Hub-and-spoke network design - Regional hubs: SF, Denver, Chicago, NYC
Source : Kosiur (1998)				
15 (RAS)	7	54%	100 (U)	- 30 home work (10 hrs/month), local call - 70 mobile work (30 hrs/month), toll call (10c/min)
37 (RAS)	21	43%	400 (U)	- 200 home work (20 hrs/month), local/toll call - 200 mobile work (5 hrs/month), international call (30c/min)
Source: Phifer (2001)				

40 (RAS)	17	57.5%	500 (U)	- 50%: mobile worker, 10%: telecommuter, 40% day extender
				- Usage: mobile worker: 30min/day
				  telecommuter: 240 min/day
				  day extender: 30 min/day
				- Line cost: US tool average: 8c/min
				  International average: 60c/min

Source: Indus River Networks (1998)				
14 (T-1)	11.4	12%	5 (S)	
Source: Munroe (2000)				
12 (FR)	8.6-12.5	28- 0%	15(S)	- Remote site access: 56/64k ($200) - Headquarter access: T-1 ($700)
Source: Nortel Networks (2000)				

variation depending on the scope of virtual connections and research assumptions. However, they consistently indicate IVPN's positive impact on communications cost.

A second benefit involving IVPNs is increased flexibility to an organization. IVPN can offer better virtual process management through improved customer service and corporate reach (Kosiur, 1998). An IVPN offers anywhere, anytime, and any-to-any connectivity (Nortel, 2000). As the global economy becomes more competitive and corporations depend more frequently on digital communications, the need to communicate quickly with multiple partners becomes a critical issue. Today, many companies may extend their corporate networks to partners and customers via leased lines or frame relay networks. These technologies; however, require long lead times for carriers (particularly in the third world nations) to provide access to corporate partners and customers.

Another strength of IVPNs is its scalability. Corporate reach can be expanded easily, because adding additional suppliers or customers to the virtual network is unlimited in the Internet (Ryan, 2000). This capacity leads to high usage and connection rates and the growth of the user population. Kosiur (1998) defined IVPN's scalability from two different dimensions: geographic scalability means the capacity of an IVPN that can grow beyond any geographical limit because of Internet's ubiquity; and bandwidth scalability means that links between client sites and ISPs can grow independently as needed (i.e., 56kbps modem, ISDN, DSL and T-1).

Also, an IVPN can become a major vehicle for promoting e-commerce (Becker & Machler, 2000; Kosiur, 1998). E-commerce is rapidly emerging as a dominant paradigm for business operations and transactions. As business interconnectivity becomes essential, being connected to the Internet is the logical choice for corporations that expect a broader use of corporate e-business applications (Ryan, 2000). Private networks, with a closed, inflexible private network infrastructure, are not well suited for supporting e-commerce for consumers and B2B partners.

An important e-commerce application of IVPNs is electronic data interchange (EDI) that involves real-time transmission of electronic documents among business partners. Corporations that could not afford EDI on expensive private networks (i.e., value added networks or VANs) can do it now through the Internet (Kosiur, 1998). EDI, in conjunction with IVPNs, make information exchange among business partners global and seamless and allow companies to restock products quickly and sell products faster. Additionally, stronger strategic relationships between organizations can result from a simple and secure exchange of data. IVPNs that combine the flexibility of the Internet and high security of private networks enable corporations to do business online (Munroe, 2000).

While an IVPN can bring about many benefits, there may be some disadvantages as well. Above all, IVPNs depend upon the speed, reliability, and performance of the Internet, which may lower quality of services (QoS). QoS is a major concern for companies who are considering IVPN implementation because of systemic problems with today's Internet infrastructure such as congestion and dropped packets (Bosemark, 1999). The QoS requirement would become even more important as organizations begin using next-generation applications such as distance learning, video conferencing, and other multimedia applications. While ISPs are upgrading their infrastructure, many customers have alternative views as to whether these upgrades will be sufficient to improve IVPN QoS.

Another main concern in deploying IVPNs involves data security (Ryan, 2000). The "private" in the IVPN means that a tunnel between two users appears as a private link, even if it is running over the public Internet. "Private" also implies security, that is, freedom from prying eyes and tampering using tunneling, access control, encryption, and user authentication. Despite IVPNs' built-in capacity to develop trust among involved parties, the lack of guaranteed information security over the Internet itself is currently a risk factor for business owners who desire to have reliable communications.

CASE STUDIES

In this section, we discuss two real-world examples of organizations planning to use IVPN solutions to solve business needs. Information was gathered through interviews and the review of company documentation. At the request of interviewees, we used fictional company names. The first case, Ocean Technologies Group, demonstrates *LAN-to-LAN* IVPN connections, and the second case, United Trucking Co., describes a future plan for *LAN-to-Client* IVPN implementation.

Ocean Technologies Group: LAN-to-LAN Case

Ocean Technologies Group (OceanTech), headquartered in the US, is a producer of outdoor products, and their main focus is on fishing equipment. The organization grosses over $50 million in revenue and has approximately 1400 employees worldwide. OceanTech owns subsidiaries in eleven countries around the world (mostly in Europe). Each subsidiary produces different products, such as fishing line and rods, and they all add up to the comprehensive line of fishing products that OceanTech offers to its customers.

OceanTech is not a stranger to cutting-edge technology. OceanTech got into EDI at a very early stage. Several of OceanTech's major customers are massive retailers including Wal-Mart and K-Mart. These customers helped (nearly forced all of their suppliers) OceanTech grow into EDI at an early stage. OceanTech is also heavily into Web technology, hosting e-commerce sites and securing them with firewalls. OceanTech's newest technology implementation was the arrival of enterprise resource planning package that embraced the entire organization from accounting to human resources. When this package was fully implemented, OceanTech's goal was to interconnect all of their subsidiaries onto the same system, hence, the problem of interconnecting highly distributed sites.

Although OceanTech is a technology-based company, by no means are they loose with the money spent on IT. The IT department drives the computer environment for the entire organization, and IT fills a definite business purpose, but OceanTech does not simply get a new technology to try something new. The IT group at OceanTech also faces the risk that they may be outsourced if they are not efficient. This stems from the fact that they do not do any program development themselves. The IT group merely provides support for vendor-purchased packages that have undergone few changes. Therefore, the director of IT is always looking to add value to the organization through efficient use of information technology.

When the issue of telecom connectivity came about, the topic of an IVPN came up. If the organization were to secure dedicated lines using a private WAN service, it would be extremely expensive due to the distance the subsidiaries are from each other. For example, subsidiaries in Taiwan, Switzerland, and Australia would require long-haul connections. Lines stretching across the world to its US headquarters in the Midwest would be extremely expensive, and OceanTech was looking for a cheaper way to provide connectivity. With its interest in IVPN technology, the company sent their network manager to training for one week that covered different IVPN technologies and services.

Figure 1 shows an organization connecting using dedicated lines and that same organization using an IVPN structure. We can easily see that an IVPN reduces the complexity of the system, because each LAN only needs access to the Internet through the use of an ISP (Figure 1 b). This is one connection per site as opposed to several in the fully meshed example (Figure 1 a). In OceanTech's case, the home office is already connected through a T1 line. The other subsidiaries already have some type of Internet connection at this time as well. Therefore, the only step missing is software that needs to be placed at the home office and each subsidiary location to facilitate the use of IVPN. For the home office, the Firewall-1 product that is already in place can run the necessary software that will allow the creation of an IVPN with its subsidiaries.

The IVPN-based virtual connections enable the entire company to become integrated and have real-time interactions across country borders. The integration of enterprise resource planning system with an IVPN allows the subsidiaries to utilize the same system as the home office. This eases foreign currency translation

Figure 1: Fully Meshed LAN-to-LAN Connection (Leased Line vs. IVPN)

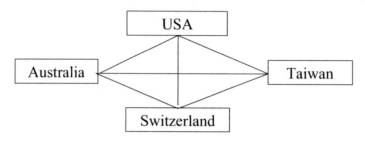

a. Fully Meshed Leased Line Network

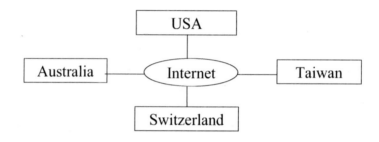

b. Fully Meshed IVPN Network

and streamlines production for customers. Order fulfillment can also be integrated across the system. For example, when an order is placed at headquarters, instead of creating a whole new transaction for each subsidiary that must fill part of the order, one transaction can be created, and the system facilitates the fulfillment of that order across the globe.

Of course, security was a big issue for OceanTech. Confidential documents are frequently sent thousands of miles across public networks. This is why OceanTech spent the time up front to determine which VPN service best suits the organization. To ensure a proper implementation, OceanTech trained important people on IVPN technology. OceanTech felt it was better to spend preparation time than to remove the technology later because of unexpected problems.

Currently, all locations are on the IVPN through UUNET, one of the largest Internet backbone service providers in the world. For the dedicated Internet connections to UUNET, the company is paying approximately $1,000 for all locations. This is in addition to $1000 for 128 kbps in Europe and $1100 for T-1 line (1.54 Mbps) in the US for local connections. IVPN software cost the company $4,000 in Europe and $20,000 in the US. It was estimated that the maintenance cost for each piece of software was 10 percent of the original cost. Such up-front cost, nonetheless, was expected to be recovered relatively soon, because connecting all locations using popular but proprietary dedicated services such as frame relay could cost the company $15,000 to $20,000 per month.

Once the IVPN was set up at the company, it became very stable in administration and network management. Management of the IVPN is centralized so that remote locations all have to go through the same location. It was learned that the key for the IVPN success was to have a good Internet provider for reliable connections. IVPN's quality of service as the major concern in terms of speed, accuracy, accessibility, and reliability of transmission has been very good. The backbone provides the company fast connections, and the scalability and flexibility of networking has been great with UUNET. Guaranteed latency and reliability for connections are offered by UUNET through service level agreements and standard access across all locations. The president of the company was pleased with the performance of IVPN communication.

United Trucking Company: LAN-to-Client Case

United Trucking Company is a carrier organization that is headquartered in Nebraska. United's primary business is short-haul trucking. Typically, they are an LTL (less-than-truckload) carrier, grossing several million in revenue and having thousands of employees. These two items in combination mean that United hauls loads for several organizations at one time and makes stops along the way for several customers dropping off and picking up freight along the path. Their whole revenue stream is based on what the trucking industry calls a trip. A trip number is given for each order of freight (trip) a customer has. For example, if a truck leaves the home office with ten different delivery stops and picks up and drops off 35 more stops before returning to the home office, every product that was picked up and delivered somewhere else must have a trip sheet.

Currently, United delivers only to the continental United States and focuses on the Midwest and Western states. United has approximately 40 terminals, where trucks stop to be serviced and where freight is loaded and unloaded to ensure efficient delivery. These terminals have their own computer systems, but they do not have a computer connection with the home office.

The billing cycle cannot be initiated until the hard copies of the trip sheets are brought back to the office. When a truck leaves, sometimes the driver and the truck do not return for 2 weeks. This means that something may be delivered today and not billed for another 2 weeks. A financial comparison does justice at this point. United creates approximately $100,000 of business per day. If the cost of capital is assumed 10 percent, United is taking an average of 10 days of revenue loss in the current situation. After doing the math ($100,000 * 10 * 10%), approximately $100,000 is being lost annually. Theoretically, United could spend ($100,000/12) $8,333 per month on the IVPN and break even.

United needed a way to get trip sheets back to the home office faster. Also, a secure approach is needed, because the trip sheets many times contain confidential information for both United and their customers. Simply e-mailing the trip sheets is not feasible due to the nature of United's industry and the intricacies of their accounting system.

As stated above, although the terminals have computers, they were not interconnected with the home office. United looked into many technologies, mainly frame relay for wide area network connections. However, the organization realized that frame relay connections to every terminal would be extremely expensive. The cost would be unbearably high for an organization the size of United. United was looking for a low-cost, secure way to send electronic documents to increase cash flow and significantly speed-up the revenue cycle, hence, the IVPN surfaced.

United has decided that an IVPN technology would work nicely in their circumstance. The setup for United will be similar to the architecture Figure 2 displays. The left side of the figure will be the home office, and the right side will be all of the terminals that will link to the home office using an IVPN. The home office will be linked to the Internet through a dedicated connection, probably a T1 connection, and the terminals will be linked to the Internet through dial-up ISP connections.

United is almost sold on IVPN products and services from IBM. This product would require ISP connections, which would cost about $20 per month per site. Local ISPs (ISPs that do not require their users to dial long-distance and pay long-

Figure 2: LAN-to-Client Configuration

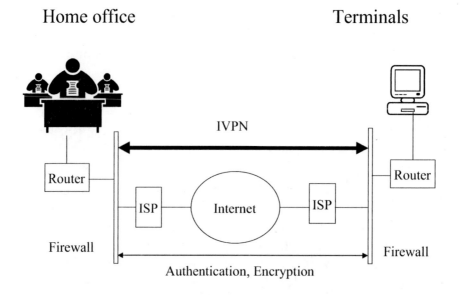

distance fees to connect to the Internet) are available nearly in every area around the country. This figures to be approximately $800 for the ISP service each month plus the cost of the product from IBM global services. The IBM products will probably consist of a fairly large firewall application for the home office, and a lightweight firewall application for each terminal. If a small firewall cost $200 for each terminal and United purchased a $1000 package for the home office, the total start-up costs would be $9,000. After the initial purchase, the only ongoing fee would be for the ISP connection and to IBM for each IVPN use.

IBM's IVPN products use IPSec, which is a standard created to add security to TCP/IP networking. This open technology provides cryptography-based protection at the IP layer and requires no changes to existing applications. United's transfers will be protected in three ways using cryptography. First, authentication will be used to identify end points in the system. Next, integrity checking is done to ensure nothing was tampered with while in transit. Finally, the information is encrypted so it is unintelligible during transit.

The actual approach United will use is called a branch-office-connection network. Small eNetwork (IBM, 1999) standalone firewalls, firewalls on routers, or even a firewall on a PC is used to act as the boundary between the terminal or the home office and the Internet. With this solution, the client and server computers would not even need to support IPSec technology, since the firewalls could provide the security using IPSec. All pricing issues could be secured from untrusted users, and attackers could also be fended off. United may also choose to utilize additional management functions available from eNetwork, such as policy management, certificate management, and secure domain name system (IBM, 1998).

As digital phones and handheld devices begin to delve into the Web, a secure mode will be needed to transfer items over wireless networks in a secure fashion. For United, this may eventually be systems on each truck that can send trip sheets back immediately after delivery from the driver while he or she is going to the next stop.

AN INTERNET-VPN DECISION MODEL

. These real-world examples provide a vision of benefits an IVPN can bring to an organization. The examples all portray the IVPN in a good light. However, organizations that use the technology are taking risks, and risk may sometimes lead to loss. Although the researchers of this paper could not find any specific examples of organizations facing losses due to the IVPN, there certainly are instances where this has occurred. For instance, although use of the Internet is expected to substantially lower the cost of creating networks, the existence of hidden cost was also reported (King, 1999).

A decision model of an IVPN is proposed as an evaluation tool for benefits and risks the technology may incur at a particular organization (Figure 3). In the model, the decision of IVPN adoption essentially rests on the tradeoff between risks and returns of the technology. We can think of many risk factors of an IVPN. They may be classified into three categories: technology challenges including client deployment, technical integration, and central manageability; overhead costs such as setup, administration, and management; and business risks including reliability, information security, performance, and other quality of service (QoS) factors (Brown, 1999; King, 1999; Kosiur, 1998). In the meantime, an IVPN can offer organizations various strategic values mainly in the form of service flexibility, scalability, e-commerce potentials, and communication cost-savings (Kosiur, 1998; Ryan, 2000).

Besides the risk and return factors, we suggest that contextual factors should be weighed. The arrows in Figure 3 indicate either facilitating or inhibiting roles of contextual factors for the IVPN endeavor. Among many possible contextual factors, availability of corporate policy on network and supportive network infrastructure is crucial (Brown, 1999). Any organization considering the deployment of an IVPN should have developed an elaborate policy on network and security plans, because the success of the IVPN solution is partially conditioned by

Figure 3: Internet VPN Decision Model

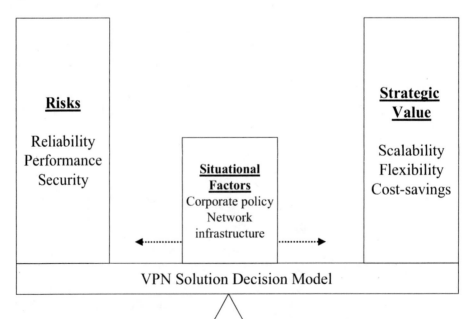

their validity and integrity (Indus River Networks, 1998). Corporate policies should govern the use of a network and all corresponding resources. These include network management (i.e., membership, access points), cost thresholds, and security strategy (i.e., physical infrastructure, human factors, audit trails, authentication, and encryption) (Brown, 1999; Indus River Networks, 1998).

There are also network infrastructure issues that directly or indirectly affect IVPN's effectiveness. For example, capabilities of current routing, security devices (i.e., firewalls), remote access servers, and modem banks in integrating IVPN should be considered (Kosiur, 1998). Ryan (2000) emphasized capabilities of ISPs in supporting reliable IVPN setup and operation.

Organizations must weigh the risks and rewards of using the IVPN system, keeping in mind that every organization is different. Success for one company may not spell success in another instance. OceanTech did a thorough analysis to determine if the IVPN was secure enough for their purposes. All companies will have to perform these types of analyses to ensure that the IVPN is the right choice. For instance, if a risk analysis proves that the money saved outweighs any potential losses caused by security breach or loss of performance, the IVPN is probably the right choice. While this is a simple depiction, this model presents a starting block for assessing the applicability of an IVPN. Organizations need to use a model such as the one below to assess how and if the IVPN fits in their strategy. In the meantime, as the IVPN becomes less risky with increased security, we expect that the Internet will increasingly become a larger portion of the communication backbone for the business world.

CONCLUDING REMARKS

The future of the IVPN is promising. Despite the technical difficulties and other threats, potential cost savings and other strategic values of the technology will be great enough to encourage many companies to at least perform a study to determine if the IVPN would work in their environment. IVPNs are no longer only feasible for organizations that have cutting-edge, risk-taking IT departments. Major telecom service providers are packaging the IVPN so it can be easily purchased and installed by many organizations.

We expect that IVPNs will have a bigger role as organizational design and operations become more distributed. Because of the intensifying competition among market players, businesses will be forced to do advanced virtual processing. Individuals will have to process transactions and do businesses in dynamic, virtual, and seamless manners. Employees will be asked to work on a project unhampered by temporal and spatial limitations. Efficiency, reliability, and security of communication among the virtual and distributed components will naturally become vital for the success of a business. On the other hand, as communication products become cheaper and more widely adopted, the role and capability of the Internet will expand even further. Although security will always be an issue due to the public nature of the Internet, the case studies confirmed the great potential of the IVPN as an effective vehicle to manage communications at a low cost. On the other hand, we believe that as IVPNs are becoming more secure, other factors such as throughput are expected to play a bigger role in the adoption of IVPN technology.

REFERENCES

Aventail Co. *Extranet VPNs: Paving the Way for E-Business.* Retrieved February 27, 1999, from http://www.aventail.com/index.phtml/solutions/white_papers/ebusiness.phtml.

Becker, M. & Machler, G. (Jan. 2000). Virtual Private Networks for the Enterprise, *Enterprise Systems Journal,* 38–43.

Bosemark, C. (1999). Quality Counts: But how to sell it? *Telecommunications International Edition*, 33(8), 24–33.

Brown, S. (1999). *Implementing Virtual Private Networks*, McGraw Hill.

Chesbrough, H. & Teece, D. J. (1996). When is virtual virtuous? Organizing for innovation, *Harvard Business Review*, 74(1), 65–73.

Davenport, T. H. & Pearlson, K. (1998). Two cheers for the virtual office, *Sloan Management Review*, 39(4), 51–65.

Davidow, W. H. & Malone, M.S. (1992). *The Virtual Corporation*, HarperCollins, New York.

Garrison, S. (1998). "'Virtual' is Key Word in Virtual Private Networking," *AS/400 Systems Management,* 26(10), 14-16.

IBM Global Services. (1998). *Internet Infrastructure*, Retrieved February 8, 1999, from http://www.ibm.com/globalnetwork/pr150299.htm.

IBM Global Services. (1999). *IBM Expands Virtual Private Network Portfolio for Intranet, Extranet, and E-Business Applications*, Retrieved February 18, 1999, from http://www.ibm.com/globalnetwork/pr150299.htm.

Indus River Networks Inc. (1998). *A Closer Look at Remote Access: Can Your Organization Benefit from VPNs?* Retrieved January 7, 2002, from http://www.adimpleo.com/library/indusrvr/wpaper.pdf.

King, C. M. (1999). Why aren't VPNs taking over? *Business Communications Review*, 29(6), 46–54.

Kosiur, D. (1998). *Building and Managing Virtual Private Networks*, Wiley.

Kovac, R. (Apr. 1999). *VPN basics.* Communications News.

Munroe, C. (2000). *Internet Growth Fuels IP VPN Growth: Corporate Confidence Increases in Lease Line Alternative.* Retrieved December 19, 2001, from http://www2.uu.net/products/uusecure/vpn/whitepapers/idcvpn1.pdf.

Nortel Networks. *Taking Care of Business—The Evolution from Frame Relay to IP VPN.* Retrieved December 19, 2001, from http://www.nortelnetworks.com.

Phifer, L. (1999). *Calculating Return on Investment for Remote Access VPNs.* Retrieved December 19, 2001, from http://www.isp-planet.com/technology/vpn-roi1.html.

Ryan, J. (2000). Managing the Costs and Complexities of VPN Deployment, *The Technology Guide Series.* Retrieved January 7, 2002, from http://www.techguide.com.

Yuan, R. (1999). Securing Your VPN, *Telecommunications, American Edition*, 33(8), 47–50.

Chapter XI

An Optimization Model for Telecommunication Systems

Bahador Ghahramani
University of Nebraska at Omaha, USA

The Optimization Model for Telecommunication Systems (OMTS) is designed and developed to optimize System Designers and Developers (SD&D) efforts in the Telecommunication Industry (TI). Using the life-cycle process, OMTS continuously evaluates business value and utility of every activity in the systems design and development process. The primary objective of the OMTS is to increase business value of the TI system and improve their performance. Through OMTS, SD&D are able to answer such critical questions as "Do modern telecommunication technologies pay off?" and "How can we best use modern technologies in the TI?" The OMTS is capable of facilitating higher business profitability and productivity by enhancing systems' strategic goals such as product position, product quality, and customer service.

INTRODUCTION

It is well understood that telecommunication systems are continuously evolving and changing. Change is the only constant attribute in the telecommunications industry (TI). To satisfy market demands, this evolution needs system designers and developers (SD&D) to constantly upgrade their expertise, be aware of up-to-date technologies, and proactively capitalize on these changes. The SD&D must be conditioned to stay ahead of this evolution and to influence the changes for the better. Today's telecommunication SD&D with extensive expertise in software, hardware, and integration know that it takes a great amount of effort and synergistic planning to develop a user-friendly product. The SD&D know that they must be constantly aware of the changes in industry, market, and technology when they are developing state-of-the-art systems. The SD&D are also aware that such design and development expertise come neither easy nor cheap. The modern SD&D are conditioned to minimize mistakes and capitalize on the scientific breakthroughs (Fitzer, 1997; Goldman, 1998).

The OMTS is a unique model, which may require integration of various hardware, software, and different expertise when it is implemented. In addition, the model sets its own dimensions, specifications, user requirements, environment, and constraints. The SD&D implementing OMTS must be aware of all the critical factors influencing their decisions, and changes that may occur during the system's development process from its concept to its production (Blanchard & Fabrycky, 1998). The OMTS is capable of optimizing SD&D efforts by increasing the system's performance payoff, application of new technologies, business value, product position in the market, and service quality (Lyu, 1995).

This chapter addresses some of the issues and concerns confronting SD&D implementing OMTS during the system design and development efforts. It also discusses the areas of expertise needed to manage the technology changes that occur during the development of telecommunication products and services (Bourrea & Dogan, 2001; Goldman, 1998). The rationale behind OMTS is an urgent need to optimize the system's design and development activities in the TI. Because most telecommunication systems are designed for change, OMTS must be able to adapt to market demands. The SD&D are aware that it is more difficult to design for the TI than industries that require modularity with a set of predetermined standards and practices. OMTS makes it easier for the SD&D to develop complex systems under adverse conditions with no predetermined standards and practices (Chong & Chow, 1999; Moyer & Umar, 2001).

In the TI, it is difficult to predict and effectively implement technology changes, because the market is constantly fluctuating, users are unique, a new product's window of opportunity is short (about 6 months), and the design and development phase is costly. OMTS capitalizes on these characteristics in the TI and is designed to adapt to the changes and use them as a driving force to open new market opportunities (Goldman, 1998). Because most of the system design and development phases are directly impacted by user demand and technology evolution, SD&D efforts are mostly reactive rather than proactive, requiring new guidelines and practices. To optimize their efforts, SD&D can use OMTS to minimize their production costs, anticipate and adapt to market changes, and be flexible at all times (Chong & Chow, 1999; Comer, 2000).

By implementing the OMTS, our readers realize the importance of modern tool applications, and the model provides successful strategies for creating business values in the TI. OMTS helps our readers to incorporate modern technologies in their systems design and development initiatives, and to be able to answer such pertinent questions as "What is the business value of information technology?" and "How can we ensure performance in the information technology?" Finally, the OMTS addresses some of the changes that a telecommunication system goes through as it is being developed, the expertise it requires, and the costs associated with these changes. This chapter also presents a cost model capable of optimizing the design and development process of a TI system.

SYSTEM EVOLUTION

As the TI evolves and proactively expands into other areas (e.g., the Internet, medical, financial), the key critical factors of OMTS also change accordingly (Forouzan, 2000; Moyer & Umar, 2001). The SD&D are becoming more aware that as the industry is evolving, user demands are changing, the market is constantly fluctuating, and system's design and development are becoming more tedious and complex. They also realize that traditional principles and system design and development techniques are no longer applicable (Amintas & Swarte, 2000; McGinity, 1999).

The SD&D realize that as ever-expanding advances in technology feed into OMTS, it expands their market shares. As the result of this expansion, there is an urgent need for cost reduction in operating costs, better services, increase in demand, and more user satisfaction. In addition, OMTS is capable of expanding a system's operations and market share by addition of other applications such as call waiting, fax usage, the Internet, remote access, word processing, e-mail, etc. (Amintas & Swarte, 2000; Ebeling, 1997; Huizing, 2000).

In the new millennium, the primary forces of change will be user needs and expectations, technology improvements, Internet applications and interfaces, and market demands. Internet applications will create an environment where each telecommunication system interfaces with others individually and collectively. These applications and standards will be guided by industry standards, practices, and polices. OMTS is conditioned to adapt to increase in Internet applications by using modern technologies such as case tools, databases, and protocols (Amintas & Swarte, 2000; McGinity, 1999; Schneider & Winter, 1998). Another hidden driving force in the TI will be a product's short window of opportunity and its shelf life. SD&D are aware that most telecommunication users constantly expect better and more modern products in the market.

This highly unpredictable user expectation is a critical driving force in today's global market. The telecommunication companies have to adapt to this to survive and maintain their shares of the market. As the TI is expanding, it will need to rely more on modern systems such as OMTS to become an effective contributor in the global market (Ebeling, 1997).

U.S. based telecommunication companies are continuously in competition with each other as well as their foreign competitors. This globalization of the industry has significantly increased the number of telecommunication products into the market, shortened their shelf lives, increased customer expectations, and created a highly dynamic market. Arrival of the new international companies into the market is adding to the competitive nature of the business and creating an urgent need for the OMTS (Ebeling, 1997; Hunter, 2001).

KEY DIMENSIONS

As user needs and requirements evolve to more complex levels, so do the key dimensions of TI technology. This continuous life-cycle process affects evolution of the TI legacy systems and increases the need for OMTS. As the interrelated TI technology advances, user needs are creating a dynamic coevolution between TI legacy systems and OMTS or dependent industries. Dynamic coevolution is also the driving force behind most advances in other dependent industries. This coevolution is further enhanced by the increase in computer processing systems and capabilities.

OMTS capabilities are changing applications of the TI networks and systems, constantly creating new leading products and services. To more effectively cope with this coevolutionary dynamics, the OMTS takes advantages of advances in programmable switches to significantly reduce costs of information exchange; direct dialing and call waiting, and other modern wireless technologies (Igobaria, 1998).

Recognizing this coevolution increases the useful life of TI products and services, and their useful lives in the competitive market. As an example, the AT&T 4ESS and 5ESS transmissions and switching systems were developed based on these principles and have been in use for three decades because their inception. OMTS recognizes that TI product and service costs are two important factors influencing useful lives of most telecommunication systems. Other factors that can be computed by OMTS are research, development, and maintenance costs (Blanchard & Fabrycky, 1998; Reinsch, 1997).

This coevolution has enhanced modern technologies and revolutionized the word processing applications through introduction of electronic mail capabilities. The broad and global application of these modern TI technologies have improved the business value of the information superhighway, increased system payoff, products and services usability, and communication within and outside organizations. OMTS uses the following key dimensions of change to optimize the business value of a system design and development process (Lied & Holmes, 1997):

- System usability—User requirements and expectations are not static. They are constantly changing as the market dynamics influence their decisions. Subsequently, system usability influences user behavior, characteristics, and profile (Dargan & Hermes, 1997).
- Competitive dynamics—TI is continuously influenced by internal and external dynamics. The internal dynamics are new scientific breakthroughs, software and hardware upgrades, applications of new tools, and standards. External dynamics are mostly market and user driven, and primarily depend upon windows of opportunity for a variety of TI products and services. An example of external dynamics is the application of digital switching in TI networks, which has decreased transmission costs and made it more practical to convert digital information into analog and vice versa. Another example is the application of packet-based network systems that have drastically decreased the price of long distance calls and have introduced flat-rate-per-minute instead of distance-sensitive models (Chong & Chow, 1999).
- Configuration and Interfaces—As technology advances and constantly evolves, modern telecommunication systems have to adapt to the new changes and increase their configurability and ability to interface with other systems and networks. Each system must be able to effectively and efficiently bridge with other systems and be capable of interfacing with different internal and external networks. Internal and external interfaces can be adopted from the International Telecommunication Union (ITU) standards and practices or other similar sources. Due to continuous changes in TI technologies, the ITU and other similar standards are constantly being upgraded. It is therefore important for SD&D to use OMTS to update the system specifications and customer requirements (Fitzer, 1997; Moyer & Umar, 2001). Unfortunately, most TI systems are built based on the existing technologies and standards. Consequently, they may become outdated after the system is completed and operational. It is therefore important to upgrade the TI software, hardware, protocols, and their integration whenever possible.
- Key design elements—As new TI systems are being designed and developed, the SD&D need to use the OMTS to identify the key design elements early to prevent bottlenecks and problems. Identifying the key design obstructions helps SD&D to identify the most effective methods of creating efficient systems (Goldman, 1998).

WHY LIFE-CYCLE PROCESS?

The OMTS relies heavily on the life-cycle process to assist the SD&D in developing the best possible system. In comparison to other models, the life-cycle process is selected for OMTS because it clearly serves as a foundation and frame of reference throughout the system's development phases. Included are the primary steps in optimizing system requirements and functional analysis, resource allocations, synthesis, cost-benefit analysis, trade-off studies and a host of other techniques. Through the life-cycle process, SD&D are able to identify new needs as well as future user demands and make appropriate adjustments (Fowler et al., 1999; Guimaraes & Darrow, 1999).

The three primary life-cycle phases of the OMTS clearly identify user needs, enhance basic understanding of the system's conceptual design and initiate appropriate steps to follow. Whenever necessary, the OMTS life-cycle process takes advantage of other interdisciplinary techniques such as operations research and other scientific tools (e.g., transportation, assignment, transshipment, integer programming, PERT/CPM, inventory, queuing, etc.) to optimize the system's operations (Fowler et al., 1999; Gamma et al., 1995).

As SD&D initiate the optimization process in the early development phase to the final testing and quality control phase, there will be a comprehensive follow-on approach to further improve the operations of the system. During the optimization process, the final phases of the system components are combined and integrated into the final system configuration. The primary advantage of the life-cycle approach is to provision for continuous feedback, improvements, and corrective actions. The life-cycle process is continuous and iterative and incorporates feedback at all times.

The OMTS optimization approach starts with a set of known user requirements. SD&D create system specifications by synthesizing a combination of the system functions. In most complex systems, the functional requirements of the system are not met the first time. After SD&D evaluate the system's performance at every level, they compare them with their specifications and systematically address the deviations. The OMTS optimization processes are iterative and time sensitive (Baker, 1997; Cockburn, 1998).

The OMTS optimization approach is initiated and employed by SD&D. It starts with user requirements and ends with a completely sound system. Elements of the subsystems are identified by their functions, characteristics, attributes, and their contributions to other interdependent subsystems.

In this approach, each element of the system is only considered for its functional behavior and utility. At its final stage, the system functional components and their values are verified and validated by synthesizing the original user requirements (Breman & Jenning, 2000; Cockburn, 1998; Lyu, 1995).

The OMTS optimization process effectively starts with evaluating the whole system, and proceeding with maximization of each one of the subsystems and their elements. In the beginning of the optimization process, the top-down approach recognizes that the sole reason for the system is to efficiently transform inputs into outputs. The optimization process therefore concentrates on functionality of a system's elements rather than their integrations (Lewis, 1994; Tai et al., 1996).

LIFE-CYCLE PROCESS

OMTS is based on the life-cycle process to assist the SD&D designing and developing their TI systems. The life-cycle process is based on three continuous quality phases: design and development, testing (alpha and beta) and maintenance. Figure 1 is an indication of these three phases. Similarly, as Figure 1 shows, the OMTS life-cycle model is a continuous quality effort in which follows the following three phases (Baker, 1997; Forouzan, 2000; Moyer & Umar, 2001):

Design and Development $\Rightarrow$ Alpha and Beta Tests $\Rightarrow$ Maintenance

Figure 1: OMTS Life-Cycle Phases

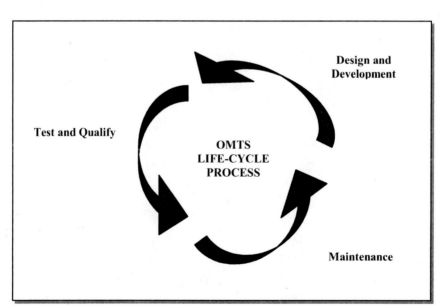

Figure 2 is also a presentation of the OMTS three-phase methodology. As Figure 2 illustrates, the OMTS life-cycle process is a user-friendly process that continuously monitors the system's three vital phases.

The OMTS life-cycle process has effectively served the industry well. The OMTS life-cycle process is a paradigm shift from more traditional system development models. The traditional models were to design and develop, test and maintain the system without re-engineering, upgrading, and continuous quality cycle (Breman & Jenning, 2000).

Figure 2: OMTS Design, Development and Testing Methodology

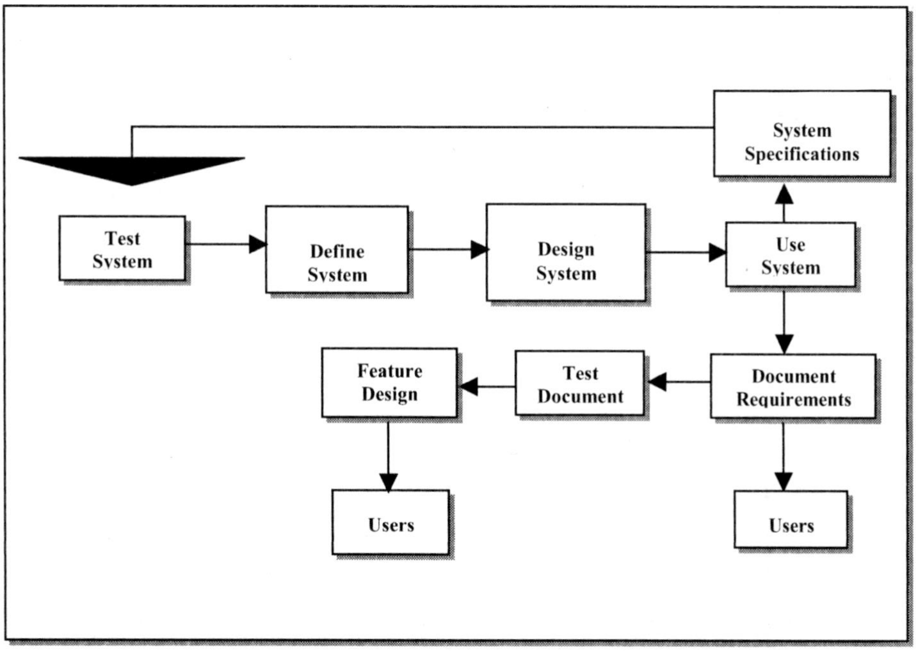

In the OMTS life-cycle process, subject matter experts implement phases: the design and development phase by SD&D; alpha and beta tests by statisticians and quality control specialists; and maintenance by system analysts (Bourrea & Dogan, 2001). Of the three OMTS life-cycle phases, most of the costs occur in the design and development phase of the process. OMTS tracks, analyzes and evaluates the costs associated with each phase of the process, which is shown in Figure 3 (Ebeling, 1997).

Although the OMTS life-cycle process has served the TI very well, recent globalization of the TI demands a more practical application of the model. The more modern version of the OMTS uses the spiral model concept which adds to SD&D

Figure 3: OMTS Architecture

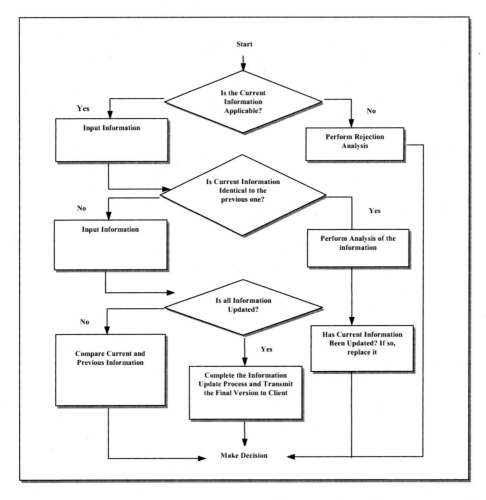

capabilities as they are developing complex and modern TI systems. This OMTS model is more practical and suitable to evolving TI systems, because it explicitly identifies the various dependencies inherent in each system.

Figure 4 is a presentation of the OMTS compatibility process. As Figure 4 indicates, each block of the process represents a new approach to reach product compatibility through information analyses, design, development, integration and testing. In the OMTS model, the arrow identifies two primary aspects of the process—capability and design dependency (Forouzan, 2000).

- *Capability* depicts compatibility between one phase of the system and another, or one release and another. As Figure 4 shows, there is a need for compatibility among all phases for the system to effectively operate and produce the right products at the right time.

- *Design and development constraints* and dependencies among various phases are identified as part of another essential characteristic of the OMTS model. This model's characteristic also highlights dependencies of one release, on another release as the system implements and proceeds through various phases (Andolfo, 2001).

The OMTS is a progression of the life-cycle process and is developed based on its principles. It has been more effective than other traditional models, because the model easily maintains awareness of the total life-cycle cost as the system is being developed. In the OMTS model, it is easier to perform cost and benefit analyses and comparative studies and to determine business value and other pertinent factors, enabling SD&D to make appropriate managerial decisions (Chong & Chow, 1999).

OPTIMIZATION MODEL

To effectively design and develop modern global telecommunications systems, SD&D need to use new models to monitor their product costs and optimize their efforts. One of these models is the OMTS spiral model, which is presented in Figure 4.

Figure 4: OMTS Compatibility Process

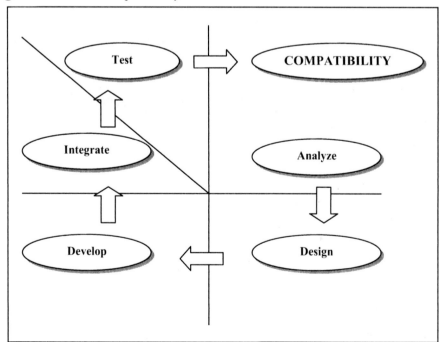

This model is suitable to compute costs and determine business values for modern dynamic and interdependent telecommunication systems. The OMTS represents a system design and development product cycle and shows its various dependencies and phases. This model consists of six interactive and interdependent phases. These phases include system's analysis, design, development, integration and tests that are essential to creating compatibility within a system. Compatibility is critical to the successful completion of a system because compatibility improves the ability to interface subsystems and various network parts. OMTS software is the framework of the model and is based on an algorithm that effectively measures SD&D efforts and computes impact of its developmental costs on system's business value (Blanchard & Fabrycky, 1998; Chong & Chow, 1999; Gailkowsky et al., 1996; Lykins, 1997).

$e \equiv$ Total efforts used developing the three phases of a system

$r \equiv$ Efforts used in developing the research part of the system

$f \equiv$ Fraction of time SD&D is used on research part of the system

$u \equiv$ Useful time SD&D spent on developing the system

$b_v \equiv$ Percent business value of the SD&D efforts developing the system

By definition:

$$f = \frac{r}{e} \tag{1}$$

$$u = e - r \tag{2}$$

We can then define B_v, the total business value in terms of the SD&D efforts, as efficiency of their useful efforts that they are capable of performing (Ireson et al., 1995).

$$b_v = \frac{u}{e} = \frac{e - r}{f} \tag{3}$$

$$b_v = 1 - \frac{r}{e} \quad \text{or} \tag{4}$$

$$b_v = 1 - f \tag{5}$$

Based on Equations (4) and (5), the percent business value of a system's design and development is directly related to efficiency of SD&D work efforts and is a fraction of their useful efforts.

Example 1.

Let us assume $e = 10,000$, and $r = 100$. Using Equation (1), we can determine f, the fraction of time that SD&D used on the research part of the system development process.

$$f = \frac{100}{10,000} = 0.01 \approx 1\%$$

Then, u, the useful time SD&D spends on developing the system, can be computed using Equation (2).

$$u = 10,000 - 100 = 9900$$

Similarly, b_v or the percent business value of the process, can be determined using Equation (5).

$$b_v = \frac{9,900}{10,000} = 0.99$$

$$b_v = 1 - f = 1 - 0.01 = 0.99 \text{ or } 99\% \text{ of the total business value}$$

To determine the most efficient method of determining the total business value or B_v of a system's design and development process, we can deduce the following important insights (Goldman, 1998; Ireson et al., 1995):

- The SD&D performance costs are significant for the first two OMTS phases. Especially when the majority of the SD&D are inexperienced or lack the expertise necessary to complete the system (Tai et al., 1996).
- The efficiency of system design and development process depends on availability of appropriate resources. In most TI development cases, the design and development phase of the process constitutes more than 70% of the completion cost (Ireson et al., 1995).
- The useful and productive time of most TI system design and development phases constitutes about 30% of the completion time and 40% of the total process time.

The above analysis and insights reinforce our assumption that the business value of a system and efficiency of its development are directly related to the useful and productive time of the SD&D (Hunter, 2001). Historical data indicates that in addition to the useful and productive time of SD&D, there are two other critical factors contributing to the business value of a system: variation in the maintenance phase and selection of the appropriate technologies used (e.g., software, hardware, integration, etc.). In OMTS, the business value of a system also depends on appropriate analysis and selection of the following (Forouzan, 2000; Hunter, 2001):

1.   Identification and implementation of an existing software framework
2.   Identification and implementation of a new software framework
3.   Identification and implementation of appropriate standards
4.   Identification and implement of appropriate case tools

OMTS is able to compute total cost of the system's business value based on the above four characteristics, and sets business value or B_v of the system by identifying types of costs from the pro forma. To compute the B_v of a system, OMTS satisfies the following three development conditions:

1.   If the B_v of design and development, testing and maintenance is *fully cost based*, the OMTS computes B_v of the systems as a cost plus of markup and sets B_v proportional to total cost. In this condition, it identifies B_v from the pro forma and adds an additional percentage to these costs as a markup. In this condition, the formula for a business value of the system is:

$$B_v = T_c + l(T_c)$$ (6)

B_v ≡ Total business value, dollars

T_c ≡ Total cost of design and development, dollars

l ≡ Performance rate on cost, decimal

Example 2.
In this model, let us assume $T_c = \$200,000$, and $l = 2\%$.

$B_v = \$200,000 + 0.02(\$200,000)$

$B_v = \$200,000 + \$4,000$ or $B_v = \$204,000$

- When costs of *software and hardware materials are insignificant* to the total development of the system, the total business value B_v can be found using the following equation:

$$B_v = \left[\sum M_O(1+O)(1+l) + M_m \right] \qquad (7)$$

$M_O \equiv$ Direct-labor cost on development operations, dollars
$O \equiv$ General overhead rate, decimal overhead dollars to direct labor costs
$l \equiv$ Markup rate, decimal
$M_m \equiv$ Direct software and hardware material costs, dollars

Example 3.

In this model, we can compute B_v for software development efforts that consist of $M_O = \$50,000$; $O = 5\%$; $l = 2\%$;   and $M_m = \$20,000$. U s i n g Equation (7), we can compute B_v of the system development process:

$$B_v = \left[\sum \$50,000(1+0.05)(1+0.02) + \$20,000 \right]$$
$$B_v = [\$53,550 + \$20,000] \text{ or } B_v = \$73,550$$

- When B_v is based on *system's investment rate of return*:

$$B_v = \left(\frac{R_i I}{N_Y} + M_f + M_V N \right) \Big/ N \qquad (8)$$

$R_i \equiv$ Desired return on investment, decimal
$I \equiv$ Investment, dollars
$N_Y \equiv$ Number of years for payback of investment
$M_f \equiv$ Development fixed costs, dollars
$M_V \equiv$ Development variable cost, dollars
$N \equiv$ Number of units sold

Example 4.

In this model, let us assume $R_i = 0.10$ or 10%;

$I = \$300,000$; $N_y = 15$; $M_f = \$40,000$; $M_v = \$70,000$; and

$N = 3$. Using Equation (8), the B_v can be computed:

$$B_v = \left(\frac{(0.10)(\$300,000)}{15} + \$40,000 + (\$70,000)(3) \right) \Big/ 3$$

$$B_v = \left(\frac{\$200 + \$40,000 + \$210,000}{3} \right) = \$8,3400$$

- When B_v is based on *direct labor and direct material* of the system development, and overhead is important and can be used to compute the B_v :

$$B_v = \left[\sum (M_O + M_m)(1+O) + C_O \right] \qquad (9)$$

$C_O \equiv$ Costs of overhead, dollars

$M_O \equiv$ Direct-labor cost on development operations, dollars

$M_m \equiv$ Direct software and hardware material costs, dollars

$O \equiv$ General overhead rate, decimal overhead dollars to direct labor cost, decimal

Example 5.

In this model, the total business value is determined using values from previous examples. Let us assume:

$$M_O = \$50,000 ; M_m = \$20,000 ; O = 5\%; \text{and } C_O = \$10,000 .$$

$$B_v = \left[\sum (\$50,000 + \$20,000)(1 - .05) + \$10,000 \right]$$

$$B_v = \left[\sum (\$66,500 + \$10,000) \right] \text{ or } B_v = \$76,500$$

2. If B_v of a system development is based on *users demand and sales' value* of the system:

$$B_v = \frac{M_t}{1 - R_m} \tag{10}$$

where

$$M_t = T_C + T_S$$

$T_C \equiv$ Total cost of design and development

$T_S \equiv$ Cost of test and sale, dollars

$M_t \equiv$ Total cost of system design, development, test and sales, dollars

$R_m \equiv$ Markup on sales, decimal

Example 6.

In this model, let us assume $T_C = \$200{,}000$; $T_S = \$45{,}000$; and $R_m = 8\%$.

$$M_t = \$200{,}00 + \$45{,}000 \ \text{ or } \ M_t = \$245{,}000$$

$$B_v = \frac{\$245{,}000}{1 - .08} \ \text{ and } \ B_v = \$12{,}250{,}000$$

3. In the TI, some costs vary with changes in the production quantity part of the system development, and others do not. Business value of a system, or B_v, is related to this variable cost and *percentage of the contribution rate* of this variable cost to the total business value. In this condition, the OMTS computes business value by incorporating the principal items of variable cost, including labor, material, marketing, and administrative costs. Upon this full variable cost or M_v value, we find the contribution based on users demand price.

$$B_v = \frac{M_v}{1 - R_c} \tag{11}$$

$B_v \equiv$ Total business value, dollars

$M_v \equiv$ Full variable cost, dollars

$R_c \equiv$ Contribution rate, decimal

Example 7.

In this model, let us assume $M_v = \$12,000$; and $R_c = 6\%$.

$$B_v = \frac{\$12,000}{0.06} = \$200,000$$

It is therefore imperative to state that the OMTS is based on the above scientific algorithms that are able to compute the business value or B_v of a system using unique and distinct equations such as Equations (6), (7), (8), (9), and (10).

RATIONALE

Developing a leading-edge-technology telecommunication system requires a solid software framework. OMTS helps the SD&D identify the best possible framework for the system before initiating its actual development. OMTS software framework will set up the foundation of the TI system and will determine its applications, upgrading capabilities, ease of use, market acceptability, across the board flexibility, development and production costs, and longevity of the system (Lykins, 1997). Figure 5 is a presentation of the Internet-based OMTS user framework that is able to set up system's foundation, to determine its applications, and to enhance other vital characteristics. As Figure 5 indicates, Internet users are able to interface with OMTS, process their information through a network of controlled activities, and receive the verified results through the multimedia chart of the model (Amintas & Swarte, 2000).

OMTS software framework selection is based on systematic identification and analyses of user requirements, SD&D specifications, applicable standards, guidelines, case tools, methodologies and policies that create form and function for the system. Proper and effective selection of software framework will be an important part of design-level and code-level segments of the design and development phase (Lykins, 1997; Schneider & Winter, 1998). OMTS implements a systematic approach to selected and documented framework specifications that ensures successful completion of the system and initiates a set of internal standards for other

Figure 5: Internet-Based User Interface Framework

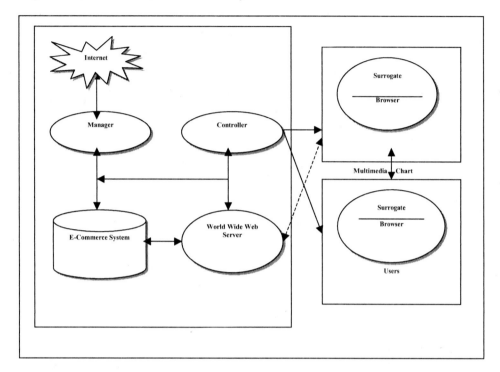

phases. OMTS workable framework reduces the total cost of the system from the market requirement documentation to the maintenance phase of the process.

As Figure 6 indicates, by implementing OMTS and application of process control, the SD&D are able to increase the effectiveness, efficiency and productivity of the process control, which may reduce the total cost of system's development from the concept to its final stage (Forouzan, 2000).

A well-developed system framework provides an effective and systematic mechanism for SD&D to follow, integrate software and hardware parts, extend new applications and implement new tools. The OMTS framework allows the SD&D to bridge newly extended applications and tools with the existing software and hardware. For a system to continue functioning, the SD&D need to be aware of the internal working of the OMTS framework and functionality of its parts and to be assured that the extension of new applications and tools fit into the overall design of the system.

OMTS uses object-oriented frameworks to support rapid iteration and prototyping of the new systems, enhance applications of new technologies and improve the learning process of the new tools. Examples of OMTS software framework extensions could be "Wizard" in Microsoft's Visual C++ development environment and other similar automatic class generation tools in Sun Microsystems's

Figure 6: SD&D Development and Process Control

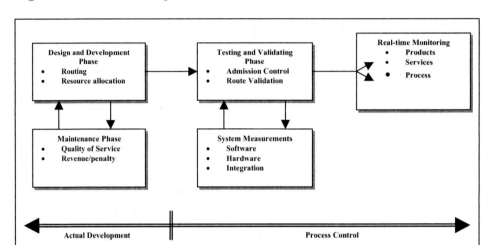

Enterprise JavaBeans technologies. The OMTS is an effective tool for developing functional system frameworks such as applications of Common Object Request Broker Architecture (CORBA), and CORBA-based software tools. The implementation of CORBA-based environments has simplified the use of OMTS and created an environment that enables SD&D to design and develop small portable software systems based on the distributed architecture. Success of developing a system framework depends on the delivery and update cycles of the tools and their availability. In addition, a framework should have user-friendly documentations with examples, limitations of the framework, software, tools and applications.

CONCLUSIONS

In this chapter, a leading-edge-technology telecommunication optimization system is discussed. OMTS enables the SD&D to determine the business value of a system and also answer such important questions as "Do modern telecommunication technologies pay off?", "How can we best use modern technologies in TI?", "What is the business value of information technology?" and "How can we ensure performance in the information technology?"

The OMTS is capable of helping SD&D develop synergistic plans to develop a user-friendly system by minimizing mistakes and capitalizing on scientific breakthroughs. The OMTS is an Internet-based unique model that ensures integration of various hardware and software and optimizes the process by increasing the system's performance payoff, application of new technologies, business value, product position in the market, and service quality (Andolfo, 2001; Amintas & Swarte, 2000). The OMTS is fully capable of adapting to increase in Internet applications by implementing modern technologies such as Case tools, databases and protocols. To optimize a system development process, OMTS takes advantage of advances in programmable switches to significantly decrease costs of information exchange. The model uses various unique key dimensions to optimize the life-cycle system development phases: system usability, competitive dynamics, configuration and interfaces, and key design elements.

The OMTS life-cycle process is based on three continuous quality phases: design and development, testing, and maintenance. The OMTS life cycle is a paradigm shift from traditional models that were not based on continuous quality of the three phases and did not adhere to system's re-engineering and upgrading. A more modern version of the OMTS implements the spiral model methodology to enhance the system's optimization process. This spiral technology helps the SD&D to increase system's compatibility through information analyses, design, development, integration, and testing.

Framework of the OMTS software is based on various algorithms for different scenarios that effectively measure SD&D efforts, and computes the impact of its development cost on system's business value. These OMTS software algorithms determine business value of a system and its development efficiency by computing the useful and productive time of the SD&D. The OMTS software framework is also based on systematic identification and selection of user requirements, SD&D specifications, application standards, guidelines, case tools, methodologies, and policies that create form and function for the system. The OMTS uses an object-oriented framework to support rapid prototyping of new systems, increases Internet applications, improves usability of its products and services, and enhances users' learning processes. Figure 7 shows the Internet-based and object-oriented framework of the OMTS (Andolfo, 2001; Amintas & Swarte, 2000).

ACKNOWLEDGMENTS

The author greatly appreciate our colleagues at the University of Nebraska at Omaha for their encouragement and support. This chapter and project would not have been possible without generous grants from the NJK Holding Corporation and its subsidiaries. The author wishes to express his appreciation for the assistance of his colleagues, Professor Theresa Stanton and Dr. Mark Pauley. Sincere thanks goes to graduate student, Louis Weitkam, for his editing and other support. In

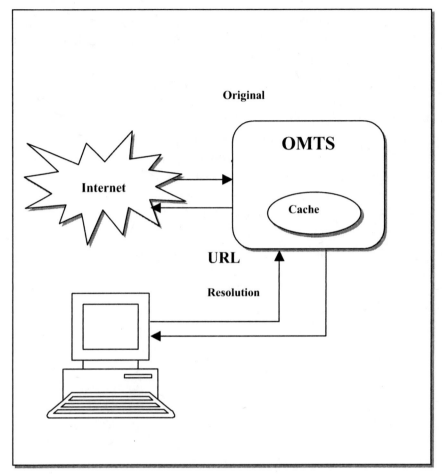

Figure 7: Internet-Based and Object-Oriented Framework of the OMTS

addition, his deepest gratitude is given to Systems Engineers in the Bell Laboratories and IBM Watson Research Center for their reviews and recommendations.

REFERENCES

Amintas, A. & Swarte, T. de. (2000). The Internet Age and the Role of Telecommunication Operations: The Case of France Telecom, *International Journal of Technology Management, 20*(1/2), 176–294.

Andolfo, T. S. (2001). Telecommunications: The Wireless Personal Communications Services Industry, *Appraisal Journal, 69*(3), 333–341.

Baker, L. (1997). Lessons Learned Applying Model-Driven System Design, *Proceedings of the Seventh Annual INCOSE Symposium,* 751–756.

Blanchard, B. S. & Fabrycky, W. J. (1998). *Systems Engineering and Analysis*. Englewood Cliffs, NJ: Prentice Hall, Inc.

Bourrea, M. & Dogan, P. (2001). Regulation and Innovation in the Telecommunications Industry, *Telecommunications Policy*, *25*(30, 167–185.

Breman, R. & Jenning, B. (2000). Evolutionary Trends I Intelligent Networks, *IEEE Communications Magazine,* June, *38*(6), 86–94.

Chong, R. B. & Chow, W. (1999). Financing Telecommunications Projects in Asia, *Federal Communications Law Journal*, *52*(1), 1–20.

Cockburn, A. (1998). *Surveying Object-Oriented Projects*, p. 9. New York: Addison-Wesley.

Comer, D. (2000). *Interworking with Transmission Control Protocol/ Interworking Protocol (TCP/IP)*, Vol. I Principles, Protocols, and Architecture, Englewood Cliffs, NJ: Prentice Hall, Inc.

Dargan, P. A. & Hermes, M. A. (1997). Challenges in Designing Open Systems, *Proceedings of the Seventh Annual INCOSE Symposium*, 799–806.

Ebeling, C. E. (1997). *Reliability and Maintainability Engineering*. New York: McGraw-Hill Companies, Inc.

Fitzer, M. M. (1997). Managing from Afar: Performance and Rewards in a Telecommunicating Environment. *Compensation and Benefits Review*, *29*(1), 65–73.

Forouzan, B. (2000). *Data Communications and Networking*, second edition, New York: McGraw Hill Companies, Inc.

Fowler, M., Beck, K., Brant, J., Opdyke, W., & Roberts, D. (1999). *Refactoring: Improving the Design of Existing Code*, New York: Addison-Wesley.

Gailkowsky, C., Sivazlian, B. D., & Chaovalitwongse, P. (1996). Optimal Redundancies for Reliability and Availability of Series Systems. *Microelectron and Reliability Journal*, *36*, 1537–1546.

Gamma, E., Helm, R., Johnson, R., & Vlisside J. (1995). *Design Patterns*, New York: Addison-Wesley.

Goldman, J. E. (1998). *Applied Data Communication: A Business-Oriented Approach.* New York: John Wiley and Son, Inc.

Guimaraes, T. & Darrow, P. (1999). Empirically Testing the Benefits, Problems, and Success Factors for Telecommuting Programmers. *European Journal of Information Systems*, *8*(1), 40–45.

Huizing, E. (2000). The Content and Design of Web Sites: An Empirical Study, *Information and Management*, *37*, 123–134.

Hunter, J. (2001). Telecommunications Delivery in the Sidney 2000 Olympic Games, *IEEE Communications Magazine*, *39*(7), 86–93.

Igobaria, M. (1998). Special Section: Managing Virtual Workplaces and Teleworking with Information Technology, *Journal of Management Information Systems*, *14*(4), 5–86.

Ireson, W. G., Coombs, C. F., & Moss, R. Y. (1995). *Handbook of Reliability Engineering and Management.* New York: McGraw-Hill Companies, Inc.

Lewis, E. E. (1994). *Introduction to Reliability Engineering.* New York: John Wiley & Sons, Inc.

Lied, R, Paulter, L. P., & Holmes, P. E. (1997). Introducing Software Reuse Technology, *Bell Laboratories Technical Journal*, *2*(1), Winter, 188–199.

Lykins, H. (1997). A framework for research into model-driven system design, *Proceedings of the Seventh Annual INCOSE Symposium*, 765–772.

Lyu, M. R., (Ed.). (1995). Software Reliability Engineering. *IEEE Computer Society Press.*

McGinity, M. (1999). Staying Connected: Flying Wireless, with a Net: Mobile Internet Providers Prepare for Takeoff. *Communications of the ACM*, *42*(12), 19–20.

Moyer, S., & Umar, A. (2001). The Impact of Network Convergence on Telecommunications Software, IEEE *Communications Magazine, 39*(1), 78–85.

Reinsch, N. L, Jr. (1997). Relationships between Telecommuting Workers and Their Managers: An Exploratory Study, *The Journal of Business Communications*, *34*(4), 343–369.

Schneider, G., & Winter, J. P. (1998). Applying Use Cases, (pp. 133–135) New York: Addison-Wesley.

Tai, A. T., Meyer, J. F., & Avizienis, A. (1996). *Software Performability: from Concepts to Applications*, New York: Kluwer Academic Publishers.

Chapter XII

Web Initiatives and E-Commerce Strategy: How Do Canadian Manufacturing SMEs Compare?

Ron Craig
Wilfrid Laurier University, Canada

INTRODUCTION

Two important forces are at work today in the Canadian and global economies. First is the traditional force of small- and medium-sized enterprises (SMEs). Statistics Canada reports SMEs account for more than 60% of Canada's private sector employment and 40% of gross domestic product. Second, Information Technology (IT) and the Internet continue to change the way businesses and individuals work, shop, and relax. In particular, the Internet and Electronic Commerce (EC) are heralded as a great opportunity for business, consumers, and governments. The impact on SMEs is somewhat uncertain and still emerging. Some argue the Internet levels the playing field, giving smaller firms greater opportunity to compete against larger firms. Others argue that, because SMEs generally have fewer resources available for IT or other initiatives, they could be left behind. In addition, because of their size, SMEs have minimal control or influence over such external forces.

In this chapter, the progress of smaller and medium-sized manufacturers in the use, and potential use, of the Internet and EC is investigated. Do they lead or lag larger firms? Is an EC strategy important for them, and what reasons do they see for pursuing it? Are firms that pursue an EC strategy more successful than the ones that do not?

Statistics Canada defines small businesses as having annual sales in the $30,000 to $5 million range. In this study, firms with sales less than or equal to $5 million were classified as small. Firms with sales in the $5 million to $30 million range were classified as medium in size, and above $30 million were classified as larger. The Canadian manufacturing sector comprises firms primarily engaged in the physical or chemical transformation of materials or substances into new products (either finished or semifinished). There are 22 major industry groups in Canada, with 238 industries (based on the North American Industry Classification System).

BACKGROUND

EC is used here in the broad sense, dealing with all aspects of business (including communication, information sharing, marketing, purchasing, logistical coordination, and payments). It is driven by improved and new business models facilitated by information technology advances and the Internet.

Obtaining consistent information concerning national and global Internet commerce is difficult, and there is often hype mixed in with reality. It is clear that business-to-business (B2B) dominates business-to-consumer (B2C) activity. Statistics Canada (2001) reports that in 1999 Canada accounted for almost 7% of worldwide Internet commerce (CDN $195 billion globally). The value of sales received over the Internet rose by 73.4% in 2000, with 80% being business to business. By 2004, it is predicted that global Internet commerce will increase to CDN $3.9 trillion, with Canada's share being CDN $151.5 billion.

Canada was recently ranked fourth in "e-readiness," a measure of the extent to which a country's business environment is conducive to Internet-based commercial opportunities (Economist Intelligence Unit, 2001). Leading the rankings was the United States, followed by Australia, and the United Kingdom. At a national level, it is recognized that one of the key issues currently facing Canada is facilitating the transition of existing SMEs into successful e-businesses (Canadian E-Business Opportunities Roundtable, 2001).

SMEs face challenges and opportunities with EC. Challenges include strategy determination and implementation, new and revised forms of business models and competition, successful technology adoption, and the pace and cost of change. Should a particular business use EC, and if so, when and how? At a basic level, the Web allows local firms to vastly extend their reach and send a much richer (content-wise) message to others (Evans & Wurster, 1999). There are opportunities to leverage corporate assets (tangible and intangible) in new ways, define new channels for communication and sales, and move toward virtual integration of the entire supply chain network. Yet the history of IT projects shows there are many difficulties and failures. The latest Standish Group (2001) data on IT projects shows 28% succeeded, 49% were challenged, and 23% failed.

EC, as an application of IT, is subject to the same excessive exuberance as exhibited with previous technology advances. Figure 1 depicts an "EC Reality Model," adapted from Feeny's (1997) "IT Reality Model." EC hype goes beyond the current capabilities of IT and EC, focusing on potential capabilities and outcomes. While it may become reality in the future, at present it is impossible. Beyond the hype, there is the current reality of EC—these are the bundle of products and services currently available, albeit not necessarily yet practical or affordable for most organizations. The domain of "Useful EC" consists of those products and services that are affordable for most organizations, providing a reasonable return on investment. Finally, there is the "Strategic EC" area, which can provide a significant contribution to organizational achievement, including substantial competitive advantage. Because of resource issues, one would expect the pool of "useful" EC to be smaller for SMEs than for larger firms.

The practical application of EC is undeniable, as is the strategic use of IT for competitive advantage. It appears that the hype is gradually being sorted from the reality and practicality, as "dot.com" firms with no sustainable cashflow or profits disappear, and the worlds of "bricks" and "clicks" converge. Yet, strong statements continue to be made, such as, "The period from 2000 to 2002 will represent the single greatest change in worldwide economic and business conditions ever, and most of the impact will occur during the next 18 months. If companies (and

Figure 1: EC Reality Model

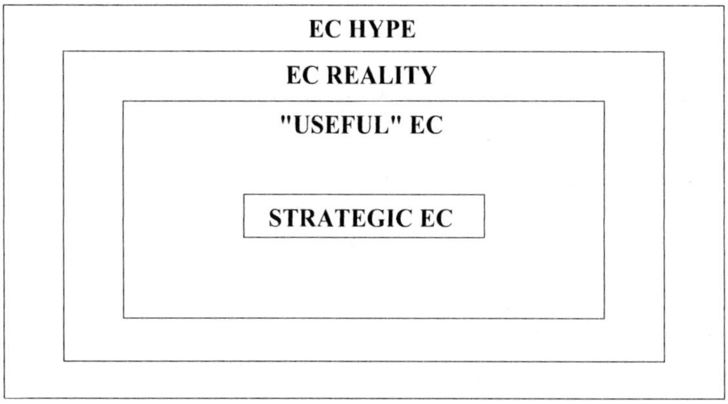

countries) do not change their assumptions and strategies during the next 12 months, they will almost certainly fall behind and probably be left behind" (Means & Schneider, 2000). Within this context, can SMEs survive or even thrive?

Strategic EC falls into the strategy domain, while Useful EC fits with tactics. The traditional strategy development approach is delineated by Fry and Killing (2000). Technology changes the environment, facilitating new approaches to utilizing the physical (Porter & Millar, 1985) and virtual (Rayport & Sviokla, 1995) value chains, and creating major disruption to historical power balances. The physical value chain model describes a series of value-adding physical activities connecting a company's supply side with its demand side. As originally proposed, the value chain model treats information as a supporting element of the value-adding process. Mimicking the physical value chain is the virtual value chain, where value is added with and through information. The virtue value chain identifies five ways of adding value via information: gathering it, organizing it, selecting it, synthesizing it, and distributing it.

While traditional strategy frameworks are still very useful, new approaches to thinking about and using them are required. In particular, technology provides a means of leveraging all the assets of a firm, including physical, financial, processes, organizational, customer, supplier, and managerial. "Value Dynamics" (Boulton et al., 2000) recommends firms design, invest in, and manage their entire portfolio of assets. Their view of assets include traditional hard assets (plant, equipment, inventory, money) plus soft assets (customers, suppliers, employees, organization). Business models are based on assembling the proper balance of assets to create the greatest value for shareholders and other stakeholders. Information technology facilitates new and improved business models, of which EC is an important development.

One can think in terms of an EC Importance Grid (Figure 2), similar to the "IT Strategic Grid" (Applegate et al., 1999). EC has both operational and strategic implications, and this grid can be applied to each. A firm in the low/low quadrant would not be highly dependent on EC for operational functioning or strategic positioning. The resource implications are that relatively few resources would be expended now, or in the future, on EC, and one would not expect senior management to spend much time, if any, on EC planning. In contrast, a firm in the high/high quadrant is dependent on smooth functioning of current EC applications and would be planning to extend applications for future competitive advantage. Management in this type of firm would spend considerable time on EC planning, and the resource implications would be significant. Understanding an organization's grid position is critical for developing an appropriate EC management strategy.

EC can also be considered within the framework of the Technology Adoption Lifecycle (Moore, 1995; Rogers, 1995), which explains how communities respond to discontinuous innovations (see Table 1 and Figure 3). Firms will adopt EC for different reasons, and at different times within the life cycle. Innovators comprise the smallest group, followed by early adopters and laggards. The early majority and late majority comprise the largest segments. While the framework is useful for considering why and when firms adopt EC, its limitations are seen if EC is only considered as a technology. Fundamentally, EC is a different approach to business and is facilitated by IT. While new forms of IT will appear, and older forms die off, EC will continue to grow as part of the common business model.

Complementing the technology adoption life cycle is the technology maturation cycle. New technologies go through an invention, development, refinement, and commercialization process. During the commercialization phase of successful technologies, the basic product is enhanced by a set of complementary products and services that enable the target customer to assimilate and use the technology. From the SME perspective, this "whole product" is more likely to be available and

Figure 2: EC Importance Grid

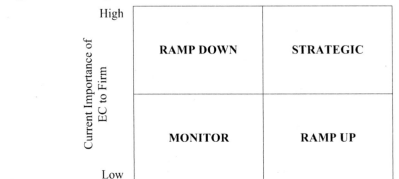

Table 1: Technology Adoption Life Cycle

Group	Alternative Name	Motivation	Approx. %
Innovators	Technology enthusiasts	Technology "high"	1-3
Early adopters	Visionaries	Competitive edge	5-15
Early majority	Pragmatists	Productivity/efficiency	30-40
Late majority	Conservatives	Conformity	30-40
Laggards	Skeptics	Compliance	10-20

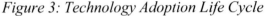

Figure 3: Technology Adoption Life Cycle

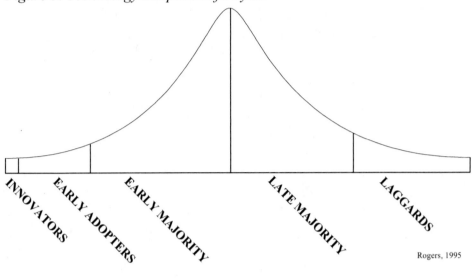

Rogers, 1995

affordable much further along the maturation curve. They usually do not have the resources to support implementations requiring substantial technical skills and investment. In contrast, larger firms have the financial and technological support resources to take on riskier projects earlier in the cycle. They also have the incentive, in terms of developing competitive advantage over other large firms. A more light-hearted, yet still realistic, view of this cycle is the Gartner Group's "Hype Cycle" (Figure 4), which ties in with the Reality Model of Figure 1.

Most academic EC research has focused on larger firms and high growth startups. Among SMEs, retailers and service providers have been studied more than manufacturers. The Canadian Federation of Independent Business (Whyte, 2000) found that, while an increasing proportion of SMEs are using the Internet, they are slow to adopt EC. Whyte concludes that servicing customers and marketing are the keys to success. Government can help by improving the national telecommunications infrastructure (easier access, high bandwidth), ensuring a fair EC tax policy, improving government Internet services, and reducing legal barriers.

Mackay et al. (2001) studied key factors affecting EC adoption in small British Columbia firms. Drawing upon the Theory of Planned Behavior (Ajzen, 1991), they found management support had the greatest influence on intention to adopt EC, followed by internal pressure and perceived benefits.

Barua et al. (2000) investigated a three-phase model of EC. E-Business drivers (IT applications, processes, e-business readiness) impact operational

Figure 4: Technology hype cycle

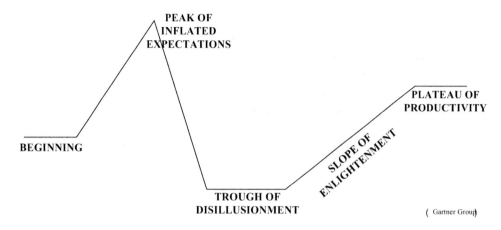

excellence measures (including % online business, % online procurement, % customer service provided online, order delivery time), which impact financial measures (including revenue/employee, gross profit margin, ROA). Results of studying some 1200 firms in the United States and Europe (a mix of retailers, manufacturers, wholesalers, and distributors), showed firms with increased financial performance had significantly better operational excellence performance and higher levels of investments in e-business drivers. In particular, smaller firms (100 or fewer employees) saw much higher percentage gains in financial performance with e-business, relative to larger firms.

Dandridge and Levenburg (1999) investigated Internet use of firms with fewer than 25 employees, finding a subset (young, with growth expectations) actively using the Internet as a marketing tool. Jentzsch and Miniotas (1999) recommend SMEs examine their value chain to determine the most effective use of the Internet. Poon (1999) outlines the state of small business Internet commerce. He found the Internet used mainly for communication and information exchange. Poon presents a "maturity model" based on business processes and EC application (technology) complexity.

Pelham (2000), although not an EC study, investigated performance factors in small manufacturing firms. He found market orientation had the strongest positive relationship with performance measures, and the most influential market orientation elements were fast response to negative customer satisfaction information, strategies based on creating value for customers, immediate response to competitive challenges, and fast detection of changes in customer product preferences. It is easy to see how the Web can be used by smaller firms to enable and support these performance factors.

STUDY PURPOSE AND SURVEY METHODOLOGY

This was an empirical study of Ontario manufacturers. Data was collected as part of a larger annual survey of manufacturers in southwestern Ontario (Canada's manufacturing center), during the final two months of the year. Firms were sampled from a database compiled from several directories (Scott's Ontario Manufacturers Directory, Dun & Bradstreet's Canadian Key Business Directory, and local Chambers of Commerce Business directories). This ensured as complete a population listing as possible, from which a random sample was taken. The sample was representative based on location, industry, and size. Respondents were senior executives of these firms. With a survey size of approximately 350, the 1999 survey had a response rate of 50.6%, while the 2000 survey was 45.0%. Firms were categorized based on sales: smaller (< $5 million), medium ($5–$30 million), and larger (> $30 million).

EC "readiness" and attitude were studied by comparing:
1.   Proportions with Web sites
2.   Whether or not EC was viewed as strategic
3.   Actual and anticipated use of EC
4.   Reasons for EC

Two research questions studied the link between EC strategy and firm performance:
1.   Is there a performance difference between manufacturers who see or do not see an EC strategy as important?
2.   Are there performance differences between different sized firms, all viewing EC as important?

Results were aggregated by size. Chi-square statistical independence tests were completed, and further analysis used difference of proportions (1-tailed t-tests). In several cases, sample sizes were too small to conduct meaningful tests. For example, a three-way classification of Table 5 (Reasons for EC) based on firm size, strategic view of EC, and reasons, would have resulted in many small cell sizes.

RESULTS AND DISCUSSION

A minimal indicator of a firm's interest in, and potential involvement with, EC is given by whether or not they have a Web site. One would expect the presence of an organizational Web site to increase with firm size (larger size equates to greater resources), and this was confirmed (0.001 level of significance). Results are shown in Table 2. While a minority of smaller firms (44%) had a Web site, this was still a considerable group. In contrast, 89% of larger firms had Web sites. In terms of technology adoption, smaller firms lagged considerably (on average) with Web site development, while larger firms led. Firms without Web sites were asked if they would have one within the coming year ("Plan to Soon" row). When this is taken into consideration ("1 Year Projection" row), the gap narrows, yet still persists. Overall, it is evident that Web sites are by now well along the adoption curve, that smaller firms have been slower (on average) to develop them, and that smaller firms have a larger laggard group. For SMEs as a group, a majority (60%) have had Web sites for some time.

When asked whether EC was an important strategy for their firm (Table 3), no statistically significant differences were found (based on firm size). However, there were two trends: the proportion of firms indicating EC as important increased with size, and the proportion of firms unsure about this decreased with size. Almost half of the smaller respondents indicated EC was important, rising to more than two-thirds for larger firms. Conversely, almost one in five smaller firms were not sure about the importance of EC to their business, while this dropped to almost one in 20 for larger firms. Given the tremendous impact B2B and B2C commerce is forecast to have, it is surprising that many firms (of all sizes) indicated it was not of strategic importance. Evidence to be examined later in this chapter shows that, while smaller firms are slower to implement supplier electronic connection, the trend is positive.

One year later (Table 4), it is seen that the percentage of firms using EC lags considerably the percentage earlier, indicating EC as an important strategy (Table 3). Even factoring in those indicating EC plans for the coming year ("1 Year Projection" row), SMEs will still lag in adoptions, while for larger firms the gap is eliminated. Though not statistically significant, there is an observable trend of increasing EC use with increasing firm size. Overall, this suggests EC adoption is not

Table 2: Presence of Web Site (1999 survey)

	Smaller	Medium	Larger	Total
Yes	43.8%	79.7%	89.1%	72.7%
No	56.3%	20.3%	10.9%	27.3%
Plan to soon	25.0%	8.7%	3.6%	11.6%
No plans	31.3%	11.6%	7.3%	15.7%
1 Year Project	68.8%	88.4%	97.7%	84.3%
Total #	48	69	55	172

as far along the curve as Web site use. SMEs are still in the "Early Majority" phase, while larger firms now have the "Late Majority" coming on-stream.

Respondents were also asked how their business will use EC in the next few years, based on a list developed from the literature. Table 5 shows their responses, for both surveys. Two things stand out: in most cases, firm size made little difference (where statistically significant differences exist, these are indicated), and there was no single dominating reason for firms to use EC. Each specific reason was selected by firms of all sizes, while the average number of reasons selected increased with size. There are also interesting differences between the two surveys, suggesting an ongoing maturation process as firms learn more about EC and are able to separate hype from reality.

Overall, the most frequently selected uses focused on sales growth, either through new markets or increased sales with current customers. A Web presence can be particularly beneficial for smaller manufacturers whose reach has been limited, and they had high expectations in the 1999 survey. Comparing the two years, the trend is to lower expectations about accessing new markets, and a continued emphasis on current customers. While this could be because new markets are becoming saturated, it is more likely that firms are realizing it is easier to increase business with current customers.

Table 3: E-Commerce Important Strategy for Firm (1999 Survey)

	Smaller	Medium	Larger	Total
Yes	48.9%	53.7%	67.3%	56.8%
No	31.9%	31.3%	27.2%	30.2%
Unsure	19.1%	14.9%	5.5%	13.0%
Total #	47	67	55	169

Table 4: Use of E-Commerce (2000 survey)

	Smaller	Medium	Larger	Total
Yes	21.1%	31.1%	48.3%	35.0%
No	65.8%	57.4%	32.8%	50.3%
1 Year Projection	34.3%	42.6%	67.3%	49.6%
Total #	38	61	58	157

Integration backward to suppliers was of concern to few small firms, while it was important for larger ones. For medium-sized firms, this became more important in 2000. This agrees with the current concern for supply chain management and optimization. Larger firms are important participants in supply chains, while smaller firms usually are not. Over time, though, electronic connection of supply chain participants will continue to expand.

Gaining access to information about the market and competition (market intelligence) was another frequently indicated reason. Rubin (1999) studied how small businesses can use the Web for competitive intelligence about competitors, industry trends, and customer opinions. All sizes of firms saw the Web facilitating this, although the trend is downwards for smaller and medium-sized firms.

One aspect of customer relationship management (CRM) is dealing with customer complaints. In both surveys, the percentage of firms mentioning this reason increased with firm size. Comparing the two years, there was an increase for medium-sized firms, and a decrease for smaller firms.

Table 5: Reason for Electronic Commerce (% Indicating)

Reason	Smaller		Medium		Larger	
Survey Year:	1999	2000	1999	2000	1999	2000
Access to new markets	64.5	36.7	46.9	28.0	45.1	26.4
More business from current customers	48.4	46.7	44.9	58.0	45.1	54.7
Market intelligence	38.7	20.0	53.1	34.0	35.3	37.7
Access to new technologies	29.0	16.7	18.4	26.0	25.5	20.8
Customer complaints (d)	22.6	16.7	24.5	34.0	39.2	37.7
Cost competitiveness (c)	22.6	3.3	22.4	18.0	29.4	24.5
Speed new products to market (c)	22.6	6.7	22.4	14.0	17.6	24.5
Integration forward (retail)	19.4	6.7	22.4	24.0	27.5	37.7
Integrate markets and technologies	19.4	10.0	22.4	28.0	21.6	26.4
Jump market barriers	19.4	3.3	32.7	14.0	15.7	11.3
Integration backward to suppliers (a, c)	16.1	16.7	28.6	36.0	47.1	43.4
Block competitors' moves	12.9	3.3	8.2	8.0	9.8	5.7
Trade/government help	12.9	3.3	10.2	4.0	3.9	1.9
Total #	n = 31	n = 30	n = 49	n = 51	n = 51	n = 53

(a) significant @ 0.00 level (1999 survey)   (c) significant @ 0.05 level (2000 survey)
(b) significant @ 0.00 level (2000 survey)   (d) significant @ 0.10 level (2000 survey)

This market orientation of many respondents aligns with the performance findings of Pelham (2000) described earlier: fast response to customer complaints, responding to competitive challenges, early detection of customer product changes, and an emphasis on a growth/differentiation strategy (rather than a low-cost strategy). Use of the Web and EC provides a means of supporting these actions.

Interestingly, cost competitiveness was not a reason given by that many firms, and its importance decreased in the 2000 survey (especially for smaller firms).

Further analysis of data in the 1999 study looked at performance measures, cross tabulating these with perceived importance of an EC strategy (Table 3). Analysis consisted of one-sided t-tests for the difference of proportions. Three surrogates of performance were employed:

1. Firm is financially better off this year.
2. Firm expects to be financially better off next year.
3. Confidence in the future (this is a good time to invest).

Table 6 shows the results within the three sizes of firms ("Yes" gives proportion viewing EC as strategic; "Gap" equals difference with firms not viewing EC as strategic). For smaller and medium-sized firms, this gap is always positive, while for larger firms it varies.

In terms of the two previously stated research questions, results support the hypothesis that SMEs can benefit from EC. Comparing performance within each size grouping, there were statistically significant differences in four of the nine measure/size pairs (asterisked cells). In another two of the pairs, the direction suggests better performance for firms viewing EC as strategically important. Comparing firms considering EC strategic, on a size

Table 6: EC Strategy Important Versus Performance (Proportion Agreeing)

Performance Measure		Smaller	Medium	Larger
Firm financially better off	Yes	0.83	0.72	0.59
	Gap	0.26*	0.22*	(0.24)
Expect better next year	Yes	0.74	0.72	0.76
	Gap	0.03	0.22*	0.12
Confidence in future	Yes	0.83	0.80	0.75
	Gap	0.21**	0.00	(0.07)

  * statistically significant @ 0.05 level
** statistically significant @ 0.10 level

basis, one significant difference was found—for the first measure (firm financially better off this year), between smaller and larger firms. Simply comparing differences among the three size groups, the direction for the first and third measures suggests an inverse relationship between size and performance. For the second measure, the results are inconclusive.

Overall, the findings are positive, suggesting that SMEs can gain disproportionately from EC. This supports the CREC study conclusions (Barua et al., 2000).

CONCLUSIONS

Early in this chapter, four frameworks were presented: the EC Reality Model, the EC Importance Grid, the Technology Adoption Life Cycle, and the Technology Maturation Cycle. Each of these can be applied to EC and SMEs.

For the EC Reality Model, this study suggests that firms are developing a better understanding of the actual benefits to be obtained from EC. Reality is being separated from hype. In particular, firms are becoming more focused with their reasons for EC. They are also becoming more realistic about potential benefits from EC (as evidenced by the decreasing importance of accessing new markets, and the continued importance of deriving more business from current customers). This study confirms that the pools of Useful EC and Strategic EC options appear to be more limited for SMEs than for larger manufacturers (larger firms gave more reasons and were more likely to already be involved in EC).

There is considerable evidence suggesting firms can fit into any of the four EC Importance Grid quadrants while still being successful. Comparing firms considering EC as strategic with those that did not, stronger performers was found in both groups. Yet, for SMEs, a higher proportion of strong performers were found in the group considering EC strategic (providing a positive response to the first research question: Is there a performance difference between manufacturers that do or do not see an EC strategy as important?). Since these are manufacturers, with physical products, the physical side of their operations (plant, equipment, and people) are important. The virtual value chain can supplement the physical but cannot replace it. So the current effect of EC does not yet appear to be significant for many manufacturers, particularly the smaller ones. While the world is changing, it is happening gradually. EC is maturing and moving along the maturation curve. Firms will need to monitor their position on the grid and make necessary adjustments at the appropriate time.

In terms of the Technology Adoption Life Cycle, larger firms clearly led SMEs. They had Web sites earlier than most SMEs, were more likely to see EC as an important strategy, were more likely to be using EC currently, and their reasons for using EC were broader. With their greater resources, and in-house IT capabilities, larger firms are better positioned to undertake adoption of technologies at an earlier point in the life cycle. As technology matures, becomes less expensive, and the "whole product" infrastructure expands, more SMEs will be able to expand their EC initiatives. With limited resources, not many SMEs can afford to be on the "bleeding edge" of EC.

Comments received indicated that some small firms felt they lacked technical understanding and resources to evaluate and implement a Web site and undertake EC initiatives. It appears that unless the owner/manager is really interested in the technology, the firm was not pressing ahead (which aligns with the findings of Mackay et al., 2001). Further investigation would be appropriate. "Resource poverty" has always been associated with smaller firms, and this is particularly relevant in the information technology area.

In response to the second research question—Are there performance differences between different sized firms, all viewing EC as important?—weak support was found suggesting that SMEs have more to gain from EC than larger firms. A higher proportion of them were stronger performers, compared to larger firms.

There were several limitations with this study. Results are representative of a particular region, rather than the entire country, at a single point or two in time, in a changing environment. The past two years have seen a period of strong economic growth in Canada, which could mask weaknesses in particular firms. This study relied on responses from senior managers, rather than observed measurements. Furthermore, differences found suggest, but certainly do not prove, causality. Nevertheless, the study provides a snapshot of what manufacturers within Canada's industrial heartland are doing, and planning to do, with EC.

REFERENCES

Ajzen, I. (1991). The theory of planned behavior. *Organizational Behaviour and Human Decision Processes, 50*(2), 179–211.

Applegate, L. M., McFarlan, F. W., & McKenney, J. L. (1999). *Corporate Information Systems Management: The Challenges of Managing in an Information Age* (5th Ed.). New York: McGraw-Hill.

Barua, A., Konana, P., Whinston, A., & Yin, F. (2000). *E-Business Value Assessment. Working Paper.* Center for Research in Electronic Commerce. Retrieved September 28, 2000, from the World Wide Web: http://cism.bus.utexas.edu/.

Boulton, R. E. S., Libert, B. D., & Samek, S. M. (2000). *Cracking the Value Code: How Successful Businesses are Creating Wealth in the New Economy.* New York: Harper Business.

Canadian E-Business Opportunities Roundtable. (2001). *Fast Forward 2.1, Taking Canada to the Next Level*. Retrieved June 6, 2001, from the World Wide Web: http://www.ebusinessroundtable.ca/english/documents/ff2.pdf.

Dandridge, T. C. & Levenburg, N. M. (1999). Small firms and the Internet: new insights on frequency and type of use. In *Proceedings of the 13th Annual National Conference*, United States Association for Small Business and Entrepreneurship, San Diego, USA.

Economist Intelligence Unit. (2001). *The Economist Intelligence Unit/Pyramid Research E-Readiness Rankings*. Retrieved June 8, 2001, from the World Wide Web: http://www.ebusinessforum.com/index.asp?layout=rich_story&doc_id=367.

Evans, P. & Wurster, T. S. (1999). Getting real about virtual commerce. *Harvard Business Review, 77*(6), 84–94.

Feeny, D. F. (1997). Introduction—Information management: Lasting ideas within turbulent technology. In Willcocks, L., Feeny, D., and Islei, G. (Eds.), *Managing IT as a Strategic Resource*, 17–28. New London: McGraw-Hill.

Fry, J. N. & Killing, J. P. (2000). *Strategic Analysis and Action* (4th Ed.). Scarborough, Ontario: Prentice-Hall.

Jentzsch, R. & Miniotas, A. (1999). The application of e-commerce to a SME. *Proceedings of the 10th Australasian Conference on Information Systems*, (pp. 435–447). Wellington, NZ.

Mackay, N., Gemino, A., Igbaria, M., & Reich, B. (2001). Empirical test of an electronic commerce adoption model in small firms. *Proceedings of the Annual Conference of the Administrative Sciences Association of Canada Information Systems Division*, (pp. 14–22). London, Canada.

Means, G. & Schneider, D. (2000). *Meta-Capitalism: The E-Business Revolution and the Design of 21st-Century Companies and Markets*, p. 15. New York: John Wiley & Sons.

Moore, G. A. (1995). *Inside the Tornado: Marketing Strategies from Silicon Valley's Cutting Edge*. New York: Harper-Business.

Pelham, A. M. (2000). Market orientation and other potential influences on performance in small and medium-sized manufacturing firms. *Journal of Small Business Management, 38*(1), 48–67.

Poon, S. (1999). Small business Internet commerce—What are the lessons learned? In Romm, C. & Sidweeks, F. (Eds.), *Doing Business on the Internet: Opportunities and Pitfalls*, (pp.113–124). Springer.

Porter, M. E. & Millar, V. E. (1985). How information gives you competitive advantage. *Harvard Business Review, 63*(4), 149–160.

Rayport, J. F. and Sviokla, J. J. (1995). Exploiting the virtual value chain. *Harvard Business Review, 73*(6), 75–85.

Rogers, E. M. (1995). *Diffusion of Innovations* (4th ed.). New York: The Free Press.

Rubin, R. S. (1999). Searching for competitive intelligence on the World Wide Web: A small business perspective. *Proceedings of the Small Business Institute Directors' Association Conference*, San Francisco, CA.

Standish Group. (2001). *GLOB of the Week*. Retrieved April 10, 2001, from the World Wide Web: http://www.pm2go.com/.

Statistics Canada. (2001). *Electronic Commerce and Technology 2000*. Retrieved June 26, 2001, from the World Wide Web: http://e-com.ic.gc.ca/english/documents/ecom_ict_2000.pdf.

Whyte, G. (2000). E-commerce—Meeting the SME challenge. *Presentation to the E-Business Capabilities in Canada Summit*, Ottawa, February. Retrieved June 26, 2001, from the World Wide Web: http://www.cfib.ca/legis/national/5064.asp.

Chapter XIII

Management's Contribution to Internet Commerce Benefit–Experiences of Online Small Businesses

Simpson Poon
Charles Sturt University, Australia
The University of Hong Kong, Hong Kong

INTRODUCTION

The importance of management and Information Technology (IT) success had been repeatedly identified in small business IT studies (for example, DeLone, 1988). When measuring information satisfaction among small firms, top management involvement was found to be one of the most important factors (Montazemi, 1988). The quest for the role of management involvement in Information Systems (IS) success in small firms continued into the 1990s. For example, Yap, Soh, and Raman (1992) studied a group of Singaporean small firms using earlier findings and discovered that CEO involvement was positively related to IS success. CEO involvement such as attending project meetings, involvement in information requirement needs analysis, reviewing consultants' recommendations and project monitoring are important to IS success. Thong, Yap and Raman (1996) pointed out that although management support was important, in cases where internal IS expertise was lacking, specialist knowledge (for example, engaging IT consultants in projects) was important to success. An in-depth study on motivators and inhibitors for small firms to adopt computing identified managerial enthusiasm as a key motivator (Cragg, 1998). The overseeing role of management during system implementation was found to be important to success. Management support was also found to be an important factor for IT success in the case of personal computing acceptance (Igbaria, Zinatelli, Craig, & Cavaye, 1997). All of these studies suggested that management involvement was critical to IS success regardless of cultural background.

Although these studies focused on small businesses, their definition of "small firms"[1] varied greatly in terms of size and turnover. I highlight this because the IT infrastructure and investment of a "large" small business (that is, with 100 or more employees) is very different from one that only has 10 or less employees. This difference might have accounted for the varying view of how important the role of management is compared to, say, external consultants. In a very small firm, the role of management is crucial, because the CEO (or owner) is the key, if not the only, decision maker. Without the very active push/participation of the CEO, no IS project can even get started. However, in a firm of 100 employees, there is likely to be someone (for example, the IT manager) who is responsible for IT development, and senior management only needs to endorse projects. Either way, the backing of management must be available for success.

In this day and age, IT applications are no longer just about in-house business software applications or local area networks. Today's IT issues are invariably linked to the Internet and Internet commerce applications. *Is there any difference between traditional IT applications and e-commerce? Can we apply what we have learned from earlier small business IT experiences to e-commerce? Does the largely external nature of e-commerce systems mean that management needs to play a different role than in the past?* These and many other questions need to be properly addressed. The aim of this study was to explore the answers to some of these questions and bridge the knowledge gap between traditional small business IT systems (such as Accounting, Inventory Management, and so forth) and Internet commerce systems. The results may help management to rethink how they can secure Internet commerce benefit and avoid activities that are noneffective.

INTERNET COMMERCE AMONG SMALL BUSINESSES

The Internet has fundamentally changed how business can and will be conducted. Statistics are pointing to increased adoption of Internet commerce by large and small companies (www.yellowpages.com.au). Given the amount of resources available, large companies have created very sophisticated Internet commerce systems (for example, those by major software vendors, publishing and information service firms). However, small firms have also benefited from Internet commerce, even with relatively little resources compared to a large firm (for example, an E-business group).

Internet commerce in this chapter is defined as *the use of the Internet and associated technologies (for example, WAP), as well as applications built upon this infrastructure to solicit, carry out and support various aspects of business activities of all levels*. This deliberately broad definition supports my belief that Internet commerce should not only cover selling and transactional activities as in the case of traditional Electronic Data Interchange (EDI) systems. The major difference between Internet commerce and traditional interorganization systems in the former is not (and should not be) limited to process-to-process business activities but also human-to-human and human-to-business communications.

Governments around the world are increasingly keen to ensure that small firms adopt Internet commerce (for example, http://www.oecd.org/dsti/sti/it/ec/index.htm). The reason for this is because most economies have a high percentage of small- and medium-sized enterprises (SMEs), some up to 95% or more. Small business success directly affects the economic health of a country.

Since the mid-1990s, more studies focus on Internet commerce among small businesses. Some are surveys on small businesses' Internet usage patterns (for example, Abell, 1996; Barker, Fuller, & Jenkins, 1997; Fink, Griese Roithmayr, & Sieber, 1997; Poon & Swatman, 1996), some into sales and marketing activities (for example, Auger & Gallaugher, 1997; Bennett, 1998; Poon & Jevons, 1997) and others on user experiences (for example, Barker, 1994) and usage strategy (for example, Cragg, 1998). We now know that small businesses are adopting very different approaches to Internet commerce as compared to large firms (Quelch & Klein, 1996). However, there is still insufficient understanding on how management can effectively help a small firm to gain benefit through Internet commerce.

Because of the still little-known linkage between the influence of management and the experience of Internet commerce success, I decided to apply the known effects of management influence from earlier studies to develop a number of propositions. The intention of these propositions was to examine if similar observations could be found in the case of Internet commerce. The outcomes would help management of SMEs to pursue a correct course of action to take advantage of Internet commerce for strategic advantage.

MANAGEMENT'S ROLE AND INTERNET COMMERCE BENEFIT

Although it is known that the role of management is instrumental to IT success among small businesses, it is not sure if we can expect the same in the case of Internet commerce. Presumably there will be similarities because the Internet can be considered a form of IT. However, there are differences between many Internet-based systems and traditional IT systems such as the focus on external and interorganizational activities rather than internal activities. Also, the openness, nonproprietary nature and easy accessibility make the Internet the most scalable and affordable IT infrastructure for SMEs to date. Because of this, measurements used in earlier studies (Montazemi, 1988; Yap et al., 1992; Thong et al., 1996), such as the number of PCs used, the existence of systems analysts and the number of internal applications, are likely to be less relevant, with the exception of management involvement. In fact, I created new indicators such as ability to convince members of the supply chain to use Internet commerce, apply Internet commerce with innovation and ability to create new business initiatives to examine their predictability of Internet commerce experience.

THE STUDY

I set up a study to investigate the effects of management on Internet commerce benefits. Apart from adapting some earlier measurements such as management push for project development, new indicators relevant to Internet commerce such as convincing firms on the supply chain to adopt Internet commerce were also used. A set of seven propositions was developed, and the rationale of each of them is explained in the following sections. A research model depicting the relationship between each of the propositions and its influence on perceived Internet commerce benefit gained is shown in Figure 1.

Push for Internet Connectivity

Management, as a driving force for technology adoption, has been repeatedly identified as key to IS success in small firms (DeLone, 1988; Martin, 1989). As such, I decided to investigate how management drives for Internet connectivity have resulted in actual benefits. Some studies (for example, Yellow Pages Australia, 1997) have suggested that one of the reasons why small firms are not using Internet commerce is because management does not see the need to use the Internet in the first place. Given the importance of management initiative (or enthusiasm) to IT success (DeLone, 1988; Martin,

Figure 1: A Research Model Proposing Management Influences on Internet Commerce Benefit

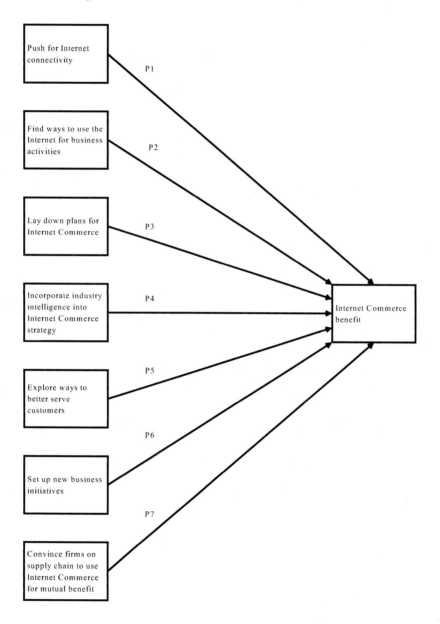

1989), I endeavoured to re-confirm if this was also true for Internet commerce adoption. I formulated Proposition 1 as below.

PROPOSITION 1: Small firms, in which management pushes for Internet connectivity, experience more benefit.

Actively Find Ways to Use the Internet for Business Activities

As Internet commerce really means using Internet technology to support business activities, how to do so effectively should be a key to success. Consequently, it is important for the user to carefully align business strategy with technology deployment. However, among the literature I found that studied how small businesses could benefit from IT, none examined the correlation between active usage and increased benefit. Logically, the more actively management experiments with Internet commerce, the more experienced management becomes in taking business advantage of such technology. Therefore, I speculated that those who actively explore using Internet commerce to support business activities would experience more benefit. I formulated Proposition 2, as follows.

PROPOSITION 2: Small firms, in which management is active in exploring how to apply Internet commerce, experience more benefit.

Lay Plans for Internet Commerce Implementation

Once a small business starts to have a rough idea of how the Internet can be used for business activities, logically, the next step for management is to lay down a plan (sometimes with external help) to implement an Internet commerce strategy. Cragg (1998) studied Internet strategy of small firms and found that management often steered the strategy development process. This concurs with findings from earlier IT studies (DeLone, 1988; Martin, 1989; Montazemi, 1988; Thong et al., 1996). I formulated Proposition 3 to test whether there was any evidence of this leading to experiencing more benefit.

PROPOSITION 3: Small firms, in which management lays down an implementation plan for Internet commerce, experience more benefit.

Incorporate Industry Intelligence into Internet Commerce Strategy

Apart from having an Internet commerce strategy, what the strategy is based on determines its quality. Industry intelligence is an important input to Internet commerce strategy, because it keeps the strategy relevant. A small business can use many economical and yet effective ways to gather industry intelligence such as publicly available information online and sources within its business networks (Hershey, 1984). By incorporating quality industry intelligence into the Internet commerce strategy formulation process, it should enhance the chances of gaining more benefit.

Therefore, I postulated that if management of a small business incorporates industry intelligence when setting Internet commerce strategy, it would benefit more from Internet commerce than firms that do not. I set up Proposition 4 follows.

PROPOSITION 4: Small firms, in which management incorporates industry intelligence when formulating Internet commerce strategy, experience more benefit.

Explore Ways to Better Serve Customers

For small businesses, Internet commerce seems to be more useful in supporting customer than supplier relationships (Poon & Swatman, 1999). Poon and Swatman suggested that this might be due to the highly customer-focused nature of most small firms. Because of this, it seems logical to assume that small firms which actively explore ways to better serve their customers would experience more benefit from Internet commerce. I formulated Proposition 5 to explore if this speculation is sustainable.

PROPOSITION 5: Small firms, in which management actively explores ways to better serve customers, experience more benefit.

Set Up New Business Initiatives Based on Internet Commerce

Apart from using Internet commerce to improve existing business processes, innovative small firms may actually set up new business initiatives to take advantage of what Internet commerce can offer. There are examples of traditional bookshops setting up virtual book clubs over the Internet, auctioneers setting up virtual auction sites to sell goods, and traditional stock brokers setting up online broker firms. These companies have taken an extra step to not just use the Internet to support existing businesses, but new business paradigms, which may be quite different.

Whether setting up new business initiatives will help a firm to experience more benefit from Internet commerce has rarely been confirmed. Because of this, I formulated Proposition 6 to examine whether setting up new business initiatives after adopting Internet commerce would lead to more benefit.

PROPOSITION 6: Small firms, in which management sets up new business initiatives through Internet commerce, experience more benefit.

Convince Firms on the Supply Chain to Use Internet Commerce for Mutual Benefit

When large manufacturing and retail firms first adopted EDI technology, they were quick to diffuse the technology to suppliers and customers (Iacovou, Benbasat, & Dexter, 1995; Webster, 1995). For an interorganizational system to succeed, it must have strong commitments from upstream and downstream of the supply chain. In the case of EDI, large firms were often found to be pressuring small suppliers and customers to adopt their technology. In such power relationships, large firms often got what they wanted, but the price to pay was the lack of full commitment from the other end. This often led to a decrease in benefit over time.

Based on earlier EDI experiences, I formulated Proposition 7 to examine whether convincing others to use the Internet helped to bring about benefit.

PROPOSITION 7: Small firms, in which management attempts to convince businesses on the supply chain to use Internet commerce, experience more benefit.

MEASURING EXPERIENCE OF INTERNET COMMERCE BENEFIT

The ideal way to measure benefit from technology adoption is to measure the change in financial performance. However, I experienced considerable difficulties in collecting financial figures from small firm management. This is shared by the obvious lack of financial analysis in earlier small business IT studies (see DeLone, 1988; Montazemi, 1988; Thong et al., 1996; Yap et al., 1992). My alternative was to measure benefit based on management's experience and perception. Although this is not as "quantitative" as financial figures, I hoped such a measurement would give me some qualitative understanding in the absence of hard figures. A five-point Likert scale (5—most positive experience, 1—least positive experience) was used for the four benefit indicators which were:

- Being more competitive than other non-online competitors
- Improved business performance
- Improved supplier/customer relationship
- Current benefit to be continued

Each of the seven propositions was measured against the four indicators above, and any significant differences were noted.

RESULTS AND DISCUSSION

A survey instrument containing questions related to the seven propositions was developed and sent to 224 small businesses via e-mail. These small companies were already online with an e-mail address and a Web page. The sample was collected from search engines which listed small businesses were interested in trading with other firms and online directories (for example, www.austrade.gov.au). For the former, I targeted search engines such as www.aussie.com.au to look for companies that did not look like a large company based on their descriptions. The sample consisted of firms from different business sectors (IT, Media and Publishing, Business and Professional Services, Tourism, Manufacturing, Retail and Wholesale); however, they were not broken down into equal portions. No firm from the Internet sector (such as Internet Service Providers and Web page developers) was included, because their responses were likely to bias the result. Among the replies collected, 67 were usable, and this gave a 30% response rate. I acknowledge that the number of responses is small in comparison to large-scale studies, but I believe the result is still useful for an exploratory study. Every effort was made to have the questionnaire reach a member of the senior management. This was done by carrying out investigations to find out the e-mail address of the CEO or a member of the management team.

The role of the respondents includes Director (48%), Owner (17.4%), Managing Director (16%), Manager (8.7%) and Partner (4.3%). This means 95% of the responses were from a member of the senior management—an important condition to ensure their answers reflected the management perspective.

For all seven propositions, a statistical method called t-test was used to examine if the two groups within the sample, those who did what was suggested in the proposition and those who did not, exhibited any significant difference in their experiences of gaining benefit from Internet commerce. The T-test was used because through visual examination of the sample distribution curve, normality could be assumed. Such a visual examination process was recommended by the statistical analysis package SPSS (in its Windows Help file), which was used to carry out all the statistical analysis in this study.

Push for Internet Connectivity

Table 1 shows that those firms which management pushed for Internet connectivity (87% of the sample did so) had more positive experiences. The difference between the two groups is significant across all four indicators. By observing the last row in Table 1 labeled *t-test (2-tailed p-value)*, one can see all four values are less than 0.05, with the one in the last column labeled *Current benefit to be continued* equal to 0.000. What all these figures mean is that there are significant differences between the two groups in terms of experiencing Internet commerce benefit when measured across the four benefit indicators. The most significant difference lies in the future view of Internet commerce, suggesting that management that pushed for Internet commerce implementation was confident of the benefit to be continued. Based on the result in Table 1, I can suggest with at least 95% confidence that Proposition 1 is a correct predictor of Internet commerce benefit based on user experience and perception.

I acknowledge that this might have been a self-fulfilling prophesy, being that those who pushed for adoption would naturally hope that Internet commerce benefit will continue. Nonetheless, the result reconfirms similar claims made in earlier small business IT studies. This also suggests that if management is not able to take the first step to acquire Internet connectivity, then it is unlikely for the firm to experience significant benefit, even if someone else in the firm gets them online.

Actively Find Ways to Use the Internet for Business Activities

My proposition that suggests firms that actively find ways to use the Internet for business activities have better experience from Internet commerce does not seem to hold true among the respondents. Eighty-eight percent of the respondents admitted they actively found ways to use the Internet for their business activities, but the experience of the two groups remained similar. One possible explanation is that once online, most firms would find ways to use the Internet anyway. The difference between those who actively did so and those who did not is insignificant. The t-test result is shown in Table 2. It is also possible that simply

Table 1: Mean Scores between Firms with Management, that Pushed for Internet Connectivity and Those Who did Not (*P = .05, **P = .01)

	More competitive than non-online competitors	Improved business performance	Improved supplier/ customer relationship	Current benefit to be continued
Pushed for Internet connectivity	3.5	3.3	3.3	4.3
Did not push for Internet connectivity	2.4	2.0	2.0	2.3
T-test (2-tailed p-value)	.032*	.016*	.015*	.000**

"finding" ways to use the Internet for business without implementing a good business strategy is insufficient for differentiation. What the result suggests is that once online, small business management must understand that looking for ways to use the Internet for business activities is a competitive necessity, not an advantage. Although the result also indicates that those who did not do so were not worse off, the future for them can be less favorable in the longer term.

Lay Plans for Internet Commerce

Although earlier studies point out the importance of management involvement in IT planning, it seems that this alone may be insufficient to guarantee benefit (see Table 3). This is again unexpected, given that management involvement in planning has proven to be critical to IT success. One explanation is that the level and the type of involvement may need to be further clarified. For Internet commerce projects, management sitting in on planning meetings might not be sufficient. Also, simply providing general guidance in planning is insufficient when working with a rapidly changing business paradigm. It is important that management works with a multidisciplinary team, including technical experts and Web page designers among others for success. Another way to interpret the result is that it may be too early to determine the effect of management planning. This is reflected by the fourth benefit indicator (current benefit to be continued) which exhibits a weak significant difference. Despite the lack of statistical differences, the mean scores for all four benefit indicators are higher for small firms that did lay down plans. Again, laying down a plan for Internet commerce is a competitive necessity instead of a competitive advantage.

Table 2: Mean Scores between Firms which Management had Found Ways to use the Internet for Business Activities and Those Who Did Not (*P =0 .05, **P = 0.01)

	More competitive than non-online competitors	Improved business performance	Improved supplier/ customer relationship	Current benefit to be continued
Found ways to use the Internet for business	3.4	3.2	3.1	4.1
Did not find ways to use the Internet for business	3.3	2.7	3.2	4.0
T-test (2-tailed p-value)	.844	.408	.935	.875

Table 3: Mean Scores between Firms with Management who Laid Plans for Internet Commerce and Those Who Did Not (*p = .05, **p = .01)

	More competitive than non-online competitors	Improved business performance	Improved supplier/ customer relationship	Current benefit to be continued
Laid plans for Internet commerce	3.5	3.3	3.2	4.3
Did not lay plans for Internet commerce	3.1	2.8	3.0	3.6
T-test (2-tailed *p*-value)	0.211	0.218	0.528	0.034*

Incorporate Industry Intelligence into Internet commerce Strategy

The effect of incorporating industry intelligence into strategy formulation has been important to the traditional planning process. Two-thirds of the respondents claimed to have incorporated industry intelligence into their strategy formulation process for Internet commerce. Therefore, it is surprising that the result in Table 4 shows that there is no significant difference between the groups. It is possible that the nature of Internet commerce rendered traditional industry intelligence less relevant. Scrutinizing what type of industry intelligence a firm is gathering and how it incorporates it into its Internet commerce strategy may provide some explanations. Because Internet commerce models change very quickly, intelligence that was useful in the past may not contribute much to future competitiveness. It may be simply a case of selecting the "right" type of intelligence and applying appropriate analysis techniques that matter.

Explore Ways to Better Serve Customers

Quality customer service is a key to the success for small businesses, because serving returning customers generally costs less than looking for new customers. If a small firm is operating with limited resources, then using Internet commerce to help service new and returning customers is important. Among the respondents, 83.6% indicated they had explored ways to better serve their customers (see Table 5). Although there is limited evidence that those respondents who explored ways to better serve customers had experienced improved business performance, it is uncertain whether they were better off than their nononline competitors or whether the current benefits would continue. Because nonmanufacturing small businesses interact more with customers than

Table 4: Mean Scores between Firms with Management that Incorporated Industry Intelligence for Strategy Formulation and Those Who Did Not (*p = 0.05, **p = 0.01)

	More competitive than non-online competitors	Improved business performance	Improved supplier/ customer relationship	Current benefit to be continued
Incorporated industry intelligence for strategy formulation	3.6	3.3	3.3	4.2
Did not incorporate industry intelligence for strategy formulation	3.1	2.8	2.8	3.9
T-test (2-tailed p-value)	.186	.135	.159	.357

suppliers, the result of the third indicator (improved supplier/customer relationship) may have been diluted by the "supplier" component.

Although both groups of respondents were exploring ways to better serve customers, interacting with customers online (for example, customer support, product delivery) can be a steep learning experience, and customers might not be ready for it yet. Consequently, the benefits gained from such efforts were not yet realized.

Set Up New Business Initiatives Based on Internet commerce

A browse on the Internet will show that many businesses come into existence because of the Internet. To take full advantage of Internet commerce, a small firm may have to transform itself to make its business "Internet commerce compatible." The result in Table 6 presents strong support for this observation. Among the respondents, 61.2% expressed that they had set up some kind of new business initiative. Interpreting this with the results from previous propositions, this is the observation. *A small firm can explore, lay down a plan for and gather information on how to deploy Internet commerce, but only those who actually set up new business initiatives tailored for the Internet will experience distinct benefits.* This means setting up totally new business initiatives around Internet commerce. This concurs with the common observations among the most successful E-businesses (for example, Yahoo!, Amazon.com, among others). Another approach is to radically transform existing business activities based on sound Internet commerce principles. This means adopting a so-called "clicks and

Table 5: Mean Scores between Firms with Management who Explored Ways to Better Serve Customers and Those Who Did Not (*p = .05, **p = .01)

	More competitive than non-online competitors	Improved business performance	Improved supplier/ customer relationship	Current benefit to be continued
Explored ways to better serve customers	3.5	3.3	3.2	4.2
Did not explore ways to better serve customers	3.0	2.2	2.7	3.6
T-test (2-tailed *p*-value)	0.330	0.025*	0.308	0.193

Table 6: Mean Scores between Firms with Management that Set Up New Business Initiatives and Those Who Did Not (*p = 0.05, **p =0 .01)

	More competitive than non-online competitors	Improved business performance	Improved supplier/ customer relationship	Current benefit to be continued
Set up new business initiatives	3.9	3.7	3.4	4.3
Did not set up new business initiatives	2.6	2.2	2.7	3.7
T-test (2-tailed *p*-value)	0.000**	0.000**	0.045*	0.038*

mortar" approach. Examples of this approach include E-enabled Supply Chain Management systems, Customer Relationship Management systems and Enterprise Resource Planning systems.

Convince Firms on the Supply Chain to Use Internet commerce for Mutual Benefit

Among the many studies of IT in small firms, this factor was not considered, because those systems studied were internal instead of interorganizational systems. Convincing partner firms on the supply chain to use Internet commerce can be quite difficult, particularly small firms which do not normally have the power to influence the others. However, streamlining exchanges (both document and information) along the supply chain was so important that in early cases of EDI adoption, some large firms actually provided the technology free for their small suppliers (Iacovou, Benbasat, & Dexter, 1995). Among the respondents, 67.2% had managed to convince others on the supply chain to use the Internet to work together. These firms also exhibited more positive experience of gaining benefit (see Table 7).

This confirms that Internet commerce, like EDI systems in the past, can only bring benefit to users when others on the supply chain are using it as well. Small firms that are planning to adopt Internet commerce need to start lobbying other firms on the supply chain to go along with them in the process. In other words, a small firm will not gain significant benefit from Internet commerce if others on the supply chain are not adopting it.

IMPLICATIONS FOR SMALL BUSINESS MANAGEMENT

This study suggests that although management needs to do many things to keep a small firm competitive through Internet commerce, only a few things make a distinct contribution to success. The key issues management needs to focus on, based on the findings from this study, are as follows:

1. **Push for Internet technology adoption**: The importance of direct intervention by management to start off the IT adoption process is not news; my results reconfirm this is "Step One" to Internet commerce success. If management adopts a "hands-on" attitude to Internet adoption, this will sound off a message to the rest of the company that management is serious about the Internet. Leadership-by-example is apparently quite important, and those companies that did so in this study found they experienced strong benefit from Internet commerce. I interpret this as a psychological strengthening effect—a change of attitude of the firm. Others in the firm who are keen to see the adoption of Internet commerce will be more encouraged to work toward this goal. The effect is significantly stronger than a firm in which management does

Table 7: Mean scores between Firms with Management Convinced Others to Use Internet Commerce and Those Who Did Not (*p = 0.05, **p = 0.01)

	More competitive than non-online competitors	Improved business performance	Improved supplier/customer relationship	Current benefit to be continued
Convinced others to use Internet Commerce	3.8	3.5	3.4	4.4
Did not convince others to use Internet commerce	2.6	2.4	2.5	3.3
T-test (2-tailed *p*-value)	0.002**	0.002**	0.010*	0.000**

not do so. The implication of this finding is that if management is not playing a leading role to start the adoption process, then even if the firm is eventually online, the experience of Internet commerce is significantly less positive.

2. **Set up new business initiatives through Internet commerce**: Setting up new business initiatives that exploit the characteristics of Internet commerce can also bring much benefit to a small firm. Compared to other less effective Internet initiatives, such as laying down a plan for implementation, it is the innovation applied by management that makes the difference. The implication of this finding to small business management is that if one wants to gain real benefit from Internet commerce, one needs to really think long and hard how to develop new business ideas which can be further enhanced through Internet commerce. Purely creating an "e-version" of the same thing may not work. For example, sending e-mail catalogues to customers instead of the printed version can be cost effective, but it is through a Customer Relationship Management strategy to customize the catalogue to address individual needs which counts. For example, one of the small businesses studied was a traditional printing business that transformed itself to become a Web page designer by focusing more on its design competence instead of its printing operation. Self-evaluation and reflection, together with a sound knowledge of Internet commerce, form the most powerful strategy.

3. **Convince those on the supply chain to adopt Internet commerce**: Internet commerce is not really useful if the size of the user community is small, particularly on the same supply chain. However, due to different reasons, some parties on the supply chain may not want to adopt Internet commerce. For example, some members on the supply chain may see allowing others to access their ordering systems as a threat. Others may see rapid exchange of information as erosion of power, because information (or the lack of it) is the bargaining chip. Unfortunately, until everyone decides to effectively use Internet commerce to streamline the supply chain, no one may gain full benefit from it. In this study, small firms that managed to convince their supply chain partners to adopt Internet commerce experienced more benefit. The implication for small business management is this: for Internet commerce, quite different from traditional IT systems, it is other members' adoption that counts for more. Consequently, a small business should, after adopting Internet commerce, try hard to convince those who do business with them to do so as well. This may not mean setting up a sophisticated supply chain management system but may be as simple as using e-mail to attach order and invoice documents. Given the limited resources (both financial and personnel) a small business has, it is more appropriate to adopt an evolutionary rather than revolutionary approach to major IT investments.

CONCLUSION

Based on earlier studies on small businesses IT success, I set up a study to examine the factors contributing to Internet commerce success among small business, with specific focus on the role of management influence. I constructed seven propositions to investigate the different ways management of a small firm influenced its Internet commerce deployment. My finding reveals that not all actions taken by management are equal—some have a more significant effect on success than others. The three most critical things management of a small firm should focus on are as follows:

1.   Push for Internet, and subsequently, Internet commerce adoption
2.   Set up new business initiatives to take full advantage of Internet commerce based on strategic rethinking and planning
3.   Convince members on the same supply chain to adopt Internet commerce and use it to conduct business with itself

In conclusion, to fully experience Internet commerce benefit, small businesses need to take proactive actions to fully exploit Internet commerce. The relationship of these most important actions is depicted in Figure 2. Moderate actions may not be sufficient because other competitors are doing so anyway. In addition, a firm cannot be inward looking as in the case of deploying traditional IT systems. Given

Table 8: A Summary of the Effect of Management Initiatives on Internet Commerce Benefit "✓" significant, "✗" insignificant

	More competitive than non-online competitors	Improved business performance	Improved supplier/ customer relationship	Current benefit to be continued
Push for Internet connectivity	✓	✓	✓	✓
Find ways to use business activities	✗	✗	✗	✗
Lay down plan for Internet Commerce	✗	✗	✗	✓
Incorporate industry intelligence	✗	✗	✗	✗
Explore ways to better serve customers	✗	✓	✗	✗
Set up new business initiatives	✓	✓	✓	✓
Convince others to use Internet for mutual benefit	✓	✓	✓	✓

Figure 2: The Benefit Value Chain for Small Business Management Involving Internet Commerce

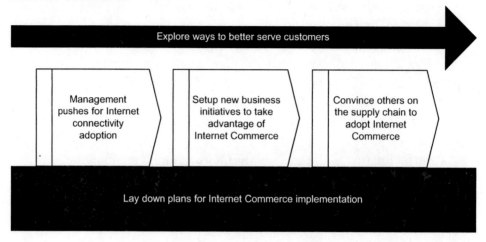

the dynamics and rapidly evolving nature of Internet commerce, small firm management needs to transform traditional ways of thinking and reconceptualize how to create new business models around the capability of Internet commerce.

ENDNOTE

1 The Australian Bureau of Statistics (ABS) defines small business as: "businesses employing fewer than 20 employees."

In addition, small businesses typically have the following management or organizational characteristics:

- They are independently owned and operated
- They are closely controlled by owners/managers who also contribute most, if not all of the operating capital
- The principal decision-making functions rest with the owners/managers

REFERENCES

Abell, W. & Lim, L. (1996). *Business Use of the Internet in New Zealand: An Exploratory Study*. Retrieved from the World Wide Web: http://www.scu.edu.au/ausweb96/business/abell/paper.htm.

Auger, P. & Gallaugher, J. M. (1997). Factors affecting the adoption of an Internet-based sales presence for small businesses. *The Information Society, 13*(1), 55–74.

Barker, N. (1994). *The Internet as a Reach Generator for Small Business.* Unpublished Masters Thesis, Business School, University of Durham, (September).

Barker, N., Fuller, T., & Jenkins, A. (1997). Small firms' experiences with the Internet. *Proceedings of the 20th ISBA National Conference,* Belfast, Northern Ireland.

Bennett, R. (1998). Using the World Wide Web for international marketing: Internet use and perceptions of export barriers among German and British businesses. *Journal of Marketing Communications, 4,* 27–43.

Cragg, P. B. (1998). Clarifying Internet strategy in small firms. *Proceedings of the 9th Australasian Conference on Information Systems, 1,* 98–107. Sydney, Australia.

DeLone, W. (1988). Determinants of success for computer usage in small business. *MIS Quarterly, 12*(1), 51–61.

Fink, K., Griese, J., Roithmayr, F., & Sieber, P. (1997). Business on the Internet—Some (r)evolutionary perspective. In Vogel et al. (Eds.), *Proceedings of the 10th International Bled Electronic Commerce Conference, 2,* 536–555. Slovenia.

Hershey, R. (1984). Commercial intelligence on a shoestring. Gumpert, D. E. (Ed.), *Growing Concerns: Building and Managing the Small Business,* (pp. 121–130). Harvard Business Review Executive Book Series. New York: John Wiley & Sons.

Iacovou, C. L., Benbasat, I., & Dexter, A. S. (1995). Electronic data interchange and small organizations: Adoption and impact of technology. *MIS Quarterly, 19*(4), 465–485.

Igbaria, M., Zinatelli, N., Cragg, P., & Cavaye, A. L. M. (1997). Personal computing acceptance factors in small firms: A structural equation model. *MIS Quarterly, 21*(3), 279–305.

Martin, C. J. (1989). Information management in the smaller business: The role of the top manager. *International Journal of Information Management, 9,* 187–197.

Montazemi, A. R. (1988). Factors affecting information satisfaction in the context of the small business environment. *MIS Quarterly, 12*(2), 239–256.

Poon, S. & Jevons, C. (1997). Internet-enabled international marketing: A small business perspective. *Journal of Marketing Management. 13*(1–4), 29–41.

Poon, S. & Swatman, P. M. C. (1996). Small business Internet usage: A preliminary survey of Australian SMEs. *Proceedings of the 4th European Conference on Information Systems,* (pp. 1103–1112). Lisbon, Portugal.

Poon, S. & Swatman, P. M. C. (1999). A longitudinal study of expectations in small business Internet commerce. *International Journal of Electronic Commerce, 3*(3), 21–33.

Quelch, J. A. & Klein, L. R. (1996). The Internet and international marketing. *Sloan Management Review, 37*(3), 60–75.

Thong, J. Y. L., Yap, C. S., & Raman, K. S. (1996). Top management support, external expertise and information systems implementation in small businesses. *Information Systems Research, 7*(2), 248–267.

Webster J. (1995). Networks of collaboration or conflict? Electronic data interchange and power in the supply chain. *Journal of Strategic Information Systems, 4*(1), 31–42.

Yap, C. S., Soh, C. P. P., & Raman, K. S. (1992). Information systems success factors in small business. *OMEGA International Journal of Management Sciences, 20*(5–6), 597–609.

Yellow Pages Australia. (1997). *Small Business Index™: A Special Report on Technology in the Small Business Sector*, August. Retrieved from the World Wide Web: http://www.yellowpages.com.au.

Previously Published in *Managing Information Technology in Small Businesses: Challenges and Solutions,* Copyright © 2002, Idea Group Inc.

Chapter XIV

Electronic Commerce Opportunities, Challenges and Organizational Issues for Australian SMEs

Mohini Singh
RMIT University, Australia

INTRODUCTION

Australian small businesses are increasingly adopting the Internet and the World Wide Web as a medium of doing business to reach new customers and suppliers, cut costs and expand business. They also use it to enhance communication between buyers and suppliers. This chapter discusses the findings of an exploratory study in Australia that identified the objectives, opportunities and challenges of e-commerce experienced by small businesses that were mostly early adopters of the Internet as a medium of trade. E-commerce issues presented in this chapter include research findings, supported by theory from literature. Electronic commerce opportunities, challenges and organizational learning by small and medium enterprises (SMEs) in Australia indicate that small businesses have created value with e-commerce, although benefits are long term and dependent on a plethora of technological, business and management issues that need to be addressed. Due to the fast-evolving nature of e-business and technological developments that are new to many small businesses, challenges such as managing the expanded flow of information, cross-border taxation, authentication, trust and security, as well as the high costs of acquiring the required technologies and skills, are prevalent. Other challenges of e-commerce range from Web site maintenance to business process reengineering for an integrated environment. Research findings also highlight the fact that small businesses need formal methods of evaluating the performance of e-commerce to realize the benefits of investment and to further expand their e-commerce venture.

ELECTRONIC COMMERCE

E-commerce generally means doing business on the Internet. It is also referred to as Internet commerce, digital business and online trade. Different authors, depending on the perspective from which it is viewed, have defined electronic commerce differently. According to Watson et al. (1999), electronic commerce is the use of computer networks to improve organizational performance. Turban et al. (2000) define it as the process of buying and selling or exchanging of products, services and information via computer networks including the Internet.

Increasing profitability and market share, improving customer service and delivering products faster are some of the organizational performance gains allegedly possible with electronic commerce. Activities such as the buying and selling of goods and services, as well as transferring funds, utilizing digital communications and all aspects of an organization's electronic interactions with its stakeholders, such as customers, suppliers, government regulators, financial institutions, managers, employees and the public at large, are included in e-commerce. All intercompany and intracompany functions such as marketing, finance, manufacturing, selling and negotiation that use electronic mail, EDI, file transfer, fax, video conferencing, workflow or interaction with a remote computer are components of e-commerce. The rapid adoption of the Internet and the World Wide Web by small businesses as a commercial medium in Australia and other parts of the world is changing the face of business. The Internet has created electronic marketplaces where buyers and suppliers meet to exchange information about prices and product and service offerings, and to negotiate and carry out business transactions (Archer & Gebauer, 2000). Archer and Gebauer are also of the opinion that although electronic marketplaces involve business-to-consumer (B2C) and business-to-business (B2B) systems, growth in B2B is estimated to be five times the value of B2C. Many small businesses are suppliers of products to larger businesses and are important entities of the supply chain.

ELECTRONIC COMMERCE ISSUES FOR SMALL AND MEDIUM BUSINESS ENTERPRISES

SMEs are embracing electronic commerce for many reasons, however, an important reason is to improve competitiveness and to reach out to customers at greater distances. New markets and distribution channels, increased communication and low-cost advertising are easily achieved with e-commerce. Although electronic commerce has been proved to be popular with large business enterprises, small and medium companies can also create value by marketing and selling goods and services electronically (Dublish, 2000). Each company is constrained by the same amount of graphics and design capability that the Internet can deliver, so everyone starts from the same position with their Web sites. This allows small companies to compete directly with larger organizations and acquire a valuable market share (Turban et al., 2000). On the Internet, it is easy for small organizations to build and maintain a professional-looking site with innovative services and capture a market share that generally belonged to larger organizations. Smaller businesses, due to their size, have the advantage of being able to implement changes faster and adapt to the demands of Internet commerce better than larger organizations, which are based on more bureaucratic structures. However, as pointed out by Baldwin et al. (2000), for small and medium-sized businesses to achieve success with e-commerce, technology must become widely available to ordinary people, and SMEs must be prepared to alter their business processes.

Poon and Swatman (1996) classified the benefits of the Internet as a medium of business for SMEs to be direct or indirect. Direct benefits include those relating to measurable cost savings in areas such as communications and marketing, and indirect benefits include shortened communication cycles, and an improved relationship and image. Whinston, Stahl, and Choi (1997) and Viehland (1998) described the opportunities of electronic commerce as savings arising from lower procurement and overhead costs, reduced inventory costs arising from electronic ordering and just-in-time delivery and reduced service costs by providing support via electronic channels. Extended markets for online businesses have resulted in increased revenue by selling to buyers from a wider geographic region. According to the Aberdeen Report (1997), business transactions conducted electronically are completed in less time and at reduced administrative costs. The reduced cost of creating, processing, distributing, storing and retrieving paper-based information is also an opportunity that can be realized from e-commerce. Small organizations can create highly specialized businesses and reduce the time between outlay of capital and receipt of goods and services. Turban et al. (2000) confirmed that e-commerce expands the marketplace to national and international buyers with minimal capital outlay and facilitates contacts with more customers, better suppliers and suitable business partners worldwide, markets to be replaced by buyers.

While business organizations can enjoy the benefits of reduced operating costs, increased revenue and effective information monitoring from electronic commerce, consumers have the advantage of convenient shopping as well as access to information regarding the product and its use. As suggested by Hoffman, Novak, and Chatterji (1999), the Web provides the ability to amass, analyze and control large quantities of specialized data to enable "comparison shopping" and speed the process of finding items. Winner (1997, p. 31) added to customer convenience by saying, "People will relish the convenience of buying things on the Net, flocking to stores whose electronic doors are always open and where parking is never a problem."

E-commerce issues discussed in this chapter have been identified from a study that investigated 20 small to medium online businesses. Of these, 17 were "bricks-and-mortar" organizations that had adopted e-commerce as a new channel of business, and three were "pure plays" that took advantage of the Internet to set up trade. The research project was exploratory in nature and aimed at identifying e-commerce issues for small and medium enterprises.

RESEARCH METHODOLOGY

For this microstudy, I adopted an exploratory study method. It involved conducting interviews with small e-business owners. The companies were selected on the basis that they had been identified as significant e-commerce initiatives within the state of Victoria. The names of companies were acquired from documents that listed them as "electronic commerce success stories" (Phillips, 1998) and from Internet searches. Victorian companies that had a presence on the Internet with online transaction capability were identified from different search engines. Although it was intended to investigate different industry sectors, the 20 case studies are representatives of those organizations with whom interviews could be arranged in the year 1999. Initial contact was made by telephone with the person who headed the electronic commerce project at the organization.

Yin (1994) describes exploratory studies to contain a number of "what" and "how many" types of inquiries, which were the types of questions included in the interview tool used to collect data. It comprised five major sections that included questions on the objectives of developing electronic commerce, its opportunities, challenges, technological requirements and its impact on business. With the permission of the interviewees, all interviews were recorded on tape and later transcribed. Findings discussed in this chapter are the outcome of a qualitative analysis of responses acquired from e-commerce project leaders and owners of 20 early adopters of e-commerce.

Companies Investigated

For reasons of confidentiality, names of companies investigated are not identified. I have referred to them as Companies A to T listed in Tables 1 and 2. Of these, Companies E, I and T are "virtual" organizations, while the others are examples of "bricks-and-mortar" organizations that have adopted the Internet as a new channel of business. E-commerce objectives, opportunities and challenges identified from the research are included in Tables 1 and 2.

E-COMMERCE OBJECTIVES AND OPPORTUNITIES

Many small and medium enterprises in Australia are adopting e-commerce to exploit the potential of new technologies such as the Internet and the World Wide Web. The opportunities and objectives of e-commerce identified from the research project include the following:

Increased Customer Base

An important advantage of Internet businesses is that they have no defined location, time zone or country. Their Web sites can be accessed 24 hours a day, seven days a week. By offering a "24x7" shop front or "we never close" customer service, Australian small businesses intend to capture customers from wider geographic regions. Online shopfronts for national and international customers allow these organizations to offer a wide variety of goods to customers from distant locations, as compared to shoppers in the vicinity of traditional outlets. Expanding business to local, regional and global customers, and offering them convenient shopping hours were important objectives of adopting e-commerce for the organizations investigated.

Increased Sales

For the sample of SMEs investigated, an increase in sales and revenue was achieved with e-commerce. An increase in revenue is usually more significant to smaller organizations as compared to larger ones. For example, a million dollars of revenue could mean a substantial increase in profits for SMEs but may be insignificant for large businesses. The sale of goods to customers in the Asia and Pacific regions who are out of reach with traditional business was already achieved by some small e-commerce enterprises. Promotion of goods to an increased number of customers and dealing with them in new ways, that is, allowing electronic ordering, online tracking of orders and sales and offering e-payment methods, escalated sales. Providing additional information about products also led to cross selling and upselling of products that may be complementary or add-ons.

Disintermediation

Disintermediation occurs with e-commerce as the services of middlemen become irrelevant. Research findings indicate that many organizations have managed to transform the market chain, that is, reach out to their customers directly. They have curtailed the role of middlemen such as brokers and dealers. Not having to deal with middle people meant reduced costs for the sellers, providing faster service and sometimes more accurate information to customers.

Improved Customer Service

Customer service and support is one of the most promising areas of electronic commerce. Delivering a better customer service and achieving improved customer relations was another important objective of e-commerce identified from this research. Organizations investigated indicated that with online trade, they intended to offer their customers access to real-time information about products, services, inventory, product updates and other relevant information. Reaching out to customers directly with correct information and personalized services via the Internet enabled their clientele to make better decisions about their purchases. With e-mail responses to confirm orders and the dispatch of goods, these organizations developed a better relationship with their customers. The supplier is able to communicate directly with the customers, thus a valuable one-to-one relationship is developed. Via e-mail responses, customers are addressed by their names, creating a more personalized service as compared to the general form of greetings offered in traditional stores. With the hyperlink capability of Web technology, organizations have been able to provide additional information about new products and services to customers. The Internet's interactive qualities allow for customers' comments and feedback for business improvements, which many small enterprises had begun to capitalize on.

Improved Efficiency and Reduced Costs

The investigated organizations improved efficiency by automating processes that were repetitive, such as sending newsletters, quotes, order and delivery confirmation, product brochures and, in some more developed e-commerce organizations, accounts and advertising. Automated processes result in efficiencies such as reduced paperwork, errors, time and overhead costs. Automated, built-in responses to customers leads to a reduction in the number of employees required by an organization to handle customer queries by phone and fax. Reduced logistics operating costs, and reduced inventory with e-ordering systems and JIT delivery, led to the reduction of overhead costs for many of the small businesses, instead of early adopters of e-commerce; however, it was more prevalent for "pure plays." As suggested by Cameron (1997), although the establishment and maintenance of a Web site has costs of its own, the price of using the Web compared to other sales channels is significantly less.

Increased Circulation of Advertisements

Most of the organizations investigated managed to increase the circulation of their advertisements on the Internet at no substantial increase in costs. As an advertising medium, promotion using a Web site results in the sale of 10 times the number of units with one-tenth of the advertising budget and one-quarter of direct-mail expenditures (Cameron, 1997). There is no time lag between publishing information on a Web site and it being accessed by customers. Research findings indicate that most organizations adopted e-commerce initiatives for advertising and marketing, and many were content with using the Internet for brochureware more than selling, which required the development and implementation of other e-processes. Others started their e-commerce with a Web site for marketing and promoting their business, followed by further "e" developments.

Improved Competitiveness

Irrespective of their size, all online businesses have the same access to potential customers. Small businesses are able to compete with well-established companies that have name recognition, an established infrastructure and purchasing power. Customers accessing online business sites are not aware of the size or location of the business. Electronic storefronts have allowed smaller organizations to compete with large multinationals by reaching out to the same set of customers. They have also been able to access and implement competitive intelligence used by larger organizations to promote business and develop new services. New product information and other marketing campaigns used by competitors can be "tweaked" at little or no cost and with very little time lag. Improved competitiveness was an important objective of e-commerce indicated by most small businesses investigated.

Educated Clients

An important intangible opportunity that resulted from electronic commerce, according to one organization, is the upgraded technology capability and business skills of consumers. To be able to take advantage of electronic commerce, consumers have to have the knowledge to use the Internet and Web technology. They have to learn to track their orders and understand secure electronic transactions and payments and other intricacies of electronic commerce. E-commerce encouraged buyers to become technology savvy.

Other objectives and opportunities of e-commerce identified from this research were to become a "smart and innovative organization," use data mining and knowledge management to predict demand and use "push technology" to win customers. Some less prevalent objectives were improved business relations, improved productivity of salespeople, "new-found" business partners, a better image and enhanced skills of employees.

ELECTRONIC COMMERCE CHALLENGES EXPERIENCED BY SMALL BUSINESSES

While the opportunities of electronic commerce are undeniable, electronic commerce is new and therefore faces a number of problems. The challenges of electronic commerce identified from this research are as follows:

An Infrastructure for Electronic Payment System

As suggested by Watson et al. (1999), when commerce goes electronic, the means of paying for goods and services must also go electronic. Paper-based payment systems cannot support the speed, security, privacy and internationalization necessary for electronic commerce. Although different electronic payment methods are available in Australia, it is clear from this research that educating consumers and business partners on secure payment systems is necessary to build their confidence and intensify electronic trade. The research highlighted the fact that electronic trade is repressed by the lack of confidence in the methods of payment systems available. As a consequence, many of these businesses depended on multichannel payment methods (checks, cash on delivery, money orders and so forth) to sustain e-commerce.

International Legal Standards

Australian organizations generally close business agreements with a handshake or a signature on a paper contract. Although small businesses could significantly expand business by contributing to various supply chains, many of them missed out on the prospect due to "fuzzy" e-agreements. They emphasized the need for a set of regulatory frameworks and authenticating policies that online merchants and buyers can turn to if disputes arose. Electronic commerce legal and security frameworks will increase the confidence of online shoppers and businesses to extend trade on the Internet.

Web Site Design and Development

Except for a few that developed their own Web sites, most of the organizations investigated outsourced its development. An important problem identified from this research was that in the process of outsourcing Web site design and development, control was given to outsiders who at times failed to adequately address the objectives of business. It was emphasized that outsourcing Web site designs meant losing creative ideas to competitor organizations taken to them by designers and developers. Another difficulty experienced was keeping up with advanced design tools and technologies. That is, by the time the e-commerce development was completed, a new and better technology for the same purpose was available. Coordination with internal people and ISPs (Internet Service Providers) during the development stage was a problem mostly due to a lack of technology knowledge in-house and the short life span of many ISPs. Striking a balance with rich graphic presentation and download speed, frequently updating and maintaining information, identifying tools for quick search and applying correct logic to e-applications were other problems identified. It was also highlighted that Web sites designed without analyzing the projected users' knowledge of technology, background and needs is a mistake. Small businesses that supplied goods to larger organizations emphasized the need for regular meetings with business partners for uniform formats for transaction data and applications of automated processes.

Technological Limitations

Although technology issues have contributed to other challenges discussed earlier, more specific ones identified were the high costs of integrating business processes, implementing networked services, incompatible software and hardware and a lack of standards and communication protocols for B2B e-commerce.

It is also worth noting that only a small percentage of organizations investigated had extranets or intranets, therefore, issues pertinent to these technologies have not been included in this chapter.

Sociotechnical Issues

The nature and number of jobs at all levels of organization is likely to change as a result of electronic commerce. A number of problems, such as job losses due to a lack of skills and having to take up new responsibilities, led to resistance from employees. The "old guards" especially felt threatened if their previous skills gained from years of experience were not valued in the electronic environment. Although electronic commerce promises new opportunities, people are still needed to make it work. Therefore, individual feelings and needs must be addressed if the benefits of electronic commerce are to be fully realized. Motivating employees to take up training for improved e-commerce skills is essential. Benefits of e-commerce are sacrificed due to a lack of employee experience and knowledge, which many of the SMEs investigated were coming to terms with.

Evaluating the Performance of E-Commerce

Although most of these organizations achieved some improvements with e-commerce, such as increased sales, they emphasized the need for formal methods of evaluating success. Participants were asked to rate the success of their e-commerce effort, both anecdotally and on a seven-point Lickert scale, with 1 representing "very successful" to 7 representing "failure" on aspects such as earnings or return on the e-commerce investment, making the business known to customers, amount of traffic on their Web sites and dollar value of sales generated online. It was interesting to note from the responses the wide variations in perceptions of success. Most e-commerce ventures thought they were successful, without knowing how to measure success. The most common methods of measuring success by the organizations was placing a counter on their homepages to keep a track of the number of times the homepages were accessed. However, these online businesses ignored the fact that some users access a site but do not buy and some end up at the same site again and again by mistake or due to 'keyword' search. Two of the organizations had implemented "cookies," which are a very small text file placed on the users' hard drive by a Web page server. It uniquely identifies a user and tells the server that a user has returned. Although the use of cookies raises privacy and security concerns, they are used to record a user's preferences when using particular sites.

Other challenges experienced by the e-commerce organizations investigated were integrating existing information technology with their e-commerce sites, transferring business from EDI systems onto the Internet and extranets, notifying their consumers that they could do business with them online and determining the best e-channels (e-malls, portals and e-hubs) to promote online business.

Organizational Learning

It is apparent from this research that in Australia, the value and potential of e-commerce has been realized by small businesses. It is also clear that although "bricks-and-mortar" organizations are adopting electronic commerce as a new channel of business, there are others who are taking advantage of the Internet and the World Wide Web to develop virtual businesses. The Internet and the World Wide Web have given small and medium enterprises the advantage of setting up global business with minimal capital. Most small businesses depend on Internet Service Providers and consultants to set up their electronic business. Online delivered content and promotion of business was hampered due to a lack of skills in-house to continuously refresh Web sites, to add information and to make it more interesting and interactive. Although many of these organizations expected to achieve much more from e-commerce, all they have managed is a Web presence, due to a lack of knowledge and the high costs of outsourcing.

Although some SMEs have been successful with disintermediation of middle-men, such as salespeople, many have not realized the need for reintermediation of business partners for quick delivery of goods, handling payments, promoting business and discovering new buyers. Reintermediation refers to the inclusion of the reliance on business partners who may enhance e-business. Forming new alliances with business outlets that allow easy pick up and return of goods sold by online stores leads to enhanced sales and stronger bonds with customers. Successful e-commerce organizations are increasingly forming alliances with other business entities for the delivery of goods, payments and other customer services. New business partnerships with gas (petrol) stations, corner stores and Australia Post are widely discussed and implemented to support e-commerce organizations. New online business alliances are promoting each other's business as well as enhancing e-commerce. One such alliance offers a discount on petrol if the goods are picked up at the nearest service station and a gift voucher for another online business that is regional and sells fruits and vegetables.

Australian e-commerce ventures placed a lot of emphasis on the development of the online business, but human inputs (employee skills) were generally left to the individuals. Supporting the development of employee skills also enhances the organization's intellectual capital, which leads to improved efficiencies and competitiveness in global markets. Continued education is required for success with e-commerce.

RECOMMENDATIONS

Discussion on the following issues, although not prescriptive, will enhance the value of e-commerce to small organizations.

Strategy

A strategy for e-commerce that provides a focus on the business advantage of the venture is required, not only for large organizations, but small and medium enterprises as well. It is also important to link the e-business strategy to the business strategy of the organization. E-business strategy should be proactive and reactive to customers, new technological developments and the environment and globalization; and it should be flexible. The e-commerce marketplace changes every 3 to 6 months, therefore flexibility to allow for the adoption of new developments and changing directions requires strategic plans to be short term and adaptable.

Technology

Security, speed and ease of Web site navigation are important characteristics for successful e-commerce. However, personalization, service orientation and incorporation of new technologies such as mobile phones, data warehousing, data mining and knowledge management are equally important. A good alignment of business and technology is needed for success. If the Internet can be applied to the right niche business, it is guaranteed to be successful.

Legal Issues

The *Electronic Signatures in Global and National Commerce Act* of 2000, otherwise known as the e-sign bill, is designed to promote online commerce by legitimizing online contractual agreements. Under the bill, digital agreements receive the same level of validity as their hard-copy counterparts. The bill also allows cooperating parties to establish their own contracts. Digital signatures, which are the electronic equivalent of handwritten signatures, are used to authenticate the participating parties and ensure the integrity of the message (Rayport & Jaworski, 2001). Small businesses will benefit tremendously as this bill gains acceptance against repudiation and the formation of new e-partnerships. Electronic commerce will be enhanced if the users know that the electronic transaction is secure, orders and payments can be traced and that it is cost effective. The nature of business is such that internationally accepted legal standards are welcomed.

Effective Web Page Design

The quality of the design of the Web page is directly correlated to its success (Cameron, 1997). Effective Web sites are those that can carry valuable information to the consumer. They must be easy to use and navigate, and updated frequently to encourage the user to return. Customers should be able to respond to the service provided either by electronic forms or e-mail. As suggested by Viehland (1998), a successful site should follow a three-click rule, allowing its visitors to find what they are looking for within these three clicks from the homepage. Winning the confidence of consumers to revisit the Web site means creating an atmosphere of continuous innovation. Outsourcing the design of Web sites will require close coordination between the organization representative and the provider to ensure that the objectives of business are adequately addressed.

New Skills

Education and training bridge the gap between development and successful implementation of new technology (Singh, 2000). Training provides new skills and methods needed to maintain the new Internet-based electronic trade. Considerable time is involved in training a person, which is usually underestimated by many organizations. A trained workforce with appropriate knowledge and skills will better procure the benefits of electronic commerce and avoid resistance to change. It is essential to consider people factors right from the onset of new technologies, and not after implementation, as usually happens. Proper planning of staffing, new job design, training, reward system and gain sharing will help organizations overcome most of the sociotechnical problems.

A Close Link with the Internet Service Providers

In cases where an organization is not well equipped with technical people, it will have to develop a close relationship with service providers. Staff in an organization will not know much about the intricacies of the electronic trade unless they work closely with technical people and technology providers. A close relationship with the e-commerce technology providers, with a high level of trust and understanding that not everything can be spelled out in a contract or specification, is required. A positive relationship with the supplier of technology promotes collaboration in the areas of technical support, backup, training and communication process.

Online Business Promotion

Encouraging the acceptance of electronic trade both within and outside organizations will lead to its success. Without promotion, a Web site will be lost in cyberspace. Press releases that present the highlights of the site and focus on information of interest to customers, the most important content, and its benefit to customers and business partners should be highlighted. Although business cards, brochures, stationery, print and TV advertisements are excellent ways of promoting the online business, the e-paradigm is evolving so fast that new models, trading hubs, e-malls, portals and other approaches should be continuously monitored and adopted for further expansion.

Business Process Re-engineering and Linking Back Office Systems to the Web

To maximize the opportunity of rapid information processing with electronic trade, some business processes will have to be re-engineered so that back-end systems are successfully integrated with the Web site. Online stores will then be able to rapidly process information and further reduce costs. Problems of inefficient and ineffective communication with manual order processing and delays caused by human error will also be eliminated. Integrated back-end systems are easily integrated to e-supply chains, which is another opportunity for e-commerce small businesses.

Evaluating the Effectiveness of the E-Commerce Strategy

Determining the effectiveness of the electronic commerce strategy will result in informed decisions about the site and the business approach. Various methods and tools for measuring the effectiveness can be applied. Electronic business effectiveness should take into account intangible benefits as well. Continuous monitoring of electronic commerce will highlight its progress and improve its utilization. Formal evaluation will identify problems for which solutions can be developed to minimize any negative repercussions. The evaluation method put in place should be one that will highlight the apparent financial and nonfinancial costs and benefits associated with the new business system. Without performance evaluation of electronic commerce, it will take a long time to identify its shortcomings and an equally long time to rectify the problems. Although different methods of evaluations and effectiveness matrices for e-commerce have been suggested by different experts (Rayport & Jaworski, 2001; Schubert & Selz, 2000), business implementation reviews most appropriate to the organization, based on its business case, can be applied.

CONCLUSION

Issues included in this chapter clearly indicate that some small and medium enterprises in Australia have realized the potential of electronic commerce and increased the use of the Internet as a business advantage. Electronic commerce in most organizations is adopted for financial rewards rather than just establishing a Web presence for image building or advertising. However, it is also clear that a lot of support and learning is required for the SMEs to be successful e-commerce ventures.

Early adopters of e-commerce have created loyalty with lucrative customers and business partners, and achieved a competitive advantage. An appropriate human, process and technology architecture for e-commerce is required for creating business value. To enhance e-commerce it is essential for small organizations to concentrate on brand recognition, customer loyalty and service, flexible and short-term strategic plans and worthwhile business alliances, and to focus on profitable e-commerce applications.

To be successful with e-commerce, full commitment of the managers/owners is required to enforce the changes and create the e-business culture in the organization. E-commerce applications should be fully integrated to avoid "islands of Web application." Information sharing, effective communication of ideas and future plans to all employees, and being business focused and not only technology focused, will lead to success. As suggested by Wigglesworth (2001), for an e-commerce venture to be successful, it will have to learn to improve and modify continuously. An attitude of "a Web fairy will come along and make it all better" will not work.

REFERENCES

Aberdeen Group. (1997). Electronic commerce to Internet commerce: The evolution of the Internetworked enterprise. *An Executive white paper*, October.

Anderson Consulting. (1999). *A Review of E-Commerce in Australia*, April. Retrieved from the World Wide Web: http://www.ac.com/services/ecommerce/ecom_australia.html.

Archer, N. & Gebauer, J. (2000). Managing in the context of the new electronic marketplace. *Proceedings of the First World Congress on the Management of Electronic Commerce*, McMaster University, Hamilton, Canada (CD ROM).

Baldwin, A., Lymer, A., & Johnson, R. (2001). Business impacts of the Internet for small- and medium-sized enterprises. *E-Commerce & V-Business: Business Models for Success*. Great Britain: Butterworth Heinman.

Cameron, D. (1997). *Electronic Commerce: The New Business Platform for the Internet*. Computer Technology Research Corporation, SC.

Dublish, S. (2000). Retailing and the Internet. *Proceedings of the First World Congress on the Management of Electronic Commerce*, McMaster University, Hamilton, Canada (CD ROM).

Hoffman, D. L., Novak, T. P., & Chatterji, P. (1999). *Commercial Scenarios for the Web: Opportunities and Challenges*. Retrieved from the World Wide Web: http://www.ascusc.org/jcmc/vol1/issues3/hoffman.html.

Phillip, M. (1997). *Successful e-Commerce*. Melbourne, Australia: Bookman.

Poon, S. & Swatman, P. (1997). Internet-Based Small Business Communication: Seven Australian Cases. *EM-Electronic Markets*, 7(2).

Rayport, J. F. and Jaworski, B. J. (2001). *e-Commerce*. Singapore: McGraw-Hill International.

Singh, M. (2000). Electronic commerce in Australia: Opportunities and factors critical for success. *Proceedings of the First World Congress on the Management of Electronic Commerce*, McMaster University, Hamilton, Canada (CD ROM).

Turban, E., Lee, J., King, D., & Chung, H. (2000). *Electronic Commerce: A Managerial Perspective*. Englewood Cliffs, NJ: Prentice Hall.

Viehland, D. (1998). *E-Commerce*. Melbourne: Australian Institute of Charted Accountants.

Watson, R. T., Berthon, P., Pitt, L., & Zinkhan, G. (1999). *Electronic Commerce*. Orlando, FL: The Dryden Press.

Whinston, A., Stahl, D., & Choi, S. (1998). *The Economics of Electronic Commerce*. Indianapolis, IN: Macmillan Technical Publishing.

Wigglesworth, K. (2001). … in the eSpace. *Lecture Notes*, RMIT, Melbourne.

Winner Langdon. (1997). The neverhood of Internet commerce. *MIT's Technology Review*, 100(6).

Yin, R. (1994). *Case Study Research Design and Methods*. New Delhi, India: Sage Publications.

Table 1: Objectives and Opportunities of Electronic Commerce

Case	Objectives and Opportunities
Company A	Increased circulation of advertisements, expanded existing market, reached out to customers at greater distances, reduced costs, reduced the time required to process an order
Company B	A better relationship with customers, expanded customer base, increased sales
Company C	Captured markets nationally and internationally, reduced the need for middle people, traced buying habits of customers, easy demand forecasts
Company D	Increased business, automated repetitive processes, reduced stock, shifted business-to-business transactions to the Internet
Company E	Increased sales, expanded customer base
Company F	Savings on labor costs, automated processes, improved customer relationship by offering 24 hr service, reached out to non-Australian customers
Company G	Online booking and payment, better account monitoring, reduced the number of middleman, increased business-to-business and business-to-customer linkages
Company H	Reduced the number of middleman, obtained new distribution channels, expanded business
Company I	Increased sales and customer base
Company J	Increased customer base nationally and internationally
Company K	Improved customer service, improved business with "smart technology"
Company L	Quick and improved transaction records, reduced paperwork, reduced costs
Company M	Better customer service with "click, talk, walk," to be competitive, 24-hr shopfront, reduced costs
Company N	Provide campus services online, better customer service, reduce face-to-face contact, increase the use of remote offices
Company O	Increase customer base, promote business, competitive advantage, gaining knowledge and technologies
Company P	Reaching clients at greater distances, quick retrieval of information, amass large amount of information
Company Q	Capture new customers, exploit new technologies to offer better customer service, offer customized products and services
Company R	Provision of updated information to customers, improved efficiency, reduced costs and thus reduced prices to consumers
Company S	Wider clientele, apply "push" technology to increase business, improve business processes, reduce overheads, reduced cost for warehousing, easy marketing, speeds negotiation process, access to international markets, improved lead times
Company T	No overheads, no cost of warehousing, quick dissemination of information, marketing on the Web

Table 2: Electronic Commerce Challenges

Case	Electronic Commerce Challenges
Company A	Integrating e-business into existing business, archive business rules about payments online, develop Web interfaces useable for users, creating Web sites that will be accessed by users and provide them with maximum support, deal with people and new technology issues
Company B	Letting people know that their business is online, winning the confidence of customers to trade electronically, international payment structure for Australian businesses, dealing with people issues in the organization such as getting them to adopt electronic business
Company C	Presenting sites in different languages to reach customers in different countries in the region
Company D	Senior management being less inclined to technology and taking a long time to accept technology initiatives
Company E	Banks not ready to accept chargebacks for credit cards (credit card companies create fear among users about other payment systems)
Company F	Getting the customers to accept the Internet as a business medium
Company G	Uncertainty, being able to keep up with rapidly changing technology, need for continuous improvement, appropriate content and Web page design, perceiving and responding to people's sensitiveness
Company H	Getting the community and the employees to accept the e-commerce culture
Company I	Support and trust for credit card payments over the Internet, difficult to measure the effectiveness of the site to compare the advertising costs
Company J	Overcoming security concerns, educating the marketplace to use e-commerce
Company K	Changing the culture within the organization and users to do things electronically
Company L	Obtain senior management support for electronic business, depending on outsiders to make technology decisions, not being able to get the users to accept electronic services
Company M	To get managers, employees, partners and users interested in electronic commerce. To educate the customers to access the solutions to their questions online
Company N	Copyright issues for hard copies of electronic material, authentication problems
Company O	Gaining consumer confidence to use online business, keeping up with technology, making transaction process user friendly, educating employees and customers to accept online business, dealing with resistance to change
Company P	Assuring users that transactions are secure, encouraging customers to use to use online business, finding ways to promote e-commerce
Company Q	Establishing online business without affecting existing business, change the culture within the organization to accept online business
Company R	The need for EC standards for data integrity, contracts with business partners, high costs of setting e-business.
Company S	Incompatible systems with business partners, technical data in different formats because business partners operate on different platforms, sociotechnical issues
Company T	Secure financial transactions

About the Authors

Namchul Shin is Associate Professor of Information Systems at Pace University. He received his PhD in MIS from the University of California at Irvine, an MBA from the University of Toledo, and a BA from Seoul National University. His current research interests lie in the areas of IT business value, organizational and strategic impacts of IT, electronic business, and enterprise commerce management. He is an associate editor of the *Journal of Electronic Commerce Research*. His work has been published in journals such as *European Journal of Information Systems*, *Logistics Information Management*, *Journal of Electronic Commerce Research*, *International Journal of Services Technology and Management*, and *Business Process Management Journal*. His recent work can be viewed at http://csis.pace.edu/~shin.

*   *   *

Susan J. Chinburg is completing a doctorate in telecommunications from the Management Department of the College of Business Administration, Oklahoma State University, Stillwater, OK. She has a BS from Mankato State University, Mankato, MN, and a MS from San Jose State University, San Jose, CA. After school Susan joined Conoco working in many areas related to oil and gas exploration and development. Her interests in technology led her into research, working on projects integrating technology into workflow. Susan returned to school to study networking and computer science. Currently, she is in the optical architecture group of Williams Communications working on developing and implementing state-of-the-art optical networks.

Ron Craig is a Professor of Business at Wilfrid Laurier University and Area Coordinator of the Operations & Decision Sciences Group. He holds a PhD and MASc in Management Sciences, and a BASc in Chemical Engineering, all from the University of Waterloo. His research interests are in the areas of small business and technology management. Co-founder of a computer peripheral manufacturer prior to joining Laurier, Professor Craig also served more recently as the university's first IT Officer.

Bahador Ghahramani is an Associate Professor in the Information Systems and Quantitative Analysis, University of Nebraska at Omaha (UNO). Prior to joining the academia, he was a Distinguished Member of the Technical Staff (DMTS) at the AT&T-Bell Laboratories. His work experience covers several years in academia, industry, and consulting. He has extensive R&D experience in Advanced Systems Design and Development, Advanced Management Information Systems, Advanced Business Applications Programming, Object Oriented Programming Environment, Expert Systems and Decision Support Systems, Database Management, Design of Human Machine Systems, Business Data Communications, Organization of Impact of Information Technology, Business Systems Analysis and Design, and Business Data Structure. Dr. Ghahramani has presented and published numerous papers and has been an active participant and officer in several national and international organizations and honor societies. He holds five patents, *"The Eye Depth Testing Apparatus," "A Method for Measuring the Usability of a System," "A Method for Measuring the Usability of a System and for Task Analysis and Re-engineering," "Electronic Depth Perception Testing Systems Apparatus for Conducting Depth Perception Tests,"* and *"Emergency Marking System, Marking Device, Components Therefore and Methods of Making the Same,"* and applied for and maintains copyrights on five other AT&T designs. Dr. Ghahramani received his Ph.D. in Industrial Engineering from Louisiana Tech University, MBA in Information Systems from Louisiana State University; MS in Industrial Engineering from Texas Tech University, MS in Applied Mathematics and Computer Science from Southern University, and BS in Industrial Engineering and Management from Oklahoma State University.

Jatinder N. D. Gupta is currently Eminent Scholar of Management, Professor of Management Information Systems, and Chairperson of the Department of Accounting and Information Systems in the College of Administrative Science at the University of Alabama in Huntsville, Alabama. Most recently, he was Professor of Management, Information and Communication Sciences, and Industry and Technology at the Ball State University in Muncie, Indiana. He holds a PhD in Industrial Engineering (with specialization in Production Management and Information

Systems) from Texas Tech University. Co-author of a textbook in Operations Research, Dr. Gupta serves on the editorial boards of several national and international journals. Recipient of the Outstanding Faculty and Outstanding Researcher awards from Ball State University, he has published numerous papers in such journals as *Journal of Management Information Systems*, *International Journal of Information Management*, *INFORMS Journal of Computing*, *Annals of Operations Research*, and *Mathematics of Operations Research*. More recently, he served as a co-editor of a special issue on *Neural Networks in Business of Computers and Operations Research* and a book entitled, *Neural Networks in Business: Techniques and Applications*. His current research interests include information and decision technologies, scheduling, planning and control, organizational learning and effectiveness, systems education, and knowledge management. Dr. Gupta is a member of several academic and professional societies including the Production and Operations Management Society (POMS), the Decision Sciences Institute (DSI), and the Information Resources Management Association (IRMA).

Daniel C. Kinsella, Jr. is with the Enterprise Risk Services (ERS) group of Deloitte & Touche. Mr. Kinsella specializes in assessing technology and business risk and developing implementation plans to mitigate those risks. Industry experience includes insurance, banking, manufacturing, health care, and managed care. Technology experience spans across a variety of computer platforms including IBM OS/390, AS400, Windows NT, and various UNIX implementations. Due to the number of clients served, Mr. Kinsella understands key business process and has the opportunity to share best practices and add value to clients.

Kenneth L. Kraemer holds the Taco Bell Chair in Information Technology for Management at the Graduate School of Management, University of California, Irvine, where he is also the Director of the Center for Research on Information Technology and Organizations (CRITO). He has studied critical issues in management, information technology and organizations for over thirty years. He is currently doing international research on the globalization of information technology production and use.

Arlyn J. Melcher is a Professor of Management at Southern Illinois University. He has an MBA from UCLA and a PhD from the Graduate School of Business at University of Chicago. He has written widely on organization and strategic management issues. He works with both small and large businesses in managing change and reengineering their organizations. Currently, his central focus is on how to design and manage high performance organizations.

Carlos J. Navarrete is Associated Professor in the Computer Information Systems Department at the College of Business Administration of the California State Polytechnic University, Pomona. He holds a BSc from Instituto Politecnico Nacional, Mexico, and a PhD in Management Information Systems from Claremont Graduate University in Claremont, California. Before joining California State Polytechnic, Professor Navarrete worked for Universidad Iberoamerican, Mexico, where he was the Chair of the Information Systems Department. His research interest is the use of Information Technology to support individuals, groups, and organizations' productivity. Professor Navarrete has received several awards through his academic carrier. He was Fulbright scholar from 1991 to 1994.

James B. Pick is Professor in School of Business at University of Redlands and former department chair of management and business. He holds a BA from Northwestern University and a PhD from University of California, Irvine. He is the author of seven books and 100 scientific papers and book chapters in the research areas of management of information systems, geographic information systems, environmental systems, population, and urban studies. In the fall of 2001, he was senior Fulbright scholar in Mexico.

Simpson Poon is Chair Professor of Information Systems at Charles Sturt University, Australia. He is also a Visiting Professor at The University of Hong Kong. Dr. Poon earned his PhD in Information Systems from Monash University, Australia. He was the Founding Director of the Centre of E-Commerce and Internet Studies at Murdoch University, Australia. Dr. Poon has been an e-business consultant and has worked with both government and business organizations in Australia and Asia. He has published widely in the area of e-business in both academic and professional journals.

Arun Rai is the Harkins Professor of Electronic Commerce in the eCommerce Institute, Robinson College of Business, Georgia State University. His research focuses on digitally enabled transformation of complex processes, enterprises and supply chains and the diffusion and infusion of information technologies and systems. His publications have appeared in several leading journals including *Communications of the ACM, Decision Sciences, Information Systems Research, Journal of MIS, MIS Quarterly*, among others. He serves as an Associate Editor of *Information Systems Research*, among other scholarly journals, and has served as associate editor of *MIS Quarterly*. Leading corporations, including Daimler-Chrysler, Comdisco, IBM, and UPS, among others, have sponsored Arun's work. He recently received an IBM faculty award for his eCommerce contributions.

Kristina Setzekorn is an Assistant Professor in Oakland University's Department of Decision and Information Sciences. She earned her PhD from Southern Illinois University at Carbondale in December, 2000. Her research interests involve information technology's (IT) effects on supply chain and firm efficiency, organizational and market structure, organizational and interorganizational information sharing, decision rights and incentives. Her dissertation studies the performance implications of IT infrastructure's alignment with market context (complexity and supply chain coordination strategy).

Ra'ed M. Shams worked initially as a general manager of a major computer system integrator in Bahrain and then joined the University of Bahrain as a research and teaching assistant and participated in establishing the MIS department at the College of Business Administration. His current research and consultancy interest is in the area of strategic IS management, especially strategic alignment. Currently, he is setting for his PhD at the University of Bradford, U.K.

Ramesh Sharda, PhD (University of Wisconsin-Madison), is currently the Conoco Chair of Management of Technology and Regents Professor of Management Science and Information Systems at Oklahoma State University. His extensive research has led to over 60 articles in major journals and books including *Management Science, Information Systems Research*, *Decision Support Systems*, *Interfaces*, *INFORMS Journal on Computing*, *Computers and Operations Research*, and many others. He started the MS in Telecommunications Management Program at Oklahoma State. His professional service includes serving as the Editor of the *Interactive Transactions of ORMS*, and on the editorial board of several journals. He is also a co-founder of iTradeFair.com, a leader in producing virtual trade fairs.

Sushil K. Sharma is currently Assistant Professor of Information Systems at the Ball State University, Muncie, Indiana. He received his PhD in Information Systems from Pune University, India and has taught at the Indian Institute of Management, Lucknow for eleven years before joining Ball State University. Prior to joining Ball State, Dr. Sharma held the position of Visiting Research Associate Professor at the Department of Management Science, University of Waterloo, Canada. Dr. Sharma's primary teaching interests are E-commerce, computer communication networks, database management systems, management information systems, and information systems analysis and design. He has extensive experience in providing consulting services to several government and private organizations including World Bank funded projects in the areas of information systems, e-commerce, and knowledge management. Dr. Sharma is the author of two books and has numerous articles in national and international journals. His current research interests include database management systems, networking environments, electronic commerce (e-commerce), knowledge management, and corporate information systems.

Bongsik Shin is an Assistant Professor in the Department of Information and Decision Systems at San Diego State University. He earned a PhD from the University of Arizona. He joined the faculty of Management Information Systems at the University of Nebraska at Omaha in 1997 through 1999. His work has been published or accepted in *Communications of the ACM, IEEE Transactions on Systems, Man, and Cybernetics, IEEE Transaction on Engineering Management, Journal of Data Warehousing, Journal of Organizational Computing and Electronic Commerce, Journal of Systems Integration,* and *Journal of Database Management.* His current research interests are data warehousing and data mining, telework, and e-commerce.

Mohini Singh is a Senior Lecturer in E-Business at RMIT University, Australia. She earned her PhD from Monash University in the area of New Technology Management. Her publications and presentations are in the area of Management and Implementation of New Technologies and Electronic Commerce. Dr. Singh was the Founding Director of the Electronic Commerce Research Unit at Victoria University, Melbourne. She has successfully completed funded research projects in the area of e-commerce, and presented and published widely both locally and internationally. Her current research focus is on electronic commerce management and business issues, evolving e-business models, e-commerce effectiveness metrics and e-business relationship management.

Bernd C. Stahl, born in 1968, Dipl.-Wi.-Ing., MA, DEA; studied mechanical engineering and commerce at the University of the German Armed Forces in Hamburg from 1990 to 1994. (degree: Diplom-Wirtschaftsingenieur) From 1994 to 1998 he studied philosophy and economics at the University of Hagen (degree: Magister Artium). From 1999 to 2000 he studied philosophy in Bordeaux, France, where he graduated with a Diplôme d'Etudes Approfondies. From 1987 to 1997 he was an officer of the German Armed Forces, his latest assignment was that of a deputy company commander in the artillery regiment 7 in Dülmen. From 1998 to 2000 he worked as research assistant at the University Witten / Herdecke (Germany), at the Institute of Economics and Philosophy. Since September 2000 he has been a Lecturer at the Department of Management Information Systems at the University College Dublin, Ireland. He works on questions of the relationship of ethics and business with a particular emphasis on the notion of responsibility. His second field of research is normative problems arising from the use of information technology in business. Another area of interest includes normative problems caused by the use of computers and IT in education.

Paul P. Tallon is an Assistant Professor of Information Technology at the Wallace E. Carroll School of Management, Boston College, and a Research Associate at the Center for Research on Information Technology and Organizations (CRITO) at the University of California, Irvine. His research interests include the economic and organizational impacts of IT, the alignment of IT with business strategy, the application of real options to IT evaluation, and IT for financial services. His work has appeared in the *Journal of Management Information Systems* and in several conference proceedings. He previously worked as an auditor with PriceWaterhouse, and as a consultant on the development of computer-based training programs for the International Trade Center, Geneva.

Mark Weiser is Director of the Masters of Science in Telecommunications Management Program at Oklahoma State University. He teaches a variety of networking topics including upper-layer routing protocols and hands-on applied labs. Dr. Weiser's research encompasses multiple areas, such as analyzing protocol proliferation, optimal packet sizes, and distance education technologies and techniques; with publications in several leading journals and books.

Frederick P. Wheeler has had a broad interest in the management and application of information for decision making. He was until recently Senior Lecturer in Management Science at the School of Management, University of Bradford, and is currently with the U.K. Competition Commission as their Statistical Adviser.

Index